'The apparent pointlessness of ı
significance and purpose are du
world at least, the . . . universe i
pointlessly grinding its way towa_____ _____ate stagnation and death;
men are tiny offshoots of the universal machine, running down to
their own private death; physical life is the only real life; mind is a
mere product of body . . .'

Aldous Huxley

'One way to define theism is that it is a story about the universe
that proclaims the reality of the true, the good and the beautiful
. . . naturalism is a story that reduces reality to physical particles
and impersonal laws, portrays life as a meaningless competition
among organisms that exist only to survive and reproduce, and
sees the mind as no more than an emergent property of
biochemical reactions . . . Theism tells us that we should by nature
want whatever is true, good and beautiful; naturalism implies that
such a unifying vision is fantasy . . .'

Phillip E. Johnson

To the 6,000 or more teenagers who attend my school conferences each year and discuss their beliefs and values with me so openly and honestly. I hope that I may help you explore spiritual and moral issues. You certainly help me to gain some insight into the impact of modern culture in your lives.

*For information on these school conferences (and to watch a video about them) see **www.damaris.org/schools***

I Wish
I Could
Believe in
Meaning
and Purpose

Peter S Williams

www.damarispublishing.com

First edition published in 2004 by
Damaris Publishing
PO Box 200, Southampton, Hampshire, SO17 2DL
www.damarispublishing.com

Website for this book:
www.IWishICouldBelieve.com

ISBN 1 904753 06 X

Acknowledgements
For various contributions to the production of this book, I would like to
thank:

Edward Babinski
Matt Beech
Steven Carr
Steve Couch (for managerial oversight of the publication process)
my colleagues in the *Damaris* office (for their prayers and
    encouragement)
Nicholas Everitt (for questions about beauty)
Richard Francis
Peter Lambros and the household Lambros (for fellowship and food)
Angus Menuge
Tom Price
Gerald Rogers (for the cover design)
Clive Thorne
Viv Wickham (my editor, for constructive criticism and easy-going
    conversation over tea, toast and Marmite)
my supporters (for their prayers and finances)
my parents (for their loving encouragement, and for introducing me to the
    meaning of life)

A catalogue record for this book is available from the British Library
Designed and typeset by AD Publishing Services Limited
Printed and bound in Malta

Contents

Introduction

Talking about serious questions is a pleasure.
G. K. CHESTERTON

A student party in Norwich at the fag end of the twenti-
eth century. My first book, *The Case for God*
(Monarch, 1999), is due for publication at the close of
this, the final semester of my M.Phil. degree at the
University of East Anglia. The dark-haired young lady
talking to me (she must be a friend of a friend) has
heard about my book. She has also had a few drinks,
and says: 'I wish I could believe in God, it would make
my life meaningful.' I respond off the cuff, but with genuine curiosity: 'If you wish you could believe in God,
why don't you?' We briefly discuss the connection
between God and the meaning of life; but this is hardly
an opportune place for 'a deep and meaningful', and the
party moves on.

My young enquirer is not alone. Research published
by the American Council on Education showed that the
number one goal among the 171,509 students surveyed
(for 68.1 per cent of them) was 'developing a meaningful philosophy of life'.[1] Another survey, conducted by
John Hopkins University, found that among 7,948 students at 48 colleges, 78 per cent ticked their primary
goal in life as 'finding a purpose and meaning to my
life'.[2] These results bear out psychologist Abraham H.
Maslow's thesis that meaning is 'an irreducible need

[and] man's primary concern'.[3]

Do you know what it means to feel (even in the midst of the party, when you really should be enjoying yourself) that life is somehow flat, like that day-old open can of Coke by that cold, half-eaten pizza? Does your heart tell you that belief in God would give life back its lost sense of meaning, purpose and worth, even as your head tells you that you should learn to live with the fact that, as Nietzsche said, 'God is dead'?

Psychologist Dr Nola Passmore is right, isn't she, when she writes that:

> The heart cry of the human race is for meaning and purpose, a sense of belonging when human relationships fail to satisfy, a need to know we are unconditionally loved in spite of our circumstances, a need to know that we are not an accident of chance but people of design, a need to know that we have a future and a hope even when everything around us seems to be falling apart.[4]

This is what we long for, and this is what our scientific culture tells us time and again that we cannot have, at least not without taking our brains out and placing a 'do not disturb' sign on them. As Nicholas Mosley writes: 'There is a subject nowadays which is taboo in the way sexuality was once taboo, which is to talk about life as if it had any meaning.'[5] Atheist and palaeontologist Stephen Jay Gould (1941–2002) summed up the cultural status of belief in meaning: 'Look, it's a tough life and if you can delude yourself into thinking that there's all some warm and fuzzy meaning to it all, it's enormously comforting. But I do think it's just a story we tell ourselves.'[6] Gould linked his negative appraisal of meaning to his belief in the theory of evolution: 'The

Darwinian revolution is about who we are – it's what we're made of, it's what our life means insofar as science can answer that question.'[7] Clearly, the not-so-subtle subtext here is that life has no meaning 'insofar as science can answer that question', and that non-scientific answers to the question of meaning are illegitimate, nothing but comforting storytelling. As Douglas Futuyama says: 'Some shrink from the conclusion that the human species was not designed, has no purpose, and is the product of mere mechanical mechanisms – but this seems to be the message of evolution.'[8]

The 'message of evolution' is presented as a nihilistic message, a message absorbed by the population at large from the cold academic heart of our secular culture as it speaks to them through the media and the arts, a message that drains the colour from their lives: 'Many authors have tied naturalism and materialism to evolution,' observes theologian Terence L. Nichols, 'as if belief in Darwin's ideas about evolution entails naturalism and materialism and rules out religion as a valid worldview.'[9] Taxi driver Jose Martinez, in a *Life* magazine story about the search for meaning, has learnt his lessons well:

> We're here to die, just live and die. I like driving a cab. I do some fishing, take my girl out, pay taxes, do a little reading, then get ready to drop dead. You've got to be strong about it. Life is a big fake. Nobody gives a damn. You're rich or you're poor. You're here, you're gone. You're like the wind. After you're gone, other people will come. It's too late to make it better. Everyone's fed up, can't believe in nothing no more. People have no pride. People have no fear. People aren't scared. People

> only care about one thing and that's money. We
> gonna destroy ourselves, nothing we can do about
> it. The only cure for the world's illness is nuclear
> war – wipe everything out and start over. We've
> become like a cornered animal, fighting for
> survival. Life is nothing.[10]

Richard Dawkins, Oxford University's Professor for the
Public Understanding of Science, is well known through
his best-selling books and media appearances for the
passionate advocacy of an atheistic worldview grounded in a scientific understanding of the world: 'Oxford
biologist Richard Dawkins' *The Blind Watchmaker* . . .
explicitly states that he intends the book as a challenge
to belief in a designer God, and he carries that further
to challenge belief in any God at all. It is a brilliant book
and a brilliant challenge.'[11]

There is no doubting Dawkins' sincerity when he says
(as everyone surely should say): 'I care about what's
actually true.'[12] Dawkins is convinced that the
Darwinian theory of evolution is what's actually true
about the world we live in, writing of 'the inescapable
factual correctness'[13] of Darwin's conclusions. He is
equally convinced that evolution excludes the truth of
any belief in God, 'the pacifier of faith in immortality',[14]
the absolute truth of any moral or aesthetic values, or,
as a consequence of all this, any objective meaning or
purpose of life: 'The universe at large is a tale told by
an idiot.'[15] In fact, the universe at large is precisely *not*
a tale, because there is no cosmic Storyteller, idiotic or
otherwise. Hence, according to Dawkins (and many
thinkers like him) we face a clear choice between
accepting the atheistic, nihilistic truth revealed to us by
science, or throwing our brains away in order to

embrace the 'warm comfortable lie'[16] that God is alive and that the cosmos is infused with value, meaning and purpose, as intelligent people once believed but Darwin disproved. Not to embrace the truth, not to stand up 'full-face into the keen wind of understanding'[17] as Dawkins puts it, is surely to succumb to 'a kind of pathetic, childish response to some failure'.[18] We must choose, explains Dawkins, to be 'people of intellect, as opposed to people of faith'.[19] As Jose said, we're just here to die, and we've got to be strong about it.

Given such a stark and momentous choice between scientific truth and spiritual comfort, perhaps you can identify with philosopher Peter van Inwagen, reading about the death of the famous composer Handel (1685–1759), who expressed 'his eagerness to die and to meet his dear Saviour Jesus Christ face to face'.[20] Inwagen's reaction to Handel:

> . . . was negative and extremely vehement, a little explosion of contempt, modified by pity. It might be put in these words: 'You poor booby. You cheat.' Handel had been taken in, I thought, and yet at the same time he was getting away with something. Although his greatest hope was an illusion, nothing could rob him of the comfort of this hope, for after his death he would not exist and there would be no one there to see how wrong he had been.[21]

Inwagen says he isn't sure that he would have disillusioned Handel if he could have done so, 'but I certainly managed simultaneously to believe he was "of all men most miserable" and that he was getting a pretty good deal'.[22] The reverse image of Dawkins' forced choice between truth and comfort, as philosopher William

Lane Craig articulates it, is that: 'Man cannot live consistently and happily as though life were ultimately without meaning, value, or purpose. If we try to live consistently within an atheistic worldview, we shall find ourselves profoundly unhappy. If instead we manage to live happily, it is only by giving the lie to our worldview.'[23]

Suppose my young enquirer's words echo your own: 'I wish I could believe in God, it would make my life meaningful.' Suppose I responded to you as I responded to her: 'If you wish you could believe in God, why don't you?' Suppose we had a clear-headed opportunity (fuelled, perhaps, by copious amounts of coffee rather than alcohol) to explore your search for meaning together, to ask if belief in God really would give life back its fizz, and whether the reasons for not believing, like Professor Dawkins' reasons, actually amount to anything. Would you take the time to talk? Or is 'the party' just too alluring?

Dr Armand M. Nicholi Jr, Professor of Psychiatry at Harvard medical school, ponders the relationship between our busy lives and our lack of meaning:

> Perhaps we distract ourselves because looking at our lives confronts us with our lack of meaning, our unhappiness, and our loneliness – and with the difficulty, the fragility, and the unbelievable brevity of life . . . Perhaps the reason we find it difficult to sit quietly and examine our lives is because doing so makes us anxious. But until we examine our lives, we can do little to make them less unhappy and more fulfilling.[24]

The iconic distractions of 'sex, drugs and rock'n'roll' undoubtedly provide fleeting relief from the meaninglessness of existence; but if, in our existential anxiety, we substitute our distractions for the task of facing up to the question of meaning, then our distractions from meaninglessness actually stand between us and any hope of finding fulfilment, and we suffer from a terminal case of substitute abuse. As G. K. Chesterton said in his last radio broadcast for the BBC:

> I am perfectly certain that all our world will end in despair, unless there is some way of making the mind itself, the ordinary thought we have at ordinary times, more healthy and more happy than they seem to be just now, to judge by most modern novels and poems. You have to be happy in those quiet moments when you remember that you are alive, not in those noisy moments when you forget.[25]

I grew up watching *The Muppet Show*, and still enjoy watching Kermit the Frog and his puppet pals. One of my favourite Muppet sketches involves the 'Pigs in Space' crew faced with a 60-second wait to discover 'the meaning and purpose of life'. When they are interrupted by the dinner-gong, Captain Link bemoans the fact that he will have to miss out on knowing the meaning and purpose of life. Miss Piggy asks whether he couldn't simply skip dinner; but Link points out that the menu for the day includes 'swill-stroganoff', and he leaves. Torn between making the great discovery or consuming swill-stroganoff, Miss Piggy gives in to temptation (seconds before the moment of truth) and rushes off to dinner, leaving 'the announcer' as the only Muppet in the know. Who gets the best deal? Which would you choose, distraction or truth, meaning or a meal?

Perhaps you feel reticent about the search for meaning because you have looked before and have found the search fruitless. The naturalists seem to have the best of the argument (science appears to be on their side), and intellectual integrity demands that their conclusions, however unpalatable, be accepted. I simply ask that you give me this opportunity to explain why I am convinced that you *can* have hope without being a 'poor booby'. Later in life, van Inwagen concluded that he could in fact embrace the former without being the latter; so he did. Perhaps thinking through the issues with the help of this book will enable you to reach the same conclusion. Since the intellectual and personal stakes are so high, it is always worthwhile re-visiting the question of meaning, especially in company (two heads are better than one). And as Chesterton might have said, reading about serious questions is a pleasure. Surely, then, you have nothing to lose and everything to gain.

In the chapters that follow I will build a case for a theistic understanding of life as objectively meaningful and purposeful because God exists, calling upon a number of prominent 'expert witnesses' as we proceed. In particular, we will give sustained attention to the thinking of Richard Dawkins, whom A. N. Wilson calls 'Darwin's most ardent representative on earth'.[26] I will defend my own conclusions on the issues we must grapple with to resolve the question of the meaning and purpose of life, but the ultimate act of conclusion naturally rests with you. Cast yourself in the role of jury-member, carefully weighing the evidence and arguments in order to arrive at your verdict. Your decision will be no less important than it would be in an actual trial, because whatever you conclude, you'll be sentencing yourself to live with the results.

[1] Frankl, Viktor, *Man's Search for Ultimate Meaning* (Cambridge, Massachusetts: Perseus Publishing, 2000), p.86.

[2] *ibid.*

[3] *ibid.*

[4] Passmore, Nola, in John F. Ashton (ed.), *On the Seventh Day* (Green Forrest: Master Books, 2002), p.116.

[5] Mosley, Nicholas, *Natalie, Natalie* (New York: Coward, McCann & Geoghehan, 1971), quoted by Frankl, *op. cit.*

[6] Quoted by Jonathan Sarfati in *Refuting Evolution 2* (Green Forrest: Master Books, 2002), p.40.

[7] Gould, Stephen Jay, Evolution, PBS Television, Episode One: *Darwin's Dangerous Idea.*

[8] Futuyama, Douglas, *Science on Trial: The Case for Evolution* (New York: Pantheon, 1983), p.12-13.

[9] Nichols, Terence L., *The Sacred Cosmos* (Grand Rapids: Brazos Press, 2003), p.12.

[10] Quoted by Ravi Zacharias in *Can Man Live Without God?* (Milton Keynes: Word, 1994), p.129.

[11] Ferguson, Kitty, *The Fire in the Equations: Science, Religion & The Search For God* (London: Bantam Books, 1995), p.149.

[12] Dawkins, Richard, 'Darwin's Dangerous Disciple' at www.skeptic.com/03.4.miele-dawkins-iv.html

[13] Dawkins, Richard, *A Devil's Chaplain*, Latha Menon (ed.), (London: Weidenfeld & Nicolson, 2003), p.11.

[14] *ibid.*, p.13.

[15] Dawkins, 'Darwin's Dangerous Disciple', *op. cit.*

[16] Dawkins, *A Devil's Chaplain, op. cit.*

[17] *ibid.*

[18] Dawkins, 'Darwin's Dangerous Disciple', *op. cit.*

[19] Dawkins, 'Time to Stand Up', *A Devil's Chaplain, op. cit.*, p.157.

[20] van Inwagen, Peter, 'Quam Dilecta', www.faithquest.com/philosophers/vaninwagen/quam.html
After conducting the *Messiah* on 6 April 1759, Handel told friends: 'I want to die on Good Friday in the hope of rejoining the good God, my sweet Lord and Saviour, on the day of his resurrection.' He died on 14 April 1759, Good Friday. cf. Jane Stuart Smith and Betty Carlson, *A Gift of Music: Great Composers and Their Influence* (Carlisle: Solway, 1998).

[21] *ibid.*

[22] *ibid.*

[23] Craig, William Lane, *Reasonable Faith* (Wheaton: Crossway Books, 1994), p.71.

[24] Nicholi, Armand M. Jr, *The Question of God* (New York: Free Press, 2002), p.6.

[25] Chesterton, G. K., 'The Spice of Life', in Russell Sparkes (ed.), *Prophet of Orthodoxy* (London: Fount, 1997), p.217.

[26] Wilson, A. N., *God's Funeral* (London: John Murray, 1999), p.177.

CHAPTER I

In which we meet a Medieval Dumb Ox and discover the Meaning of Meaning

'Let's play the Weakest Link' says Anne Robinson, and another episode of the hit BBC game show begins. A group of contestants answer a string of general knowledge questions that secure the opportunity to 'bank' increasingly large amounts of money. Each round of questions is followed by a round of voting where the contestants can get rid of the 'weakest link', the contestant who holds back the bank balance by getting the most questions wrong. In the end, only one person can take the money home with them. As contestants decide whom to vote off, a voice lets the audience at home know who has actually answered the least number of questions correctly and poses a rhetorical question along the lines of 'But will the votes follow the facts?' The show's drama and suspense comes from the fact that people are sometimes voted 'the weakest link' when they clearly do not merit the label. They have been picked on by ruthless contestants willing to be branded 'cowards' by Anne in order to dispose of anyone they consider to be an intellectual threat. Whether or not the votes follow the facts, the 'weakest link' must leave the studio as Anne remarks: 'You are the weakest link, goodbye.' But of course, sometimes we all know that they are *not* the weakest link, but victims of others' greed. I find it interesting that such a show, based upon giving true answers to general knowledge questions and casting votes that have dramatic results according to whether or not they correspond to reality, should be watched and enjoyed by many people who would say that all truth is subjective.

*. . . the best way to approach a problem of any
kind is usually not to talk or even think very
much about the ultimate answer until I have
made sure that I am asking all the right
questions in the right order.*
PHILLIP E. JOHNSON[1]

'Suppose', wrote G. K. Chesterton, 'that a commotion arises in the street about a lamp post, which many influential people want to pull down. A grey-clad monk, who represents the spirit of the Middle Ages, is approached about the matter, and begins to say: "Let us first of all consider, my brethren, the value of Light. If Light be in itself good . . ." At this point he is somewhat excusably knocked down. All the people make a rush for the lamp post, the lamp post is down in ten minutes, and they go about congratulating each other on their unmedieval practicality.'[2] However, the story is far from over:

Some people have pulled the lamp post down
because they wanted the electric light; some
because they wanted old iron; some because they
wanted darkness, because their deeds were evil.
Some thought it not enough of a lamp post, some
too much; some acted because they wanted to
smash municipal machinery; some because they
wanted to smash something. And there is war in
the night, no man knowing whom he strikes. So,
gradually and inevitably . . . there comes back the
conviction that the monk was right after all, and
that all depends on what is the philosophy of
Light. Only what we might have discussed under
the gas lamp, we must now discuss in the dark.[3]

This parable illustrates the wisdom of starting at the beginning. If we are to make any progress on the question of meaning, we must emulate Chesterton's monk: 'Let us first of all consider, my brethren, the meaning of meaning . . .' This may seem a typically philosophical project, and so it is (nor is it any the worse for that). The question of meaning 'is not a straightforward empirical question that can be settled by observation. The question itself needs to be analysed and better understood . . . We need to make it specific, so that it can be answered.'[4] As the American philosopher Peter Kreeft explains with characteristic wisdom: 'There is nothing more pointless than an answer to a question that is not fully understood . . . We are far too impatient with questions, and therefore far too shallow in appreciating answers.'[5]

In pursuing the question of life's meaning, or lack of meaning, we are seeking nothing less than the *true* account of the *facts* about the *meaning*fulness (or meaninglessness) of existence in general and human existence in particular. We need, therefore, to begin by getting the nature of 'truth', 'facts' and 'meaning' clear in our minds.

Lessons about truth from a 'Dumb Ox'

While the assertion 'You are now reading' is true (because it describes what you are currently doing), it is the fact of your reading which is *the truth*. 'You are now reading' wouldn't be true if you were not, in fact, now reading. This distinction was noted by the Italian philosopher-theologian Thomas Aquinas (1225–1274), who wrote that 'all knowledge is . . . the conformity or match of thing and understanding . . . So that the existence of things precedes their being true . . . what is true is first true understanding and then the thing that matches it.'[6]

Chesterton may well have had Aquinas in mind when he wrote his parable of the monk and the lamp post, for he wrote a deservedly famous biography of the Italian 'schoolman'. Those who knew Aquinas 'describe him as a large, heavy-set figure who plodded about rather slowly and silently. When he was studying under Albert the Great, his fellow pupils derisively called him the Dumb Ox.'[7] His wise old lecturer, on the other hand, saw that although Thomas was physically slow, he had a mind that was sure. He defended his pupil with prophetic accuracy: 'You call him a Dumb Ox; I tell you this Dumb Ox shall bellow so loud that his bellowings will fill the world.'[8]

Thomas was innately inquisitive: 'The thing that killed the cat keeps alive the philosophers. Aquinas was curious about everything . . .'[9] It is said that at the age of four Aquinas asked his mother the simple question 'What is God?' Since this question is rather harder to answer than it is to ask, especially when the questioner is four years old, Tom's theological curiosity was not satiated by his mother's answer (whatever it was), and as Peter Kreeft comments: 'he set about writing the *Summa Theologiae*'.[10] (The *Summa* is a highly influential textbook for theology students still studied today by professional theologians and philosophers.)

Aquinas may have grown up to be 'a huge heavy bull of a man, fat and slow and quiet . . . mild and magnanimous . . . shy . . . and abstracted',[11] but when asked for what he thanked God, he simply answered: 'I have understood every page I ever read.'[12] The impressive nature of this claim can only be truly appreciated by someone who has at least a passing acquaintance with the works that Aquinas read. I well remember how a course I took on Aristotle (a major influence upon Aquinas) at Cardiff University was the most mind-expanding experience legally available on campus. And yet Aquinas was so full of the things he read and thought about that he could not be full of himself. As Chesterton wrote:

> His bulk made it easy to regard him humorously as the sort of walking wine-barrel, common in the comedies of many nations; he joked about it himself. It may be that he . . . was responsible for the sublime exaggeration that a crescent was cut out of the dinner-table to allow him to sit down. It is quite certain that it was an exaggeration; and that his stature was more remarked upon than his stoutness.[13]

Aquinas mixed with 'the great and the good', but it didn't go to his head, because his head was elsewhere: 'this absentminded professor has his head in the clouds and his feet on the ground – obviously the proper place for both. *Not* to have one's head in the clouds is to be an intellectual midget.'[14] For example, one tale that reveals how Aquinas had his mind set on higher things tells how in travelling to Paris he 'came to a place where the road turned to reveal the whole city gleaming in the sun beneath him. His companion remarked, "How beautiful it is! Wouldn't it be grand to own everything you can see from here?" Aquinas' laconic reply was: "I'd rather have the missing manuscript of Saint John Chrysostom." First things first.'[15] As Peter Kreeft comments: 'When someone has as accurate a scale of values as that, he appears eccentric.'[16]

Aquinas was a widely travelled chap, 'but he did not ride on a donkey, as his companions did. He walked. The obvious reason was his bulk. It was out of courtesy to the donkey that he did not impose the formidable burden on the poor innocent beast.'[17] Aquinas was courteous in his writings as well as in his travel arrangements. He was especially courteous to his opponents:

> He always states their position more perfectly and clearly and convincingly than they do before he refutes it. This is the exact opposite of the methods of modern politicians and even most modern philosophers: the making and unmaking of straw men . . . And of course, Aquinas always refutes his opponent's position, not his opponent. He is almost always impersonal rather than personal. That is because he believed so strongly in . . . objective truth.[18]

Although he died at the relatively early age of 49, Aquinas bequeathed to the world a *massive* body of work: 'commentaries on Aristotle, on scripture, and on other important authors, records of hundreds of disputations (public debates) on theological and philosophical subjects, small and large works on questions of the day, and several comprehensive text-books of theology. These writings stretch to over eight and a half million words – an average of some 1,190 words a day every day for twenty years.'[19] Aquinas has long since been recognized as 'an intellectual luminary with very few counterparts then or now'[20], and 'one of the dozen greatest philosophers of the western world'.[21] He also wrote prayers and poems.

Telling it like it is

*The First Noble Truth of theism (and of common
sense) is the reality of truth itself.*
STEPHEN R. L. CLARK[22]

In response to the question 'Whether there is only one
truth . . . ?'[23] Aquinas said that 'truth resides primarily
in the intellect; and secondarily in things . . .'[24] The secondary meaning of truth is what we commonly call 'the
facts of the matter'. Thus, Aquinas asserts, 'it is from
the fact that a thing is or is not, that our thought or
word is true or false, as the Philosopher [i.e. Aristotle]
teaches'.[25] This is the primary meaning of 'truth'.
Aristotle's definition of the primary meaning of truth, to
which Aquinas refers, is framed in words of one syllable:

> If one says of what is that it is, or of what is not
> that it is not, he speaks the truth; but if one says
> of what is that it is not, or of what is not that it is,
> he does not speak the truth.[26]

So there are two sides to 'truth'. The first side of truth,
which depends upon the second as sunlight depends
upon the sun, is a quality of beliefs and propositions
(sentences that make claims about what is the case). It
is not a quality of *all* beliefs and propositions, but only
those beliefs and propositions that correspond to the
facts: 'truth in the mind . . . isn't determined by how the
mind sees things but by how things are: for *statements*
– and the understanding they embody – *are called true
or false inasmuch as things are or are not so . . .*'[27]
As Aristotle wrote: 'it is by the facts of the case, by their
being or not being so, that a statement is called true or
false'.[28] The other side of truth, then, is 'the facts' that
determine whether or not our understanding of reality

is correct, because they are the reality we are trying to know. To understand something, as Peter Kreeft points out, is to stand under its authority as reality to determine how we think about it. The foundational importance of such understanding, of a humble dedication to truth rather than falsehood and deception, is encapsulated by a line from a poem by Chesterton: 'There is one sin, to call a green leaf grey.'[29] Like Richard Dawkins, we need to 'care about what's actually true'.[30]

This understanding of truth is not something Aquinas or Aristotle *invented*, but something they *discovered* at the foundation of all thought, argument and communication. Any attempt to think, argue or communicate an alternative theory of truth would contradict itself by relying upon the nature of truth as described by our slow but sure medieval 'Dumb Ox' and his ancient Greek master. As Peter Kreeft and Ronald Tacelli argue:

> All theories of truth, once they are expressed clearly and simply, presuppose the commonsensical notion of truth that is enshrined in the wisdom of language and the tradition of usage, namely the correspondence . . . theory. For each theory claims that it is really true, that is, that it corresponds to reality, and that the others are really false, that is, that they fail to correspond to reality.[31]

Aquinas pointed out that from the mere acceptance that *there is a fact* flowed an appreciation of the ground rules of logic:

> Aquinas . . . says emphatically . . . that something is something. Perhaps it would be best to say very emphatically (with a blow on the table), 'There *is* an Is.' That is as much monkish credulity as St.

Thomas asks of us . . . Aquinas insists very profoundly, but very practically, that there instantly enters, with this idea of affirmation, the idea of contradiction . . . Therefore there has already entered *something* beyond even the first fact of being; there follows it like its shadow the first fundamental creed or commandment; that a thing cannot be and not be. Henceforth, in common or popular language, there is a false and true. I say in popular language, because Aquinas is nowhere more subtle than in pointing out that being is not strictly the same as truth; seeing truth must mean the appreciation of being by some mind capable of appreciating it . . . In other words, the essence of . . . common sense is that two agencies are at work; reality and the recognition of reality; and their meeting is a sort of marriage, because it is fruitful; the only philosophy now in the world that really is fruitful. It produces practical results, precisely because it is the combination of an adventurous mind and a strange fact . . . [32]

As J. P. Moreland explains: 'This is why truth is so powerful. *It allows us to cooperate with reality, whether spiritual or physical, and to tap into its power.*' [33]

Anthony O'Hear draws attention to the fact that 'Right from the start, our experience is already rooted in activity in a real world which is not of our making, and to which our desires and thoughts have to conform . . .' [34] F. C. Copleston explains that 'Aquinas . . . uses the proposition "I exist" as an example of a proposition which I know to be true if I enunciate it. And in knowing it to be true I know that I can attain truth.'[35] As Thomas wrote: 'The meaning of true consists in a matching of thing and understanding, and matching presupposes diversity, not identity.'[36] These first principles are, as Peter Kreeft says, 'indubitable. Only hypocrites and mad-men pretend to doubt the Law of Non-contradiction.'[37] If we want to keep thinking, we'd better stick with the insights of Aquinas, for as O'Hear argues: 'The reason why we should not contradict ourselves is because if we do, we will simply lapse into incoherence. You cannot, for example, think both that it is five o'clock in the afternoon and not five o'clock in the afternoon. The one thought cancels out the other. You end up thinking nothing.'[38]

Unified realism

Paul Helm summarizes the implications of the 'perennial philosophy' developed by thinkers like Aquinas:

> . . . the universe . . . exists, as such, in an intelligible and orderly manner, a manner that holds true irrespective of what men or women may think or hope about it. We may make all sorts of mistakes in our belief, due to our incapacity, our ignorance, carelessness and a lack of imagination, but this does not alter the fact that there is one objective state of affairs to which, as far as possible, we ought to make our beliefs conform and which, because of its objective character, often corrects our beliefs in unexpected ways.[39]

As scientist turned theologian Alister McGrath points out, this realist understanding of truth underlies the scientific enterprise:

> Modern philosophy of science [insists] that a rigorous distinction must be made between

epistemological and ontological issues – that is, between how something can be known and whether something is actually there . . . A critical realist position holds that something can be there without our being aware of it . . . reality does not depend upon human observation to come into existence. It is already there; the question is how we discern it, coming to know what is already there, in advance of its being known.[40]

The early practitioners of science, from Copernicus through Galileo, Kepler and Newton, all regarded the search for order behind the flux of nature 'as a worthy and legitimate response to a universe regulated by an intelligent Creator, who had also created the human mind in such a way that it was fitted to the intelligibility of nature'.[41] As Thomas Dubay explains, for Aquinas, 'nature lies between the divine mind, which creates, and our human minds, which discover'.[42] This double-sided belief, in the rationality of creation and the suitability of our faculties to understand that rationality 'secured the possibility of scientific knowledge and a foundation for the scientist's confidence in the reliability of his most fundamental assumptions'.[43] Today, atheistic scientists continue to make the same assumptions, but without any metaphysical guarantee of their validity.

Helm calls the medieval view of a fit between creation and rationality, which laid the foundations for the birth of modern science, *'unified realism'*[44] in that it holds that: '[objective] truths about the universe hold independently of the decisions or theorisings of human beings, and these truths form one consistent set'.[45] He goes on to explain that: 'For this tradition . . . theology is a branch of metaphysics. And the metaphysical account [Aquinas and others] give of the relation between God and the world is a unified realist conception. Such an account of God and the world, if it is true, would be true even if religious belief ceased.'[46] For Aquinas, theology is a science because it is about applying the truth-orientated tools of reason to discover objective truth about an objective reality: 'Theology is a science for Aquinas. It depends on principles established by a higher science, as music depends on mathematics . . . The higher science is the science of God; that is, the knowledge God has of us, not the knowledge we have of God. The data of theology is divine revelation, God's word about man rather than man's word about God.'[47]

Peter Kreeft observes that: 'There are in the long run only three philosophies: that there are more things, fewer things, or the same number of things in heaven and earth, that is, in objective reality, as in our philosophies and dreams, that is, in our subjective consciousness.'[48] Like Hamlet, Aquinas said that there are more things in heaven and earth than in our philosophies and dreams; but he also said that humans may come to know some of those things because we are made in the image of God, who knows them all:

Practical understanding causes things and is the measure of what it makes [i.e. a carpenter is shown to be skilled if the chair he makes turns out the way he intended it to be]; but theoretical understanding acquires knowledge from things . . . so that things are the measure of it [i.e. 'knowledge is . . . the conformity or match of thing and understanding']. So clearly the things of nature, from which our mind draws its science, are the measure of the human mind, as Aristotle says [i.e. scientific theories are judged by how well they model reality], but are themselves measured by God's mind, in which everything exists in the way a craftsman's handiwork exists in a craftsman's mind . . . Since a thing's relationship to God's mind precedes its relationship to human minds, its truth in the first sense precedes its truth in the second; so, if the human mind did not exist, things would still be called true in relation to God's mind . . .[49]

And as he says in *Summa Contra Gentiles*, 'The knowledge of the principles that are known to us naturally has been implanted in us by God, for God is the Author of our nature.'[50] While our knowledge of these basic principles is thus innate, one of the important consequences of realism is that it 'permits the possibility of ignorance'.[51] Unified realism is ultimately a humbling understanding of reality. As Phillip Johnson points out, 'For statements about the difference between appearance and reality to be meaningful, there must truly be a way things really are, and this is metaphysical realism.'[52]And this implies 'that the world that we live in is richer in meaning than our experience of it'.[53]

University challenge

> . . . parts of our universities are going through what Plato described as the last stages of democracy, when . . . nihilism is both preached and practiced.
> PHILLIP E. JOHNSON[54]

Professor of Psychology Paul C. Vitz comments that:

'Universities are so deeply secularised that most academics can no longer articulate why they are opposed to Christianity. They merely assume that for all rational people the question of being a Christian was settled – negatively – at some time in the past.'[55] Ironically, the University was a medieval institution founded by Christians on the assumption of unified realism:

> The medieval university was established on the premise that all knowledge is ultimately coherent and unified. The very word *university* was borrowed from the word *universe*, which derives from two different and opposite words, *unity* and *diversity*. A universe is a place where the many (diversity) come together into the unified whole (unity). The working assumption was that all diverse particulars of knowledge discovered and analyzed in the specialized academic disciplines, found their coherency in God. It was the unifying power of theology that elevated her to the queen of sciences, being assisted by her handmaiden philosophy.[56]

Today, theology has been dethroned as the queen of sciences. Ravi Zacharias observes how: 'The idea of God's non-existence now either explicitly or implicitly permeates almost every major discipline in secular universities.'[57] As a result: 'The university has become the multiversity and students feel the impact of the disintegration of higher education.'[58] According to Jimmy H. Davies and Harry L. Poe, in the last three centuries, 'The palette has shrunk from many complementary ways of knowing that mutually informed one another to only one or two recognized ways of knowing. This transition corresponds to the general fragmentation of knowledge over the last three centuries. We have witnessed an explosion is some kinds of knowledge, but a poverty in other areas of knowledge.'[59]

The disintegrating effect of atheism upon academia is well illustrated by the history of the Encyclopaedia. Between 1751 and 1789 a group of French intellectuals known as the Encyclopaedists published the 35 volumes of *L'Encyclopedie* (edited by Denis Diderot), a reference work that became a major voice for the enemies of the French establishment's interpretation of the theistic worldview: 'Its stance can be seen from the way in which it was complied', explains John Blanchard:

> In previous encyclopaedias, information was classified under such headings as 'animal kingdom' and 'plant kingdom'. In Diderot's work the connecting link between previously related entries was broken and everything was arranged in alphabetical order. This arrangement . . . carried a clear message: all entities exist independently of each other and the hierarchy of man and animals, things and ideas has disappeared . . . Some 250 years later, many people take exactly the same line as the French Encylopaedists, but one wonders whether they have thought through the implications. If all the elements in the universe, human and otherwise, are unconnected or unrelated, where can human life find meaning or purpose?[60]

Today, students study an ever-wider assortment of subjects in an ever-decreasing depth (knowing less and less about more and more), and without anyone encouraging them to ask how all these particulars can be integrated into an intellectually satisfying worldview.[61] The result is a compartmentalized intellectual schizophrenia:

> The chaos of secularistic education is keenly felt
> by the students enduring it. Some are driven to
> despair as the message of nihilism gets through.
> Some seek to quiet the haunting questions of the
> mind by indulging in forms of escapism. Others
> seek solace in the acceptable practice of
> specialization in which the conflict of the
> disciplines can be avoided by preoccupation with a
> highly specialized, singular field of endeavor . . .
> With the death of god must come the death of the
> 'Renaissance man'.[62]

Having lost the focal point of theology, the university has also lost the ability to answer the existential needs of its students: 'Within the university, students and professors scrutinize every possible aspect of our universe – from the billions of galaxies to subatomic particles, electrons, quarks – but they assiduously avoid examining their own lives.'[63] The modern university is consequently a pragmatic institution actively draining students of every idealistic pretension:

> . . . universities . . . have unrealistically
> encouraged careerism for a pragmatic reason:
> they desperately need enrolments to stay in
> business. But the universities have also disparaged
> and ground down all other ideals. Faculty
> members pushing pluralistic relativism have
> destroyed once-common forms of idealism. As a
> result, the romance of the career – unsupported by
> such ideals as truth (for those in education),
> justice (for those in law), patriotism (for those in
> the military), life (for those in medicine) – soon
> collapses into just a job.[64]

Allan Bloom opened his noted book *The Closing of the American Mind* with the assertion that: 'There is one thing a professor can be absolutely certain of: almost every student entering the university believes, or says he believes, that truth is relative.'[65] In fact, '70 percent of today's generation. . . claim that absolute truth does not exist, that all truth is relative'.[66] (In one poll, 64 per cent of Americans agreed that the self-contradictory statement 'there is no such thing as absolute truth,'[67] was true!) This is an opinion many find endorsed rather than challenged by their time at university. Claire Fox, Director of the Institute of Ideas, laments that: 'In our universities, current relativist orthodoxy celebrates all views as equal as though there are no arguments to win. Whatever the cause, many in academia bemoan the loss of the vibrant contestation and robust refutation of ideas in seminars, lecture halls and research papers.'[68] Indeed, disregard for objective truth has negative ramifications for the whole of society, as a 1994 survey of 3,795 'churched youth' in America revealed: 'When our youth do not accept an objective standard of truth they become: 36 per cent more likely to lie to you as a parent . . . 48 per cent more likely to cheat on an exam . . . 2 times more likely to try to physically hurt someone . . . 3 times more likely to use illegal drugs . . . 6 times more likely to attempt suicide . . . 65 per cent more likely to mistrust people . . . 2 times more likely to be angry with life . . . 2 times more likely to be lacking purpose.'[69]

Jay Budziszewski recalls with horror how, fresh out of graduate school, he stood in the Government Department of the University of Texas to give his 'here's-why-you-should-hire-me lecture':

I wanted to teach about ethics and politics, so as

academic job seekers do everywhere, I was
showing the faculty my stuff. So what did I tell
them? Two things. The first was that we human
beings just make up the difference between good
and evil; the second was that we aren't responsible
for what we do anyway . . . Does that seem to you
a good plan for getting a job teaching the young?
Or does it seem a better plan for getting
committed to the state mental hospital? Well, I
wasn't committed to the state mental hospital, but
I did get a job teaching the young.[70]

John Leo complains that: 'A growing number of professors accept the postmodernist notion that there is no
such thing as truth, only rhetoric. The result is the blur-
ring of distinctions between history and literature, fact
and fiction, honesty and dishonesty.'[71] For example,
although it is one of the best-documented genocides in
history, a small number of 'deniers' argue that the
Holocaust is a hoax: 'Professor Deborah E. Lipstadt
carefully documents their activities in her book
*Denying the Holocaust: The Growing Assault on
Truth and Memory* (1993). Professor Lipstadt suggests that one reason deniers have gained a hearing on
university campuses is because of the relativistic thinking that permeates the academy.'[72] (According to one
poll, one-third of Americans do not believe the
Holocaust happened![73]) No attitude is more calculated
to denigrate the importance of truth and reason, and to
support the tyranny of mere rhetoric, than the attitude
that 'there is no such thing as truth, only rhetoric'. No
attitude could be more calculated to instil students with
a sense of lethargic purposelessness and meaninglessness. As a graduate student lamented in a Harvard com-

mencement address: 'The freedom of our day, is the freedom to devote ourselves to any values we please, on the mere condition that we do not believe them to be true.'[74]

A university, writes Phillip Johnson, 'is fundamentally about knowledge. Without a strong sense of what knowledge is and why the increase of it is good for everyone, it may seem that the university is little more than a playground for intellectuals.'[75] Universities have evolved, as Josh McDowell and Bob Hostetler observe, 'from institutions that aid in a search for knowledge to institutions that deny the possibility of knowing anything objectively!'[76] Johnson asks why taxpayers, donors and tuition-fee payers should support a university department of literature:

> When I went to college as a literature major
> almost forty years ago, the answer was clear. By
> studying great literature with proficient scholars,
> one supposedly learned something about what is
> really good and beautiful and why the really good
> works are better than the ones that seem good to
> persons whose tastes are uninformed.[77]

Today, such a justification is hard to sustain on the assumptions adopted by most universities: 'If the literature and philosophy professors now believe that "good" is just what the most influential people happen to like, or if they start from assumptions that make relativism hard to avoid, the rationale for paying their salaries may well be called into question.'[78] I remember the frustration I felt as a student in Cardiff University's postmodern English department, where one of our lecturers taught that texts have no inherent meaning ('The author is dead' as Roland Barthes put it, echoing Nietzsche), and that since texts only mean what they mean *to the reader*, Shakespeare has no more inherent value than the text on the back of a breakfast-cereal packet. How he expected his students to value the *inherent* meaning of his 'deconstructionist' theory, I will never know!

Universities have become largely self-defeating institutions: 'Universities are centres of unreason in the . . . profound sense that they are based on a metaphysical position that will not support a concept of rationality in the value realm, and hence ultimately will not support it anywhere.'[79] Of course, universities are also wonderful places that can open up whole new worlds of academic and personal exploration to their students. I certainly benefited hugely from my six years in higher education. Nor is adherence to the incoherence of postmodernism universal. Many university departments (notably departments of science and philosophy) stand out as islands dedicated to truth in the midst of a relativistic academic sea. Unfortunately, even departments committed to truth often subscribe to philosophical assumptions that lead to its disintegration and demise. Studying at university today all too often means having to grapple with wolves in sheep's clothing.

Unified realism and the mind of God

While 'unified realism' has a natural fit with, and derives support from, belief in 'the Mind of God', it isn't necessary to begin with a belief in God to discover that unified realism is the inescapable philosophy of common good sense. Aristotle wasn't a theist in the traditional sense of the term, and Aquinas argued in support of 'unified realism' simply from the inherent implications of the admission that *something*, anything (like

Augustine's 'If I err, I exist', or Descartes' 'I think therefore I am'), *is the case.*

If you want to deny that *something is the case*, you will have to find a way of doing so without claiming either that your denial is the case, or that something that contradicts unified realism is itself the case! You won't be any more successful in this task than you would be trying to lift yourself off the ground by tugging at your shoe laces, or in convincingly denying your ability to speak English by saying: 'I do not speak English.' As Aquinas concluded, 'We must, therefore, have recourse to the natural reason, to which all men are forced to give their assent.'[80]

Nevertheless, the natural fit between unified realism and belief in the Mind of God is of the utmost importance; for as Aidan Nichols points out: 'The rejection of the great discovery or rediscovery of Thomas's metaphysics worked itself out as nihilism, in which the world, once seen as God's beautiful effect, filled with wisdom and goodness, becomes an indifferent or even threatening place where these qualities of created being cease to be present since they are no longer considered as enjoying extra-mental reality.'[81] Hence, 'The denial of God destroys the inherent value and meaningfulness of the world.'[82]

Facts: subjective or objective

Objective truth is truth that is not dependent on any creature's subjective feelings, desires or beliefs.
DOUGLAS GROOTHUIS[83]

Facts are 'states of affairs that obtain', they are 'things

that are the case'; but facts come in two varieties: there are objective facts, and there are subjective facts. The categories of objective and subjective facthood are central to discussing the meaning of life. Philosopher John Searl writes of the difference between 'those features of the world that exist intrinsically, or independently of human observation and conscious attitudes, and those features of the world that are dependent on human attitudes'.[84] Those intrinsic features of the world that exist independently of human observation and conscious attitudes are objective facts, and they include 'the sorts of things discussed in physics and chemistry'.[85] An objective fact is 'Something independent of me, my mind, my opinions and feelings and beliefs and desires and experiences.'[86] Raindrops on roses and whiskers on kittens, bright copper kettles and warm woollen mittens, not to mention brown paper packages tied up with string, are all objective facts. The fact that these are a few of someone's favourite things is, on the other hand, a subjective fact. Subjective facts do not exist independently of human observation and conscious attitudes, but depend entirely upon the attitude, opinion or belief of one or more finite subjects (and are therefore relative to the subject/s).

A liking for brown paper packages tied up with strings is a subjective fact that *depends upon*, and is therefore *relative to*, the individual whose liking it is having that liking. However, the fact that brown paper packages tied up with strings exist to be liked by anyone is an objective fact that does not depend upon human consciousness or attitudes. Such packages may exist because we made them, but *that they exist* is not something that depends upon what you, or I, or we think or feel or decide. If no one liked brown paper packages, then it would still be true that brown paper packages exist, even though no one would like them. If no one believed that brown paper packages existed, they would still exist all the same. When it comes to objective reality, it is reality that calls the shots, not us. This is an especially important truth to remember when we are dealing with matters of metaphysics and religious belief. As Richard Purtill explains:

> When something is a matter of personal preference what is right for one person can be wrong for another . . . A career as a college teacher can be right for me, but perhaps wrong for you, and so on. But religion deals with such questions as 'Is there a God?' and 'Do we continue to exist after death?' And it looks as if the answers to such questions depend on how things are, not on our attitudes or tastes. If we exist after death, we will exist after death no matter what our present opinions are. If God doesn't exist, then no matter how much we want God to exist, He still doesn't exist.[87]

The transcendentals

> *. . . we may enumerate . . . beauty, goodness, and truth as comprehensive descriptions under which many particular experiences of value may be brought . . .*
> W. R. SORELYL[88]

Garreth Thomson observes that 'In part, the question of the meaning of life is a request to clarify the nature of value . . .'[89] As our quest for meaning progresses we will find ourselves getting well acquainted with questions about what medieval philosophers like Aquinas called the 'transcendental' values of truth, goodness and beauty (so called because they are 'qualities that "transcend" the divisions between classes of things'[90]). Stephen Ian McIntosh writes: 'The grouping of beauty, truth and goodness is hardly coincidental; it is not merely a convenient list of desirable qualities. Beauty, truth and goodness have been associated together ever since people started thinking about these values.'[91] As Mortimer J. Aldler explains:

> Truth, goodness, and beauty form a triad of terms which . . . have been called 'transcendental' on the ground that everything which is is in some measure . . . subject to denomination as true or false, good or evil, beautiful or ugly. But they have also been assigned to special spheres of . . . subject matter – the true to thought and logic, the good to action and morals, the beautiful to enjoyment and aesthetics. They have been called 'the three fundamental values' with the implication that the worth of anything can be exhaustively judged by reference to these three standards . . .[92]

Questions of meaning are intimately bound up with questions of value. Things (like raindrops on roses, whiskers on kittens, and human existence) are obviously only worthwhile in so far as they have worth; and that means *in so far as they have truth, goodness, or beauty*. Hence Richard Harries' lament:

> One of the unfortunate characteristics of the modern world is the way we have split asunder thinking, feeling and morality. Beauty is too often thought of simply in terms of an emotional

response. Conscience is usually understood to be a feeling of guilt whilst pure hard thinking is reserved for science. In contrast, our Christian forebears had a unified vision in which mental processes always had a role to play and beauty was an aspect of objective reality.[93]

In a similar vein, theologian Jeremy S. Begbie insightfully comments:

> The three great transcendentals of traditional philosophical enquiry – truth, goodness and beauty – are no longer seen to be at all universal features of our world existing in harmonious interrelationship. The outcome is that truth – if objective truth is believed to exist at all – is widely thought to be the province solely of the scientist, whose work accordingly appears either to be unrelated to the deeper meaning of things or, worse, to impose a view of an empty and meaningless universe. It is part of the paradox of the modern age that science's discoveries of the sheer beauty, unity and rationality of the universe co-exist with assertions of its essential meaninglessness or indifference to moral values.[94]

Many thinkers have seen truth, beauty and goodness as objective facts, on a par with bright copper kettles and warm woollen mittens, grounded in the objective existence and nature of Ultimate Reality. As C. E. M. Joad explains in a passage that had a formative influence on my own view of the matter:

> In regard to the nature of Value, the traditional view . . . seems to me to be correct. The Values, on this view, reduce themselves to three, Goodness, Truth and Beauty . . . they are both

> objective in the sense that they are found by the
> human mind – found as given in things – and not
> projected into things or contributed to them by
> our own minds, and ultimate, in the sense that
> whatever we value can be shown to be valued
> because of the relation of the thing valued to some
> one or other of the three Values. Thus while other
> things are valued as means to one or other of
> these three, *they* are valued as ends in themselves.
> Moreover, these Values are not just arbitrary,
> pieces of cosmic furniture lying about, as it were,
> in the universe without explanation, coherence or
> connection, but are revelations of a unity that
> underlies them, are, in fact, the ways in which God
> reveals himself to man.[95]

This belief, that ultimate reality combines and explains
the good, the true and the beautiful in one package, has
been gradually discarded over the last two centuries by
Western culture:

> Once upon a time . . . our society, by and large,
> explained the universe, humanity, and the purpose
> of life from the Judeo-Christian tradition: a belief
> that truth existed . . . A clear understanding of
> what was right and wrong gave society a moral
> standard by which to measure crime and
> punishment, business ethics, community values,
> character, and social conduct. It became the lens
> through which society viewed law, science, art,
> and politics – the whole of culture. It provided a
> cohesive model that promoted the healthy
> development of the family, united communities,
> and encouraged responsibility and moral
> behaviour. That has changed drastically . . . Our

> children are being raised in a society that has
> largely rejected the notions of truth and morality,
> a society that has somewhere lost the ability to
> decide what is true and what is right. Truth has
> become a matter of taste; morality has been
> replaced by individual preferences.[96]

The unavoidable cost of this philosophical shift has
been the abolition of the belief that truth, goodness and
beauty are objective realities and, in turn, the abolition
of meaning and purpose.

In his classic biography of Aquinas, G. K. Chesterton
warned: 'God made Man so that he was capable of coming in contact with reality; and those whom God has
joined, let no man put asunder.'[97] A loss of belief in God
has inevitably led to a (self-defeating) loss of belief in
objective truth (and the objectivity of the other transcendental values), and in the human capacity to know
these objective realities: 'the secularised intellect denies
the existence of any truth beyond what is humanly con-
trived, and this denial . . . manifests itself in the wild,
manic-depressive intellectual swings so characteristic
of modernity, between self-congratulatory claims of
omniscience and self-pitying lamentations of complete
scepticism'.[98] As Oxford philosopher Keith Ward cautions:

> Deprived of the traditional Christian support that
> the cosmos itself is the product of supreme reason
> . . . human reason can easily come to seem an
> ephemeral and unreliable mechanism . . . And
> once it is dethroned, it may be hard to find
> anything to put in its place, which can provide a
> firm basis for giving human life purpose, dignity
> and value, and which can give us faith to go

> without despair when our dreams are not
> realised.[99]

Hence we find ourselves in a situation where 'All truth, all value, all beauty must be measured without appeal or recourse to eternal verities or absolute standards'[100]; and it is hardly surprising that, having discarded any way to measure truth, goodness or beauty against an absolute standard, we fail to measure anything as being objectively true, good, or beautiful! We have become like the fisherman who complained that he never caught any fish smaller than the holes in his net. This situation has obvious implications for the question of meaning: 'When you separate the natural world from the world of transcendent reality, as many people do these days, then life has meaning only to you personally, and not to the world as a whole.'[101] Meaning has been relegated to the objectively meaningless realm of the merely subjective.

Nevertheless, to affirm the objectivity of truth, goodness and beauty, upon which the objectivity of meaning rests, is to place oneself in good company, for as C. S. Lewis wrote: 'Until modern times no thinker of the first rank ever doubted that our judgements of value were rational judgements or that what they discovered was objective . . .'[102] Peter Kreeft confirms, for example, that: 'To pre-modern man, pagan as well as Christian, moral laws were absolute: unyielding, non-negotiable, and unquestionable. They were also objective: discovered rather than created; given, in the nature of things.'[103] Such an objective conception of value can be traced back to Aristotle's teacher Plato, who argued that the human mind does not create values, but discovers what is in itself objectively and inherently good. Deciding which view of value, the subjective or the objective view, presents us with the truth about the world, will obviously be a crucial issue for us to grapple with as our study progresses.

What is the question of meaning?

Those who wish to succeed must ask the right preliminary questions.
ARISTOTLE

We have patiently followed the advice of Chesterton's monk, and have assembled the philosophical tools for the task ahead. We are now ready to attend to the question in hand, the question of meaning.

Questions about the meaning, purpose or value of life are all *existential* questions, questions that 'concern how we exist in the world, how we should view existence, and how we ought to exist . . . These are the questions most fundamental to getting our bearings and finding our way.'[104]

Some philosophers argue that since meaning is a linguistic thing, and since life is not a linguistic thing, life just isn't the sort of thing that could have a meaning. Questions about the meaning of life are, they suggest, meaningless. Julian Jaynes writes: '*words* have meaning, not life or persons, or the universe itself . . .'[105] However, this argument is far from convincing: 'Body movement can have meaning. We can make meaningful discoveries. We can give meaningful looks. And there is no syntax or semantics sufficient to justify the claim that there is really a linguistic phenomenon operative in every such case. A meaningful experience need not refer, or modify, or express action. It is not a category mistake to ask whether life has meaning. It is not nonsense to suppose it does.'[106]

Like the intrepid 'Pigs in Space' from the Muppet Show we often speak about 'the meaning and purpose of life'. In doing so, we make two assumptions, both of which I think are correct. The first assumption appears to be that meaning and purpose, while connected, are nevertheless distinct. The second assumption is that what we are seeking when we ask after 'the meaning and purpose of life' is an objective fact.

Whether or not life is subjectively meaningful *to us* (in the same sense that a certain flavour of ice cream tastes nice *to us*), we are here asking whether life is objectively meaningful. The answer to this question is either that it is or that it isn't, and we want to know one way or the other (only then can we go on to ask what the answer to the question of meaning means *to us*). Either way, what we are interested in is an objective state of affairs that obtains independently of our consciousness. This is implied by the use of the definite article: *the* meaning and purpose of life. Thomas V. Morris writes:

> What is the meaning of life? This has often been said to be the deepest question that can be asked about life in this world. But there is a deeper question: Is there any meaning to life? When we ask merely what the meaning of life is, we are presupposing that it has a meaning. And it is just this presupposition that many intellectuals began to question in the early twentieth century.[107]

What we should make of the answer to this objective question, positive or negative, (in terms of our subjective intellectual, emotional and practical responses) is a separate kettle of fish; but the answer must at least be sought. If we seek an answer, our search may fail. However, if we never seek the truth, we shall never find it.

[1] Johnson, Phillip E., *The Right Questions* (Downers Grove: IVP, 2002), introduction.

[2] Chesterton, G. K., 'Heretics' in Russell Sparkes (ed.), *Prophet of Orthodoxy* (London: Fount, 1997), p.227.

[3] *ibid*.

[4] Thomson, Garreth, *On the Meaning of Life* (London: Wadsworth, 2003), p.4.

[5] Kreeft, Peter, *Making Sense out of Suffering* (Ann Arbor, Michigan: Servant, 1986), p.27.

[6] Aquinas, Thomas, *Questiones Disputatae de Veritate*, in Timothy McDermott (ed.), *Aquinas – Selected Philosophical Writings* (Oxford University Press, 1998), p.53-54, 57.

[7] Change, Curtis, *Engaging Unbelief* (Downers Grove: IVP, 2000), p.64.

[8] Quoted by G. K. Chesterton, *St. Thomas Aquinas* (London: Hodder & Stoughton, 1933), p.79.

[9] Kreeft, Peter, 'When Philosophy and Life are One', in *The Ever Illuminating Wisdom of St. Thomas Aquinas* (San Francisco, Ignatius, 1996), p.28.

[10] *ibid*.

[11] Chesterton, *op. cit.*, p.15.

[12] *ibid.*, p.16.

[13] *ibid.*, p.142-143.

[14] Kreeft, 'When Philosophy and Life are One', *op. cit.*, p.15.

[15] Kreeft, *op. cit.*, p.24.

[16] *ibid.*

[17] *ibid.*, p.25.

[18] *ibid.*, p.26.

[19] McDermott, Timothy (ed.), *Aquinas – Selected Philosophical Writings* (Oxford University Press, 1998), Introduction, p.xv.

[20] Graham, Gordon, *Genes: A Philosophical Inquiry* (London: Routledge, 2002), p.151.

[21] Kenny, Anthony (ed.), *Aquinas, A Collection of Critical Essays* (London, 1969), p.1.

[22] Clark, Stephen R. L., *God, Religion and Reality* (London: SPCK, 1988), p.36.

[23] Aquinas, *Summa Theologica*, article 6.

[24] *ibid.*

[25] *ibid.*, Part I, Question 16, Objection 3.

[26] Quoted by Peter Kreeft, *Between Heaven and Hell* (Leicester: IVP, 1982).

[27] Aquinas, *Questiones Disputatae de Veritate*, in McDermott (ed.), *Aquinas – Selected Philosophical Writings* (Oxford University Press, 1998), p.58.

[28] Aquinas, quoted by Norman L. Geisler and Paul D. Feinberg, *Introduction to Philosophy* (Grand Rapids: Baker, 1987), p.247.

[29] Chesterton, G. K., 'Ecclesiastes', in *The Collected Poems of G. K. Chesterton* (New York: Dodd, Mead & Co., 1911), p.310.

[30] Dawkins, Richard, 'Darwin's Dangerous Disciple' at www.skeptic.com/03.4.miele-dawkins-iv.html

[31] Kreeft, Peter and Tacelli, Ronald, *Handbook of Christian Apologetics* (Crowborough, Monarch, 1995), p.366.

[32] Chesterton, *St. Thomas Aquinas*, *op. cit.*, p.198-200, 221.

[33] Moreland, J. P., *Love Your God With All Your Mind* (NavPress, 1997), p.81.

[34] O'Hear, Anthony, *Philosophy* (London: New Century, 2001), p.35.

[35] Copleston, F. C., *Aquinas* (Hardmondsworth: Penguin Books, 1957), p.49.

[36] Aquinas, *Questiones Disputatae de Veritate*, in McDermott (ed.), *op. cit.*, p.58-59.

[37] Kreeft, 'When Philosophy and Life are One', *op. cit.*, p.27.

[38] O'Hear, *op. cit.*, p.39.

[39] Helm, Paul, *Faith and Understanding* (Edinburgh University Press, 1997), p.53-54.

[40] McGrath, Alister, *The Re-Enchantment of Nature* (London: Hodder & Stoughton), p.180-181.

[41] Stewart, W. Christopher, 'Religion and Science' in Michael J. Murray (ed.), *Reason for the Hope Within* (Grand Rapids: Eerdmans, 1999), p.327.

[42] Dubay, Thomas, *The Evidential Power of Beauty* (San Francisco: Ignatius, 1999), p.320.

[43] Stewart, *op. cit.*, p.327.

[44] Helm, *op. cit.*, p.54.

[45] *ibid.*, p.54, 76.

[46] *ibid.*

[47] Kreeft, *op. cit.*, p.27.

[48] Kreeft, Peter, *Heaven, The Heart's Deepest Longing* (San Francisco: Ignatius, 1993), p.246.

[49] Aquinas, *Questiones Disputatae de Veritate*, *op. cit.*, p.57.

[50] Aquinas, *Summa Contra Gentiles*, 1.7.2, p.74.

[51] Thomson, Garreth, *On the Meaning of Life* (London: Wadsworth, 2003), p.111.

[52] Johnson, Phillip E., *Reason in the Balance* (Downers Grove: IVP, 1995), p.128.

[53] Thomson, *op. cit.*, p.112.

[54] Johnson, Phillip E., 'Harter's Precept' in *Objection Sustained* (Downers

Grove: IVP, 1998), p.160.

[55] Vitz, Paul C., *Psychology as Religion* (Grand Rapids: Eerdmans, 2001), p.xvi.

[56] Sproul, R. C., Gerstner, John and Lindsay, Arthur, *Classical Apologetics* (Grand Rapids, Michigan: Zondervan/Academic Books, 1984), p.9-10.

[57] Zacharias, Ravi, 'An Ancient Message, Through Modern Means, To A Postmodern Mind' in D. A. Carson (ed.), *Telling the Truth* (Grand Rapids: Zondervan, 2000), p.21.

[58] Sproul, Gerstner and Lindsay, *op. cit.*, p.10.

[59] Davies, Jimmy H. and Poe, Harry L., *Designer Universe: Intelligent Design and the Existence of God* (Nashville, Tenessee: Broadman & Holman Publishers, 2002), p.209.

[60] Blanchard, John, *Does God Believe in Atheists?* (Darlington: Evangelical Press, 2000), p.53.

[61] cf. Moreland, J. P., 'Integration and the Christian Scholar' at http://capo.org/premise/96/april/p960406.html

[62] Sproul, Gerstner and Lindsay, *op. cit.*, p.11.

[63] Nicholi, Armand M. Jr, *The Question of God* (New York: Free Press, 2002), p.6.

[64] Vitz, *op. cit.*, p.165.

[65] Bloom, Allan, *The Closing of the American Mind* (New York: Simon & Simon, 1987), p.25.

[66] McDowell, Josh and Hostetler, Bob, *Right from Wrong* (Milton Keynes: Word, 1994), p.17.

[67] Andrus, Michael P., 'Conversion Beyond Mere Religious Preference' in Carson (ed.), *op. cit.*, p.158.

[68] Fox, Claire, *Designer Babies: Where Should We Draw The Line?*, Preface (London: Hodder & Stoughton, 2002), p.viii.

[69] McDowell and Hostetler, *op. cit.*, p.21.

[70] Budziszewski, Jay, 'Escape from Nihilism: A Christian scholar chronicles his journey from faith to nonreason, and back', at www.leaderu.com/real/ri9801/budziszewski.html

[71] Leo, John, 'Nobel Prize for Fiction?', *U.S. News and World Report*, January 25, 1999, p.17.

[72] Netland, Harold A. and Johnson, Keith E., 'Why Is Religious Pluralism Fun – And Dangerous?' in Carson (ed.), *op. cit.*, p.62.

[73] Kreeft, Peter, *C. S. Lewis for the Third Millennium* (San Francisco: Ignatius, 1994), p.110.

[74] Quoted by Francis J. Beckwith and Gregory Koukl, *Relativism* (Grand Rapids: Baker, 1998), p.20.

[75] Johnson, Phillip E., *Reason in the Balance* (Downers Grove: IVP, 1998), p.130.

[76] McDowell and Hostetler, *op. cit.*, p.17.

[77] Johnson, *op. cit.*, p.130.

[78] *ibid.*

[79] *ibid.*

[80] Aquinas, *Summa Contra Gentiles*, 1.2.3, p.62.

[81] Nichols, Aidan, *Discovering Aquinas* (London: Darton, Longman & Todd, 2002), p.43.

[82] *ibid.*

[83] Groothuis, Douglas, *Truth Decay* (Downers Grove: IVP, 2000), p.67.

[84] Searle, John, 'I Married a Computer' in Jay W. Richards, (ed.), *Are We Spiritual Machines?* (Seattle: Discovery Institute, 2002), p.67.

[85] *ibid.*, p.68.

[86] Kreeft, Peter, *The Journey* (Leicester: IVP, 1997), p.29.

[87] Purtill, Richard, *Thinking About Religion* (Englewood Cliffs: Prentice-Hall, 1978), p.4.

[88] Sorely, W. R., *Moral Values and the Idea of God* (Cambridge University press, 1921), p.27, 123.

[89] Thomson, *On the Meaning of Life*, *op. cit.*, Preface.

[90] Nichols, *op. cit.*, p.153.

[91] McIntosh, Stephen Ian, *Creating Beauty as a Spiritual Practice*, Chapter 2, 'Beauty, Truth & Goodness' at www.beautytruthgoodness.org/chapter2.html

[92] Adler, Mortimer J., *The Great Ideas, A Syntopicon of Great Books of the Western World* (Encyclopaedia Britannica), quoted by McIntosh, *op. cit.*

[93] Harries, Richard, *Art and the Beauty of God* (London: Mowbray, 1993), p.69.

[94] Begbie, Jeremy S., *Voicing Creation's Praise* (Edinburgh: T&T Clark, 1998), p.xi.

[95] Joad, C. E. M., *The Recovery of Belief* (London: Faber & Faber, 1952), p.177.

[96] McDowell and Hostetler, *op. cit.*, p.15.

[97] Chesterton, *op. cit.*, p.221.

[98] Wiker, Benjamin, 'Does Science Point to God?: The Intelligent Design Revolution' at www.arn.org/docs2/news/doessciencepointtogod040903.htm

[99] Ward, Keith, *The Turn of the Tide* (London: BBC, 1986), p.23.

[100] Sproul, Gerstner and Lindsay, *op. cit.*, p.7.

[101] Bickel, Bruce and Jantz, Stan, *Bruce & Stan Search For The Meaning of Life* (Word: Nashville, 2001), p.28.

[102] Lewis, C. S., 'The Poison of Subjectivism', in *Christian Reflections* (London: Fount, 1998).

[103] Kreeft, Peter, *Fundamentals of the Faith* (San Francisco: Ignatius, 1998), p.103.

[104] Morris, Thomas V., *Philosophy for Dummies* (IDG Books, 1999) p.282.

[105] Julian Jaynes, quoted in Thomson, *op. cit.*, p.147.

[106] Morris, *op. cit.*, p.287.

[107] *ibid.*, p.281.

CHAPTER 2

Meaning, Purpose and Nihilism – Three Responses

Naturalism is the philosophical equivalent of J. K. Rowling's Dementors: creatures that guard the wizarding prison of *Azkaban* and who 'drain peace, hope and happiness out of any human who comes too close to them . . .' As psychiatrist Richard Winter writes: 'An attempt to live while believing that there is no ultimate meaning or purpose, that there is no point in even looking for these, can be very depressing; at the very least, life becomes profoundly boring. Nothing is of real significance or importance.'[1]

Is the most basic truth about ultimate reality a personal truth, or is it an impersonal truth?
THOMAS V. MORRIS[2]

For anything to have a purpose, it must be purposed by someone. As atheist Antony Flew notes: 'objects acquire whatever [point or] purpose they may have from people'.[3] There can be no objective purpose without a purposer, a personal agent who creates the thing in question to achieve a goal they consider worth achieving. Hence, only if human life is purposed by a pre-existent person can it have an ultimate purpose. Daniel Hill's argument is right on target:

> . . . life has a [purpose] only if there is an
> explanation of it in terms of the purposes of an
> agent that brought life about . . . Belief in a

creator and designer is essential, then, for anyone
that thinks that life has a [purpose] . . . Therefore,
atheists must necessarily deny that life has a
[purpose], since no overall complete explanation
of the existence of living things could be given in
terms of the purposes of any set of non-divine
agents.[4]

Indeed, atheist Kai Nielsen admits: 'If there is no God
. . . there is no purpose to life; you weren't made for a
purpose.'[5]

Purpose vs. purposes

*The problem is apparent for those who believe the
world and human life began by chance: if no meaning
was put in, then no meaning can be taken out.*
PETER J. GRANT[6]

Nielsen attempts to mitigate the effect of his admission
that if there is no God then there is no purpose to life
by arguing that: 'Even if you weren't made for a purpose, you could still find plenty of purposes in life,
things worth doing and having and believing and strug-
gling for.'[7] However, there are problems with this
response to the purposelessness of life in a godless universe. Doesn't the suggestion that although I *have* no
purpose I can *confer* purpose upon myself sound like
the suggestion that someone who doesn't have any
money can bail themselves out of jail by simply printing
their own currency? If there is no God who purposes my
existence, then I can certainly have *subjective* purposes; but neither I, nor my subjective purposings, are to
any *objective* purpose. I can't give myself an *objective*
purpose. As William Lane Craig, Research Professor of

Philosophy at Biola University, argues: 'It is inconsistent to say life is objectively absurd [meaningless] and then to say one may create meaning for his life.'[8]

What's it worth?

Nielsen says that even if we are not made for a purpose, we can still have *subjective* purposes that are worthwhile. However, unless there are *objective* values, Nielsen's 'things worth doing' can only have *subjective* worth. Unless atheism can provide a basis for objective worth (a question we will investigate later), atheists can't comfort themselves with Nielsen's thought that although they lack an objective purpose, they nevertheless have subjective purposes that are worthwhile (at least, not objectively worthwhile). Instead, they are simply set adrift with their subjective purposes. As C. S. Lewis argued: 'Either there is significance in the whole process of things as well as in human activity, or there is no significance in human activity itself . . . You cannot have it both ways. If the world is meaningless, then so are we; if we mean something, we do not mean alone.'[9]

Purpose, values and meaning

Julian Baggini, editor of *The Philosopher's Magazine*, acknowledges in his book *Atheism: A Very Short Introduction* that atheism faces a public relations problem due to 'the idea that without God nothing has a purpose. Sure, you can do what you want because there's no divine power there to stop you, but what is the point of doing anything at all?'[10] The heart of this public relations nightmare, writes Baggini, is that: 'Many people think that atheists believe that there is no God *and* no

morality; or no God *and* no meaning to life . . .'[11]
Indeed, many atheists (e.g. Richard Dawkins) candidly
affirm that without God there is no *objective* purpose,
meaning or value to human existence, no *objective*
point in doing anything at all.

Baggini aims to counter atheism's negative image by
arguing that: 'Atheism is only intrinsically negative
when it comes to belief about God, it is as capable of a
positive view of other aspects of life as any other
belief.'[12] However, Baggini makes exactly those negative affirmations that give rise to the public relations
problem he sets out to solve! Baggini thinks that there
is no *objective* God, no *objective* morality, and no
objective meaning to life. Like Kai Nielson, Baggini can
only clutch at subjective straws: 'we can choose our
own purposes . . . and thus be the authors of *our own
meaning* . . .'[13]

Baggini recognizes that belief in God implies belief in
objective purpose: 'since he made us with some purpose in mind'.[14] Just as a knife has a purpose because it
was made for a purpose, so life would have a purpose if
(and only if) it were made for a purpose. As an atheist,
Baggini naturally concludes that there is no such purpose to life. However, he tries to soften the blow by
arguing that being created by God would provide 'a
very unsatisfactory form of meaning in life'.[15] He makes
his point with an illustration: 'Although it is true that the
knife has meaning and purpose because of its creator,
this kind of purpose is hardly significant *for the
knife*.'[16] Well of course not, because the knife isn't self-
aware! However, Baggini takes this example to show
that 'when we ascribe a purpose to something in virtue
of what it was made for, this locates the significance of

that purpose with the creator or the user of the object, not in the object itself'.[17] He seeks to drive the point home with a *Brave New World* thought experiment, wherein humans are 'bred in laboratories to fulfil certain functions'.[18] The knowledge that one had been bred for the purpose of cleaning lavatories, for example, would hardly answer 'the important existential question about the meaning of life'[19] because 'a purpose or meaning given to a creature by its creator just isn't necessarily the kind of purpose or meaning that we are looking for in life'.[20] This fact leads Baggini to conclude that 'belief in a creator God does not automatically provide life with a meaning'.[21]

Baggini's argument is muddled, but it is useful, because it highlights the importance of a distinction he blurs. Although he begins by talking about purpose he ends by talking about meaning (or 'significance'), without having made a clear distinction between the two. As Baggini admits, only if something is made for a purpose can it have an objective purpose. Whether or not that something can make anything of its purpose (knives can't, people can), and what it makes of 'the significance of that purpose' if it can make something of it, are separate issues. This becomes obvious if we ask: 'Would having an objective purpose be enough to make life objectively meaningful?' Clearly not, for as Thomas V. Morris reminds us: 'Purposes are connected with values.'[22] What if the purpose of life was not objectively valuable? Worse, what if it were positively evil? (This is the point of Baggini's *Brave New World* story.) Either way, life would surely not count as *meaningful*, despite having an objective purpose.

Having a purpose is not a sufficient condition of life's

being objectively meaningful. Indeed, having a purpose isn't even a necessary condition of being objectively meaningful. Of course, if life has an objectively good purpose then it is objectively meaningful *and* purposeful; but if life is not objectively good then it cannot be objectively meaningful, whether or not it has an objective purpose. The question of purpose is truly separate from that of meaning. Nevertheless, the two questions are related, for if life has a purpose it is only meaningful if that purpose is good, and if life is meaningful then it might well have a purpose. Finding out what the purpose of life is (and how to engage with it) would then be an important part of the search for meaning, because discovering the purpose of creation would give life a rational and moral directionality.

The problem with Baggini's laboratory-bred lavatory cleaner is clearly that this purpose is not an objectively good purpose to have imposed upon him. His lavatorial purpose lacks the significance we feel a human life ought to have, and unjustifiably limits the freedom of choice we feel he ought to have. Cleaning toilets is not a bad thing *per se*, but being created for the sole purpose of cleaning toilets is intolerable. But why do we feel this, if not because we are assuming that creating a human with such a purpose contradicts some significance or value that attaches to what a human is meant to be? Does it make sense to say that the scientists who created our lavatory cleaner did something they were 'not meant to do' if humans are not objectively *meant* to do anything at all?

Baggini correctly points out that for life to be meaningful 'life's ultimate purpose must be something which is *good in itself*',[23] and he affirms that 'life seems meaningful enough, since the overall package is a *good in itself*[24]; but he also believes that such evaluative judgements are purely subjective claims that it is 'possible for someone to disagree with . . . *without saying something that is factually false*'[25]; and he believes this because he sees that without God 'there is no single moral authority . . . we have to in some sense "create" values for ourselves . . . moral claims are not true or false in the same way as factual claims are.'[26] Ironically, the thought experiment Baggini uses to argue that God is unnecessary for a meaningful life suggests that God *is* needed to make sense of the concepts, such as human dignity, upon which it depends (after all, if humans have no objective value or purpose, why not re-shape them through genetic engineering for any task we choose?[27]). This being so, Baggini ought to acknowledge not only that naturalism is unable to accommodate life having an objective purpose, but that it is unable to accommodate life being objectively meaningful. Having set out to counter the negative perception that atheists believe in 'no God *and* no morality; or no God *and* no meaning to life',[28] Baggini ends up affirming that there is no objective purpose or meaning to life precisely because there is no God, and hence no objective value. Hence we face a crucial question: Is there such a thing as objective value?

The reality of goodness

'If I think stealing a person's money or making love to his wife is alright', asks Dr Armand M. Nicholi Jr, 'is that wrong?'[29] More importantly, 'If you disagree with me, who is right? If we have no moral point of reference, what you think is no more right or wrong than what I think.'[30] Moral subjectivism (sometimes called 'moral relativism') is the philosophical position that says that stealing a person's money or making love to his wife is not objectively wrong, and if you disagree with me then neither of us is right, because 'there are no objective values'[31]; there is 'no single moral authority',[32] and the only values are the subjective values that we create for ourselves. Hence, as Baggini affirms, moral claims 'are not true or false in the same way as factual claims are'.[33] Indeed, it is 'always possible for someone to disagree with [a moral claim] *without saying something that is factually false*'.[34]

Relativist Gilbert Harman explains his belief that: 'What is right in relation to one moral framework can be morally wrong in relation to a different moral framework. And *no moral framework is objectively privileged as the one true morality*.'[35] In other words, different people or societies can have contrary opinions about good and evil (e.g. 'cannibalism is good' vs. 'cannibalism is wrong') without the implication that anyone is factually right or wrong! Harman concludes that moral disagreements are 'not objectively true or false',[36] because there are no objective moral facts to get right or wrong: 'there is no such thing as objectively absolute good . . . What someone takes to be absolute rightness is only rightness in relation to (a system of moral coordinates determined by) that person's values.'[37] As J. L. Mackie argued: 'Morality is not to be discovered, but to be made: we have to decide what moral views to adopt, what moral stands to take.'[38]

Moral subjectivism can be seen as the application to meta-ethics (the study of right and wrong) of a Protagorean relativism which announces that, 'Man is the measure of all things; of those things that are, that they are; of those things which are not, that they are not . . .'[39] This is the very opposite of realism. The obvious problem for Protagoras, and for those who would keep company with him, is that in expressing the opinion that 'man is the measure of all things' he affirms everyone's opinion, 'including the opinion that his own opinion is false'.[40]

For example, when Julian Baggini rejects the existence of an objective moral law, saying that moral claims 'are not true or false in the same way as factual claims are',[41] he candidly admits that his claim raises serious philosophical questions, but he suggests that these questions don't matter 'for practical purposes'.[42] However, taking seriously the claim that moral claims are not objectively true or false could have rather dramatic practical consequences. Baggini seems to rely upon people being good in order to keep the concept of goodness on the straight and narrow, a project that gets the horse and the cart entirely the wrong way around. What would happen if I accepted Baggini's atheism, but declared that since he had convinced me that moral judgements can never be factually false, I was nevertheless going to continue supporting theism because I no longer believed myself to be under any factual obligation to deal consistently with evidence? I suspect Baggini would think this a rather dire practical consequence of his views!

Moral objectivism, on the other hand, is the philosophical position that says that stealing a person's money or making love to his wife is objectively wrong, and if you disagree with me then one of us is wrong, because there *are* objective moral facts that we *can* (and do) get right or wrong: 'Just so, if a certain line is crooked, it is crooked, and though I may possibly not remark this, or may even think that the line is straight, or may wish that it were straight, it is none the less crooked for all that.'[43] Our moral opinions are true or false as they correspond or fail to correspond to an objective moral reality that, despite being non-physical, is on a par with the reality of raindrops on roses and whiskers on kittens:

> To say that morality is objective is to say that there exists an objective entity independent of any human being . . . We don't determine or control it. It does not change from one person to another. Nor does it go away because we don't appreciate it . . . Objective morality is simply there for us to discover and measure our actions against.[44]

As Stuart C. Hackett explained: 'far from it being the case that we legislate these principles by opting for them, it is rather the case that our legislative options are themselves to be evaluated by these principles considered as objective.[45] *Contra* J. L. Mackie, moral values are discovered, not invented. As atheist Colin McGinn argues:

> When I assert 'this is good' or 'that is evil,' I do not mean that I experience desire or aversion, or that I have a feeling of liking or indignation. These subjective experiences may be present; but the judgement points not to a personal or subjective state of mind but to the presence of an objective value in the situation. What is implied in this objectivity? Clearly, in the first place, it implies independence of the judging subject. If my assertion 'this is good' is valid, then it is valid not for me only but for everyone. If I say 'this is

good,' and another person, referring to the same situation, says 'this is not good,' one or other of us must be mistaken . . . The validity of a moral judgement does not depend upon the person by whom the judgement is made . . . In saying that moral values belong to the nature of reality . . . the statement implies an objectivity which is independent of the achievements of persons in informing their lives with these values, and is even independent of their recognising their validity. Whether we are guided by them or not, whether we acknowledge them or not, they have validity . . . objective moral value is valid independently of my will, and yet is something which satisfies my purpose and completes my nature . . .[46]

There are obviously subjective 'values' in the sense of personal preferences that differ according to the feelings and decisions of human beings. The question is, can these subjective 'values' be objectively true or false? In other words:

Are there any objective facts about value?

An experience is the awareness of a subject, but not necessarily a merely subjective awareness. This is an important point. While every experience is something had by a subject, not all experience is wholly subjective, in that *at least some experiences have objective referents*. For example, your subjective experience of reading this book has an objective referent: this book. Awareness of moral value is, I suggest, another example of a subjective experience that has an objective referent.

I think that Richard Swinburne's analysis of moral values as facts 'which nag at us'[47] and are felt as a 'force

. . . from without'[48] captures something irreducibly true about moral goodness. Moral goodness *matters*. There is certainly an emotional content to our understanding of moral values but these values cannot be reduced to, or explained away, as 'nothing but' subjective facts about either ourselves or our communities: 'We who believe it wrong to torture children, believe it would still be wrong if we had been brought up to think otherwise. We who believe it our duty to help the starving, feel the force of a moral obligation from without.'[49]

One may employ the principle of credulity here, that we should take experiences at face value unless we have some sufficient reason not to do so. This places the burden of proof on those who hold that moral values are not objective. Indeed, it would seem to be a heavy burden of proof, for as Kai Nielsen says: 'moral truisms . . . are as available to me or to any atheist as they are to the believer. You can be . . . confident of the correctness or, if you will, the truth of these moral utterances . . . They are more justified than any sceptical philosophical theory that would lead you to question them.'[50]

For example, it is sometimes suggested that the reality of moral disagreement supports the theory of moral subjectivism. However, the fact that people disagree about ethics indicates, not that moral values are subjective, but that they are objective. People disagree about matters of objective truth such as how old the universe is, and whether there are objective moral values or not. When it comes to subjective truths, however, people don't disagree. For example, unless you had reason to think I was lying, you wouldn't disagree with me when I make the subjective claim that I prefer Pepsi Cola to Coca Cola. This is a subjective truth (constituted by my mental state): I personally do prefer Pepsi Cola to Coca Cola. My claim is not that Pepsi Cola is objectively better than Coca Cola, but simply that I prefer it. The fact that people disagree about ethics is therefore an indication that ethics concerns matters of objective fact rather than subjective preference: 'it is not subjective things but objective things that people argue about . . . So disagreement about something is a reason not for thinking that something is subjective, but rather for thinking that it is objective . . .'[51] As McGinn writes: 'The fact that people disagree, rather than just express different preferences, already shows that they take there to be some truth over which they are contending.'[52] Why do moral decisions and debates matter so much, justify so much thought and effort, if we literally cannot get it wrong?

Moral subjectivism implies hugely counterintuitive results. For example, it would be impossible to say that one society (e.g. twenty-first-century Germany) is morally better than any other society (e.g. Nazi Germany), a fact that renders the concept of moral progress mute (since the idea of progress requires an objective goal one can progress towards). If moral relativism is true, then moral reformers such as William Wilberforce (who campaigned for the abolition of slavery) cannot have been *right* to challenge the majority moral opinions of their societies. But surely contemporary German society is a real improvement on Nazi Germany, and surely Wilberforce was right to oppose slavery, in which case relativism is wrong. As Francis Beckwith and Gregory Koukl argue, a wide range of moral concepts, such as moral accountability, goodness, evil, blame, justice, fairness, moral improvement and tolerance: 'seem to be concepts that have meaning apparent to our moral common sense. Each is justified by moral intuition, and yet relativism renders them all meaningless. If these moral notions are valid but yet are inconsistent with moral relativism, then relativism must be false.'[53] The validity of these moral notions isn't something that we choose or decide, but something that we simply intuit:

> All moral reasoning must start with foundational concepts that can only be known by intuition, which is why one doesn't carry the burden of proof in clear-case examples of moral truth . . . People who can't see this . . . are morally handicapped. We shouldn't allow their impaired vision to call into question what is clearly evident. Those who deny obvious moral truths . . . do not merely have a different moral point of view; they have something wrong with them . . .[54]

Any theory that denies (directly or indirectly) such powerfully obvious intuitions as that rape is an objectively evil thing and that the proposition 'rape is an objectively evil thing' is *true*, faces, to say the least, an uphill struggle for acceptance.

The entailment of objective goodness

The central question about moral and ethical principles concerns their ontological foundation. If values are [not] anchored in some transcendent ground they are purely ephemeral.
PAUL KURTZ[55]

The crucial thing to realize at this juncture is that Julian Baggini's recognition that *if* God doesn't exist *then* objective moral values don't exist, is equivalent to the proposition that *if* objective value is a reality *then* God must be an objective reality.[56] J. L. Mackie acknowledged that objective moral values would provide evidence for the existence of God:

> . . . if we adopted moral objectivism, we should
> have to regard the relations of supervenience
> which connect values and obligations with their
> natural grounds as synthetic; they would then
> be in principle something that a god might
> conceivably create; and since they would
> otherwise be a very odd sort of thing, the
> admitting of them would be an inductive ground
> for admitting also a god to create them.[57]

Mackie rejected the objectivity of moral value, embracing subjectivism and retaining his atheism: 'if we adopted instead a subjectivist . . . account of morality, this problem would not arise'.[58] But which is really the greater 'problem', accepting the existence of God or accepting moral subjectivism? As we saw above, atheist Colin McGinn isn't prepared to embrace subjectivism. He defends the objectivity of moral value, and brushes aside Mackie's concern that doing so is to start out on a logical road leading to God. McGinn writes that it is possible 'to detach moral objectivity from any religious world-view – so that we do not need to believe in God in order to find morality both important and binding.'[59] I agree that it is possible to believe that morality is important and binding without believing in or defending either the existence of God or the truth of any particular religious tradition (indeed, we have done just this above). However, I agree with Mackie that the existence of objective moral value is evidence for the existence of God. As I see it, Mackie is right to think that the existence of objective morality and the existence of God are linked, but wrong to think that morality is not objective, whereas McGinn is right to think that morality is objective, but wrong to think that the existence of objective morality and the existence of God are not linked. True enough, they are not linked *epistemologically* (that is, like McGinn, one can know and defend the reality of objective moral value without mentioning God), but they are linked *ontologically* (that is, one cannot fit the reality of objective moral value within a non-theistic worldview). McGinn may try to have his cake and eat it, but God and objective value are factually (ontologically) inseparable. As philosopher Paul Copan argues: 'while the atheist . . . correctly believes (*epistemologically*) in moral realism, his own *ontological* foundation furnishes no basis for this belief'.[60]

The ontological foundation of objective values

If one believes that objective moral value is a reality, one might well ask what sort of existence we are to attribute to objective moral value. Obviously it has some sort of *objective* existence, but what sort of objective existence? Is it material or immaterial? Personal or impersonal? Necessary or contingent? Well, the fact that an objective moral value is *objective* shows, by definition, that its existence cannot be explained in terms of finite minds. The fact that an objective moral value is a *moral value* (i.e. that it has the form of an ideal prescription we are obligated to heed) shows that its existence cannot be explained in terms of any impersonal reality. A number of arguments show why the existence of moral value cannot be given a non-personal explanation. For example:

1) In the moral law we meet commands. Only personal beings can issue commands; when did you last hear an article of cutlery order anything? Pointing out that a computer, which is not a personal being, could 'make a demand' doesn't weaken this argument, since computers must be built and programmed by personal beings that can and do make demands. As Beckwith and Koukl argue: 'A command only makes sense when there are two minds involved, one giving the command and one receiving it.'[61] Therefore, if a moral value is an objective command that humans receive, then there must be an objective and personal moral law Commander beyond individual or collective humanity.

2) I often have a duty to do or to refrain from doing something. But how could something impersonal obligate me? The law of gravity is an impersonal force that operates on me such that without any opposing force, I fall down. When I trip up, falling to the ground is something I am *caused* to do; but is it something I *ought* to do? Moral laws, on the other hand, prescribe things I objectively ought (or ought not) to do, but which I am not caused to do. After all, while I never fail to 'obey' the laws of gravity, I often fail to 'do the right thing'. A moral law, unlike a physical law, does not describe something that simply *is* the case, but rather prescribes something that *ought* to be the case. Since I cannot be morally obligated to something non-personal, I must be obligated to something personal. After all, I can't break a promise made to a fishbowl.

The idea of a moral obligation more important and binding than those imposed upon us by other individuals or by the state is only intelligible if we make reference to a lawmaker higher than the state. Ethicist Richard Taylor explains:

> A duty is something that is owed . . . But something can be owed only to some person or persons. There can be no such thing as duty in isolation . . . the idea of an obligation higher than this, and referred to as moral obligation, is clear enough, provided reference to some lawmaker higher . . . than those of the state is understood . . . This does give a clear sense to the claim that our moral obligations are more binding upon us than our political obligations . . . But what if this higher-than-human lawgiver is no longer taken into account? Does the concept of a moral obligation . . . still make sense? . . . the concept of moral obligation [is] unintelligible apart form the idea of God. The words remain, but their meaning is gone.[62]

State and community transcending obligations can only be rationally understood as being owed to God. Our obligations towards other people must derive from our obligation to a transcendent personal reality to whom our primary obligation is owed.

3) Since objectively right moral value judgements require an objective moral standard, and as no *moral* standard could exist in matter, and no *objective* moral standard could exist in finite minds, there must be an objective moral standard in an infinite mind. It follows that this personal ground of objective moral values must be ultimate goodness personified.

In summary: since something non-personal cannot make moral prescriptions, morally obligate us, or contain a moral ideal, the moral law must have some sort of *personal* ground and explanation. However, by definition, an *objective* moral law cannot depend upon any finite individual or collection of individuals. Therefore, the objective moral law must be grounded in the existence of an infinite personal being. Indeed, we are led to conclude, by a process of elimination, that there must be an objective, transcendent, necessary, personal and wholly good reality: God. As Francis J. Beckwith argues:

> . . . moral obligation, though resting on abstract principles, is deeply connected to our obligations *toward* other persons . . . the source of morality could not be a contingent being, one whose existence and moral authority are dependent on something outside itself. For in order to be *the ground* of morality, a being must not receive its existence and moral authority from another . . . [Moreover] the source of morality must be the sort of being who has the moral authority to enforce universal moral norms. Thus, if moral laws are known nonmaterial realities that are a form of communication for which we have a sense of incumbency . . . it seems that the moral law must have a personal, eternal, transcendent, and perfect source . . . God . . . [63]

The relation between God and meaning

Taking care over our definitions has begun to pay dividends in terms of enabling us to arrive at some important conclusions. If God does not exist, then objective goodness can no more exist than a cosmic purpose can exist without a cosmic purposer. Since for life to be objectively meaningful it is necessary for life to be an objectively good thing, if God does not exist, then life is not objectively meaningful. As Paul Copan writes of the naturalistic worldview: 'Why consider human beings of any moral worth and under any moral obligation at all given their nonmoral, valueless, impersonal origins and development? No wonder atheists and sceptics such as Bertrand Russell, Aldous Huxley, J. L. Mackie, William Provine, Daniel Dennett, and Richard Dawkins have rejected the existence of such values as completely incompatible with atheism.'[64] Belief in cosmic meaning (and worthwhile purpose) presupposes the existence of objective value, and hence of a wholly good, transcendent, personal being: God. If God does not exist, life is objectively devoid of objective meaning. On the other hand, if life is objectively meaningful (and/or if life has an objectively worthwhile purpose), then God must exist. So, the million-dollar question is: 'Is life objectively meaningful?'

Three possible answers

There are three ways we could go about answering this fundamental question:

First answer

The first answer, embraced and disseminated by atheists like Richard Dawkins, is the negative answer of nihilism, which one can express by saying that life is without objective meaning or purpose because God does not exist:

1) **Life (including human existence) is objectively meaningless and without purpose, unless God exists.**

2) **God does not exist.**

3) **Therefore, life (including human existence) is objectively meaningless and without purpose.**

Alternatively, nihilism can be asserted as an argument against the existence of God:

1) **Life (including human existence) is objectively meaningless and without purpose, unless God exists.**

2) **Life (including human existence) is objectively meaningless and without purpose.**

3) **Therefore, God does not exist.**

The affirmation that life is objectively meaningless entails either an explicit or an implicit affirmation that God does not exist. Either way, nihilism denies meaning by denying God.

Suppose you accept that in the absence of God life has no *objective* meaning, having no *objective* purpose and being devoid of *objective* value; why should you find in this situation any cause for concern? In the film *AntZ*, comedian Woody Allen plays an angst ridden Ant called Z. The film begins with Z talking to his psychiatrist: 'I feel insignificant,' says Z. 'We've made a breakthrough' says his psychiatrist. 'We have?' asks Z. 'Yes' says his psychiatrist, 'You *are* insignificant.' Like Z's psychiatrist, nihilism says that we are all insignificant. There is no objective meaning or purpose to life. Nevertheless, we keep on going, even though we don't matter. Why? As the opening scene of *AntZ* comes to its close we see Z going to work, picking up his pickaxe and telling himself that he has to maintain 'a positive attitude, even though I'm utterly insignificant'. The French philosopher Albert Camus defined 'the absurd' as the existence of a miss-match between the way the world is and the way we behave in it. Isn't Z's comment about having a positive attitude even though he is utterly insignificant funny precisely because it is absurd? Why bother having a positive attitude to life if doing so is absurd? As Thomas S. Hibbs asks: 'If meaninglessness is the ultimate framework, then what's the point of striving at all? What's all the fuss about?'[65] Thus Camus said that the fundamental question for philosophy was: 'Why not suicide?' Why choose to live when the choice to live is absurd? If you are thinking to yourself that the choice to live is not absurd – then your thinking so entails that you ought to think that God exists!

There is a wide and bipartisan agreement on the existence of an absurd discrepancy between thought and action at the heart of nihilism, an agreement between both theists and atheists that should give us pause for thought. Kai Nielsen acknowledges: 'There is a strong and widespread tendency . . . both among the intelligentsia and other people to believe that in a world without God, nothing matters. (It's a Nietzche thing.) In a world without God, everything is permitted; our lives will be fragmented and pointless. Our morality itself will be pointless. We can't know that anything is good or bad.'[66] Douglas Groothuis explains that, having proclaimed the 'death of God', Nietzsche:

> . . . rejected any transcendently warranted system of ethics . . . there are only moralities, which come in two basic types: slave morality and master morality. Slaves compensate for their lack of power by their feelings of resentment toward their masters, whom they label as 'evil' . . . Masters, however, discharge their powers . . . in accordance with their expansive ambitions. They are fettered neither by humility nor altruism, although they may elect to show kindness – when it suits them. For Nietzsche, the herd of slaves exists for the sake of the master who realizes that 'exploitation . . . belongs to the nature of living beings as . . . a consequence of the intrinsic Will to Power, which is presently the Will to Life.' Nietzsche champions the ultimate master as the Ubermensche, or Overman, who actualises himself by destroying the old values and creating his own values *ex nihilo* [out of nothing]. 'Overman is the meaning of the earth,' declares Nietzsche's Zarathustra (who elsewhere says life has no meaning) . . . [67]

Nietzsche's particular brand of atheistic amoralism was represented by the character of The Green Goblin (played by Willem Defoe) in the movie *Spider-Man*. The alter ego of businessman Norman Osborn, the Goblin uses his power in an attempt to dominate New York. In a crucial scene from the film, the Green Goblin tempts Spider-Man to join him because they are both 'extraordinary people' and the masses exist 'for the sole purpose' of lifting such extraordinary individuals onto their shoulders. Spider-Man refuses to join forces with the Green Goblin because, as he says, 'It's the right thing to do.' Spider-Man thinks there is such a thing as 'the right thing to do' (he is a moral objectivist), but the Goblin doesn't (he is a moral subjectivist: 'to each his own'). Why do we side with Spider-Man in this difference of opinion? Is it because he is the hero and the Goblin is the bad guy? But that assumes there is objective good and evil, rather than merely different opinions about how to behave. Choosing to do something because 'it's the right thing to do' assumes that there is such a thing as 'the right thing to do'. The whole film relies upon the audience making the same assumption as Spider-Man about the objectivity of morality – or else they might watch the whole thing applauding the Goblin's struggle to become New York's 'Overman'! As Groothuis observes: 'this reduction of ethics to force is nothing but a classic example of "might makes right" . . . given his rejection of objective moral standards . . . neither Nietzsche's condemnations nor commendations have any real moral consequence for anyone else, however passionately he ventilates them'.[68]

Atheist William Provine doesn't shrink from acknowledging the nihilistic worldview implied by his rejection of God: 'No life after death; no ultimate foundation for ethics; no ultimate meaning for life; no free will.'[69] Little wonder philosopher Thomas V. Morris concludes that 'Naturalism is ultimately a pessimistic world view.'[70] Morris explains:

> The nihilist's answer to the question of whether
> life has meaning is a simple and emphatic No. Life
> itself has no meaning. Your life has no meaning.
> My life has no meaning. Existence is without
> meaning of any kind. There is a void of

significance to everything. There is no purpose in life. No plan. No reason. There are no ultimate values that we are here to embrace or embody. And nothing is finally of any importance whatsoever . . . There is no room in a naturalistic universe for meanings . . . In a reality consisting only of matter in motion, it's hard to see what the ultimate status of anything as different from an atom as a meaning would be. And if we think that we can give anything meaning, we are fooling ourselves, according to a consistent development of this worldview. Any attempts to create meaning are themselves nothing more than empty, meaningless gestures in a universe that just doesn't care.[71]

Christian apologist Ravi Zacharias agrees that: 'Having killed God, the atheist is left with no reason for being, no morality to espouse, no meaning to life, and no hope beyond the grave.'[72] Christian astronomer Hugh Ross argues that: 'If the universe is simply uncreated, eternally self-existent or randomly self-assembled, then it has no purpose and consequently we have no purpose. Determinism rules. Morality and religion are ultimately irrelevant, and there is no objective meaning to life.'[73] As Os Guinness says: 'For those who find themselves without faith in God and who conclude that the world they desire does not fit with the world they discover, life is fundamentally deaf to their aspirations. And in fact, it is literally *absurd*.'[74] I can't imagine how anyone can understand the difference between the theistic belief that life is objectively meaningful and the non-theistic belief that life is objectively meaningless without recognizing that they represent a truly significant existential difference without any middle ground.

Second answer

Alternatively, one could affirm or argue that God exists, and then reason that since God exists, life *is* objectively meaningful:

1) **Life (including human existence) is objectively meaningless and without purpose, unless God exists.**

2) **God exists.**

3) **Therefore, life (including human existence) is objectively meaningful and purposeful.**

This argument shows that, *if* theism is true, *then* the theistic answer to the question of meaning (that life is objectively meaningful) is true. Life would be objectively meaningful if, and only if, God exists. Hence, *if* God does exist, *then* life is objectively meaningful.

Third answer

Finally, one might simply *affirm* that life is objectively meaningful without argument. Such an affirmation would of course (given the cogency of our preceding argument) entail an affirmation of God's existence; but it would not directly draw upon God's existence in order to justify the affirmation that life is objectively meaningful.

What would it mean for someone to simply *affirm* that life is meaningful? Why would someone do that? Well, perhaps they simply find themselves with what philosophers call a 'properly basic belief' that life is objectively meaningful. Recognizing the discrepancy between how they experience life as meaningful and how they think about life as meaningless, someone might reasonably decide, on that basis alone, to change how they think about life rather than how they feel about it.

A basic belief is 'a belief which is not believed on the basis of some underlying belief but is rather a foundational belief which we simply form in certain situations'.[75] For example, we don't see a tree and then consciously engage in reasoning and weighing evidence in order to arrive at the carefully justified conclusion that there is indeed a tree before us! Under normal conditions, seeing a tree simply 'triggers our belief-forming faculties, which produce in us the belief that a tree is there'.[76]

In order to be *properly* basic, a basic belief must be 'grounded in appropriate circumstances'.[77] That is, the apparent circumstances of belief formation must *cohere* with the nature of the object of belief. Hence: 'If I look at my office wall and form the belief "There is a tree," then such a belief is not warranted, since it is not grounded in appropriate circumstances.'[78] Basic beliefs that appear to be appropriately grounded should be accepted (on the principle of credulity) as being properly basic *until and unless there is sufficient reason to doubt their truth*: 'Such a belief is justified at face value (*prima facie*).'[79] As William Lane Craig explains using the example of belief in God: 'What makes belief in God basic for some person is the fact that this person holds it without founding it on arguments or other beliefs, and what makes it properly basic for him is that it is not held arbitrarily but is grounded in his experience.'[80]

A 'properly basic belief' is really just another name for 'an intuition' (remember our discussion of moral intuition). An intuition can be defined as the exercise of 'our capacity to recognize a state of affairs as in fact the case and to form the belief that it is so without any mediating process of reasoning'.[81] Intuition is 'a foundational way of knowing that does not depend on following a series of facts or a line of reasoning to a conclusion. Instead, intuitional truth is simply known by a process of introspection and immediate awareness.'[82] As Professor of philosophy Roy Clouser reminds us: 'Proving is actually an inferior way of coming to know something, a way we resort to when we can't directly experience what we want to know.'[83] Examples of properly basic beliefs include 'belief in the reality of the past, the existence of the external world, and the presence of other minds like your own'.[84] Properly basic beliefs are not arbitrary or 'made up', because 'they are grounded, in the sense that they're formed in the context of certain experiences'[85]; but neither are they invulnerable to evaluation. They can in principle be overturned by further data, but only if that data is strong enough to overwhelm the inherent strength of the basic belief in question.

Can someone have a properly basic intuition that life is meaningful? I don't see why not. It wouldn't seem any harder to specify what would count as an appropriate experience to ground a basic belief in the objective meaningfulness of life than it is to specify what would count as an appropriate experience to ground a basic belief in objective moral values or God (indeed, the relevant circumstances would appear to overlap somewhat). Meditating upon your experience of existence with reference to its meaning (perhaps in the process of reading this book) would surely be the right sort of circumstance!

Consider the experience of Christian writer Teresa Turner Vining, who as a university student began to doubt the existence of God: 'questions had been flooding my mind and sweeping away every certainty I had thought I had held securely. The atheistic worldviews held by some of my professors were having an effect on me, but that wasn't all. For some time there had been a gnawing uncertainty deep inside me, insistently whispering, *What if it is all a lie?*'[86] It was only when Teresa hit rock bottom that she discovered a strong properly basic belief, or intuition, that countered her scepticism and started her on the journey back to belief:

> Tears ran down my face as I returned to my empty apartment. Lying in bed surrounded by darkness, I tried to grasp the significance of it all. There is no God, I told myself. This life is all there is. No one really knows why we are here or how we got here. There is nothing more than self-centred, imperfect humanity in which to hope. There is no real meaning, no basis for knowing what is right and what is wrong. It doesn't matter what we do or how we live. There is no foundation, no right and wrong, no hope.
>
> *No!* Something deep inside of me screamed. It could not be true. I couldn't believe that life was just a sick joke with humans and their capacity for love, appreciation of beauty, and need for meaning as the pitiful punch line. That went against all my experience as a human being. There had to be something more!
>
> That night was the beginning of a new no-holds-barred search for truth in my life . . .

because the one thing I *did* know after that night was that I couldn't believe this life is all there is. Something deep inside me seemed to testify that somehow 'good' is better than 'bad' and 'love' is better than 'hate,' and that must be something more than just a sum of atoms.[87]

A rearrangement of our premises, based on a properly basic affirmation of meaning, yields the following argument for God's existence:

1) **Life (including human existence) is objectively meaningless, unless God exists.**

2) **Life is objectively meaningful.**

3) **Therefore, God exists.**

Once again, this is a logically valid argument. The only question is whether the premises are both true. If you think that life is not only subjectively meaningful *to you*, but that it is intrinsically and objectively meaningful, then the argument from meaning should convince you that God exists.

The way ahead

By carefully defining some crucial terms (e.g. 'truth', 'facts', 'objective, 'subjective', 'purpose', 'meaning') and our question ('Is life objectively meaningful?') we have managed to map out the answers we might give to the question of meaning. Either life is objectively meaningful or it isn't. Whether or not life is objectively meaningful depends upon whether or not God exists, because only God can ground objective value or give the universe an objective purpose. On the one hand, if God exists then life is objectively meaningful; and if life is objectively meaningful that can only be because God exists. On the other hand, if God does not exist, then life is objectively meaningless; and if life is objectively meaningless, that can only be because God does not exist. Whether or not life is objectively meaningful, and whether or not God exists, turn out to be inseparable questions.

You might feel that life is meaningless and that God therefore does not exist. Even so, it would be worthwhile asking whether there isn't sufficient reason to believe in God to overturn your belief in nihilism. After all, who would want to miss out on knowing the meaning of life if there is one? Only the Muppet crew of the *Swine Trek*! As Aldous Huxley, author of *Brave New World*, advised: 'That so many philosophers and mystics, belonging to so many different cultures, should have been convinced, by inference or by direct intuition, that the world possesses meaning and value is a fact sufficiently striking to make it worth while at least to investigate the belief in question.'[88] Then again, you might think that life is objectively meaningful (and that God therefore exists), or that God exists and that life must therefore be objectively meaningful. If so, then perhaps the rest of this book can function to reinforce your belief in God and meaning.

Maybe, like the student who talked to me at that party in Norwich, you 'wish you could believe' that life has an objective meaning and purpose, but you are impressed by the confident atheism of those, like Richard Dawkins, who argue that science has shown belief in God to be a childish, if understandable, mistake – and that anyone who cares about truth must ultimately choose between the 'warm comfortable lie'[89] of theism and the grown-up cosmic nihilism of the factually inescapable Darwinian worldview (a worldview in which we are all insignificant cogs in an indifferent cosmic mechanism that lacks objective meaning and purpose). If so, I hope that the following material will prove to be an intellectually satisfying encouragement to the opposite conclusion.

Doubting Dawkins

In an open letter written to his daughter Juliet on her tenth birthday, Richard Dawkins encouraged her to reject any beliefs that come from tradition, authority and revelation and to think for herself:

> Next time somebody tells you something that sounds important, think to yourself: 'Is this the kind of thing that people probably know because of evidence? Or is it the kind of thing that people only believe because of tradition, authority or revelation?' And next time somebody tells you that something is true, why not say to them: 'What kind of evidence is there for that?' And if they can't give you a good answer, I hope you'll think very carefully before you believe a word they say.[90]

One might question why the accumulated wisdom of a well-founded tradition (such as a scientific or theological tradition), the authority of those rationally judged to be in a good position to speak authoritatively on this or that (such as a scientist speaking on matters of science or a theologian on theology), or the tenets of some particular revelation – if it is indeed a revelation – should not count as evidence, but should instead be dismissed as 'bad reasons for believing anything'.[91] Dawkins circumscribes what can count as evidence so tightly – conflating evidence with empirical evidence – that his definition of evidence ends up suffocating itself, because it cannot be justified with anything that it would count as evidence! What empirical evidence is there to support the important sounding claim that one should only believe important sounding claims if there is empirical evidence to support them? There is no such evidence, in which case Dawkins' important sounding claim counts against itself in a fit of self-contradiction that labels Dawkins himself as someone about whom we should think very carefully before we believe a word he says. His bold assertion that scientists are 'the specialists in discovering what is true about the world and the universe'[92], is a self-defeating assertion (because its truth cannot be discovered by scientists *as such*), an assertion that leaves no room for philosophy or theology and which therefore has profound implications for his worldview and its answer to the question of meaning.[93]

With these points in mind we can proceed to take Dawkins' advice by applying it to his own views. When Dawkins promulgates the message that 'God is dead' because science reveals a world without purpose or design, posing us with a no-brainer choice between scientific truth and spurious religious comfort, he certainly says something that sounds important. So let's ask ourselves: Is this the kind of thing that Dawkins knows because of the evidence (broadly construed)? Or is it the kind of thing that he believes because he stands in the atheistic tradition and accepts the authority of fellow atheists and the Darwinian 'revelation' that the facts of biology somehow undermine belief in God and thereby belief in cosmic meaning and purpose? Why don't we examine Dawkins' naturalistic views asking: 'What kind of evidence (scientific *and* philosophical) is there for that?' And if we don't receive a good answer, we should think very carefully before we believe what he has to say about the question of meaning. But first I want to introduce you to a scientist of an all-together different metaphysical persuasion . . .

[1] Winter, Richard, *Still Bored in a Culture of Entertainment: Rediscovering Passion & Wonder* (Downers Grove: IVP, 2002), p.90.

[2] Morris, Thomas V., *Making Sense of it All: Pascal and the Meaning of Life* (Eerdmans, 1992), p.21.

[3] Flew, Antony, *God and Philosophy* (London: Hutchinson, 1974), p.105.

[4] Hill, Daniel, 'The Meaning of Life', *Philosophy Now*, Issue 35, March/April 2002.

[5] 'Nielsen's Opening Statement' at www.leaderu.com/offices/billcraig/docs/craig-nielsen2.html

[6] Grant, Peter J., 'The Priority of Apologetics in the Church', in Zacharias, Ravi and Geisler, Norman L., *Is Your Church Ready?* (Grand Rapids: Zondervan, 2003), p.60.

[7] *ibid.*

[8] Craig, William Lane, *Reasonable Faith* (Crossway Books, 1994), p.65.

[9] Lewis, C. S., *The Personal Heresy: A Controversy* (London: Oxford University Press, 1965), p.29-30.

[10] Baggini, Julian, *Atheism: A Very Short Introduction* (Oxford University Press, 2003), p.57.

[11] *ibid.*, p.3.

[12] *ibid.*

[13] *ibid.*, p.62, my italics.

[14] *ibid.*, p.58.

[15] *ibid.*, p.59.

[16] *ibid.*

[17] *ibid.*

[18] *ibid.*

[19] *ibid.*

[20] *ibid.*

[21] *ibid.*

[22] Thomas V. Morris, *Philosophy for Dummies* (IDG Books, 1999), p.284.

[23] Baggini, *op. cit.*, p.65, my italics.

[24] *ibid.*

[25] *ibid.*, p.51, my italics.

[26] *ibid.*, p.41-51.

[27] cf. Williams, Peter S., 'Mere Humanity' at www.arn.org/docs/williams/pw_merehumanityreview.htm

[28] Baggini, *op. cit.*, p.3.

[29] Nicholi, *op. cit.*, p.57.

[30] *ibid.*

[31] Mackie, J. L., *Ethics: Inventing Right and Wrong* (London: Penguin, 1990), p.15.

[32] Baggini, *op. cit.*, p.41.

[33] *ibid.*, p.41-51.

[34] *ibid.*, p.51, my italics.

[35] Harman, Gilbert, 'Moral Relativism' in Harman and Thomson, *Moral Relativism and Moral Objectivity* (Blackwell, 1995), p.3, my italics.

[36] *ibid.*, p.63.

[37] *ibid.*, p.17.

[38] Mackie, *op. cit.*, p.106.

[39] Quoted by Holmes, *op. cit.*, p.8.

[40] *ibid.*

[41] Baggini, *op. cit.*, p.41-51.

[42] *ibid.*, p.52.

[43] Taylor, A. E., *Does God Exist?* (London: Fontana, 1945), p.103.

[44] Chamberlain, Paul, *Can We Be Good Without God?* (IVP, 1996), p.55.

[45] Hackett, Stuart C., *Reconstruction of the Christian Revelation Claim* (Grand Rapids: Baker, 1984).

[46] Sorely, *op. cit.*, p.93, 238-239.

[47] Swinburne, Richard, *Responsibility and Atonement* (Oxford: Clarendon Press, 1989).

[48] *ibid.*

[49] *ibid.*, p.17-18.

[50] 'Kai Nielsen's Opening Statement' at www.leaderu.com/offices/billcraig/docs/craig-nielsen2.html

[51] Kreeft, Peter, *The Journey* (Leicester: IVP, 1997).

[52] McGinn, *op. cit.*, p.49.

[53] Beckwith, Francis J. and Koukl, Gregory, *Relativism* (Grand Rapids: Baker, 1989), p.59, 61.

[54] *ibid.*, p.59.

[55] Kurtz, Paul, quoted by Tom Price, unpublished dissertation (2004), conclusion.

[56] 'Strictly speaking the conditional "if objective value is a reality then God must be an objective reality" is the contrapositive of (and therefore equivalent to) the conditional "if God is not an objective reality then objective value is not a reality" . . . it is the same claim, viewed differently, since "If A then B" is equivalent to "if Not-B then Not-A."' – Angus Menuge, personal correspondence.

[57] Mackie, J. L., *The Miracle of Theism* (Oxford University Press, 1982), p.118.

[58] *ibid.*

[59] McGinn, Colin, *Ethics, Evil and Fiction* (Oxford: Clarendon Press, 1999), p.vii.

[60] Copan, Paul, 'Can Michael Martin Be a Moral Realist?: Sic et Non' at www.gospelcom.net/rzim/publications/essay_arttext.php?id=4

[61] Beckwith and Koukl, *op. cit.*, p.166.

[62] Taylor, Richard, *Ethics, Faith, and Reason* (Englewood Cliffs, N.J.: Prentice-Hall, 1985), p.83-84.

[63] Beckwith, Francis J., 'Moral Law, the Mormon Universe, and the Nature of the Right We Ought to Choose' in Francis J. Beckwith *et al.* (eds), *The New Mormon Challenge* (Jonathan Ball Publishers, 2002), p.227-240.

[64] Copan, Paul, *That's Just Your Interpretation* (Grand Rapids: Baker Books, 2001), p.14.

[65] Hibbs, Thomas S., *Shows About Nothing* (Dallas: Spence, 1999), p.161.

[66] 'Nielsen's Opening Statement', at www.leaderu.com/offices/billcraig/docs/craig-nielsen2.html

[67] Groothuis, Douglas, 'Nietzsche and Postmodernist Nihilism' at www.gospelcom.net/ ivpress/groothuis/nietzsch.html

[68] *ibid.*

[69] Provine, William B., 'Darwinism: Science or Naturalistic Philosophy?' in debate with Phillip E. Johnson, 30 April 30, 1994.

[70] Morris, *Philosophy for Dummies, op. cit.*, p.281.

[71] *ibid.*, p.286-287.

[72] Zacharias, Ravi, *The Shattered Visage* (Grand Rapids: Baker, 1990), p.102.

[73] Ross, Hugh, 'Astronomical Evidences for a Personal, Transcendent God', in *The Creation Hypothesis* (Downers Grove: IVP, 1994), p.141.

[74] Guinness, Os, *Time for Truth* (Leicester: IVP, 2000), p.78.

[75] Craig, William Lane, *Time and Eternity* (Crossway Books, 2001), p.131.

[76] Clouser, Roy, *Knowing with the Heart* (Downers Grove, IVP, 1999), p.65.

[77] *ibid.*, p.73.

[78] *ibid.*

[79] *ibid.*, p.131.

[80] Craig, William Lane, 'Reason Enough', in *God?* (Oxford University Press, 2004), p.74.

[81] *ibid.*, p.65.

[82] Beckwith and Koukl, *op. cit.*, p.56.

[83] Clouser, *op. cit.*, p.11.

[84] Craig, *op. cit.*, p.26.

[85] *ibid.*, p.26.

[86] Vining, Teresa Turner, *Making Your Faith Your Own* (Downers Grove: IVP, 2001), p.11.

[87] *ibid.*, p.12-13.

[88] Huxley, Aldous, *Ends and Means* (Chatto & Windus, 1966), p.277.

[89] Dawkins, *A Devil's Chaplain* (London: Weidenfeld & Nicholson, 2003), p.13.

[90] *ibid.*, p.248.

[91] *ibid.*, p.243.

[92] *ibid.*, p.242.

[93] On the epistemological issues here cf. Bibliography.

CHAPTER 3

Unweaving the Rainbow

When comedian Ricky Gervais (famous for playing David Brent in *The Office*) says that God does not exist and that life is pointless and futile, he seems intellectually adamant, but existentially resigned:

> I've never prayed since I became an atheist. People invent God, because the alternative is too scary. They can't cope with the pointlessness and futility of existence without something else. I believe in physics and nature and I think life is brilliant. It's amazing and I try to make it as nice as I can. I like running and drinking wine and playing with my kitten. I enjoy laughing all the time and eating too much. If I ever said 'Oh, God help me,' I'd be kidding myself. What's the point? I know there is no God as strongly as I know two and two is four.

We can agree with Gervais that it won't do to shy away from the scary pointlessness and futility of an existence without God by kidding ourselves that He exists and can answer our prayers. And perhaps if the belief that God doesn't exist were on a par with the belief that two and two is four, we'd all have to join Gervais in making the best of a bad deal, distracting ourselves with experiences that give us subjective enjoyment but which, we would know, are ultimately meaningless. But maybe belief in God isn't irrational. Maybe we can believe in physics and nature *and* God. Maybe we can even believe in God *because of* what we know about physics and nature and how brilliant life is. Indeed, if life really is 'amazing' and 'brilliant', does that square with thinking that life is also pointless and futile?

Thence came forth Maul, *a giant. This* Maul *did use to spoil young Pilgrims with sophistry.*
JOHN BUNYAN

In 1664 an undergraduate student at Cambridge University who had a knack for beating his fellow students at draughts and would one day invent the cat-flap, wrote out a list of questions, organizing his ignorance about the natural world under 45 headings. His 'Quaestiones' (standardized English spelling had yet to be invented) began with the nature of matter, place and time, took in cosmic order, and proceeded to the nature of light, colour and vision, among other things. All the while he was thinking not so much of *arguments* for or against this or that answer to his questions, but of *experiments* he could carry out to discover the answer. The name of this inquisitive, draughts playing student was Isaac Newton.

Newton's curiosity helped him to become one of the most eminent 'natural philosophers' (scientists) of his age.[1] Albert Einstein, the first natural philosopher to improve on Newton's insights in two hundred years, 'never doubted that Newton was the greatest scientific genius of all time'.[2] Newton became the Lucasian Professor of Mathematics at Cambridge University at a mere 27 years of age. Today, the same chair is held by Stephen Hawking.

Newton was largely self-taught. The curriculum at Cambridge (which was still based on Aristotle) held little interest for him, so he spent most of his time reading books other than those recommended by the university. Dr Robert Iliffe, lecturer in the History of Science at Imperial College London, comments: 'we have a number of his notebooks, and, in one of those, there are some notes on Aristotle. One gets the impression from reading them that he took those notes and then very quickly became bored with them and moved on to the new philosophers then in vogue . . .'[3] Rather than Aristotle, Newton read Descartes, Galileo and Robert Boyle. When an exam approached he would 'cram', and pass, so he could get back to his real learning, until, 'with no help beyond the books he had found for himself, he had made himself the foremost mathematician in Europe and the equal of the foremost natural philosopher'.[4] For example, quite independently of Leibniz's discovery of the method, Newton hit upon mathematical calculus (which he called 'fluxions'), 'an innovation that has been called the greatest accomplishment in mathematics since ancient times'.[5]

Newton learnt early on that people can be more irritated than impressed by a display of intellect or skill greater than their own. As biographer Richard Westfall says: 'Genius of Newton's order does not find ready companionship in any society in any age.'[6] He kept himself to himself, spending his time making working mechanical models from a book called *The Mysteries of Nature and Art* by John Bate. John Gribbin notes:

> [Newton] was a good practical experimenter, he built telescopes and so on, and this goes right back to his childhood when he would make really sophisticated toys . . . His particular thing, which people wrote about years afterwards when he was famous, was that he made a working windmill which was driven by mice running round a treadmill . . . The other thing was kites: he flew kites with lanterns attached to them and caused one of what must have been the first UFO scares in England . . .[7]

Newton's childhood sweetheart remembered him as 'a

sober, silent, thinking lad'.[8] Other people observed that Newton would be 'silent and thoughtful for above a quarter an hour together, and look all the while almost as if he was saying his prayers; but that when he did speak, it was always very much to the purpose',[9] and that 'he was hardly ever alone without a pen in his hand and a book before him . . .'[10]

Newton's roommate at Cambridge recollected how: 'Once at work on a problem, he would forget his meals. His cat grew very fat on the food he left standing on his tray.'[11] As another of his compatriots at Trinity College, Humphry Newton (no relation), mused: 'I believe he grudged the short time he spent in eating and sleeping.'[12] As a Professor, Newton seldom dined in hall, unless it was upon some public holiday, and even then, as Humphry wrote, he would go 'very carelessly [with] shoose down at heels, stockings untidy . . . and his head scarcely combed'.[13] Not that turning up to dinner necessarily meant that Newton ate anything. William Stuckely, a friend of Newton who had been a student at Cambridge reported: 'when he had been in the hall at dinner, he has quite neglected to help himself, and the cloth has been taken away before he has eaten anything . . .'[14] Stuckley also recalled: 'That when he had friends to entertain at his chamber, if he stept in to his study for a bottle of wine, and a thought came into his head, he would sit down to paper and forget his friends.'[15] Newton appears to have been the archetypal absent-minded professor.

Natural philosophy and ultimate explanations
Newton's absent-minded fascination with nature paid dividends. When Newton was asked how he had discov-

ered the law of universal gravitation, he simply replied that it was 'by thinking on it continually'.[16] According to Voltaire's *Lettres sur le Anglais*, it was while walking in the garden at Woolsthorpe, his family home, 'that the fall of an apple suggested to him the greatest and most famous of his later discoveries – the law of universal gravitation'.[17] Newton is best known for the findings he published in 1687 in his *Philosophiae Naturalis Principia Mathematica*, which built upon and combined Galileo's law of falling bodies with Kepler's law of the periodic times of the planets. Newton elucidated his three laws of motion and explained in mathematical terms that the orbit of the moon is due to its delicately balanced continual falling towards the Earth away from a straight line: 'His calculating tool was his famous inverse square law: each object in the universe behaves as if it attracts every other object with a force proportional to the product of the masses and inversely proportional to the square of the distance between them. Thus the gravitational influence of one body upon another becomes one fourth as strong when the distance between them is doubled, one ninth as strong when the distance is tripled, and so on.'[18] Astronomer Royal, Sir Martin Rees, explains that in the *Principia* Newton demonstrated the power of mathematics in understanding the natural world:

> What Newton managed to do was to subsume all that was known about the orbits of the planets and the moon in a single law of nature . . . the so-called Inverse Square Law . . . sciences aspire to the ability to unify as much as possible in terms of simple laws that you can write down on a single sheet of paper . . . and Newton was the first

scientist who actually achieved something in that direction.[19]

Newton's *Principia* has been called 'perhaps the single most important book in the history of science'.[20]

Nancy Pearcey and Charles Thaxton note that 'Newtonian physics tends to be identified as materialistic and deterministic. Yet Newton himself was neither a materialist nor a determinist . . . A highly religious man, Newton even used his physical theories . . . to persuade his contemporaries of the existence of God.'[21] Newton did not think that the inverse square law of gravity somehow pushed God aside by giving Him less to do: 'Though the deists later took Newton's laws as evidence for a universe that ran by itself, Newton himself believed in a God who "governs all things".'[22] Robert Iliffe observes that 'Newton was a very religious man. He was reading in the book of nature which God had written. In a sense he saw himself as a priest of nature.'[23] Regius Professor of Divinity at Oxford University, Keith Ward reports how: 'Newton remarked that his search for simple underlying laws of nature was prompted by the belief that a wise creator would have designed the universe to run on such simple principles.'[24] Ward points out that: 'Newton's assumptions have been vindicated in a spectacular way by the success of science, which has shown how physical objects are indeed related in ways describable by elegant and mathematically simple expressions . . . This is indeed a universe founded on intelligible wisdom.'[25] Newton himself concluded *Principia Mathematica* with the rumination that: 'this most beautiful System of the Sun, Planets and Comets could only proceed from the counsel and dominion of an intelligent and powerful Being'.[26]

Nor did the fact that Newton's laws made it possible 'to predict the behaviour of many aspects of nature because the same laws were seen to rule everywhere'[27] cause Newton to reject the possibility of miracles, for Newton held that God 'is more able by His Will to move Bodies . . . and thereby to form and reform the Parts of the Universe, than we are by our Will to move the Parts of our own Bodies'.[28] Newton took the inverse square law 'to be a mere description of how gravity works',[29] and explained the nature of gravity itself 'in terms of the activity of the Spirit of God'.[30] He thought of these two explanations, one scientific and the other theological, as being wholly compatible and forming together a more adequate description of reality than could be offered by science (natural philosophy), or theology, alone. For Newton, natural philosophy consists 'in discovering the frame and operations of Nature, and reducing them, as far as may be, to general Rules or Laws, – establishing these rules by observations and experiments, and thence deducing the causes and effects of things . . .'[31] As Pearcey and Thaxton write: '[Newton] insisted that the concept of force he had introduced was not an ultimate explanation at all . . . It was merely a postulate used to explain observations. Ultimate explanations, Newton said, should be left out of science.'[32]

For ultimate explanations, and much more besides, Newton turned to religion: 'he spent much of his time studying the Scriptures in depth, producing books on chronologies in the Old Testament and on the book of Revelation. After many years of diligent Bible study, Newton concluded: "We account the Scriptures of God to be the most sublime philosophy. I find more sure marks of authenticity in the Bible than in any profane history whatsoever."[33]

Unweaving the rainbow

Aside from formulating the law of universal gravitation, Newton is famous for his work in optics (he invented the reflecting telescope), especially his work on the rainbow. Newton proved, experimentally, and in contradiction to the prevailing thought of the day, that a prism does not *impose* the colour spectrum upon the light shone through it, but *unweaves* the different colours of light *from out of the white light itself*:

> By experimenting with sunlight passing through various configurations of prisms, Newton showed not only that white light could be separated into its component colours, each refracted to a different degree to produce a spectrum, but that these could be re-combined to form white light again . . . Further, he showed that objects have colour only because they 'reflect one sort of light in greater plenty than another'.[34]

A prism separates out the mixture of colours in white light because different colours of light are bent by different amounts as they pass through the glass: 'slowly moved rays are refracted more than swift ones'.[35]

The little boy who stood on the shoulders of giants

When Newton died in 1727 he was accorded a state funeral in Westminster Abbey, an event that prompted Voltaire to say 'that England was honouring a mathematician as other nations honoured a king'.[36] Shortly before his death, Newton looked back over his life in natural philosophy and summarized it thus: 'I don't know what I may seem to the world, but, as to myself, I seem to have been only like a small boy playing on the sea shore, and diverting myself in now and then finding a smoother pebble or a prettier shell than ordinary, whilst the great ocean of truth lay all undiscovered before me.'[37] Newton also acknowledged his debt to those who came before him, saying 'if I have seen further it is by standing on the shoulders of giants'.[38] Alexander Pope wrote a famous couplet honouring Newton's achievements:

Nature and Nature's laws lay hid in night
God said 'Let Newton be', and all was light.[39]

Two hundred and seventy-one years later . . .

The strongest arguments for naturalism have come from evolutionary biologists, such as Richard Dawkins . . .
TERENCE L. NICHOLS[40]

Another well-known British scientist recounts the effect his first book had on some of his readers:

A foreign publisher of my first book confessed that he could not sleep for three nights after reading it, so troubled was he by what he saw as its cold, bleak message. Others have asked me how I can bear to get up in the mornings. A teacher from a distant country wrote to me reproachfully that a pupil had come to him in tears after reading the same book, because it had persuaded her that life was empty and purposeless. He advised her not to show the book to any of her friends, for fear of contaminating them with the same nihilistic pessimism.[41]

The contrast with public reaction to Newton's work could hardly be starker. We have already met the scientist in question: Zoologist[42] Dr Richard Dawkins (b. 1941). Dawkins has been described as 'materialistic, reductionist and overtly anti-religious'.[43] Julia Hinde writes that 'Dawkins, Oxford University's professor of the public understanding of science, and a vocal atheist, is quick to dismiss religious belief. He has called anyone advocating a creator God "scientifically illiterate".'[44] Of course, such rhetoric dismisses 40 per cent of Dawkins' fellow scientists in one ill-thought-out generalization![45] Even Stephen Jay Gould recognized that 'Unless at least half my colleagues are dunces, there can be – on the most raw and empirical grounds – no conflict between science and religion.'[46] Indeed, when Dawkins says, with exasperation: 'I don't understand why so many people who are sophisticated in science go on believing in God',[47] he acknowledges that people who believe in God are *not* necessarily 'scientifically illiterate'. As Professor Alister McGrath – molecular biologist, theologian, and Principle of Wycliffe Hall in Oxford – observes: 'Dawkins often seems like the polemical inversion of the Bible-bashing fundamentalist preacher, peddling his own certainties, excoriating the views of his rivals, and mocking the mental and moral abilities of those foolish enough to disagree with him.'[48]

Dawkins' attitude towards religious believers is not unique. It reflects a naturalistic snobbery that currently pervades much of Western academia. But as Cambridge University's Professor of Divinity, David F. Ford protests:

> Among the world's estimated one and a half billion Christians there are many millions of university-

educated believers who are at least as
sophisticated and intelligent as their unbelieving
or other-believing fellow human beings . . . the
assumption – which I find actually quite common
in our Common Rooms – that there is something
irrational or intellectually suspect about believing
in God is patronizing and even insulting to all
those people . . . It is a prejudice often
accompanied by considerable ignorance of the
rigorous intellectual engagements, past and present, with the reality and identity of God.[49]

Charles Simonyi, head of the Intentional Programming
team in Microsoft's research division, endowed Oxford
University with the funds to establish a professorship
for the public understanding of science (which Paul
Johnson called 'Oxford's first Chair of Atheism'[50]) with
Dawkins specifically in mind:

Evolution's first great advocate, 1860s biologist
Thomas Henry Huxley, earned the nickname
'Darwin's bulldog' from his fellow Victorians. In
our own less decorous day, Dawkins deserves an
even stronger epithet: 'Darwin's Rottweiler, perhaps', Simonyi suggests. Now, thanks to Simonyi's
gift of £1.5 million sterling to England's venerable
Oxford University, the Rottweiler is unleashed.[51]

Dawkins comments: 'if I am asked for a single phrase to
characterize my role as Professor of Public
Understanding of Science, I think I would choose
Advocate for Disinterested Truth'.[52] (Here at least I find
common ground with Dawkins, for 'both of us have little in common with those so-called relativists who see
no reason to prefer scientific views over whatever
beliefs any person or group of people may happen to

feel comfortable with irrespective of any objective truth criteria'.[53]) Dawkins' new role does mean that he is no longer a *practising* scientist:

> A controversial lecturer, best-selling author, and leading evolutionary theorist, Dr. Dawkins is clearly at home in the glare of television lights, on radio talk shows, and in book-tour interviews. 'Do I miss doing laboratory research?' he says, craning his neck around the make-up artist. 'A bit, but I can probably make more of an impact by going out and writing books, doing radio broadcasts, and writing articles in newspapers. If I could guarantee that from my lab work I would be another Francis Crick, it would be another matter. But given that I would end up being another Joe Blow, I might as well do what I do best.'[54]

Dawkins' was awarded the title 'Humanist of the Year' in 1996 by the atheistic British Humanist Association, since when he has been its Vice President. His skill as a science writer was recognized by the Royal Society of Literature in 1997, when they elected Dawkins as a Fellow. In the same year, Dawkins received the fifth *International Cosmos Prize* (from the Expo '90 Foundation[55]) for the 'tremendous impact on our view of the world'[56] his books have: 'Dawkins tries to show us that all living things on earth appear, exist and advance as a result of an endless battle of genes. This entirely new perspective challenges our concept of harmony with the natural world and totally reverses our understanding and perception of the world . . . This perspective compels us to essentially switch our fundamental views.'[57]

Dawkins' first book, which had such a profoundly

unsettling effect on some of his readers, was *The Selfish Gene*, in which he argued that 'we are survival machines – robot vehicles blindly programmed to preserve the selfish molecules known as genes'.[58] Dawkins' Oxford colleague Keith Ward, reviewing the selfish gene hypothesis, observes: 'It is just like saying that the important goal of cookery is the production of recipes. The cakes themselves are unintended by-products of the recipes. Something has gone seriously wrong!'[59] Cambridge University scientist Dr Denis Alexander makes some key points when he replies to Dawkins: 'The fact that the operations of pistons, spark plugs and carburettors in a car engine are "mindless" does not imply the car-driver has no chosen destination. The fact that the various mechanisms that comprise the operating parts of jet engines are "mindless" has no implications for the existence of Frank Whittle who originally designed the jet engine.'[60] Nevertheless, it was an atheistic view of reality, a view that treats people as inconsequential by-products of nothing but chance and necessity, that was purveyed by *The Selfish Gene*, and as physicist Professor J. Roy Shambles complains: 'This atheistic message from the lofty spires of Oxford has gone almost unchallenged for far too long – and many people – often scientifically ill-informed – hear and believe – because of who Dawkins is . . .'[61]

Cold philosophy

An atheist is a man who believes himself an accident.
FRANCIS THOMPSON[62]

Theologian Paul Haffner observes that 'Darwinists and neo-Darwinists who base their vision of the evolution of life on chance often display a nihilist tendency.'[63] Atheist and philosopher Daniel Dennett calls Darwin's theory of evolution by natural selection 'Darwin's Dangerous Idea' because, he says, it bears 'an unmistakable likeness to universal acid – it eats through just about every traditional concept'.[64] Indeed, according to Dennett: 'Darwin's dangerous idea cuts much deeper into the fabric of our most fundamental beliefs than many of its sophisticated apologists have yet admitted, even to themselves.'[65]

In *Unweaving the Rainbow* (1998) Richard Dawkins is intent upon assuring his readers that science doesn't eat through the wonder or meaning of the world and replace it with nihilistic pessimism. Dawkins takes as his point of departure a poem by Keats, a man who, according to Dawkins, believed that the 'cold philosophy' of science spoils the beauty of the rainbow 'by reducing it to the prismatic colours'[66]:

Do not all charms fly
At the mere touch of cold philosophy?
There was an aweful rainbow once in heaven:
We knew her woof, her texture; she is given
In the dull catalogue of common things.
Philosophy will clip an Angel's wings,
Conquor all mysteries by rule and line,
Empty the haunted air, and gnomed mine –
Unweave a rainbow . . .[67]

Dawkins seeks to illustrate how a scientific understanding of reality (such as Newton obtained when he split white light into the rainbow using a prism, thereby 'unweaving the rainbow'), far from draining life of meaning (by its constant de-mystification of reality), can actually deepen our sense of awe and mystery before the universe: 'The feeling of awed wonder that science can give us is one of the highest experiences of which the human psyche is capable.'[68]

In an article for *The Humanist*, Dawkins again speaks of the emotional rewards of science: 'All the great religions have a place for awe, for ecstatic transport at the wonder and beauty of creation. And it's exactly this feeling of spine-shivering, breath-catching awe – almost worship – this flooding of the chest with ecstatic wonder, that modern science can provide.'[69] This says more about Dawkins' religious devotion to science than it does about the ability of science to provide a substitute for the sense of meaning once derived from 'the great religions'. As Kirsten Birkett comments:

> Christians feel awe in looking at creation because they know it is creation – and they know the creator personally. It is this juxtaposition of images, that the creator who could accomplish so much on such an overwhelming scale would care to concern himself with the most insignificant of humans, that is the inspiration to awe and wonder . . . Dawkins awe of 'creation' is in stark contrast to his actual belief about its origins and destiny.[70]

Dawkins may 'almost worship'; but theists can go further, into actual worship.

With Phillip E. Johnson, we may happily concede Dawkins' defence of science at the outset, for 'pleasure in the rainbow is not spoilt by knowing how Newton explained the prism effect'.[71] Indeed, if anything, Newton has doubled our pleasure by allowing us to wonder not only at the beauty of the rainbow, but at the beauty of the physical process that causes rainbows as well. But perhaps Keats has a more significant point to

make, for as Johnson says, 'Behind this seemingly triv-
ial argument there are deeper issues . . . involving the
long-standing dilemma of whether and how Darwinian
ideology is to be reconciled with human dignity and
freedom.'[72] Alister McGrath is more sensitive to Keats'
concerns:

> For Keats, a rainbow is meant to lift the human
> heart and imagination upwards, intimating the
> existence of a world beyond the bounds of experi-
> ence. For Dawkins, the rainbow remains firmly
> located within the world of human experience. It
> has no transcendent dimension. The fact that it
> can be explained in purely natural terms is taken
> to deny that it can have any significance as an
> indicator of transcendence. The angel that was, for
> Keats, meant to lift our thoughts heavenwards has
> had its wings clipped; it can no longer do anything
> save mirror the world of earthly events and princi-
> ples . . .
>
> Despite Dawkins's insistence to the contrary,
> Keats had no fundamental problems with scientific
> explanations of the rainbow. His criticisms were
> directed against those who insisted that this was
> *all* that there was to a rainbow – who denied that
> the rainbow could have any *symbolic* significance,
> both heightening the human yearning for a tran-
> scendent realm and hinting at means of its resolu-
> tion.[73]

With McGrath I think it is 'a matter of profound regret
that Dawkins makes no attempt to empathise with Keats
– to try to understand the fear that Keats expresses and
its wider resonance within Western culture. Keats react-
ed against materialism, which he feared would rob

human life of its purpose and meaning.'[74]

Dawkins rightly defends science against the charge of de-mystification (showing how it reveals new vistas of grandeur and delight to the inquiring mind), but his apology ('a rational defence of one's views') is undermined by his insistence upon seeing science through the distorting lens of his naturalistic worldview. It is not Dawkins' science *per se* that clips the angel's wings to produce a bleak, nihilistic pessimism in his readers, rather, it is his 'cold philosophy'. In *Unweaving the Rainbow* Dawkins mistakenly defends his 'cold philosophy' from the charge of nihilism by defending his science (a natural enough mistake for someone who constantly confuses science with philosophy). Physicist Stephen M. Barr's review of *Unweaving the Rainbow* is spot on:

> This book is based in its entirety on a simple mistake. It is not often that one can find exactly the point where an author goes off track, but here one can. It is in the fifth sentence of the preface of the book, which begins, 'Similar accusations of barren desolation, of promoting an arid and joyless message, are frequently flung at science in general.' However, what people object to in Dawkins is not the science but the atheism. Because he cannot see the difference, he writes a book that is a 300-page *non sequitur*.[75]

As Johnson notes: 'The cold philosophy that causes a sensitive human spirit to recoil is not scientific investigation but scientific materialism, the philosophical dogma that insists that only mindless matter is ultimately real and that only science holds the key to knowledge.'[76] Interestingly enough, when I mentioned to an educated friend (then completing his doctorate in political philosophy) that I was writing a book that examined Dawkins' views, he was under the impression that Dawkins was a philosopher and was surprised to learn that he was a zoologist. Perhaps this is a reflection of Dawkins' own public confusion of science and naturalism.

Why don't you just grow up?

Father Christmas and the Tooth Fairy are part of the charm of childhood. So is God. Some of us grow out of all three.
RICHARD DAWKINS[77]

We are to be children in heart, not in understanding.
THOMAS AQUINAS[78]

Some grown-ups feel that everything child-like is childish, and that since adults shouldn't be childish, they should never be child-like. They don't realize that the fear of being thought childish by one's peers because of child-like behaviour (e.g. enjoying *The Muppets*, having a go on the swings, etc) is in itself very childish. It is only rebellious children who are desperate to 'grow up'. Commenting on a newspaper report that Dawkins had called belief in God 'childish, like belief in Santa Claus . . .',[79] Professor Denys Turner said:

> I am not sure what Dawkins does understand, but
> he clearly does not understand children if he
> thinks that the childishness of theism makes
> theism like belief in Santa Claus . . . Children only
> believe in Santa Claus . . . because adults persuade

them to, and often for unimpressive reasons of
their own, like contriving cover for the choice of
inappropriate presents; whereas theism is closely
connected not with adult myths foisted upon
children, but with more spontaneous forms of
thought which are natural to children's own
minds; and adults seem often to want to suppress
such childish thoughts . . .[80]

Atheists have been alternatively nagging humanity to
'grow up', and predicting that humanity will inevitably
'grow up', for a long time (without seeming to notice
the tension between these pessimistic and optimistic
sides to their atheistic coinage). For example, Nietzsche
alleged that religion originates with 'an early, immature
intellectuality in man [that] takes lightly the duty to tell
the truth'.[81] Those who make such accusations never
stop to think that maybe some forms of belief in the
supernatural are more akin to the child-like ability to
enjoy a go on the swings rather than the childish inability to take turns nicely. Jesus said: 'unless you change
and become like little children, you will never enter the
kingdom of heaven' (Matthew 18:3). But the child-like-
ness Jesus taught has everything to do with a child's
capacity for trust and nothing to do with a childish
inability to reason: 'When I was a child,' said Paul, 'I
thought like a child, I reasoned like a child. When I
became a man, I put childish ways behind me' (1
Corinthians 13:11): 'When Jesus said you had to enter
the kingdom like a child, he means you have to enter
with a child's trust, not with a child's understanding.'[82]
As Paul C. Vitz comments: 'The pose of rebellion, the
clichés of hostility to authority . . . that have gone
unchallenged for years in the modern world are wearing

out. The time has come for a childlike philosophy to reassert its superiority to an adolescent one.'[83]

In the tired and tested traditional manner of sceptics, Dawkins expresses his faith that the onward march of grown-up (we might say jaded) science will inevitably falsify traditional views of reality (and with them, belief in cosmic meaning):

> As time goes by and our civilization grows up more, the model of the universe that we share will become progressively less superstitious, less small-minded, less parochial. It will lose its remaining ghosts, hobgoblins and spirits, it will be a realistic model, correctly regulated and updated by incoming information from the real world.[84]

Physicist turned theologian Dr John Polkinghorne calls this sort of unsubstantiated assertion 'promissory naturalism'. If all the evidence isn't in yet, how can Dawkins be so confident of the end result? Because the answers that Dawkins' allows science to give are restricted from the outset by his commitment to the naturalistic worldview, a worldview summed up by the late Carl Sagan's claim that 'The Cosmos is all that is or ever was or ever will be.'[85] As William Hasker explains: 'Philosophical naturalism insists that the natural world is complete in itself, self-contained and self-sufficient. According to naturalism, everything which exists or occurs lies entirely within the domain of natural processes. Nothing comes into nature or influences it from outside. There is no "outside"; nature is all there is.'[86]

According to Dawkins: 'Science shares with religion the claim that it answers deep questions about origins, the nature of life and the cosmos. But there the resemblance ends. Scientific beliefs are supported by evidence, and they get results. Myths and faiths are not and do not.'[87] Science and religion certainly overlap, since both make truth claims about the real world, including claims that make a difference to the way the world should be discovered to be if those claims are true. As Dallas Willard claims: 'The life and words that Jesus brought into the world came in the form of information and reality. He and his early associates overwhelmed the ancient world because they brought into it a stream of life at its deepest, along with the best information possible on the most important matters.'[88] Or as Polkinghorne affirms: 'there is a cousinly connection between the dwellers in science-land and the dwellers in theology-land. Their common cause for truth means that the frontier between them will always be busy with traffic across its open border.'[89] At least Dawkins doesn't do religion the disservice of seeing it as restricted to a privatised realm of feelings and opinions that are merely 'true for you'. However, Dawkins' accusation that religious faith is not interested in, or supported by, evidence (or that it doesn't 'get results'[90]) is far from being either significant or true.

As for the significance of evidence, philosopher Del Ratzsch points out that: 'If one believes something on the basis of evidence, then one presumably has to believe that the evidence is reliable. But if one can only believe things on the basis of evidence, then one must have evidence for one's evidence. The chain, as you can see, is going to get a bit unwieldy.'[91] In other words, evidence can't be the be-all and end-all of rational belief, and religious beliefs might therefore be perfectly rational in the absence of 'evidence'.[92] As for the truth of Dawkins' accusation, Alister McGrath responds:

> Dawkins's caricature of Christianity may well carry weight with his increasingly religiously illiterate or religiously alienated audiences, who find in his writings ample confirmation of their prejudices, but merely persuades those familiar with religious traditions to conclude that Dawkins has no interest in understanding what he critiques . . . Christian tradition has always valued rationality and does not hold that faith involves the abandonment of reason or the absence of evidence.[93]

Unfortunately, 52 per cent of university students in a recent survey agreed with the statement: 'Scientific thinking is based on evidence, religion is based just on faith,' while 49 per cent affirmed that: 'Science is about objective facts, religion is about feelings and subjectivity.'[94] It would be less of a distortion to say that Dawkins' scientific thinking is based just on faith and feelings! Science and religion both involve people making a personal investment in beliefs about objective reality based upon publicly available evidence and personal feelings – but unlike science, religion (in its Judeo-Christian form at least) is construed by believers as an objectively real, personally transforming relationship with the object of their belief.

Dawkins' derisory view of religion is grounded in the fact that, far from leaving ultimate explanations out of science as Newton counselled, he believes that science is the ultimate explanation, a belief that 'grants an epistemological sovereignty to science which would astonish most philosophers – not to mention the founders of modern science'.[95] In promoting science as the provider of ultimate explanations, Dawkins effectively turns science into a religion called *scientism*; a religion that prefers to dismiss the really deep questions as meaningless than to admit any answers that exceed the limited competency of a naturalistically restricted science to meet – even if that means embracing nihilism: 'we know from the second law of thermodynamics that all complexity, all life, all laughter, all sorrow, is hell-bent on levelling itself out into cold nothingness in the end', says Dawkins, 'They – and we – can never be more than temporary, local buckings of the great universal slide into the abyss of uniformity.'[96] Dawkins clearly sees that a universe lacking a creator is a universe 'lacking all purpose'.[97] But he doesn't take into account the fact that science does not (indeed cannot) reveal a universe without design; or that if there is a Designer, then the universe might be destined for something other than 'the abyss of uniformity'.

Conclusion

There is, as W. Christopher Stewart comments:

> . . . something logically suspect about the claim that 'science proves metaphysical naturalism'. More precisely, this argument seems to commit the fallacy logicians call 'begging the question' – assuming the very thing one is attempting to prove. If science presupposes naturalism for methodological purposes, then there is something singularly uninteresting and downright misleading about the claim that science proves that there is no such thing as supernatural agency operative in the universe.[98]

Due to his devotion to scientism, Dawkins routinely confuses science and metaphysics, and so fails to see that his supposedly 'scientific' beliefs about ultimate reality and meaning are, ironically, a product of his philosophical rejection of God rather than the result of scientific evidence. As A. N. Wilson wisely observes: 'the Science versus Religion match is usually conducted most loudly by people who would benefit from a few months spent reading a third discipline – philosophy'.[99]

[1] The term 'scientist' was invented by Rev. William Whewell, Master of Trinity College, Cambridge, in the early nineteenth century.

[2] Bragg, Melvyn, *On Giants' Shoulders* (London: Sceptre, 1998), p.97.

[3] *ibid.*, p.78.

[4] Westfall, Richard S., *The Life of Isaac Newton* (Cambridge University Press, 1993), p.60.

[5] Heeren, Fred, *Show Me God: What the Message from Space Is Telling Us About God* (Wheeling, Illinois: Daystar, 2000), p.351.

[6] Westfall, *op. cit.*, p.23.

[7] Bragg, *op. cit.*, p.77.

[8] Westfall, *op. cit.*, p.13.

[9] *ibid.*, p.306.

[10] *ibid.*, p.307.

[11] *ibid.*, p.35.

[12] *ibid.*, p.66.

[13] *ibid.*, p.63.

[14] *ibid.*

[15] *ibid.*

[16] *ibid.*, p.40.

[17] Anonymous, *One Hundred Great Lives* (London: Odham Press), p.37.

[18] Heeren, *op. cit.*, p.352.

[19] Bragg, *op. cit.*, p.84.

[20] *ibid.*, p.85.

[21] Pearcey, Nancey R. and Thaxton, Charles B., *The Soul of Science* (Wheaton: Crossway, 1994), p.79.

[22] Heeren, *op. cit.*, p.352.

[23] Bragg, *op. cit.*, p.95.

[24] Ward, Keith, *God, Faith & the New Millennium* (Oxford: OneWorld, 1998), p.52.

[25] *ibid.*, p.69.

[26] Newton, *Principia Mathematica*, quoted by Fred Heeren, *op. cit.*, p.352.

[27] Broom, Neil, *How Blind is the Watchmaker?* (Downers Grove, Illinois: IVP, 2001), p.213.

[28] Heeren, *op. cit.*, p.352.

[29] Moreland, J. P., 'The Explanatory Relevance of Libertarian Agency', in William A. Dembski (ed.), *Mere Creation* (Downers Grove, Illinois: IVP, 1998), p.279.

[30] *ibid.*

[31] Newton, *op. cit.*, p.248-249.

[32] Pearcey and Thaxton, *op. cit.*, p.90.

[33] Heeren, *op. cit.*, p.353.

[34] *ibid.*, p.351-352.

[35] Newton, *Principia Mathematica*, quoted by Fred Heeren, *op. cit.*, p.53.

[36] Bragg, *op. cit.*, p.75.

[37] Newton, quoted by Bragg, *ibid.*, p.309.

[38] Newton, quoted by Fred Heeren, *op. cit.*, p.351.

[39] Bragg, *op. cit.*, p.91.

[40] Nichols, Terence L., *The Sacred Cosmos* (Grand Rapids: Brazos Press, 2003), p.89.

[41] Dawkins, Richard, *Unweaving the Rainbow* (London: Allen Lane/The Penguin Press, 1998), p.ix.

[42] A zoologist is a biologist who specializes in the study of animals.

[43] Nelkin, Dorothy, 'Less Selfish than Sacred? Genes and the Religious Impulse in Evolutionary Psychology', in *Alas, Poor Darwin* (London: Vintage, 2001), p.15.

[44] Hinde, Julia, 'Does God Exist?', in Harriet Swain (ed.), *Big Questions in Science* (London, Jonathan Cape, 2002), p.2.

[45] 'a 1996 survey still found 40 percent of US scientists believed in God' – Hinde, *ibid.*, p.4. cf. Tim Holt, 'Science Resurrects God' at www.id.ucsb. edu:16080/fscf/LIBRARY/HOLT/science.html

[46] Gould, Stephen Jay, quoted by Denis Alexander, *Rebuilding the Matrix* (Oxford: Lion, 2001), p.330.

[47] Dawkins, Richard, at www.pbs.org/faithandreason/

[48] McGrath, Alister, *The Re-Enchantment of Nature* (London: Hodder & Stoughton, 2003), p.153.

[49] Ford, David, *God in the University* (Gatehouse Occasional Papers No. 1.), p.2-3.

[50] Johnson, Paul, 'If there is no God, what is the Oxford atheist scared of?', *Spectator*, 16 March 1996, p.19.

[51] Downey, Robert, in *Eastsideweek*, 11 December, 1996, at www.world-of-dawkins.com/Media/seattle.htm

[52] Dawkins, Richard, *A Devil's Chaplain* (London: Weidenfeld & Nicolson, 2003), p.37.

[53] Steer, Roger, *Letter to an Influential Atheist* (Carlisle: Authentic Lifestyle/Paternoster Press, 2003), p.7.

[54] *The Chronicle of Higher Education*, 29 November 1996, www.world-of-dawkins.com/Media/chron.htm

[55] cf. www.expo-cosmos.or.jp/about_e.html

[56] 'International Cosmos Prize Press Release' at www.world-of-dawkins.com/Dawkins/Prizes/cosmos.htm

[57] *ibid.*

[58] Dawkins, Richard, *The Selfish Gene* (Oxford University Press, 1976), Preface.

[59] Ward, Keith, *God, Chance & Necessity* (Oxford: OneWorld, 1996), p.137.

[60] Alexander, Denis, *Rebuilding the Matrix* (Oxford: Lion, 2001), p.352.

[61] Shambles, J. Roy, in Steer, *Letter to an Influential Atheist, op. cit.*, Foreword, p.x.

[62] Backhouse, Robert, 5,000 *Quotations for Teachers & Preachers* (Eastbourne: Kingsway, 1994), p.10.

[63] Haffner, Paul, *The Mystery of Creation* (Gracewing, 1995), p.17.

[64] Dennett, Daniel, *Darwin's Dangerous Idea: Evolution and the Meaning of Life* (New York: Simon & Schuster, 1995), p.63.

[65] *ibid.*, p.18.

[66] Dawkins, Richard, *Unweaving the Rainbow* (London: Allen Lane/The Penguin Press, 1998), p.x.

[67] Keats, John, 'Lamia' (1820), quoted by Richard Dawkins, *ibid.*, p.39.

[68] Dawkins, *Unweaving the Rainbow, op. cit.*, p.x.

[69] Dawkins, 'Is science a religion?' in *The Humanist*, Jan/Feb 1997, p.27.

[70] Birkett, *The Essence of Darwinism, op. cit.*, p.99-100.

[71] Johnson, Phillip E., 'The Robot Rebellion of Richard Dawkins – A Review of *Unweaving the Rainbow* by Richard Dawkins' at www.arn.org/docs/johnson/pj_robotrebellion.htm

[72] *ibid.*

[73] McGrath, *op. cit.*, p.176-177.

[74] *ibid.*, p.178.

[75] Barr, Stephen M., 'Prophet of Pointlessness', *First Things*, August/September 1995.

[76] Johnson, 'The Robot Rebellion of Richard Dawkins – A Review of *Unweaving the Rainbow* by Richard Dawkins', *op. cit.*

[77] Dawkins, Richard, *Thirdway Magazine*, June 2003, Vol. 26, No. 5, p.5.

[78] *5,000 Quotations for Teachers & Preachers, op. cit.*, p.220.

[79] Turner, Denys, *Faith Seeking* (London: SCM, 2002), p.19.

[80] *ibid.*, p.19-20.

[81] Neitzche, Friedrich, *Daybreak*, trans. R. J. Hollingdale, (Cambridge: Cambridge University Press, 1985), p.53.

[82] Budziszewski, J., *How To Stay Christian In College* (Colorado Springs: NavPress, 1999), p.29.

[83] Vitz, Paul C., *Psychology as Religion* (Grand Rapids: Eerdmans, 2001), p.85.

[84] Dawkins, Richard, *Royal Institute Christmas Lecture*, 1991, Lecture 5, 'The genesis of purpose'. I don't care for ghosts or hobgoblins, but on the existence of spirits *per se*, see my *The Case for Angels* (Carlisle: Paternoster, 2002).

[85] Sagan, Carl, *Cosmos* (Random House, 1980), p.4.

[86] Hasker, William, *Metaphysics: Constructing a World View* (Leicester: IVP, 1983), p.108.

[87] Dawkins, Richard, *River Out of Eden: A Darwinian View of Life* (London: Windfield & Nicolson, 1995), p.33.

[88] Willard, Dallas, *The Divine Conspiracy* (Fount, 1998).

[89] Polkinghorne, John, *Traffic in Truth: Exchanges Between Science & Theology* (Norwich: The Canterbury Press, 2000), p.50.

[90] cf. Chamberlain and Hall, *Realized Religion* (Templeton, 2002).

[91] Ratzsch, Del, *Science & Its Limits* (Downers Grove: Apollos, 2000), p.103.

[92] cf. Plantinga, Alvin, *Warranted Christian Belief* (Oxford, 2000).

[93] McGrath, *op. cit.*, p.156-157.

[94] cf. Alexander, *op. cit.*, p.29.

[95] Birkett, *op. cit.*, p.99.

[96] Dawkins, 'Is science a religion?', *op. cit.*

[97] Dawkins, *River out of Eden*, *op. cit.*, p.296.

[98] Stewart, W. Christopher, 'Religion and Science' in Michael J. Murray (ed.), *Reason for the Hope Within* (Grand Rapids: Eerdmans, 1999), p.325. There is no good reason for science to presuppose even a 'methodological' naturalism, cf. Alvin Plantinga, 'Methodological Naturalism?' at http://id-www.ucsb.edu/fscf/library/plantinga/mn/home.html

[99] Wilson, A. N., *God's Funeral* (London: John Murray, 1999), p.202.

CHAPTER 4

From Ideology to Science

January 2004 saw the UK's TV Channel Five producing a series of documentaries on *The Big Questions*. The advertising for these programmes implied that only through science had it now become possible to answer these questions. The third programme in the series featured Richard Dawkins tackling the question 'Why Are We Here?' He told viewers that the answer given by previous generations to this question (i.e. 'We were created by God') was unsatisfying because it was 'made up rather than properly investigated'. The real answer, according to Dawkins, was revealed by Victorian naturalist Charles Darwin, who proposed a scientific theory that 'shook the spiritual foundations of his age' because it meant that humans were *not* the product of design. Still, 'we've got over it now', said Dawkins, and most of us are happy to accept that we are (nothing but) apes. Dawkins affirmed that the scientific answer to the question 'Why Are We Here?' is that there is no reason for which we exist, life has no purpose, we just happen to exist as the unintended product of a natural process he describes as 'harsh', 'bloodthirsty', 'callous' and 'wasteful'. Paradoxically, Dawkins also affirmed that his scientific answer to the question 'Why Are We Here?' is 'optimistic', 'inspiring', and 'uplifting'. Can it really be both? How much blind faith does it take to be optimistic if humanity is nothing but an ape in the uncaring hands of a harsh, bloodthirsty, callous and wasteful reality? And if Dawkins' naturalistic worldview is true, can he justify the validity of such value judgements as underpin his calling evolution either callous or uplifting?

*Darwinism is a philosophical preference, if by
that we mean we choose to discuss the material
Universe in terms of material processes
accessible by material operations.*
ARTHUR SHAPIRO[1]

Plato noted that 'all things do become, have become
and will become, some by nature, some by art, and
some by chance',[2] and he argued that either Mind
comes before matter (and the world is a work of art), or
matter comes before Mind (and the world is purely the
result of chance and natural regularities). The theistic
doctrine of Creation says that Mind came before matter
– it is a work of art. To be an atheist, on the other hand,
means being committed to a 'matter first' view of things
– the cosmos is not a work of art, and everything *must*,
therefore, be the result of *nothing but* natural regularities and chance: 'Naturalistic rules require that theories
employ only two kinds of forces – chance and necessity, random variation and impersonal law.'[3]

Why Dawkins' work reveals a philosophy without scientific support

Darwin's theory of evolution is an attempt to explain
biological diversity in terms of a finely balanced combination of natural regularities and chance working over
long periods of time. For an atheist like Dawkins, evolution is not so much the result of an assessment of the
scientific evidence as it is a necessary assumption
brought to its interpretation. Dawkins lets the cat out of
the bag when he writes that: 'even if there were no actual evidence in favour of the Darwinian theory . . . we
should still be justified in preferring it over all rival the-

ories'.[4] As William A. Dembski notes: 'We are dealing with a naturalistic metaphysic that shapes and controls what theories of biological origins are permitted on the playing field in advance of any discussion or weighing of evidence.'[5] Taking a historical view, molecular biologist Michael Denton argues:

There can be no question that Darwin had nothing like sufficient evidence to establish his theory of evolution . . . yet despite the weakness of the evidence, Darwin's theory was elevated from what was in reality a highly speculative hypothesis into an unchallenged dogma in a space of little more than twenty years after the publication of the *Origin*. To understand how this came about we have to look beyond the facts of biology. As is so often the case and as the history of science so amply testifies, the acceptance of new ideas is often dependent on the influence of non-scientific factors of a social, psychological and philosophical nature and the Darwinian revolution was no exception.[6]

As Phillip Johnson says: 'in the last analysis . . . Darwinism is not really based on empirical evidence. Its true basis is in philosophy, and specifically the metaphysics of naturalism.'[7] Of course, evidence is presented[8]; but when it comes to Dawkins' favourite subject of Darwinism, the data has been interpreted through an atheistic worldview that required some sort of evolution *on purely philosophical grounds* long before Darwin proposed his theory of evolution by means of natural selection: 'We suppose that Darwin discovered evolution in the early nineteenth century,' observes Benjamin Wiker, 'but in reality he was mainly repeating an ancient argument, and adding to it what he took to be a body of supporting evidence.'[9] As Kirsten Birkett writes: 'it is polemically convenient for atheists if evolutionary theory is believed to be purely scientific . . . Then when they claim that evolution disproves Christianity they can present this as a conclusion based on science. It is not; it is a conclusion based on ideology, in fact a conclusion drawn before evolutionary theory was formulated at all.'[10]

For example, the fifth-century BC philosopher Empedocles of Acragas postulated that the universe was composed of four basic elements: earth, air, fire and water. These elements were stirred by Love and Strife (i.e. 'attraction' and 'repulsion'):

> The constant interplay of these elements . . . formed the universe. Empedocles claimed that the Earth had given birth to living creatures, but that the first creatures had been disembodied organs. These organs finally joined into whole organisms, through the force of Love, but some of these organisms, being monstrous and unfit for life, had died out . . . Empedocles had come up with a sort of evolutionary theory: past natural selection is responsible for the forms we see today. Empedocles also ascribed the origin of the life of today to *the interplay of impersonal forces, in which chance, not the gods, played the major role.*[11]

Empedocles' story is not as plausible as the one Dawkins tells; but in both cases, 'what drives the show is not the facts but the philosophy'.[12]

In his groundbreaking study, *Moral Darwinism: How We Became Hedonists*, Dr Benjamin Wiker traces

the roots of evolution back to the materialistic philosophy of ancient Greek Epicureanism:

> The materialist evolutionary account had existed
> as part of Epicurean materialism for almost two
> millennia, and the goal of its design was to
> eliminate the divine. The modern acceptance of all
> the essentials of Epicurean materialism necessarily
> led to the acceptance of the entire theoretical
> construct, of which evolution was a necessary
> part . . . Epicurus himself, living three hundred
> years before the birth of Christ, forged his
> materialism for the particular task of eliminating
> the pernicious influence of Greek religion. But
> when Epicurean materialism was revived in the
> Renaissance and Enlightenment . . . its modern
> adherents reforged ancient Epicureanism for the
> task of destroying Christianity. [13]

Agnostic Michael Ruse's explanation of Darwin's
motives is revealing:

> . . . evolution was little more than a
> pseudo-science on a par with . . . phrenology
> (brain bumps), used as much by its practitioners
> to convey moral and social messages as to
> describe the physical world . . . Charles Darwin . .
> . set out to change all of this. First, he wanted
> to give an empirically grounded basis for belief
> in the fact of evolution. Second, he wanted to
> persuade his readers of a particular mechanism
> of evolution, the natural selection of the
> successful brought on by the struggle for
> existence. [14]

Note that a pseudo-scientific belief in 'the fact of evolution' came *before* Darwin's project to *provide*

evidence for evolution and to advocate his particular theory as to its mechanism. As Johnson writes: 'A theory of biological origins that is in a general way like Darwinism follows fairly straightforwardly from the proposition that God is an illusion and nature is therefore all that exists . . . Darwinian selection is simply the most plausible candidate for that process that has ever been suggested.'[15]

The above observations do not mean that the theory of evolution is false, but they do raise serious questions about its use in the hands of atheists, like Dawkins, to justify a naturalistic worldview. As Dean L. Overman cautions, 'Starting with the result one wants and working backwards is not unusual and not always an incorrect procedure. In many circumstances reasoning backwards is a very useful device for constructing plausible hypotheses, but it cannot be substituted for a rigorous proof.'[16]

The significance of an *a priori* commitment to naturalistic explanations can be clearly seen in Dawkins' *The Blind Watchmaker* (which John Gribbin described as perhaps 'the most important evolution book since Darwin'[17]). Dawkins' title derives from William Paley's argument for God from the similarities between the complex workings of a watch, which we know has a designer, and the analogous complex workings of nature, which therefore probably has a designer too.[18] As William Dembski explains:

> For the watch there is no question that it actually is intelligently designed. For the organism, on the other hand, this is not so immediately clear. Yet because the watch and the organism share several features in common . . . (like functional

> interdependence of parts, self-propulsion, etc.),
> we are, according to the argument from analogy,
> warranted in concluding that organisms are also
> intelligently designed.[19]

This design argument does not lead us directly to the conclusion that God exists, but the identification of the designer with God would be a reasonable one. Such design as life exhibits, like the design exhibited by a watch, suggested Paley, requires something more akin to human intelligence than to unthinking instinct or reflex; the designer (it is simpler to postulate one designer than several) must be capable of intelligent intentional agency: 'Thus, we are more like our Creator than anything else we have experience of.'[20] As Paley said of his argument: 'Among other things, it proves the *personality* of the Deity, as distinguished from what is called nature . . . that which can contrive, which can design, must be a person . . . the acts of a mind prove the existence of a mind.'[21]

Dawkins fundamentally fudges the issue here. According to him, Paley was right about the complexity of nature, but wrong about its explanation: 'The only thing he got wrong – admittedly quite a big thing – was the explanation itself. He gave the traditional religious answer . . . The true explanation is utterly different, and it had to wait for one of the most revolutionary thinkers of all time, Charles Darwin.'[22] It's crucial to realize that Dawkins has just 'pulled a fast one' (albeit unintentionally). He has just implied that *either* Paley was right to argue that nature is a work of art, *or* Darwin was right to argue that biological organisms are the result of nothing but nature and chance. But of course, as Michael Poole explains, this is a false dilemma:

> When giving causal explanations, it needs to be
> made clear whether the causes in question are
> primary (ultimate) or secondary (immediate,
> proximate) ones and also whether they are to be
> given in terms of an agent or a process. There is
> no logical blunder being committed if it is claimed
> both that 'God made the universe' and 'the universe
> was the result of a "Big Bang"'. It *is* a logical error
> to hold that an explanation of cosmological
> mechanisms involved necessarily excludes divine
> agency. It certainly appears to be a common error
> to regard explanations of agency and explanations
> of process as alternatives. Perhaps the form of this
> mistake which generates most heat and least light
> is the claim that one has to choose between 'God
> created humankind' and 'humankind was the
> result of an evolutionary process'. [23]

In other words, it's possible that Paley and Darwin are
both right:

> Evolutionary theory does not, of course, prove
> that there is no creator God. But evolutionary
> theory held by a theist is a completely different
> theory of origins from evolutionary theory held by
> an atheist. One is telling the details of how a
> loving Father created us to be fully human and
> capable of becoming his children. The other is
> telling the details of how a bizarre accident
> incidentally brought about a meaningless set of
> intelligent apes. [24]

As Paul Copan interjects: 'The greatness of God's creative genius is not diminished if he created gradually
rather than instantaneously. God's majestic power is
not lessened if he acts indirectly rather than directly.' [25]

Explanatory compatibility

Aristotle pointed out that there are different types of logically compatible explanation. For example, if we are to give a comprehensive explanation for the existence of a watch we must appeal to the existence of the stuff the watch is made out of (its material cause), take into account the arrangement of that stuff in that form (its formal cause), explain how that stuff came to be in that form (its efficient cause) and finally we must provide the reason why the watch exists, the goal that this arrangement of matter serves (its final cause – to tell the time). Atheist Anthony Flew calls the compatibility of different types of explanation the 'first moral' of explanation (a moral ignored by Dawkins):

> Explanations answering different questions are not necessarily rivals . . . The first moral, therefore, is that there is not just one single, *the* explanation for anything which we may wish to have explained. There may instead be as many, not necessarily exclusive, alternative explanations as there are legitimate explanation-demanding questions to be asked.[26]

Science explains things in terms of contingent material, formal and efficient causes. It cannot explain *why* there is any matter, or *why* the laws of physics (and so chemistry, and so biology) take the form they do, let alone *why* there is a universe in the first place. Nor can science say the universe hasn't got an efficient cause beyond itself that created the universe according to a pre-conceived formal cause for a purpose (a 'final cause'). The scientific description of a physical system, be it evolution or anything else, is *in principle* incapable of ruling out what Richard Swinburne calls 'personal explanations', explanations in terms of the desires and intentions of agents. This fact can be recognized in such mundane situations as cooking something in a microwave: Why is the potato getting hot? Scientific answer: because the microwaves are causing the water molecules to vibrate. The microwaves are the 'efficient cause' of the potato getting hot. But why is this happening? Because I want my lunch! This is a *teleological* explanation in terms of a goal (Greek: '*telos*') purposefully aimed at by an agent. My goal of having a cooked potato is the 'final cause' of the potato getting hot, and saying so does not conflict with the scientific explanation of the potato's hotness.

Moreover, the fact that we can give a scientific description of the physical mechanism of a microwave machine does not disprove the existence of a microwave machine designer. Similarly, a scientific description of a physical mechanism that results in living organisms (such as the mechanism Darwin proposed) would not disprove the existence of a designer of that system. As Thomas Dubay writes: 'There are no theological problems with evolution, provided it remains firmly within scientifically verifiable facts and sheds any baseless philosophical bias against design.'[27] Evolution, as a scientific theory, cannot and does not exclude design. Dawkins' naturalistic philosophy *demands* a world without design, but the evidence of the natural world itself, as Paley observed, seems to point to the existence of a designer.

Dawkins' suggestion that evolution contradicts creation (and thus meaning and purpose) can only be swallowed if we agree to define evolution and creation as mutually exclusive concepts. But why do that? As Phillip Johnson writes:

> 'Evolution' contradicts 'creation' only when it is explicitly or tacitly defined as fully naturalistic evolution – meaning evolution that is not directed [or intended] by any purposeful intelligence. Similarly, 'creation' contradicts evolution only when it means *sudden creation*, rather than creation by progressive development . . . The essential point of creation has nothing to do with the timing or the mechanism the Creator chose to employ, but with the element of design or purpose. In the broadest sense, a 'creationist' is simply a person who believes that the world (and especially mankind) was *designed*, and exists for a *purpose*.[28]

When it comes to the question of purpose, and to evaluating the competing worldviews of atheism and theism: 'This is the real issue: not whether evolution is true or not, but whether or not we are created. If not, then we are meaningless accidents.'[29]

Dawkins admits that living things are analogous to watches in their complexity, and that they appear to be designed. In conversation with Keith Ward Dawkins said:

> When a biologist looks at particular organs or organisms, an eye or a brain, what he sees is a machine, which has every indication of being designed for a purpose. In that sense, living things quite obviously do have a purpose. But natural selection manages to explain how they came into being without there being an ultimate purpose. There is admittedly a strain between the thought

of blind chance and design. For living beings are not only designed, they are supremely well designed, beautifully designed and far more complicated than any man-made machine. But what is so magnificent about Darwinian explanation is that it does manage to show how blind forces of physics could, given enough time, build these highly complicated machines.[30]

In *The Blind Watchmaker* Dawkins defines biology as 'the study of complicated things that give the appearance of having been designed for a purpose'.[31] Here we see Dawkins recognizing that: '1) biological systems are complex, 2) they have the appearance of design, and 3) the design is apparently for a purpose. It is only the assumption of naturalism that prevents him from saying, "What looks like a duck, acts like a duck, sounds like a duck, and smells like a duck, must *be* a duck."'[32] Indeed, Dawkins' own reductionism actually *strengthens* Paley's analogy: 'Each one of us is a machine, like an airliner only much more complicated.'[33] Paley's analogy stands. In which case, how does Dawkins know that design in living things is only *apparent* and not real? Because, says Dawkins, 'Natural selection, the blind, unconscious, automatic process which Darwin discovered, and which we now know is the explanation for the existence and apparently purposeful form of all life, has no purpose in mind . . . it is the *blind* watchmaker.'[34] There are a number of questionable aspects to this assertion, not least the fact that although the subtitle of *The Blind Watchmaker* (in its American edition) is 'Why the evidence of evolution reveals a world without design', Dawkins 'actually excludes design on philosophical grounds'.[35] As Dawkins writes in the preface: 'I want to persuade the reader, not just that the Darwinian world-view *happens* to be true, but that it is the only known theory that *could*, in principle, solve the mystery of our existence.'[36] This claim is repeated in the concluding chapter: 'Darwinism is the only known theory that is in principle *capable* of explaining certain aspects of life.'[37] As biologist Jonathan Wells points out: 'claiming that a theory is true "in principle" is the hallmark of a philosophical argument, not a scientific inference. The latter requires evidence, and as Dawkins himself admits, evidence is unnecessary to prove the truth of Darwinism.'[38] Unnecessary, that is, if one begins with the philosophical *assumption* that Paley's divine 'watchmaker' does not exist; since then there *must be* a '*blind* watchmaker': 'Darwinism is the answer to a specific question that grows out of philosophical naturalism . . . The question is: How must creation have occurred if we assume that God had nothing to do with it?'[39] Answering this question is not at all the same thing as asking this question: 'How did creation occur?'

An even more fundamental point is this: Natural selection may be a 'blind watchmaker' with no purpose in mind (because it has no mind), but *natural selection may itself be the tool of a designer who does have purposes in mind*. After all, human engineers use computers running genetic algorithms as part of the design process. Neither the computer nor the algorithm has a purpose *in mind*; but the engineers who design and run such systems certainly do. Perhaps natural selection is analogous to such a purposefully designed system: 'What is there to preclude us from saying that this is the machinery that God devised and through which he works in order to people the planet with various and changing forms of life?'[40]

Dawkins' philosophical objections to design

Dawkins' objection to design is not scientific, but philosophical. Indeed, he employs two explicitly philosophical arguments against design. One is an argument against the explanatory usefulness of design. The other is an argument based on the supposed imperfections of biological systems. I will examine each argument in turn.

The superfluity argument against design

An opposition between design and evolution is of fundamental importance to Dawkins' atheism, as revealed in his interview with Nick Pollard: 'Of all the classical arguments for the existence of God,' said Dawkins, 'only the argument from design seemed to me to carry any weight, and I finally toppled that in my mind when I learned about evolution.'[41] In interview with Keith Ward, Dawkins expounded his argument against the explanatory power of design: 'I do not think it would be possible to rule out a designing God, but natural selection does make God superfluous. My own view is that where something is both superfluous and exceedingly complicated and therefore improbable in its own right, we are better off being positively sceptical about it.'[42]

This argument calls for two points of reply. The first is that whether or not God is 'complicated' in a relevant sense is debateable. J. P. Moreland and William Lane Craig point out that: 'A mind's ideas may be complex, but a mind itself is a remarkably simple thing, being an immaterial entity not composed of pieces or separable parts.'[43] Richard Swinburne argues that, as 'the greatest possible being', God is metaphysically simple in a way that finite entities are not. With a finite entity one always has questions about why it has this or that property and why it has this or that degree of this or that property. Such questions do not arise with God, because, as a matter of definition, God must have the maximum possible amount of every great making property (goodness, power, knowledge, etc).

The second point of reply is that when Dawkins says natural selection makes God 'superfluous', he clearly means something like 'superfluous to the provision of a direct causal explanation for all examples of biological design'. Even if we are prepared to grant Dawkins this much, should we be willing to grant his implicit assumption that once direct causal explanations have been accounted for, there are no further types of explanation, or evidence for explanations, remaining? I think not. What Dawkins fails to recognize is that, since evolution cannot 'rule out a designing God', and since nothing he says undermines Paley's analogy, there remains evidence for regarding the hypothesis of design as less than superfluous. Design can be superfluous as *a direct causal explanation* without being superfluous as *an explanation*.

Dawkins puts a different spin on the superfluity argument in *The Blind Watchmaker*:

> To explain the origin of the DNA/protein machine
> by invoking a supernatural designer is to explain
> precisely nothing, for it leaves unexplained
> the origin of the designer. You have to say
> something like 'God was always here', and if you
> allow yourself that kind of lazy way out, you might
> as well just say 'DNA was always there,' or

'life was always there', and be done with it.[44]
Underlying this objection is Dawkins' reductionist view
of scientific explanation. Dawkins writes that 'a complex entity at any particular level in the hierarchy of
organization [must be explained] in terms of entities
only one level down the hierarchy'.[45] Hence Dawkins
has no problem with embodied designers, because he
thinks they will submit to reductive explanations, but an
un-embodied designer is a different matter, because it
clearly won't submit to a reductive explanation: 'In
responding to the who-designed-the-designer question'
says William A. Dembski, 'it is therefore best first to dis-
pense with Dawkins' reductionist view of science. This
is easily done . . . The divide-and-conquer mode of
analysis behind reductive explanation has strictly limited applicability within science. Complex systems theory has long since rejected a reductive bottom-up
approach to complex systems.'[46] Michael Denton takes
a more holistic approach to the study of life:

> . . . proteins are very much less modular than
> machines, which are built up from a set of
> relatively independent modules or compartments.
> Remove the cog from a watch and it still remains a
> cog . . . Remove a fragment of a protein and its
> form disassembles. What a protein represents is
> an object in which all the 'parts' are in a
> reciprocal formative relationship with each other
> and with the whole. The parts of the final whole
> are shaped and finished by reciprocal interaction
> with each other.[47]

Living things, I suggest, are sufficiently *like* machines
to support a viable argument for design by analogy (all
analogies are by nature partial). As Neil Broom, associ-

ate professor in the department of chemical and materials engineering at the University of Auckland, writes: 'Living systems at one level of description are unquestionably marvellous mechanical contrivances. The living cell operates in principle just like any man-made mechanical system with all the appearance of having been carefully constructed according to principles of engineering design . . .'[48] However, a scientific analysis that treats organisms as if they are *nothing but* machines can only take us so far:

> Although still widely described in the biological
> literature as molecular machines, proteins
> transcend mechanism in their complexity, in the
> intense functional integration and interdependence
> of all their components, in the holistic way that
> the form and function of each part is determined
> by the whole and vice versa and in the natural
> formative process by which the amino acid chain
> is folded into the native function. In these ways,
> they resemble no structure or object constructed
> or conceived by man . . . Although organisms do
> exhibit mechanical or machine-like properties they
> also possess properties which no machine exhibits
> even to a minor degree.[49]

Dawkins' commitment to reductionism is a commitment to a form of analysis that fails to capture the holistic nature of nature, and as philosopher Jakob Wolf observes: 'if you insist on resolving the dual-directional causality [of organisms] into a unidirectional version, blind dogmatism will invariably result'.[50] Facing up to what we know about organisms *may* leave the analogical design argument somewhat weakened (although Angus Menuge argues that: 'The reasons that Denton gives for saying that living things transcend machines arguably point to more design, indeed a higher design than transcends the paradigm of human artefacts, not less design.'[51]), but it certainly doesn't render it dead in the water.

How should we respond to Dawkins' regress argument itself? The simplest rebuttal is that even if we can't explain the existence of the designer, this does nothing to invalidate the conclusion that there is a designer. Dawkins fundamentally misunderstands the nature of explanation. William Lane Craig comments: 'It is widely recognized that in order for an explanation to be the best explanation, one needn't have an explanation of the explanation (indeed, such a requirement would generate an infinite regress, so that everything becomes inexplicable) . . . believing that the design hypothesis is the best explanation . . . doesn't depend upon our ability to explain the designer.'[52] As Dembski notes: 'The who-designed-the-designer question invites a regress that is readily declined . . . because such a regress arises whenever scientists introduce a novel theoretical entity . . . the question is whether design does useful conceptual work.'[53] Moreover, no one would make a similar objection to the design hypothesis in any other field of explanation: 'If someone explains some buried earthenware as the result of artisans from the second century BC, no one complains, "Yeah, but who made the artisans?"'[54]

The necessity of God
This said, theists not only hold that 'God was always there', but that God exists necessarily rather than contingently, and that it therefore makes no more sense to

demand an explanation for God's existence than it does to ask why contradictory assertions can't both be true. Philosophers, like parents, sometimes have to answer a question with: 'Just because!' DNA and life, on the other hand, clearly do not exist necessarily. Saying that they exist 'just because' simply won't wash. While it doesn't make sense to try to explain God's existence beyond noting that if God exists he does so necessarily (necessity being the opposite of impossibility), it does make sense to try to explain why DNA and life exist. Dawkins doesn't believe that 'DNA was always there' or that 'life was always there' any more than he believes that God was always there. Saying that DNA or life 'was always there' would contradict his understanding of them both. On the other hand, saying that 'God was always there' makes perfect sense given the classical understanding of God as a necessary being.

Having it both ways

Dawkins' objection to design is a very odd argument for a scientist to give, because it counts against all scientific explanations, *including evolution*. One might as well say that positing evolution explains nothing because it leaves unexplained the origin of life capable of evolving; that invoking the supposed chemical evolution of life from non-life explains precisely nothing because it leaves unexplained the existence of chemicals; or that invoking the finely-tuned laws of physics that underlay the big bang and the subsequent cosmic evolution that produced chemicals explains nothing because it leaves unexplained the origin and fine-tuning of the laws of physics. Naturally, Dawkins wants to invoke all of these theories; he just wants to exclude design. However, trying to have it both ways involves him in the use of a double standard, 'a fallacy in which a person applies standards, principles, rules, etc. to others while taking herself (or those she has a special interest in) to be exempt, without providing adequate justification for the exemption'.[55]

The devil's chaplain argument from imperfections[56]

Writing in the essay that gives its title to *A Devil's Chaplain*, Dawkins suggests that 'Darwin was less than half joking when he coined the phrase Devil's Chaplain in a letter to his friend Hooker in 1856,'[57] saying: 'What a book a Devil's Chaplain might write on the clumsy, wasteful, blundering low and horridly cruel works of nature.'[58] Dawkins quotes Darwin once again with approval: 'I cannot persuade myself that a beneficent and omnipotent God would have designedly created the *Ichneumonidae* [a parasitic wasp] with the express intention of their feeding within the living bodies of caterpillars.'[59]

Christian theology has never held that nature, in this 'fallen' world, is exactly as God ideally wants it to be. Any argument that assumes nature is 'perfect' is not an argument that can be directed against Christian theology. Nevertheless, we might profitably question Darwin's squeamishness about the natural world. It is hard to imagine that a caterpillar *suffers* when being eaten from within (especially since the *Ichneumonidae*'s sting anaesthetizes the caterpillar). Indeed: 'at least a great deal of what appears to be animal suffering need not be suffering in any real sense'.[60] Nor does the 'suffering' of an animal caused by the actions of another animal encompass the dimension of moral evil, for as

Richard Swinburne notes: 'given that animals do not have free will or moral concepts, the actions which they perform do not have a moral character . . .'[61] According to C. S. Lewis: '"Life" in the biological sense has nothing to do with good and evil until sentience appears. The very words "prey" and "ruthless" are mere metaphors . . . A forest in which half the trees are killing the other half may be a perfectly "good" forest: for its goodness consists in its utility and beauty and it does not feel.'[62]

A consistent natural world in which material forces can impinge upon one another is a necessary means to the end of physically embodied finite creatures with genuine and wide-ranging freedom of action, and the total value of such a world and the ends it makes possible would seem sufficient justification for such a creation. Paul Copan points out that: 'the very conditions in the universe that make human life possible, if only slightly different, would not support life at all and thus no free human beings. For all we know, there may not be a more suitable world that is governed by laws that have no natural evil as a by-product.'[63] As Herbert McCabe argues:

> . . . you cannot make material things that develop in time without allowing for the fact that in perfecting themselves they will damage other material things . . . You may be tempted to argue that it would be better not to have lions at all – but *if you think along those lines you have to end up thinking that it would be better not to have any material world at all* . . . No reasonable person objects to an occasional withdrawal of natural cause, a miracle from time

> to time; but a world without any natural causes . . .
> would not be a natural material world at all. So the
> people who would like [God] to have made a
> material world without suffering . . . would have
> preferred him not to have made a [material]
> world . . . But . . . *most people are pleased he
> made such a world . . . The accusation that
> God made it does not seem very damning.*[64]

The caterpillar dies, but the *Ichneumonidae* lives – and
perhaps it is better to have both than it is to have only
one (the former) or neither.

Keith Ward suggests that Darwin's gloomy view of
nature as 'a continual battle for survival between ego-
tistical organisms was suggested',[65] not by his observation of nature, but by reading Thomas Malthus, 'who
had predicted that the inevitable tendency to over-pop-
ulation could only be remedied by repeated wars and
plagues if life on earth was to survive'.[66] John Randell
suggests that many adherents of Darwin's gloomy view
of nature are actually attracted by its very gloominess:
'Many believed it *because* it was so dreadful; they prid-
ed themselves on their courage in facing facts.'[67] It is
certainly true to say that Richard Dawkins, for one,
takes pride in 'standing up full-face into the keen wind
of understanding [the] daemonic alternative urged by
my matured devil's Chaplain . . .'[68] It is at least worth
considering whether the devil's chaplain doesn't play
up the 'cruelty' of nature in the service of scoring
rhetorical points against belief in God. Indeed, Darwin
comments in the *Origin* that: 'The wonder indeed is, on
the theory of natural selection, that more cases of the
want of absolute perfection have not been observed.'[69]
In other words, Darwin observes that the world is actually

more 'perfect' than his own theory leads him to predict, an observation that surely *supports* belief in design!

Keith Ward points out that:

> In biology, the model of isolated units in competition has for some time now been opposed by a model of a unified web of interrelated and intricately balanced forces . . . Those who find Lovelock's Gaia hypothesis more apt will see all planetary life interlinked in a web of mutually supporting relationships. This may help one to see the beauty and wisdom of the natural world in a much more positive light.[70]

Earth abounds with examples of symbiotic relationships among both plants and animals that illustrate the ecological balance which sustains life: 'nature presents to us the most impressive picture of universal co-operation', writes Dr Paul Tournier: 'The chemical cycles, all the symbioses, the interdependence of vegetative and animal life, of the organs of the body, of the various species, and of all the functions and cells of an organism – all this bespeaks community and solidarity.'[71] On a theistic interpretation, argues Ward: 'It is not just a blind will to power that drives evolution forward. It is also a striving to realise values of beauty, understanding and conscious relationships.'[72]

Dawkins sees evolution as a process full of 'waste'.[73] But as Ward asks in response:

> . . . why should we consider all the organisms that do not produce offspring, all the species that become extinct, a waste? The dinosaurs were not a waste of time, just because they, or their descendents, did not live forever. They have value that lies in their sheer existence, whether or not

> they left descendents . . . They probably had many
> sorts of experience that were worthwhile . . . And
> their diverse and fascinating forms would be of
> value to God . . .[74]

Of course, Dawkins assumes that there is no God to appreciate the dinosaurs; but Ward makes a significant point here when he observes: 'We would only call the evolutionary process wasteful if we assumed that it only had one point, which was for everything to have descendents. But what if the point lies in the complex and varied forms of life that it produces?'[75] In other words, if God exists, then evolution is not the wasteful process it appears to be on the naturalistic view of things. In which case, any argument against God's existence from the supposed wastefulness of evolution is guilty of begging the question!

Laura L. Garcia, adjunct Professor of Philosophy at Rutgers University, replies to the atheist's objection that a creator 'would not use a mechanism as inefficient as the evolutionary process to produce the universe'[76] (and perhaps he didn't) by noting that it assumes a materialistic conception of nature as a mere mechanism, whereas the theist has additional conceptual descriptions of nature to take into account, such as seeing creation as a work of art: 'Works of art, especially those of narrative form, are evaluated by very different criteria than mechanical efficiency.'[77]

The place of Darwinian theological themata in evolutionary reasoning

In his paper, 'Jettison the Arguments, or the Rule? The Place of Darwinian Theological Themata in Evolutionary Reasoning', university of Chicago philosopher Paul

A. Nelson observes with interest that: 'While presenting a line of evidence or argument for evolution, the author will, as a premise of his argument, make a theological claim.'[78] This is significant, for 'why does an argument for evolution have to resort to theology?'[79] Perhaps it might be suggested this is because, as Huston Smith affirms, Darwinism is 'supported more by atheistic philosophical assumptions than by scientific evidence'.[80]

Nelson teases out the general form of arguments from imperfection:

1. If p is an instance of organic design, then p was produced either by a wise creator, or by descent with modification (evolution).

2. If p (an instance of organic design) was produced by a wise creator, then p should be perfect (or should exhibit no imperfections).

3. Organic design p is not perfect (or exhibits imperfections).

From these premises, the conclusion follows that:

4. Organic design p was not produced by a wise creator, but by descent with modification.[81]

Nelson argues that 'Each premise of the argument is attended with difficulties.'[82] In fact, there are so many difficulties in the argument that by the time one adds up the results one may well conclude that the overall strength of the argument has dropped below making its conclusion more reasonable than its denial. For one thing: 'the first premise of the imperfection argument is a false dichotomy'.[83] In reality, as we have seen, if p is an instance of organic design, then p may be produced by a wise creator *using* an *intended* process of descent with modification.

The second premise requires a high degree of confidence in making statements of the sort, 'I don't believe you wanted to do that . . .', directed at the designer. As Nelson writes, 'any exponent of the argument must explain (1) what a "wise creator" or a "sensible God" is, and (2) what a "wise creator" would do'.[84] Such judgements are not as easy to make as one might think. After all, we are not sensible gods! Trying to second guess how a wise creator ought to have arranged things is surely analogous to the folly of an undergraduate engineering student attempting to critique the designs of a postgraduate.

'Is it possible that biological entities judged imperfect when considered individually, might combine to form a macro-system judged perfect?'[85], asks Nelson, noting that 'there is no reason for a creator to optimise one part of the universe at the expense of the whole'.[86] Take Darwin's own example of the *Ichneumonidae*, for which he could see no good purpose. The *Encyclopaedia Britannica* reports: 'The group as a whole is beneficial to man because it parasitizes many insect pests.'[87] When caterpillars eat corn seedlings, the corn releases a hormone that attracts the wasps, which destroys the caterpillar, thus saving the corn:

> . . . while on the surface it appears that the wasps
> weren't designed with the well-being of the
> caterpillars in mind (i.e. it appears to have sub-
> optimal design), from a higher order perspective
> we see that their purpose is not only beneficial to
> corn plants, but also to humans and the ecosystem
> as a whole! Without the wasps, the caterpillars
> might endlessly reproduce, thus destroying any
> chance for corn to grow, humans to eat the crops,

and in the end, for the caterpillars themselves to survive.[88]

As William Dembski observes: 'higher-order designs of entire ecosystems might require lower-order designs of individual organisms to fall short of maximal function'.[89] Casey Luskin argues that: 'true sub-optimalities can never be proven, for one never knows that there *isn't* a higher level of order in which the apparent sub-optimality is actually perfectly fulfilling the exact function it was intended to perform'.[90] As a proposed logical problem for the design hypothesis, sub-optimality is unverifiable.

Reformulating the argument in terms of probability doesn't help, for as philosophers such as William P. Alston, Gregory E. Ganssle and Stephen John Wykstra have pointed out, the inability of finite human beings to discern a good reason for God allowing particular states of affairs to exist is a less than compelling reason to suppose that he doesn't have one: 'The inference from the claim that it seems as though there is no sufficient reason to be found to the conclusion that it is probably the case that there is no sufficient reason at all is not a strong inference [in this case].'[91] After all, if a novice at chess were to see a grand-master sacrifice one of his pieces in a game, and couldn't work out what greater good this apparently sub-optimal move served (especially before the game is over), would that be a sufficient reason to doubt the ability or wisdom of the chess master? Clearly not (especially if the novice has some evidence that the chess master is indeed good at chess). Given that the cognitive difference between ourselves and a wise creator is at least as great as that between a chess novice and a grand-master, it follows that our inability to see why the creator causes or permits this or that state of affairs can hardly count as a knock-down reason to doubt the creator's ability or wisdom (especially if our evidence includes some indications that the designer is wise): 'If in fact our knowledge set is limited when compared to that of the Creator of the universe, or even when compared to what we think is out there in the natural world, perhaps we ought to reserve judgment until we have a complete and accurate physical and metaphysical picture of what's really going on in the world.'[92]

We don't need to prove anything concerning what God's good reasons are, or even what they could be, in order to rebut an argument premised on the mere assumption that there are none. We simply need to show that the assumption that there are none is no more plausible than its denial. Besides, given the correctness of the type of analogy given above, it would follow that humans might expect to have difficulty comprehending God's actual reasons; hence a failure to adduce any would hardly be an overwhelming failure in our rebuttal of the suboptimality argument!

In fact, I think we have a surprising degree of insight into God's reasons for permitting evil in various forms (e.g. the famous 'free-will' theodicy for moral evil, which can be extended to cover natural evils via the anthropic fine tuning of the universe – about which, more later). However, given the chess analogy, there are probably good reasons that we do not know about as well.

I am not advocating a general pessimism about human cognitive abilities, or taking refuge in a simplistic 'God moves in mysterious ways' response. Rather, I am pointing out that a rational assessment of our cognitive situation in this particular instance undermines a simplistic move from 'I don't see why a wise designer would do it that way' to 'Therefore a wise designer didn't do it'. The missing premise is obviously: 'Whenever I can't see a good reason for a supposedly wise designer doing something, there probably isn't one.' My reaction to *this* universal assumption is a sceptical one, and this scepticism is supported by the above analogies.

The third premise of the argument from imperfections likewise calls for judgements that are far from straightforward. Nelson takes as an example Stephen Jay Gould's suggestion that the panda's thumb is inefficient: 'in finding existing pandas to be imperfect, Gould must have some notion of an ideal panda, departure from which evokes a judgement of imperfection. So what does an ideal panda look like?'[93] As Maynard Smith points out: 'it is clearly impossible to say what is the "best" phenotype [body-plan] unless one knows the range of possibilities. If there were no constraints on what is possible, the best phenotype would live forever, would be impregnable to predators, would lay eggs at an infinite rate, and so on.'[94] Other biologists make more favourable judgements about the panda's 'thumb'.[95] Dr Jonathan Sarfati argues that 'there is nothing clumsy at all about the panda's design. Instead, the "thumb" is part of an elaborate and efficient grasping structure that enables the panda to strip leaves from bamboo shoots.'[96] A recent study of the panda's 'thumb' concluded: 'The radial sesamoid bone and the accessory carpal bone form a double pincer-like apparatus in the medial and lateral sides of the hand, respectively, enabling the panda to manipulate objects with great dexterity.'[97] Indeed, Sarfati comments: 'Evolutionists have produced a long list of examples of "bad design," but nothing on the list stands up under scrutiny.'[98]

For example, Dawkins is keen to point out apparent defects in the vertebrate eye:

Any engineer would naturally assume that the photocells would point towards the light, with their wires leading backwards towards the brain. He would laugh at any suggestion that the photocells might point away from the light, with their wires departing on the side nearest the light. Yet this is exactly what happens in all vertebrate retinas . . . The wire has to travel over the surface of the retina, to a point where it dives through a hole in the retina (the so-called 'blind spot') to join the optic nerve. This means that the light, instead of being granted an unrestricted passage to the photocells, has to pass through a forest of connecting wires, presumably suffering at least some attenuation and distortion (actually probably not much but, still, it is the principle of the thing that would offend any tidy-minded engineer!).[99]

The implied conclusion is that the vertebrate eye was not designed by a 'tidy-minded engineer'. Is Dawkins right to think that any engineer would laugh at the design of the vertebrate eye? William Dembski's reply is systematic:

A visual system needs three things: speed, sensitivity, and resolution. Speed is unaffected by the inverted wiring. Resolution seems unaffected as well (save for a blind spot, which the brain seems to work around without difficulty). Indeed, there is no evidence that the cephalopod retina of squids and octopuses, which is said to be 'correctly wired' by having receptors facing forwards and nerves tucked behind, is any better at resolving objects in its visual field. As for sensitivity, however, it seems that there are good functional reasons for an inverted retina. In the human body, for instance, retinal cells require the most oxygen of any cells. But when do they require the most oxygen? Their oxygen require-ment is maximal when incident light is minimal. Having a blood supply in front of the photoreceptors guarantees that the retinal cells will have the oxygen they need to be as sensitive as possible when incident light is minimal.[100]

Indeed:

The light-sensing cells in the eyes of higher verte-brates are extremely efficient at amplifying faint light [they can respond to a single photon]. The efficient, hard working tips of the light-sensing calls need a lot of energy, and they also need to be constantly regenerated. The energy is provided by a dense bed of capillaries, and the regeneration is facilitated by a special layer of epithelial cells. If the tips of the light-sensing cells faced forward . . . incoming light would be blocked by the dense cap-illary bed and the epithelial layer. Such an eye would be much *less* efficient . . . It's true that the present arrangement causes the optic nerve to leave a blind spot as it passes through the retina; but vertebrates have two eyes, and the blind spots cancel out when both are used to focus on the same object . . . the vertebrate eye seems to be a masterpiece of engineering![101]

As George Ayoub, of the Department of Biology at Westmont College Santa Barbara, concludes, having reviewed the design of the vertebrate eye: 'The vertebrate retina provides an excellent example of functional – though non-intuitive – design. The design of the retina is responsible for its high acuity and sensitivity. It is simply untrue that the retina is demonstrably suboptimal, nor is it easy to conceive how it might be modified without significantly decreasing its function.'[102] Strangely, in *Climbing Mount Improbable* Dawkins himself writes that: 'Eyes . . . impress us by their obvious perfection of engineering. An engineer can recognize them as the kind of thing that he would design, if called upon to solve a particular problem',[103] and has been quoted as saying that 'eyes are perfections of engineering – should any parts be rearranged then that would make them worse'.[104]

Besides, as it stands, this 'argument from imperfection' does not directly contradict belief in a wise creator; for a wise creator may be directly responsible for some examples of organic design without being directly responsible for every example. As Nelson points out:

> The imperfection argument presupposes a static theory of creation, according to which an organic design p appears today as it was originally created. [However, even on the questionable assumption that each and every thing a wise creator brings into being must be perfect as originally created] extant organic designs are the products not just of original creative intent, but also of the perturbating effects of secondary causes, e.g. natural selection, mutation, genetic drift.[105]

It is perfectly possible to believe in a world purposefully designed, and with good reason, to do a large measure of 'blind watchmaking'. There is no reason to think that the *Ichneumonidae* is a directly intended part of the designer's plan; it may be wholly the result of secondary causes allowed, for good reasons, to do their own thing. 'We do not know,' argues Keith Ward, 'what possibilities are so linked to other possibilities that one could not be realised without the other . . .'[106]:

> It may be, then, that if God intends to realise some possible states, they are necessarily linked to the realisation of other possible states that God does not intend . . . [For example] beings like us simply could not exist in a universe with very different laws . . . if God wanted to create human beings, the fundamental laws of the universe would have to be very much as they are, and they would, it seems, necessarily involve all the possibilities of suffering that we see.[107]

Bearing this point in mind, we might think twice before complaining about our existence.

Darwin got himself trapped between seeing everything in the biological world as the result of direct divine design, and seeing everything as the result of an unintended evolutionary process: 'I am conscious that I am in an utterly hopeless muddle. I cannot think that the world, as we see it, is the result of chance; and yet I cannot look at each separate thing as the result of Design.'[108] The way out of Darwin's muddle is to reject this false dilemma by hypothesising that the world as we see it is the result of *a combination* of primary, direct creative activity (which may be limited to creating the necessary conditions for an intended process of evolution, but which may extend to creating particular biological features) *and* the secondary, indirect causes of an intended evolutionary process. Such a view would seem to reflect the early church's conception of God's transcendent power *over*, and his immanent power *in* creation, as 'balanced and complementary'.[109] As philosopher E. L. Mascall explains: 'classical Christian philosophy, while it insisted upon the universal *primary causality* of God in all the events of the world's history, maintained with equal emphasis the reality and the authenticity of *secondary causes*'.[110] On such a view, 'creation is not autonomous. It is not self-originating or self-sustaining; it was created by God and depends continually upon Him. On the other hand, God does not work in the world by perpetual miracle. He has set up a network of secondary causes that act in a regular and consistent pattern.'[111]

Furthermore, in order to generalize the conclusion of the argument from imperfection to exclude the existence of a wise creator, one would have to add Darwin's implied premise that:

5. Either every instance of organic design is produced directly by a wise creator and appears today as it was originally created, or every instance of organic design is produced by evolution (descent with modification)

to arrive at the atheistic conclusion that:

6. Therefore, every instance of organic design is produced by evolution (descent with modification) and not by a wise creator.

However, this crucial fifth premise is doubly flawed, depending upon the false dichotomy between creation and evolution *and* upon the questionable 'static' theory of creation.

The 'argument from imperfection' embodies what Michael J. Behe calls: 'the seeming *non sequitur* that because biological feature A appears malevolent, therefore all biological features arose by natural selection or some other unintelligent process'.[112] The most basic flaw in the argument from imperfection, as Behe points out, is that it demands perfection at all:

> . . . designers who have the ability to make better designs do not necessarily do so. For example, in manufacturing, 'built-in obsolescence' is common – a product is intentionally made so it will not last as long as it might, for reasons that supercede the simple goal of engineering excellence. Another example is a personal one: I do not give my children the best, fanciest toys because I don't want to spoil them, and because I want them to learn the value of a dollar. The argument from imperfection overlooks the possibility that the designer might have motives, with engineering excellence oftentimes relegated to a secondary role. Most people throughout history have thought that life was designed despite sickness, death, and other obvious imperfections.[113]

The devil's chaplain and the argument from evil

> *You do not get out of your philosophical troubles arising out of the fact of evil by rejecting God. For . . . the real problem is not the problem of evil, but the problem of good, not the problem of cruelty and selfishness, but the problem of kindness and generosity, not the problem of ugliness, but the problem of beauty.*
> LORD HAILSHAM[114]

The argument from imperfection is simply an application within biology of the standard, and increasingly questioned, 'argument from evil' against the existence of God. The most such an argument can hope to support is the conclusion that the designer is not good, or not wise, or not all-powerful. Such considerations have no bearing on the fundamental question of *design*: 'Many cars are noticeably imperfect, though they are all designed.'[115] A sound argument from evil, if one existed, would not rebut belief in design, or establish the truth of naturalism.

Moreover, the 'problem of evil' is vulnerable to a number of standard and widely accepted philosophical rebuttals. Atheist William Rowe observes that few contemporary philosophers press the traditional charge of there being a logical contradiction between the existence of God and the existence of evil:

> Some philosophers have contended that the existence of evil is *logically inconsistent* with the existence of the theistic God. No one, I think, has succeeded in establishing such an extravagant claim. Indeed, granted incompatibilism [i.e. free will], there is a fairly compelling argument for the view that the existence of evil is logically consistent with the existence of the theistic God.[116]

Rowe is referring to Alvin Plantinga's articulation of the 'free will defence':

> A world containing creatures who are significantly free . . . is more valuable, all else being equal, than a world containing no free creatures at all . . . To create creatures capable of moral good . . . [God] must create creatures capable of moral evil; and he can't give these creatures this freedom to

> perform evil and at the same time prevent them
> from doing so.[117]

Adding the admittedly implausible suggestion that all natural (non-moral) evil is caused by fallen angels (demons) is sufficient for Plantinga to prove the *logical compatibility* of God and evil. More minimally, and without even relying on the mere possibility of free will, William Lane Craig explains that: 'the atheist presupposes that God cannot have morally sufficient reasons for permitting the evil in the world. But this assumption is not necessarily true. So long as it is even *possible* that God has morally sufficient reasons for permitting evil, it follows that God and evil are logically consistent.'[118] Plantinga's free will *defence* is simply an unpacking of what God's morally sufficient reason *might possibly be*. If this logically possible reason is advanced as being God's *actual* reason (or one among a number of reasons), then it constitutes a *theodicy*. A defence proves *that* God and evil are not logically incompatible, a theodicy attempts the more ambitious task of explaining *how it is that* God and evil are not incompatible (the biblical tale of Job gives a defence rather than a theodicy, prefiguring several themes in the contemporary philosophical debate about the problem of evil). According to Michael Bergmann, there is a 'nearly unanimous agreement among both theistic and nontheistic philosophers of religion that the logical version of the argument from evil doesn't work'.[119] The success of theistic defences means, as Daniel Howard-Snyder writes, that the logical problem of evil 'has found its way to the dustbin of philosophical fashions'.[120] Even Dawkins admits: 'We cannot prove that there is no God . . .'[121] However, having conceded that

God cannot be ruled out, Dawkins retreats to the next best line of defence: 'but we can safely conclude that He is very, very improbable indeed'.[122]

Arguments that attempt merely to show that evil makes God's existence *unlikely*, or that it at least *counts against* God's existence (called 'evidential arguments from evil') are not only vulnerable to some of the same rebuttals as the defunct logical problem, but suffer from difficulties of their own,[123] and must anyhow be weighed in the balance against the positive evidence for God. As Daniel Howard-Snyder points out, any argument from evil is a problem only for the theist 'who finds all its premises and inferences compelling and who has lousy grounds for believing theism'.[124]

As we have seen, it is harder to convict the design in nature of imperfection than many atheists assume. Nevertheless, just as when playing a chess master one has good reason to expect them to win (if one is not a master oneself), so the theist, when contemplating creation, believes they have good reason to think that God is good, even if this information is hard for them to square with the facts of nature in so far as they understand them. As C. Stephen Evans says: 'it's perfectly possible to have strong evidence that someone has a good reason for an action without knowing what that reason might be'.[125] Thus the argument from imperfections against belief in a good designer must be set in the balance against the evidence for the existence of a good God (e.g. the moral argument for God, religious experience, etc). Indeed, one cannot argue that a non-theistic (naturalistic) worldview provides a better explanation of our world *given the suffering it contains*, without asking whether the theistic or non-theistic worldview provides the best overall explanation of *our world* (including suffering) full stop. As Gregory E. Ganssle argues:

> Since the existence of sentient beings that experience biologically useful pain and pleasure is required [for the devil's chaplain's argument] and this entails that the universe *can* sustain sentient creatures, the teleological argument is relevant to the problem of evil . . . The probability of a universe suitable to these kinds of creatures is too small to allow that it came to be solely by chance.[126]

Most significantly, doesn't the judgement that nature contains 'imperfections' that a *good* and *wise* creator would not allow or be responsible for, itself imply the existence of an objective ideal of goodness and wisdom that could only find its ultimate ground in the perfect being of God? As Stephen E. Parrish notes: 'One of the greatest weaknesses of arguments against God's existence from the problem of evil is the fact that they assume notions of objective moral value that have no metaphysical basis in the naturalistic worldview. Their arguments assume a notion of moral value that is viable only if the God they are trying to disprove actually exists.'[127] This rebuttal applies equally to the 'logical' and 'evidential' forms of the argument from evil.

In *A Devil's Chaplain*, Dawkins considers the implications of his atheistically inspired belief in naturalistic evolution, which actually means the implications of his atheistic assumption that are transmitted *through* his *naturalistically interpreted* belief in evolution. The first implication highlighted by Dawkins is that 'Nature is neither kind nor cruel but indifferent'.[128] Of course, even theists believe *that*; it's just that they believe in a loving creator of a natural world that is fundamentally good (theists don't anthropomorphise nature as do certain forms of pantheism). However, what Dawkins means is that Ultimate Reality is impersonal and material, having no attitude towards life whatsoever, thus being incapable of grounding any objective moral values. In a naturalistic universe, objective moral values cannot possibly exist; objectively speaking, there is 'no evil and no good'.[129] But Dawkins doesn't notice that this first implication of Darwinism completely undermines his argument for Darwinism from the imperfections of nature that a *good* God supposedly would not create or permit if he existed! Dawkins relies upon values in order to justify belief in a naturalistic worldview that denies the reality of the values that his argument for naturalism relies upon! As Peter van Inwagen argues:

> . . . we must be able to speak of correct value judgements if the Problem of Evil is to be of any interest. An eminent philosopher of biology has said in one place that God, if He existed, would be indescribably wicked for having created a world like this one, and, in another place, that morality is an illusion, an illusion that we are subject to because of the evolutionary advantage it confers. These two theses do not seem to me to add up to a coherent whole.[130]

Rather than argue against God from the existence of evil, Dawkins would be better advised to try arguing against God *from the non-existence of evil* – for if God exists, then, and only then, would we be justified in saying that anything was objectively evil. In *River Out Of*

Eden, Dawkins concludes that:

> If the universe were just electrons and selfish genes, meaningless tragedies . . . are exactly what we should expect, along with equally meaningless good fortune. Such a universe would be neither evil nor good in intention . . . In a universe of blind physical forces and genetic replication, some people are going to get hurt, other people are going to get lucky, and you won't find any rhyme or reason in it, nor any justice. The universe we observe has precisely the properties we should expect if there is, at bottom, no design, no purpose, no evil and no good, nothing but blind pitiless indifference.[131]

He is partially right. In any universe of reliable physical forces some people are going to get hurt and others are going to get lucky, there will be both 'tragedies' and 'good fortune'. But if even a single instance of such 'fortune' is objectively *good*, or a single instance of such tragedy is objectively *bad* (rather than being literally meaningless), then naturalism is false. Dawkins cannot distinguish between 'tragedies' and 'good fortune' without making some sort of value judgement. As Angus Menuge comments: 'Dawkins' phrase "meaningless tragedies" is surely oxymoronic: if nothing matters there are no tragedies, since if nothing has value, then nothing can (tragically) lose it . . .'[132] If Dawkins, in making those judgements, inconsistently draws upon the concepts of objective good and evil, then his argument is subverted by the moral argument for God's existence: 'The problem of evil actually points us in the direction of God, whose character is good and the ultimate standard by which we judge something as good or evil.'[133] If Dawkins keeps faith with naturalism, and really does mean to say that there is no objective distinction between 'tragedies' and 'good fortune', that both are literally 'meaningless' and that there is 'no evil and no good', then I can only reply: 'The universe we observe simply does not lack these properties.'

Dawkins approvingly quotes 'one of Darwin's most thoughtful successors',[134] George C. Williams: 'What with other than condemnation is a person with any moral sense supposed to respond to a system in which the ultimate purpose in life is to be better than your neighbour at getting genes into future generations . . . ?'[135] The obvious problem with this assertion is that a naturalistic worldview provides no basis for objectively legitimizing such a 'moral sense'. If the ultimate 'purpose' (result) of life is indeed to be better than your neighbour at getting genes into future generations, then it is clear that morality doesn't matter on its own terms – but only as a pragmatic unintended evolutionary means to the pragmatic unintended evolutionary end. With film star Mae West, we could say: 'Goodness had nothing to do with it.' Neither did any genuine purpose. There are only material causes and their material results.

Dawkins chides Bernard Shaw for embracing 'a confused idea of Lamarckian evolution purely because of Darwinism's moral implications',[136] quoting Shaw's comments in the preface of *Back to Methuselah*: 'When [Darwinism's] whole significance dawns on you, your heart sinks into a heap of sand within you. There is a hideous fatalism about it, a ghastly and damnable reduction of beauty and intelligence, of strength and purpose, of honour and aspiration.'[137] However, this nihilistic conclusion is not one that is read *off* reality by scientific observation, or implied by the theory of evolution, but read *into* reality as a logical consequence of an assumed atheism. Shaw was wrong to reject the theory of evolution by natural selection because of its moral implications, but only because, as a scientific theory, it has no moral implications. On the other hand, there is nothing wrong in rejecting Dawkins' naturalistic *framing* or *support* for evolutionary theory on the grounds that it is contradicted by the reality of objective moral values. Nor is there anything wrong with rejecting Dawkins' *atheism* on the grounds that the reality of objective moral values proves the existence of God (as I argued in the previous chapter).

Dawkins' dismisses the moral argument for God's existence as the 'The same kind of thing [that] drives today's populist opposition to evolution.'[138] (By which, of course, he means naturalistic evolution.) Once again, Dawkins obscures the real issue by confusing evolution and the *naturalistic* interpretation of evolution. He quotes apologist Kyle Butt: 'The most evolution could produce would be the idea that "might makes right". When Hitler exterminated approximately 10 million innocent men, women and children, he acted in complete agreement with the theory of evolution and in complete disagreement with everything humans know to be right and wrong . . .'[139] (Hitler certainly didn't act in contradiction to evolutionary theory.) Noting that the 'opposite response to the callousness of natural selection is to exult in it'[140] like Hitler, Dawkins agrees with George Williams and Kyle Butt that doing so is wrong, only (and this is the crucial point Butt is making) *without providing a sufficient basis for adopting such a position*. As William Lane Craig argues:

> If there is no God, then any ground for regarding the herd morality evolved by *Homo sapiens* as objectively true seems to have been removed. After all, what is so special about human beings? They are just accidental by-products of nature which have evolved relatively recently on an infinitesimal speck of dust lost somewhere in a hostile and mindless universe and which are doomed to perish individually and collectively in a relatively short time. Some action, say, incest, may not be biologically or socially advantageous and so in the course of human evolution has become taboo; but there is on the atheistic view nothing really wrong about committing incest . . . the non-conformist who chooses to flout the herd morality is doing nothing more serious than acting unfashionably.[141]

In requiring an acknowledgement of objective moral values that are alien to the ontology of naturalism, the problem of evil backfires on the atheist; for as philosopher Norman L. Geisler writes: 'to disprove God via evil one must assume the equivalent of God by way of an ultimate standard of justice beyond this world . . .'[142]

Dawkins concludes *A Devil's Chaplain* with the affirmation that: 'There is deep refreshment to be had from standing full-face into the keen wind of understanding.'[143] Understanding, that is, that one faces a choice between 'being satisfied with easy answers and cheap comforts, living a warm comfortable lie',[144] sucking 'at the pacifier of faith in immortality'[145] or accepting 'the daemonic alternative urged by my mature Devil's Chaplain'.[146] At this juncture it is worth noting with Peter van Inwagen that:

Atheists often preach on the emotional attractiveness of theism. It needs to be pointed out that atheism is also a very attractive thesis . . . for at least two reasons. First, it is an attractive idea to suppose that one may well be one of the higher links in the Great Chain of Being – perhaps even the highest. (This idea is attractive for several reasons, not the least of which is that most people cannot quite rid themselves of the very well justified conviction that a being who knew all their motives and inmost thoughts might not entirely approve of them.) Secondly, there are very few atheists who do not admire themselves for possessing that combination of mental acuity and intellectual honesty that is, by their own grudging admission, the hallmark of atheists everywhere.[147]

So what is the 'daemonic' alternative proposed by Dawkins? It is 'the joy of knowing that you have grown up, faced up to what existence means [i.e. nothing]; to the fact that it is temporary and all the more precious for it'.[148] Strip away the fine flourish of rhetoric, and we find nothing here but the cold undergrowth of nihilism. Life is *not* 'all the more precious' for being 'temporary', because *nothing has any objective value within the naturalistic worldview*. This is the whole point of Dawkins' observation that nature, which he sees as the ultimate reality, is 'indifferent'.[149] Why accept the nihilistic truth of naturalism if doing so is not an objectively good thing to do and embracing the 'warm comfortable lie' of religious belief is not an objectively bad thing to do? Of course, if embracing a warm comfortable lie *is* an objectively bad thing to do then the moral argument for God would lead us to conclude that it is naturalism, and not theism, that constitutes the lie. We do *not* face a choice between truth and meaning as Dawkins mistakenly implies – because God's truth is meaningful truth.

To recap: Dawkins believes that evolution is true and (mistakenly) that evolution contradicts creation. He believes that evolution contradicts creation because he insists on interpreting evolution naturalistically, and he insists upon interpreting evolution naturalistically *because he doesn't believe in God*. And what justification does our professor for the public understanding of science give for not believing in God? He doesn't present us with scientific evidence (such a thing is impossible), although he gives the impression that science does away with God. Rather, he provides philosophical justifications, and deeply flawed justifications at that. Dawkins uses unsound *philosophical* arguments against belief in God in the belief that the theory of evolution thereby wins by philosophical default, a theory that elsewhere he presents as if it discredits belief in God!

Did Darwin make it possible to be 'an intellectually fulfilled atheist'?

The atheist's problem before Darwin's theory of evolution by natural selection was that there was no plausible candidate for a physical mechanism to fill in the blank labelled '*blind* watchmaker'. Atheists were left without a plausible causal explanation for why there were things that looked designed even though, on their worldview, they weren't. By filling in that blank, says Dawkins, 'Darwin made it possible to be an intellectually fulfilled atheist.'[150] Once again, Dawkins' motives for believing in evolution are revealed as primarily philosophical: 'Ironically, scientific naturalism is just as religious as the overtly religious naturalism of Hinduism. Only with scientific naturalism there is the pretence that science has finally established naturalism once and for all. In fact, science provides no evidence for naturalism . . . though the assumption of naturalism profoundly affects how we do science.'[151]

Michael Ruse calls himself 'an ardent evolutionist', yet he objects when 'evolution is promoted by its practitioners as . . . an ideology, a secular religion'.[152] According to Ruse: 'If people want to make a religion of evolution, that is their business [but] we should recognize when people are going beyond the strict science, moving into moral and social claims, thinking of their theory as an all-embracing world picture. All too often, there is a slide from science to something more.'[153] *The Blind Watchmaker* sees Dawkins making just such a slide from science to something more (i.e. to atheistic ideology; or rather, from atheistic ideology to naturalistic science). Darwin's theory of evolution may fill in a blank created by the assumption of atheism, but that doesn't prove atheism. Santa Claus may fill in a blank left by the assumption that parents don't deliver Christmas presents, but that hardly proves the existence of Santa Claus!

Wider teleology

The theist, no less than the atheist, can acknowledge the existence of a 'blind watchmaker', simply by attributing that 'blind watchmaker' to God's design. The theist may simply say: 'The laws of nature are themselves the regular and principled ways in which God acts to produce the future out of every present.[154] As Antony Flew argued: 'it is . . . useless to try to dispose finally of the [design] argument with a reference to the achievement of Darwin . . . the regularities discovered and explained with the help of the theory of evolution by natural selection, like all other regularities in nature, can be just so much more grist to the mill'.[155] Theists can argue that the evolutionary account *supports* the design inference:

> Christians believe . . . that God wills the existence of rational beings . . . so we can say that the probability of their evolving . . . is as high as it could be . . . We also know that there are vast numbers of possible outcomes to any evolutionary process, so that the prior probability of any one of them ensuing is quite low. Since rational beings do exist, it looks much more probable that God should have influenced events to produce them, than that they should have evolved by blind chance . . . it would become highly probable, and still remain within the laws of nature, if selection within the possible mutations available at any time was influenced by an intelligent consciousness . . . If the very unlikely happens, a good explanation is that somebody has made it happen . . .[156]

Indeed, argues Keith Ward: 'if one is asking . . . whether a very improbable process is compatible with intelligent design, the answer is that *if the process is elegantly structured to a good end, then the more improbable the process, the more likely it is to be the product of intelligent design*'.[157] Hence, 'The argument that the

evolutionary process is incompatible with design misses the mark completely.'[158]

Suppose someone who disbelieves in watch-designers
says that although watches *look* designed, they can be
explained without the hypothesis of design. We could
ask the obvious question, 'So what does account for the
design of watches?' If our sceptic had no answer, just an
explanatory blank left by their exclusion of the design
hypothesis, we wouldn't find their scepticism very
impressive. This is analogous to the position of atheists
before Darwin. Now, let's suppose that our sceptic
comes up with a brilliant explanation to fill in their
explanatory blank. Watches must originate in an automated machine-making factory that operates using
Darwinian principles of design. (After all: 'Genetic
algorithms (GAs) are modelling techniques which
attempt to apply the theory of evolution to a real life
problem such as the design of a new mechanism.'[159])
Such a suggestion parallels the theory of evolution
which Dawkins thinks makes it possible to be an intellectually fulfilled atheist. But even supposing that the
existence of an automated machine-making factory
were to be confirmed, would we find our design sceptic's disbelief any more plausible than before? Wouldn't
we simply suppose that some designer(s) had decided
to create machines though the intermediary mechanism
of a robotic factory? Our understanding of how watches come to exist may have become more complicated
(and more accurate) than in the days when we thought
they were directly intended and cobbled together by a
watchmaker; but surely our belief in design wouldn't
have become any less rational.

Indeed, while the sceptic may point to the factory to

explain watches without the necessity of mentioning designers, and they may claim that the design hypothesis is thereby rendered superfluous, might we not ask *how they explain the design of the factory*? Even allowing that the design of watches is wholly derived from the design of the factory, that doesn't explain away the evidence for design in the watches, or negate the design hypothesis as such, unless the factory can be given a superior design-free explanation. But factories don't explain themselves. Likewise, 'Science cannot demonstrate that the order of the world is intrinsic to it.'[160] The factory, no less than the watches it produces, is composed of a complicated arrangement of interacting parts, etc. Surely the best explanation of a machine-producing factory is the existence of a machine-factory designer. Far from explaining away design, then, the Darwinian suggestion that an automated factory manufactures the watches actually *compounds* the design-sceptic's problem by adding into the mix an additional entity that appears to be designed (the factory)! Likewise, the physical structures and entities that are a necessary precondition of evolution (and therefore cannot be explained by evolution) are no less analogous to a watch – consisting of an intricately related set of co-adapted parts (physical laws), etc. – than are the organisms they supposedly produce. Surely the best explanation of an organism-producing cosmos would be the existence of an organism-producing-cosmos designer. As Richard Swinburne argues: 'men make not only machines, but machine-making machines. They may therefore naturally infer from nature which produces animals and plants, to a creator of nature similar to men who make machine-making machines.'[161]

De-bunking the heart of the cosmos

*Atheists put on a false courage and alacrity in the
midst of their darkness and apprehensions, like
children who, when they fear to go into the dark,
will sing with fear.*
ALEXANDER POPE[162]

In *Unweaving the Rainbow* Dawkins writes that 'accusations of barren desolation, of promoting an arid and
joyless message, are frequently flung at science in general, and it is easy for scientists to play up to them'.[163]
For example, he quotes from Peter Atkins' book *The
Second Law* (1984):

We are children of chaos, and the deep structure
of change is decay. At root, there is only
corruption, and the unstemmable tide of chaos.
Gone is purpose; all that is left is direction. This is
the bleakness we have to accept as we peer deeply
and dispassionately into the heart of the
Universe.[164]

Dawkins calls this 'a very proper purging of saccharine
false purpose',[165] a 'laudable tough-mindedness in the
debunking of cosmic sentimentality'.[166] He has no beef
with Atkins' scientistic description of 'the heart of the
Universe'. He does not point out that Atkins' assertions
are philosophical and not scientific. When Atkins
asserts that science reveals a universe without purpose,
he does not ask, as J. Budziszewski asks, 'How could
science "show" a thing like that? Could I point a mean-
ing-meter at the wonder of life and see the needle swing
to "empty"?'[167] Instead, he simply says that questions
about the ultimate nature of reality are irrelevant to
questions about personal meaning:

> Presumably there is indeed no purpose in the ultimate fate of the cosmos, but do any of us really tie our life's hopes to the ultimate fate of the cosmos anyway? Of course we don't; not if we are sane. Our lives are ruled by all sorts of closer, warmer, human ambitions and perceptions. To accuse science of robbing life of the warmth that makes it worth living is so preposterously mistaken, so diametrically opposite to my own feelings and those of most working scientists, I am almost driven to the despair of which I am wrongly suspected.[168]

This is, one must admit, a fine piece of rhetoric; but as a philosophical reply to his critics this is a non-starter, because questions about the ultimate nature of reality are of crucial relevance to questions about personal meaning.

The red herring of insanity (and its three equally fallacious friends)

What we do in time echoes in eternity.[169]

Dawkins' assertion that 'Our lives are ruled by all sorts of closer, warmer, human ambitions and perceptions' is factually incorrect. For example, Christians place a great deal of hope in their belief that the ultimate fate of the universe is to be recreated by its Creator to form 'a new heaven and a new earth, the home of righteousness' (2 Peter 3:13). This is 'Heaven', where believers expect to spend an eternity with a God who will 'wipe every tear from their eyes', and wherein 'There will be no more death or mourning or crying or pain, for the old order of things has passed away' (Revelation 21:4).

John Polkinghorne argues: 'The significance of [Jesus'] empty tomb is that the Lord's risen and glorified body is the transmuted form of his dead body. Thus matter itself participates in the resurrection transformation, enjoying thereby a foretaste of its own redemption from decay. The resurrection of Jesus is the seminal event from which the whole of God's new creation has already begun to grow.'[170] Polkinghorne might be deluded (mistaken) about this hope, but he certainly isn't delusional to entertain it. If Polkinghorne is right, then the ultimate fate of the cosmos is clearly something that one might rather sensibly look forward to and to which one would be irrational *not* to tie one's 'life's hopes'. (If Polkinghorne is wrong, then the ultimate fate of the cosmos still has a bearing on our 'life's hopes', in that anyone sharing his hope would be deluded and anyone who was not thus deluded would lack this particular hope. Without the hope of heaven, our 'life's hopes' must restrict themselves to the finite span of time allotted to us by an uncaring universe. Either way, the ultimate fate of the cosmos hardly seems irrelevant to our 'life's hopes'.)

A great many people, like Polkinghorne, tie their life's hopes to 'the ultimate fate of the cosmos', and argue that doing so is perfectly rational. Now, you might not believe in Heaven (Dawkins doesn't), but to call people who do believe 'not . . . sane' is not only impolite, but it hardly counts as a telling argument for the irrelevancy of Atkins' predicted cosmic doom when it comes to questions of personal meaning. In fact, Dawkins' insinuated charge of insanity embodies a number of informal logical fallacies (and giving Dawkins the benefit of the doubt in our interpretation of 'not . . . sane' – perhaps he means 'irrational' or 'stupid' or 'ignorant' rather than 'mentally ill' – has little if any effect on these fallacies).

To start with, Dawkins' argument is *ad hominem*: 'In this fallacy, one argues against an opponent's position by attacking the other arguer and not the argument.'[171] It simply won't do to counter Polkinghorne's argument that the resurrection of Jesus validates the Christian hope of Heaven simply by calling him 'not . . . sane'! Of course Dawkins is not actually responding to Polkinghorne's argument here – but he *is* trying to score a point against a generic category of belief into which Polkinghorne and his form of hope certainly fits.

Perhaps Dawkins means to critique the belief that our 'life's hopes' can and should be tied to 'the ultimate fate of the cosmos' on the grounds that the people who believe this are 'not . . . sane'. If so, he is committing *the genetic fallacy*: 'This fallacy occurs when someone confuses the origin of an idea with the reasons for believing the idea and faults the idea because of where it came from . . . and not because of the adequacy of the grounds for the idea . . . When we answer the question, "Why do you believe in x?" we need to keep separate a psychological or originating "why" from a rational "why" . . . Motives are one thing, rational grounds and evidence are another.'[172]

Dawkins implies that we *either* tie our 'life's hopes to the ultimate fate of the cosmos', *or* we tie them to 'all sorts of closer, warmer, human ambitions and perceptions'. By inviting us to agree that our lives are of course dominated by 'closer, warmer, human ambitions and perceptions' (a description implying that to disagree with this premise would be to sign up to distant, cold and inhuman ambitions and perceptions), Dawkins hopes to secure our acquiescence in making this distinction. But this is clearly a false dilemma, in that we might tie our life's hopes to 'all sorts of closer, warmer, human ambitions and perceptions' *in the light of* our beliefs about the ultimate fate of the cosmos. Indeed, as a Christian, this is just what I do. By suggesting otherwise, Dawkins has in effect attacked a *straw man*: 'This fallacy is committed when an arguer distorts an opponent's position for the purpose of making it more easy to destroy, refutes the distorted position, and concludes that his opponent's actual view is thereby demolished.'[173]

To imply that people who tie their life's hopes to 'the ultimate fate of the cosmos' are insane is nothing but thinly veiled intimidation. Such intimidation embodies an informal logical fallacy called *an appeal to the people*: 'In this fallacy, one argues that if you want to be accepted, included in the group, loved, or respected, then you should accept the conclusion X as true. Here the arguer incites group emotions or the enthusiasm of the crowd, appeals to people's vanity or snobbery, or challenges people to jump on the bandwagon to support a conclusion.'[174] No doubt there are some insane people who believe that life's hope is tied to the ultimate fate of the cosmos, just as there are probably some insane people who believe that such a view is mistaken. In either case, the mention of insanity (together with the coercive appeal to our desire not to be counted as insane) is a diversionary 'red herring': 'This fallacy gets its name from a procedure for training dogs to follow scent. A red herring would be dragged across the trail with the intent of leading the dogs astray with its potent scent. Well-trained dogs do not follow red herrings but stick to the original scent. In logic, a red herring fallacy takes place when someone diverts the reader's or listener's attention by changing the subject to some different and irrelevant issue.'[175] Whether or not anyone actually ties their life's hopes to the ultimate fate of the cosmos (and they do), and whether or not people who tie their life's hopes to the ultimate fate of the cosmos happen to be 'not . . . sane', the issue at hand is whether or not the ultimate fate of the cosmos actually has any bearing on life's hopes such that we *ought* to tie our life's hopes (whether negatively or positively) to the ultimate fate of the cosmos.

This ship is unsinkable! Dawkins' *Titanic* mistake

Dawkins' focus on the ultimate fate of the cosmos (as predicted by science on the un-prove-able assumption that God will not intervene in His creation) actually overlooks the issue of cosmic purpose raised by Atkins. Both Atkins and Dawkins agree that, on a cosmic scale, the idea of purpose must give way to the idea of mere direction: a direction that results from the unintended chance interplay of physical cause and effect. To the question, 'What is the purpose of the cosmos?', Dawkins' answer is that the very idea of the cosmos having a purpose is 'false'. There is no purpose behind our existence, no goal or target towards which our existence is launched; and while this may mean that our lives can never fail to live up to our cosmic potential, it also means that they can never succeed so to do. Dawkins agrees with physicist Steven Weinberg's comment that 'the more the universe seems comprehensible, the more it seems pointless'.[176] He thinks, as

Shakespeare wrote, that life is 'a tale told by an idiot, filled with sound and fury, signifying nothing'. But he says: 'I want to guard against . . . people therefore getting nihilistic in their personal lives.'[177] Isn't this another case of Dawkins trying to have it both ways? Dawkins says he sees no contradiction here: 'You can have a very happy and fulfilled personal life even if you think the universe at large is a tale told by an idiot. You can still set up goals and have a very worthwhile life and not be nihilistic about it at a personal level.'[178] Thus Dawkins attempts to launch an unsinkable ship of personal meaning on a pointless cosmic ocean:

> As an academic scientist I am a passionate
> Darwinian, believing that natural selection is . . .
> the only known force capable of producing the
> illusion of purpose which so strikes all who
> contemplate nature. But at the same time as I
> support Darwinism as a scientist, I am a
> passionate anti-Darwinian when it comes to
> politics and how we should conduct our human
> affairs . . . I have always held true to the closing
> words of my first book, 'We, alone on earth, can
> rebel against the tyranny of the selfish
> replicators.'[179]

As an aside, it is worth noting that Dawkins doesn't explain how or why the freedom to purposely act against the grain of our selfish evolutionary programming could or would have evolved in a naturalistic universe. As Phillip E. Johnson comments:

> This is not only absurd but embarrassingly naïve.
> If human nature is actually constructed by genes
> whose predominant quality is ruthless selfishness,
> then pious lectures advocating qualities like

> generosity and altruism are probably just another strategy for furthering selfish interests . . . Selfish genes would produce not a free-acting self, but rather a set of mental reactions that compete with each other in the brain before a winner emerges to produce a bodily reaction that serves the overall interests of the genes.[180]

Nevertheless, Dawkins is sure that 'If you seem to smell inconsistency or even contradiction, you are mistaken.'[181]

However, the fact remains that in Dawkins' worldview, 'purpose' is nothing but a euphemism for the contingent outworking of chance and necessity, and that the whole cosmic process is heading towards a state of chaos:

> If there is a bridge over a gorge which spans only half the distance and ends in mid-air, and if the bridge is crowded with human beings pressing on, one after another they fall into the abyss. The bridge leads nowhere, and those who are pressing forward to cross it are going nowhere. It does not matter where they think they are going, what preparations for the journey they may have made, how much they may be enjoying it all. The objection merely points out objectively that such a situation is a model of futility.[182]

Drawing on Aristotle's distinctions between causes, Nick Pollard suggested to Dawkins that different types of explanation can complement each other: 'if I asked, "Why is that kettle boiling?" we could talk in terms of the processes or we could consider another meaning of 'why', which is to do with purpose. The reason it's boiling is because your wife Lalla put the kettle on to make a cup of tea.'[183] Dawkins replied that he was not impressed:

. . . because the explanation that somebody
switched on the kettle and had a purpose in doing
so simply is not a different kind of explanation.
It's just a more complicated problem that we now
have to solve. We now have to look at her brain
and ask what it is that made her want to switch
the kettle on. And that takes us back to the
workings of her brain, to why she has a brain in
the first place, which gets us back to evolution.[184]

In embracing this reductionistic explanation, Dawkins
has effectively given up on the notion of humans as
free, morally and rationally responsible agents – replacing it with the assumption that humans are 'a product
of brains',[185] that brains are the unintended product of
evolution, and that evolution is the unintended product
of matter plus time plus chance: 'To me, human consciousness is a deep, philosophically mysterious manifestation of brain activity and is in some sense a product of Darwinian evolution. But we don't yet really have
any idea how it evolved and where it fits into a
Darwinian view of biology.'[186] (Many philosophers
would argue that such a reductive, materialistic understanding of the mind is not at all plausible,[187] and that
we have no idea how the mind fits into a Darwinian view
of biology for the simple reason that it does not fit.[188])
Dawkins tries to compartmentalize 'personal meaning'
from 'cosmic meaning', but here he rips through the
insulting hull of this artificial dichotomy with the giant
iceberg of Darwinian evolution, drowning the personal
in the sea of impersonal material reality, reducing the
free to the determined, the moral to the a-moral,
the rational to the a-rational, and so sinking his
supposedly unsinkable ship of 'personal meaning' in the

icy depths of cosmic meaninglessness.

Dawkins is quite right when he says that scientific Darwinism doesn't justify moral Darwinism:

> I can show that from a Darwinian point of view there is more Darwinian advantage to a male in being promiscuous and a female being faithful, without saying that I therefore think human males are justified in being promiscuous and cheating on their wives. There is no logical connection between what is and what ought . . . The Darwinian world is a very nasty place: the weakest go to the wall. There's no pity, no compassion. All those things I abhor, and I will work in my own life in the interests of thoroughly un-Darwinian things like compassion.[189]

However, the crucial point is that Darwinism provides no grounds for saying that someone who takes the opposite moral point of view is in any absolute sense *wrong* to do so – either way, it's all just a matter of fac-tually unjustified choice, because there is no logical connection between a material *is* and a moral *ought*:

> If somebody used my views to justify a completely self-centred lifestyle, which involved trampling all over other people in any way they chose – roughly what, I suppose, at a sociological level social Darwinists did – I think I would be fairly hard put to it to argue on purely intellectual grounds. I think it would be more: 'This is not a society in which I wish to live. Without having a rational reason for it necessarily, I'm going to do whatever I can to stop you doing this.' . . . I couldn't, ultimately, argue intellectually against somebody who did something I found obnoxious. I think I

could finally only say, 'Well, in this society you can't get away with it' and call the police.[190]

In other words, in the final analysis 'might makes right' and in the 'law of the jungle' Dawkins wants to avoid rules. As relativist Richard Rorty affirms: 'there is no neutral, common ground to which a philosophical Nazi and I can repair to argue out our differences'.[191] The choice between lifestyles, between Nazism and Liberal Democracy, is nothing but a non-rational manifestation of a Neitzchian 'will to power'. As Thomas S. Hibbs asks: 'if there is nothing beyond me in light of which I might understand myself and appraise my actions and goals, then how is any particular course of action more worthy of choice than any other?'[192] Dawkins' atheistic worldview doesn't justify 'a completely self-centred lifestyle', but then *it doesn't justify or condemn any lifestyle*. Hence Anthony O'Hear says of Dawkins: 'this particular Darwinian is quite unable to explain why we have an obligation to act against our 'selfish' genes'.[193]

This moral vacuum follows quite straightforwardly from Dawkins' scientism. Dawkins acknowledges that 'Science has no methods for deciding what is ethical.'[194] But he also thinks that science is the only way to really know anything factual, saying that the way we 'know the things that we know'[195] is through empirical 'evidence'[196] such as 'hearing, feeling, smelling'[197] and that scientists are 'the specialists in discovering what is true about the world and the universe'.[198] Therefore, it is little wonder that Dawkins ends up relegating ethics to the realm of subjective personal opinion, however passionately held. Philosopher Karl Popper hit the meta-ethical nail on the head when he wrote: 'the fact that science cannot make any pronouncement about ethical principles has been misinterpreted as indicating that there are no such principles whilst in fact the search for truth presupposes ethics'.[199] Dawkins himself admits: 'I realise this is very weak, and I've said I don't feel equipped to produce moral arguments in the way I feel equipped to produce arguments of a cosmological and biological kind. But I still think it's a separate issue from beliefs in cosmic truths.'[200] It *is* a separate issue in that truths about an amoral reality can never discredit Dawkins' moral choice to give money to Oxfam; but it *is not* a separate issue in that truths about an amoral reality can never discredit Hitler's moral choice to exterminate the Jews:

> . . . scientific man . . . may construct private absolutes of faith and morality, but, in public, he must inhabit a fluid, relative world. So, for example, his moral choices cannot be made by referring to an outside order or system, they can only be *his* choices. Given that, he will always be aware that there are different choices made by other people. He cannot argue absolutely against these different choices, he can only say that he thinks they are wrong . . . There is only relative right or wrongness; there is no absolute form of either . . . he cannot even tell his children with any conviction that they must believe what he does because it is true. They can simply point out that he is offering them not a fact but just another opinion among countless others.[201]

Dawkins may try to have his cake and eat it, but when push comes to shove he has to admit that, given his scientistic worldview: 'The universe we observe has precisely the properties we should expect if there is at bottom no design, no purpose, no evil and no good, nothing but pointless indifference.'[202] However, Dawkins' nihilistic conclusion has not, as he implies, been read off reality by observation. Rather, it has been read *into* reality as a logical consequence of an atheism assumed on the basis of some deeply flawed (self-contradictory) philosophical arguments and assumptions.

[1] Shapiro, Arthur, 'Did Ruse give Away the Store?', *NSCE Reports* (Spring, 1993).

[2] Plato, *The Laws*, book X.

[3] Johnson, Phillip E., *Reason in the Balance* (Downers Grove: IVP, 1995), p.106.

[4] Dawkins, Richard, *The Blind Watchmaker* (Penguin, 1990), p.287.

[5] Dembski, William A., 'What Every Theologian Should Know about Creation, Evolution, and Design' at www.arn.org/docs/dembski/wd_theologn.htm

[6] Denton, Michael, *Evolution: A Theory in Crisis* (Woodbine House, 1996), p.70.

[7] Johnson, *op. cit.*, p.16.

[8] Johnson observes: 'There is a whole lot of evidence [data] out there, and even a false theory is likely to be supported by some of it.' (*Testing Darwinism*, Downers Grove: IVP, p.38.) In detective dramas evidence may initially mislead police into suspecting the wrong character, but first impressions are overturned by taking into account a wider range of evidence. The important question is not 'does any available evidence support such and such a theory?' (e.g. evolution), but 'does the preponderance of available evidence support such and such a theory?' Robert C. Newman highlights the role of philosophical assumptions in the evaluation of evidence by telling a story about a detective so fixated on 'getting his man' that he overlooks the otherwise glaringly obvious conclusion that the victim was crushed to death by an elephant.

[9] Wiker, Benjamin, *Moral Darwinism* (Downers Grove: IVP, 2002), p.63.

[10] Birkett, Kirsten, *Unnatural Enemies* (Matthias Press, 1997), p.118.

[11] 'Evolution and Palaeontology in the Ancient World' at www. ucmp.berkeley. edu/history/ancient.html, my italics.

[12] Pearcey, Nancy, in Phillip E. Johnson, *The Right Questions* (Downers Grove: IVP, 2002), Foreword, p.13.

[13] Wiker, *op. cit.*, p.25, 216, 133, 224.

[14] Michael Ruse, 'Is Evolution a Secular Religion?' atwww.arn.org/docs2/news/rusesecularreligion031003.htm

[15] Johnson, *Reason in the Balance, op. cit.*, p.16.

[16] Overman, Dean L., *A Case Against Accident and Self-Organization* (New York: Rowman & Littlefield, 1997), p.17.

[17] Dawkins, *The Blind Watchmaker, op. cit.*, dust cover.

[18] cf. William Paley, *Natural Theology* at www.hti.umich.edu/cgi/p/pd-modeng/pd-modeng-idx?type=HTML&rgn=DIV1&byte=53054870

[19] Dembski, William A., *No Free Lunch* (Lanham, Rowman & Littlefield, 2002), p.31.

[20] Geivett, R. Douglas, 'Is Jesus the Only Way?' in *Jesus Under Fire* (Paternoster Press, 1995), p.199.

[21] Paley, *op. cit.*

[22] Dawkins, *op. cit.*, p.41.

[23] Poole, Michael, 'Explaining or Explaining Away', *A Guide to Science and Belief* (Lion Manual) (Lion Publishing, 1997)

[24] Birkett, *op. cit.*, p.122-123.

[25] Copan, Paul, *That's Just Your Interpretation* (Grand Rapids: Baker, 2001), p.145.

[26] Flew, Anthony, *Thinking About Social Science* (Oxford: Blackwell, 1985), p.40.

[27] Dubay, Thomas, *The Evidential Power of Beauty* (San Francisco, Ignatius, 1999), p.204.

[28] Johnson, Phillip, *Darwin on Trial* (Downers Grove: IVP, 1993), p.4, 115. According to a 1991 Gallup poll, creation in this broad sense is accepted by 87 per cent of Americans.

[29] Birkett, *op. cit.*, p.119.

[30] Dawkins in Keith Ward, *The Turn of the Tide* (BBC, 1986), p.28-29.

[31] Dawkins, *The Blind Watchmaker, op. cit.*, Preface, p.x. 'Francis Crick similarly writes that, "Biologists must constantly keep in mind that what they see was not designed, but rather evolved."' (*What Mad Pursuit*, New York: Basic Books, p.138.)

[32] Muncaster, Ralph O., *Dismantling Evolution: Building the Case for Intelligent Design* (Eugene, Oregon: Harvest House, 2003), p.185.

[33] Dawkins, *The Blind Watchmaker, op. cit.*, p.3.

[34] *ibid.*, p.1.

[35] Wells, Johnathan, *Icons of Evolution* (Washington DC: Regency Publishing, 2000), p.204.

[36] Dawkins, *op. cit.*, Preface.

[37] *ibid.*, p.287.

[38] Wells, *op. cit.*, p.205.

[39] Johnson, Phillip E., 'What is Darwinism', *Objection Sustained* (Downers Grove: IVP, 1998), p.33.

[40] Joad, C. E. M., *The Recovery to Belief, op. cit.*, p.109.

[41] 'Nick Pollard Talks to Dr. Richard Dawkins', *op. cit.*

[42] Dawkins in Ward, *op. cit.*, p.29.

[43] Moreland, J. P. and Craig, William Lane, *Philosophical Foundations For A Christian Worldview* (Downers Grove: IVP, 2003), p.490.

[44] Dawkins, *op. cit.*, p.141.

[45] *ibid.*, p.13.

[46] Dembski, *No Free Lunch*, *op. cit.*, p.353.

[47] Denton, Michael J., 'Organism and Machine', in Jay W. Richards (ed.), *Ray Kurzweil vs. the Critics of Strong A.I.* (Seattle: Discovery Institute Press, 2002), p.91.

[48] Broom, Neil, *How Blind is the Watchmaker?* (IVP, 2001), p.46-47.

[49] Denton, *op. cit.*, p.91-95.

[50] Wolf, Jakob, 'Two Kinds of Causality – Philosophical Reflections on Darwin's Black Box' at www.iscid.org/papers/Wolf_TwoKinds_110802.pdf

[51] Menuge, Angus, personal correspondence.

[52] Craig, William Lane, 'Why I Believe in God', in Norman L. Geisler and Paul K. Hoffman (eds), *Why I Am A Christian* (Baker, 2001), p.73.

[53] Dembski, *No Free Lunch*, *op. cit.*, p.354.

[54] Richards, Jay, quoted by Dembski, *ibid.*, p.255.

[55] www.nizkor.org/features/fallacies/special-pleading.html

[56] Thanks to Edward Babinski for his critical correspondence with me on this argument.

[57] Menon, Latha (ed.), *A Devil's Chaplain: Selected Essays by Richard Dawkins* (London: Weidenfeld & Nicolson), p.8.

[58] *ibid.*

[59] *ibid.*

[60] Lewis, C. S., *The Problem of Pain* (London: Fount, 1977), p.106.

[61] Swinburne, Richard, *Providence and the Problem of Evil* (Oxford: Clarendon Press, 1998), p.172.

[62] Lewis, C. S., *The Problem of Pain* (London: Fount, 1977), p.104.

[63] Copan, Paul, *That's Just Your Interpretation*, *op. cit.*, p.99.

[64] McCabe, Herbert, *God Matters* (London: Mowbray, 1987), pp. 31-33, my italics.

[65] Ward, Keith, *God, Chance & Necessity* (Oxford: OneWorld, 1996), p.62.

[66] *ibid.*

[67] Randell, John, quoted by Pearcey and Thaxton, *op. cit.*, p.116.

[68] Dawkins, *A Devil's Chaplain*, *op. cit.*, p.13.

[69] Darwin, Charles, *The Origin of Species* (Ware: Wordsworth Editions Limited, 1998), p.356.

[70] Ward, *op. cit.*, p.87, 92.

[71] Tournier, Paul, *Escape from Loneliness* (London: SCM, 1974), p.31.

[72] Ward, *op. cit.*, p.87-88.

[73] Dawkins, *A Devil's Chaplain*, *op. cit.*, p.8.

[74] Ward, Keith, *God, Faith & The New Millennium* (Oxford: OneWorld, 1998), p.113.

[75] *ibid.*

[76] Garcia, Laura L., 'Teleological and Design Arguments', in Philip L. Quinn and Charles Taliaferro (eds), *A Companion To Philosophy Of Religion* (Oxford: Blackwell, 1999), p.339.

[77] *ibid.*, p.339.

[78] Nelson, Paul A., 'Jettison the Arguments, or the Rule? The Place of Darwinian Theological Themata in Evolutionary Reasoning' at www.arn.org/docs/nelson/pn_jettison.htm

[79] ARN guide to *Evolution*.

[80] Smith, Huston, 'Huston Smith replies to Barbour, Goodenough, and Peterson', *Zygon* 36, No. 2 (June 2001).

[81] Nelson, *op. cit.*, p.3-4.

[82] *ibid.*, p.4.

[83] *ibid.*

[84] *ibid.*, p.5.

[85] *ibid.*

[86] *ibid.*

[87] *Encyclopaedia Britannica* at www.britannica.com/bcom/eb/article/4/0,5716,42934+1+41986,00.html

[88] Luskin, Casey, 'Bad Theology and Good Design' at www-acs.ucsd.edu/~idea/badtheolgooddesn.htm

[89] Dembski, William A., *The Design Revolution* (Downers Grove: IVP, 2004), p.61.

[90] Luskin, *op. cit.*

[91] Ganssle, Gregory E., 'God and Evil', in *The Rationality of Theism, op. cit.*, p.263. cf. William P. Alston, 'The Inductive Argument from Evil' and Stephen John Wykstra, 'Rowe's Noseeum Arguments from Evil', in Daniel Howard-Snyder (ed.), *The Evidential Problem of Evil* (Indiana University Press, 1996).

[92] Luskin, *op. cit.*

[93] Nelson, *op. cit.*, p.7.

[94] Quoted *ibid.*

[95] cf. Woodmorappe, John, 'The panda thumbs its nose at the dysteleological argument of atheist Stephen Jay Gould' at www.answersingenesis.org/home/area/magazines/tj/v13n1_panda.asp

[96] Sarfati, Jonathan, *Refuting Evolution 2* (Master Books, 2003), p.122.

[97] Endo, Hideki, Yamagiwa, Daishiro, Hayashi, Yoshihiro, Koie, Hiroshi, Yamaya, Yoshiki and Kimura, Junpei, 'Role of the giant panda's psuedo-thumb', *Nature*, January 28, 1999, Vol 347 # 6717, p. 309-310.

[98] Sarfati, *op. cit.*, p.125.

[99] Dawkins, *The Blind Watchmaker, op. cit.*, p.93.

[100] Dembski, William A., 'Becoming a Disciplined Science' at www.designinference.com/documents/2002.10.27.Disciplined_Science.htm

[101] ARN guide to *Evolution*. cf. Michael J. Denton, 'The Inverted Retina: Maladaptation or Pre-adaption?' at www.arn.org/docs/odesign/od192/invertedretina192.htm

[102] Ayoub, George, 'On the Design of the Vertebrate Retina' at www.arn.org/docs/odesign/od171/retina171.htm

[103] Dawkins, *Climbing Mount Improbable* (Viking, 1996), p.69-70.

[104] Dawkins, Richard, quoted by Dover, Gabriel, 'Anti-Dawkins', in Hilary Rose and Steven Rose (eds), *Alas Poor Darwin* (London: Vintage, 2001), p.49.

[105] Nelson, *op. cit.*, p.4-5.

[106] Ward, *God, Faith & The New Millennium, op. cit.*, p.92.

[107] *ibid.*, p.92, 95.

[108] Darwin, Charles, as quoted in Gillespie, N. C., *Charles Darwin and the Problem of Creation* (Chicago: University of Chicago, 1979), p.87.

[109] Pearcey and Thaxton, *op. cit.*, p.80.

[110] Mascall, E. L., *Christian Theology and Natural Science* (Hamden: Archon Books, 1965), p.198.

[111] Pearcey and Thaxton, *op. cit.*, p.80.

[112] Behe, Michael J., *Darwin's Black Box* (FreePress, 1996), p.166.

[113] *ibid.*, p.223.

[114] Lord Hailsham, *The Door Wherein I Went* (Collins, 1975), p.41-42; quoted by John Blanchard, *Does God Believe in Atheists?*, p.523.

[115] ARN Guide to *Evolution, op. cit.*

[116] Rowe, William L., 'The Problem of Evil and Some Varieties of Atheism', *American Philosophical Quarterly*, 16 (1979).

[117] Plantinga, Alvin, 'The Free Will Defence' in Basil Mitchell (ed.), *The Philosophy of Religion* (Oxford: Oxford University Press, 1971).

[118] William Lane Craig in debate with Kai Nielson.

[119] Bergmann, Michael, *Philosophia Christi*, Series 2, Vol. 1, Number 2, 1999, p.140.

[120] Howard-Snyder, Daniel, *The Evidential Problem of Evil* (Bloomington, Indiana: Indiana University Press, 1996), p.xiii.

[121] Dawkins, Richard, Channel 4 interview with Sheena McDonald at www.geocities.com/ResearchTriangle/Facility/4118/misc/dawkins

[122] *ibid.*

[123] cf. Howard-Snyder (ed.), *op. cit.*

[124] *ibid.*, p.xi.

[125] Evans, C. Stephen, *Quest for Faith* (Downer's Grove: IVP, 1986), p.97.

[126] Ganssle, Gregory E., 'God and Evil', in Paul Copan and Paul K. Moser (eds), *The Rationality of Theism* (London: Routledge, 2003), p.273-274.

[127] Parrish, Stephen E., 'A Tale of Two Theisms', footnote 53, in Francis J. Beckwith *et al.* (eds), *The New Mormon Challenge* (Zondervan, 2002), p.459-460.

[128] Dawkins, *A Devil's Chaplain, op. cit.*, p.9.

[129] Dawkins, Richard, *River Out Of Eden* (New York: Basic Books, 1995), p.133.

[130] van Inwagen, Peter, 'The Problems of Evil, Air, & Silence' in Daniel Howard-Snyder (ed.), *The Evidential Problem of Evil, op. cit.*, p.162.

[131] Dawkins, *op. cit.*, p.132-133.

[132] Menuge, Angus, personal correspondence.

[133] Copan, *op. cit.*, p.91-92.

[134] Dawkins, *A Devil's Chaplain*, *op. cit.*, p.9.

[135] *ibid.*

[136] *ibid.*

[137] *ibid.*

[138] *ibid.*

[139] Butt, Kyle, 'Ideas have Consequences', quoted in Dawkins, *ibid.*

[140] Dawkins, *ibid.*

[141] Craig, William Lane, 'The Indispensability of Theological Meta-Ethical Foundations for Morality' at www.leaderu.com/offices/billcraig/docs/meta-eth.html

[142] Geisler, Norman L, *Christian Apologetics* (Grand Rapids: Baker, 1995), p.233.

[143] Dawkins, *op. cit.*, p.13.

[144] *ibid.*

[145] *ibid.*

[145] *ibid.*

[146] van Inwagen, Peter, *God, Knowledge & Mystery* (Cornell University Press, 1995), p.159.

[148] Dawkins, *op. cit.*, p.13.

[149] *ibid.*, p.9.

[150] Dawkins, *The Blind Watchmaker*, *op. cit.*, p.6.

[151] Dembski, William A., *Intelligent Design* (Downers Grove, Illinois, IVP, 1999), p.101.

[152] Ruse, Michael, quoted by Johnathan Wells, *Icons of Evolution* (Washington DC: Regency Publishing, 2000), p.227-228.

[153] Ruse, quoted by Johnathan Wells, *Icons of Evolution* (Washington DC: Regency Publishing, 2000), p.227.

[154] Ward, *God, Faith & The New Millennium*, *op. cit.*, p.104.

[155] Flew, Antony, *God and Philosophy* (London: Hutchinson, 1974), p.60.

[156] Ward, *God, Faith & The New Millennium*, *op. cit.*, p.106, 111.

[157] *ibid.*, p.118-119, my italics. This seems to be a pre-theoretic form of William Dembski's Explanatory Filter – cf. Chapter Eight.

[158] *ibid.*, p.119.

[159] Burgess, Stuart, *Hallmarks of Design* (Epsom: Day One, 2002), p.29.

[160] Dembski, *Intelligent Design*, *op. cit.*, p.100.

[161] Swinburne, Richard, *The Existence of God* (Oxford, 1991).

[162] Pepper, Margaret (ed.), *The Macmillan Dictionary of Religious Quotations* (London: Macmillan, 1996), p.40.

[163] Dawkins, Richard, *Unweaving the Rainbow* (London: Allen Lane/The Penguin Press, 1998), p.ix.

[164] Atkins, Peter, quoted by Richard Dawkins in *Unweaving the Rainbow*, p.ix.

[165] Dawkins, *ibid.*

[166] *ibid.*

[167] Budziszewski, J., *How To Stay Christian In College* (Colorado Springs: NavPress, 1999), p.121.

[168] Dawkins, *op. cit.*, p.ix-x.

[169] *Gladiator*, Dir. Ridley Scott (Dreamworks/Universal Pictures, 2000).

[170] Polkinghorne, John, *The God of Hope and the End of the World* (London: SPCK, 2002), p.113.

[171] Moreland, J. P., *Love God With All Your Mind* (NavPress, 1997), p.122.

[172] *ibid.*

[173] *ibid.*

[174] *ibid.*, p.121.

[175] *ibid.*, p.123.

[176] Weinberg, Steven, *The First Three Minutes*, quoted by Frank Miele, 'Darwin's Dangerous Disciple – An Interview with Richard Dawkins', *The Skeptic*, vol. 3, no. 4, 1995.

[177] Dawkins, Richard and Miele, Frank, 'Darwin's Dangerous Disciple – An Interview with Richard Dawkins', *ibid.*

[178] *ibid.*

[179] Dawkins, *A Devil's Chaplain*, *op. cit.*, p.10-11.

[180] Johnson, Philip E., 'The Robot Rebellion of Richard Dawkins' at www.arn.org/docs/johnson/pj_robotrebellion.htm

[181] Dawkins, *op. cit.*, p.11.

[182] Blackham, H. J., 'The Pointlessness of it All', in H. J. Blackham (ed.), *Objections to Humanism* (London: Constable, 1965), p.119.

[183] 'Nick Pollard talks to Dr. Richard Dawkins', *Thirdway*, April 1995, vol 18, no 3.

[184] *ibid.*

[185] *ibid.*

[186] Dawkins, 'Darwin's Dangerous Disciple', *op. cit.*

[187] cf. Bibliography.

[188] cf. Swinburne, Richard, 'The Justification of Theism' at www.leaderu.com/truth/3truth09.html

[189] Dawkins, 'Nick Pollard talks to Dr. Richard Dawkins', *op. cit.*

[190] *ibid.*

[191] Rorty, Richard, 'The Priority of Democracy to Philosophy', quoted by Phillip Johnson, in *Reason in the Balance*, *op. cit.*, p.121.

[192] Hibbs, Thomas S., *Shows About Nothing* (Dallas: Spence, 1999), p.161.

[193] O'Hear, Anthony, *Beyond Evolution* (Oxford), p.103.

[194] Dawkins, *A Devil's Chaplain*, *op. cit.*, p.34.

[195] *ibid.*

[196] *ibid.*

[197] *ibid.*

[198] *ibid.*

[199] Popper, Karl, 'Natural Selection and the Emergence of Mind', *Dialectica*, 32, 1978, pp. 339-355.

[200] Dawkins, 'Nick Pollard talks to Dr. Richard Dawkins', *op. cit.*

[201] Appleyard, Bryan, *Understanding the Present: Science and the Soul of Man* (London: Picador, 1993), p.11.

[202] Dawkins, *Science*, 277, (1997): 892.

CHAPTER 5

Reducing Reductionism

Steven Spielberg's 2002 film *A.I. Artificial Intelligence* follows the life of robot boy David (Haley Joel Osment), the first android ever built to feel human emotions: 'A mecha of a qualitatively different order . . . a robot that can love . . . A mecha with a mind . . .' Used as a substitute for a couple who have had their own son cryogenically frozen until a cure is found for his terminal illness, David's world collapses when his human brother comes out of cold storage. Abandoned by his human mother, David's journey of self-discovery is just beginning. *A.I.* is a modern retelling of Pinocchio, and one of a number of films asking what, if anything, sets humans apart from machines. Of course, it's easy to suspend our disbelief in the cinema when the robots are played by human actors and the special effects (by the Stan Winston Studio and Industrial Light & Magic) are this good. It's even easier to suspend our disbelief given the naturalist's assumption that humans are really nothing but machines anyway. But is this assumption fact or fiction?

> *Richard Dawkins's ideas necessarily invite philosophical questions about things like determinism, reductionism and scientism.*
> JULIAN BAGGINI AND JEREMY STANGROOM[1]

Richard Dawkins' view of reality goes by many names whose meanings overlap one-another: atheism, metaphysical naturalism (or naturalism for short), materialism, monism (because it only acknowledges one type of reality: the physical), scientism, etc. One of its most descriptive names is 'ontological reductionism', because it seeks to explain everything by *reducing* it to

nothing but naturalistically acceptable, material categories. Dawkins complains that: 'If you read trendy
intellectual magazines, you may have noticed that
"reductionism" is one of those things, like sin, that is
only mentioned by people who are against it.'[2] William
Hasker affirms that: 'No sensible person should want to
avoid reductionism altogether. Many of the greatest
successes of the sciences have come through reductive
explanations.'[3] However, there are different kinds of
reductionism, and: 'The kind of reductionism to be
avoided is the kind that gives reductive explanations
which deny or ignore the reality and importance of that
which is in fact real and important.'[4] Dawkins also complains: 'Reductionism is one of those words that makes
me want to reach for my revolver. It means nothing. Or
rather it means a whole lot of different things, but the
only thing anybody knows about it is that it's bad,
you're supposed to disapprove of it.'[5] J. P. Moreland
and William Lane Craig define reductionism as: 'the
continued belief in some entity X, but X is no longer
thought to be what theory S said it was; rather, it is now
"reduced to" being Y, which the new theory claims it
is.'[6] For example, Dawkins asserts: 'The kind of explanation we come up with must not contradict the laws of
physics. Indeed *it will make use of the laws of
physics, and nothing more than the laws of physics.*'[7]
Hence, for any entity X that is not just obviously physical (e.g. the human mind), X must be reduced (if only
hypothetically) to nothing but physically describable
realities (e.g. the functioning of the human brain). Such
reductionism is the inevitable methodological corollary
of naturalism. Unsurprisingly then, Dawkins is committed to the ontological reduction of mind to matter (the

hypothesis of 'physicalism'): 'philosophically I am committed to [physicalism] because I think that . . . consciousness must be a manifestation of the evolutionary process, presumably via brains. . . consciousness is ultimately a material phenomenon'.[8]

According to philosophers Paul Moser and David Yandell: 'Explanation in philosophy and science is ultimately unifying, subsuming a multiplicity of phenomena under classificatory unity – for example, under a unifying cause in the case of causal explanation. Explanation contributes unity and thus organization to what may otherwise appear as mere diversity.'[9] Ontological reductionism doesn't just seek to bring explanatory unity and organization to apparent diversity by *subsuming* a multiplicity of phenomena under a classificatory unity, but by *reducing* a multiplicity of phenomena to a single class of reality. Moser and Yandell warn that proponents of naturalism, who begin with an *a priori* commitment to explaining everything in terms of material reality: 'must attend to the risk of neglecting genuine data and truths resistant to a monistic explanatory scheme. What monism gains by unification of multiplicity in data may be lost by neglect of genuine recalcitrant data. Explanatory unity may be a virtue, but it will be virtuous only if pertinent truths and data are not excluded for the sake of theoretical simplicity.'[10] This is the danger of reductionism, that the legitimate search for the simplest adequate unifying explanation will be pursued with such dogmatic commitment that the demand for simplicity will outweigh the primary explanatory demand *that explanations must be adequate to the nature of the data they are meant to explain*. If this happens, facts are *reduced* to fit a single, simplistic and inadequate explanation, rather than explanations being expanded or multiplied to fit the facts. When the demand for simplicity outweighs the demand for adequacy, explanation becomes explaining-away as data is dismissed as 'only apparent' on the basis that if it were genuine it wouldn't fit *the explanation*! Such a reductionistic approach to explanation is clearly base over apex, but it is an approach that Dawkins takes time and again.

Dawkins writes as if reductionism is acknowledged by all right-thinking people to be an unqualified good, a good opposed only by misguided religious fundamentalists (and 'trendy intellectual magazines') who reject such explanations for sentimental reasons: 'Reductionist explanations are true explanations', said Dawkins in his interview with Nick Pollard, 'It's the only kind of explanation I find satisfying. I wish I could persuade you that it's the only kind of explanation that is satisfying.'[11] However, Dawkins' fellow atheist Thomas Nagel isn't satisfied, and his book *The Last Word* shatters Dawkins' caricature of the truth, as Hasker's review explains:

> *The Last Word* is a sustained attack on a number of different varieties of reductivism. With respect to logic, science, history, and ethics he argues that none of these intellectual practices can be understood by taking up a viewpoint external to the practice in question and 'explaining' the practice from that viewpoint. Such reductive explanations invariably issue in judgements which conflict with the first-order judgements made within the disciplines themselves – and in a fair competition, the disciplines win out over the reductive explanations.[12]

It seems to me that Nagel's rejection of reductive explanations is at odds with his naturalism. I think Dawkins is the more consistent thinker in embracing the reductionistic implications of naturalism. If so, Nagel's arguments against reductionism are in reality arguments against naturalism, and Dawkins can't explain away anti-naturalism arguments that seek to exploit problems with ontological reductionism as nothing but the product of sentimental religious prejudice.

The march of reductionism

> . . . science has either killed the soul or is in the
> process of doing so.
> RICHARD DAWKINS[13]

C. S. Lewis traced the march of reductionism, and commented on its results, half a century ago:

At the outset the universe appears packed with will, intelligence, life and positive qualities; every tree is a nymph and every planet a god . . . The advance of knowledge gradually empties this rich and genial universe: first of its gods, then of its colours, smells, sounds and tastes, finally of solidity itself as solidity was originally imagined. As these items are taken from the world, they are transferred to the subjective side of the account: classified as our sensations, thoughts, images or emotions. The Subject becomes gorged, inflated, at the expense of the Object.[14]

However, observed Lewis, reductionism doesn't stop there: 'The same method which emptied the world now proceeds to empty ourselves. The masters of the method soon announce that we were just as mistaken (and mistaken in much the same way) when we attributed "souls" . . . to human organisms, as when we attributed Dryads to trees.'[15] The problem with taking reductionism to this, its logical extreme, is that it reduces away the reducers: 'While we were reducing the world to almost nothing we deceived ourselves with the fancy that all its lost qualities were being kept safe (if in a somewhat humbled condition) as "things in our own mind". Apparently we had no mind of the sort required. The Subject is as empty as the Object.'[16]

Lewis thinks that ontological reductionism commits a common sort of mistake:

> We start with a view which contains a good deal of truth, though in confused or exaggerated form. Objections are then suggested and we withdraw it. But [then] we discover that we have empted the baby out with the bathwater and that the original view must have contained certain truths for lack of which we are now entangled in absurdities. So here. In emptying out the dryads and the gods (which, admittedly, 'would not do' just as they stood) we appear to have thrown out the whole universe, ourselves included.[17]

As Richard Purtill argues, not all progressions can be reasonably carried to zero:

> Consider the joke about the miserly farmer who fed his longsuffering cow less and less each day; but just when he thought that he had weaned the cow from eating altogether, the unfortunate animal died. Many cows (and people) could get along with less food, but they cannot get along with none. So showing that we do not need as many gods as early man believed does not show

that we need no gods at all; that must be argued on its own merits.[18]

Indeed, if we consider belief in non-material (i.e. supernatural) realities *in general* (rather than 'gods' in particular), it would seem that following the logical progression of reductionism to zero is self-defeating. Daniel Dennett's 'universal acid' of Darwinian evolution is so corrosive that it eats away at the naturalistic worldview flask in which it is so triumphantly displayed. As Purtill frames the conundrum: 'if the universe is purely material and has no intelligence or purpose, then our minds are the result of something with no intelligence or purpose. However, if this is true, then what confidence can we have in the workings of our minds?'[19]

Many philosophers think the naturalistic hypothesis that mind is reducible to matter justifies so little confidence in the workings of our minds that naturalism is self-referentially absurd, because it saws off the very branch (reason) upon which it depends. Rather than breaking the law of non-contradiction by reasoning our way to the conclusion that reason is untrustworthy (as naturalism entails), we should conclude that naturalism is untrustworthy, because reason is inescapably worthy of trust.

Reductionism and the Anti-Naturalism Argument from Reason

Our minds . . . are rational to a significant degree, and it's to this rationality that we owe whatever ability we have to grasp the truth about things – including, of course, the truth about the mind itself. A theory of mind that can't account for this rationality has little to be said for it.

WILLIAM HASKER[20]

William A. Dembski observes that although the literature attempting to account for human agency in materialistic terms is vast:

> . . . the materialist's options are in fact quite
> limited. The materialist world is not a mind-first
> world. Intelligent agency is therefore in no sense
> prior to or independent of the material world.
> Intelligent agency is a derivative mode of
> causation that depends upon underlying natural –
> and therefore unintelligent – causes. Human
> agency in particular supervenes on underlying
> natural processes, which in turn usually are
> identified with brain function.[21]

The materialist's commitment can be described by three
theses: First, causality in the physical world is mechanistic and non-purposive (nothing in the physical order
of nature happens in order to achieve a goal; things just
happen because they are caused to happen: 'The physical universe . . . proceeds by physical law rather than
by reason. If rocks fall down in an avalanche, they do
not go where they go because it would be a good idea
for them to go there . . . rather, the rocks go where the
initial conditions and the laws of physics say they must
go . . . In the last analysis, there are no intended purposes in the naturalist's universe.'[22]). Second, the physical order is a closed system (nothing apart from the
physical order can cause anything to happen within the
physical order). Third, every state of affairs supervenes
on the physical facts. As Dembski explains: 'Supervenience makes no pretence at reductive analysis. It
simply asserts that the lower level determines the higher level – how it does it, we don't know.'[23] For example:
'To say . . . that intelligent agency supervenes on neu-

rophysiology is to say that once all the facts about neu-rophysiology are in place, all the facts about intelligent agency are determined as well.'[24] The supervenience thesis amounts to the thesis of reductionism, for as Hasker writes: 'What supervenience guarantees is that *the mind cannot vary independently of the body*, and this seems to be an inescapable implication of the physicalist claim that the physical facts determine all the facts.'[25] Naturalism inevitably reduces the mind to nothing but matter, as Dr Steven Lovell observes:

> The naturalist will want to say that things ultimately possess the features that distinguish the personal, the purposive, and the mental in virtue of possessing other features that are not of these kinds. For example, in so far as the naturalist accepts the reality of mental states at all, she will think each is really just (constituted by) a certain kind of physical state.[26]

The naturalistic reduction of mind to matter entails a mechanistic and therefore deterministic conception of 'mental' reality: 'Any genuinely naturalistic position requires that all instances of explanation in terms of reasons be further explained in terms of non-purposive substratum. For if some purposive or intentional expla-nation can be given and no further analysis can be given in non-purposive and non-rational terms, then reason must be viewed as a fundamental cause in the uni-verse.'[27] Such a conclusion is inimical to naturalism, for as Bertrand Russell wrote, it follows from naturalism that: 'Man is a part of nature, not something contrasted with Nature. His thoughts and his bodily movements follow the same laws that describe the motions of stars and atoms . . . we are subordinated to nature, the outcome of natural laws, and their victims in the long run.'[28] (It is worth noting with William Hasker that this conclusion follows from the philosophy of naturalism and not from the evidence of nature: 'determinism [is] purely a metaphysical hypothesis [which] entirely lacks empirical evidence . . .'[29])

The crucial question is, can acts of reasoning, such as Russell's deduction that *if* naturalism is true *then* his thoughts are 'the outcome of natural laws', be adequately accounted for on the metaphysical hypothesis that they are 'the outcome of natural laws'? Is the fact that Dawkins makes the deduction that *if* evolutionary naturalism is true *then* consciousness must be a wholly material phenomenon, compatible with his conclusion?

The concern that naturalistic accounts of rationality are in some sense incoherent finds philosophical expression in a number of arguments commonly referred to under the overarching label of 'the anti-naturalism argument from reason'. The core of the anti-naturalism argument from reason can be stated as follows:

> **1.** Naturalism reduces reasoning to a closed, mechanistic, deterministic system of physical cause and effect.
> **2.** This reduction is unable to accommodate acts of reasoning (including the naturalist's acts of reason).
> **3.** Therefore, naturalism is self-contradictory.

As we have seen, the first premise follows from the core commitments of naturalism and (as the quotation from Russell demonstrates) is accepted by naturalists. As atheist Paul M. Churchland writes: 'The important point about the standard [naturalistic] evolutionary story is that the human species and all of its features are the wholly physical outcome of a purely physical process . . . We are creatures of matter.'[30] Therefore, if the second premise can be defended as being at least more plausible than its denial, the conclusion will be supported.

'The cardinal difficulty of naturalism'

> *If physical determinism is true, then that is the end of all discussion . . .*
> JOHN ECCLES[31]

In his classic work *Miracles: a preliminary study*, C. S. Lewis presented a famous version of the argument from reason.[32] Lewis set the scene by arguing that: 'If Naturalism is true, every finite thing or event must be (in principle) explicable in terms of the Total System [of material realities and relations] . . . If any one thing exists which is of such a kind that we see in advance the impossibility of ever giving *that kind* of explanation, then Naturalism would be in ruins.'[33] In particular, Lewis pointed out that: 'A theory which explained everything else in the whole universe but which made it impossible to believe that our thinking was valid, would be utterly out of court. For that theory would itself have been reached by thinking, and if thinking is not valid that theory would . . . have destroyed its own credentials.'[34] If naturalism excludes the reality of such necessary components of our rationality as thinking that premises are true, or drawing a conclusion because it is seen to follow from premises that we think are true, then any argument advanced for naturalism is self-contradictory. Indeed, as soon as a naturalist reasoned about anything they would contradict themselves and falsify their worldview.

The argument from logical relations (it all depends on what you mean by 'because'!)

> *The presupposition of the uniformity of natural causes in a closed system seems to involve serious epistemological difficulties . . .*
> THOMAS V. MORRIS[35]

The easiest way to exhibit the fact that naturalism discredits reason, writes Lewis, is to begin by noting that there are two different senses of the word 'because', as in the statement 'I believe X because of Y.' One sense is the relation of *physical cause and effect*, as in: 'Grandfather is ill today *because* (cause–effect) he ate lobster yesterday.'[36] The other is the relation of *logical ground and consequent*, as in: 'Grandfather must be ill *because* (ground–consequent) he hasn't got up yet (and we know he is an invariably early riser when he is well).'[37] Grandpa's failure to get out of bed does not *cause* Grandfather to be ill, nor does it *cause* us to conclude he is ill; rather, it is our *grounds* for making the logical inference that he is ill. The cause–effect sense of because indicates 'a dynamic connection between events';[38] the ground–consequent sense of because indicates 'a logical relation between beliefs or assertions'.[39] Lewis explains:

> . . . a train of reasoning has no value as a means of finding truth unless each step in it is connected with what went before in the Ground–Consequent relation . . . If what we think at the end of our reasoning is to be [a valid conclusion], the correct

answer to the question, 'Why do you think this?'
must begin with the Ground–Consequent *because*.
On the other hand, every event in Nature must be
connected with previous events in the Cause and
Effect relation. But [if Naturalism is true] our acts
of thinking are events [in Nature]. Therefore the
true answer to 'Why do you think this?' must
begin with the Cause–Effect *because*.[40]

As soon as we reduce thinking to naturalistically acceptable
categories, the ground–consequent sense of *because*
gets pushed out of the picture by the all-determining
cause–effect sense of *because*. This is a problem because:

To be caused is not to be proved. Wishful
thinkings, prejudices, and the delusions of
madness, are all caused, but they are ungrounded . . .
The implication is that if causes fully account for a
belief [as they must do if naturalism is true], then,
since causes work inevitably [naturalism requires
determinism], the belief would have had to arise
whether it had grounds or not . . . even if grounds
do exist, what exactly have they got to do with the
actual occurrence of the belief as a psychological
event? If it is an event, it must be caused. It must
in fact be simply one link in a causal chain which
stretches back to the beginning and forward to the
end of time. How could such a trifle as lack of
logical grounds prevent the belief's occurrence or
how could the existence of grounds promote it?[41]

If naturalism is true, our thinking is *nothing but* the
effect of non-rational physical causes connected one to
another by the cause–effect sense of because. But 'a
train of thought loses all rational credentials as soon as
it can be shown to be wholly the result of non-rational

causes'.[42] As Hasker observes: '*In a physicalist world, principles of sound reasoning have no relevance to determining what actually happens.*'[43] If naturalism is true: 'our thoughts . . . are governed by biochemical laws; these, in turn, by physical laws which are themselves actuarial statements about the . . . movements of matter'.[44] Nowhere in this closed chain of mechanistic physical cause and effect is there room for an efficacious relationship of ground and consequent to influence or explain our arrival at this or that conclusion:

> . . . each mental event is [on the hypothesis of naturalism] either identical with or supervenient on a physical event. By hypothesis, the physical event in question has a complete causal explanation in terms of previous events *with which it is connected according to the laws of physics* . . . each such event has whatever causal powers it has solely in virtue of its physical characteristics . . . No causal role for the mental characteristics as such can be found . . . [Hence] *On the assumption of the causal closure of the physical, no one ever accepts a belief because it is supported by good reasons.* To say that this constitutes a serious problem for physicalism seems an understatement.[45]

Defending Lewis' argument, Victor Reppert writes that: 'if all thoughts are the result of nonrational causes such that, given those causes, it is impossible that the particular thought should not occur, it is incompatible with the claim that some particular thought is produced by the good reasons there are for believing it'.[46]

As rational beings, humans can of course construct physical mechanisms that act *in accordance with rea-*

son (e.g. a chess computer), but naturalism cannot accommodate anything that acts *from reason* (e.g. humans programming a computer so that it will act in accordance with the chains of reasoning they perceive). If naturalism is true it cannot be said that computer programmers act from reason in the sense of doing what they do because (ground–consequent) they have good reasons, because (cause–effect) their behaviour must be the outcome of nothing but a mechanistic sequence of physical cause and effect.[47] As Reppert observes, chess computer Deep Blue's ability to defeat world chess champion Gary Kasparov in their notorious 1997 match: 'was not the exclusive result of physical causation, unless the people on the programming team (such as Grandmaster Joel Benjamin) are entirely the result of physical causation. And that, precisely, is the point at issue.'[48] In other words, one can't point to computers as a counter-example to Lewis' argument against naturalism from logical relations without begging the question: 'while some events in nature can be explained in terms of purely mechanistic causes, rational inference cannot'.[49]

Intentionality and truth

> *The directedness, or 'about-ness' of thought is a basic fact of experience, and there appears nothing to which it could possibly be reduced in analysis.*
> GEOFFREY MADELL[50]

Lewis pointed out that 'Acts of thinking are no doubt events; but they a very special sort of events. They are "about" something other than themselves and can be true or false.'[51] However, '[physical events] are not about anything and cannot be true or false'.[52] Hence thinking 'events' in our minds cannot be reduced to physical 'events' in our brains. As J. P. Moreland explains: 'Mental states point beyond themselves to other objects even if those objects do not exist. I have a thought *about* my wife, I hope *for* a new car, I dream *of* a unicorn.'[53] A thinking event – such as: 'The anti-naturalism argument is a piece of reasoning' – cannot be a merely physical event, because the former possess qualities that the latter cannot: the quality of being *about* something, and the quality of being *true*:

> We are compelled to admit between the thoughts of a terrestrial astronomer and the behaviour of matter several light-years away that particular relation which we call truth. But this relation has no meaning at all if we try to make it exist between the matter of the star and the astronomer's brain, considered as a lump of matter. The brain may be in all sorts of relations to the star no doubt: it is in a spatial relation, and a time relation . . . But to talk of one bit of matter as being true about another bit of matter seems to me to be nonsense.[54]

'We experience,' says Lewis, 'thoughts, which are "about" or "refer to" something other than themselves . . . but physical events, as such, cannot in any intelligible sense be said to be "about" or to "refer to" anything.'[55] Electrical activity in a computer chip or a brain has all sorts of physical qualities and stands in all sorts of physical relations, but a list of such qualities and relations would not include the quality of 'being about' anything: 'no such property or combination of properties *constitutes* a representation of anything, or qualifies their bearer as being *of* or *about* anything'.[56] Hence philosopher of mind John Searle argues that: 'Any attempt to reduce intentionality to something nonmental will always fail because it leaves out intentionality.'[57] Naturalism is 'nonsensical' or 'unintelligible' as a worldview, argues J. P. Moreland, because it: 'denies intentionality by reducing it to a physical relation . . . thereby denying that the mind is genuinely capable of having thoughts *about* the world'.[58] And if thoughts cannot be about anything, then they cannot be true or false; and if thoughts cannot be true or false, then knowledge is impossible (and the claim to know that naturalism is true is self-contradictory). Since many things are known, observes Dallas Willard, 'naturalism must be false. It cannot accommodate the ontological structure of knowing and knowledge.'[59]

Determinism and rational oughts

> *I recognize that philosophically speaking determinism is a difficult issue . . .*
> RICHARD DAWKINS

'In the area of rationality,' writes J. P. Moreland, 'there are rational oughts . . . Reasons and evidence imply or support certain conclusions, and if one is to be objectively rational, one "ought" to accept these conclusions . . . Failure to do so makes one irrational.'[60] However, on the naturalistic account of the mind it is impossible to see how one mental state can stand to another in an inferential relation which prescribes that one *ought* to have the latter mental state: 'because one physical state does not . . . prescribe that the other "ought" to occur logically. It either causes or fails to cause the second state.'[61] Stephen Clark argues along similar lines: 'If my opinions are just chemical events, they . . . can't be something I *ought* or *ought not* to have. And in that case my beliefs aren't rational at all.'[62] Clark concludes: 'consistent materialists ought not to claim that their arguments are ones which anyone ought to accept . . .'[63]

Naturalism and the end of reason

> *When we hear of some new attempt to explain*
> *reasoning . . . naturalistically, we ought to react as if*
> *we were told that someone had squared the circle . . .*
> PETER GEACH[64]

Lewis was right: 'Naturalism . . . offers what professes to be a full account of our mental behaviour; but this account . . . leaves no room for the acts of knowing . . . on which the whole value of our thinking, as a means to truth, depends.'[65] Dawkins commits the *faux pas* of trying to reduce thinking to nothing but a consequence of physics: 'The body is a complex thing with many constituent parts, and to understand its behaviour you must apply the laws of physics to its parts, not to the whole. The behaviour of the whole will then emerge as a consequence of interactions of the parts.'[66] The failure of ontologically reductionistic explanations of rationality entails the failure of naturalism, for as Hasker observes: 'In order to avoid this kind of reductionism, one must abandon a cornerstone of contemporary naturalism, namely the causal closure of the physical domain.'[67] Instead, one must accept that 'human beings possess rational powers that are impossible for beings whose actions are governed entirely by the laws of physics . . .'[68]

The rationality argument for theism

The argument from reason first argues that if we are capable of rational inference, then the basic explanation for some events in the universe must be given in terms of reasons, not in terms of the blind operation of nature obeying the laws of nature. Only subsequently does the argument attempt to show that theism . . . best accounts for this explanatory dualism.
VICTOR REPPERT[69]

C. S. Lewis turned the conclusion of the anti-naturalism argument into the first premise of an argument for God:

It is . . . an open question whether each man's reason exists absolutely on its own or whether it is the result of some (rational) cause – in fact, of some other Reason. That other Reason might conceivably be found to depend on a third, and so on; it would not matter how far this process was carried provided you found reason coming from reason at each stage. It is only when you are asked to believe in Reason coming from non-reason that you must cry Halt, for if you don't, all thought is discredited. It is therefore obvious that sooner or later you must admit a Reason which exists absolutely on its own. The problem is whether you or I can be such a self-existent Reason.[70]

Lewis thought not:

This question almost answers itself the moment we remember what existence 'on one's own' means. It means that kind of existence which Naturalists attribute to 'the whole show' and Supernaturalists attribute to God . . . Now it is clear that my reason has grown up gradually since

> my birth and is interrupted for several hours each night. I therefore cannot be that eternal self-existent Reason . . . yet if any thought is valid, such a Reason must exist and must be the source of my own imperfect and intermittent rationality. [71]

Lewis concluded that: 'Human minds . . . are not the only supernatural entities that exist. They do not come from nowhere . . . each has its tap-root in an eternal, self-existent, rational Being, whom we call God.'[72]

Many contemporary thinkers follow Lewis in taking the negative conclusion of the anti-naturalism argument from reason and turning it into the first premise of a positive argument from rationality for theism. According to J. P. Moreland: 'Mind appears to be a basic feature of the cosmos and its origin at a finite level of persons is best explained by postulating a fundamental Mind who gave finite minds being and design.'[73] Victor Reppert concludes: 'the force of the argument from reason is to show that the fundamental fact of the universe must be rational. Theism is a world-view that fits this requirement . . . Naturalism, theism's chief rival for the mind of the West, does not.'[74] Even non-theistic philosophers feel the force of this argument. Antony O'Hear admits that: 'in a contest between materialistic atheism and some kind of religious-cum-theistic view, the materialistic conclusion leaves even more mysteries than a view which sees reason and consciousness as part of the essence of the universe'.[75]

Welcome to Wales

C. S. Lewis argued that:

> It would be impossible to accept naturalism itself if we really and consistently believed naturalism.

> For naturalism is a system of thought. But for
> naturalism all thoughts are mere events with
> irrational causes. It is, to me at any rate, impossible
> to regard the thoughts which make up naturalism
> in that way and, at the same time, to regard them
> as a real insight into external reality.[76]

In phrasing his argument in terms of whether it is rational for naturalists to regard their thoughts as giving 'a real insight into external reality', Lewis pre-figured an ingenious version of the anti-naturalism argument from reason put forward three decades later by philosopher Richard Taylor. Taylor began with a thought experiment: Suppose that you are travelling by train and, glancing out of the window, you see some stones on a hillside spelling out the words 'Welcome to Wales'. Taylor points out that if, on the basis of this observation alone, you formed the belief that you are entering Wales: 'you would, in fact, be presupposing that they were arranged that way by an intelligent and purposeful being or beings for the purpose of conveying a certain message having nothing to do with the stones themselves'.[77] It would be unreasonable to continue holding the belief that you are entering Wales, purely on the basis of observing these stones, if you came to believe that the stones had *not* been arranged on purpose to give a real insight into a reality external to themselves, but had ended up in this formation merely as a result of nothing but natural laws and/or chance: 'it would be *irrational* for you to regard the arrangement of the stones as evidence that you were entering Wales, *and at the same time to suppose that they might have come to that arrangement accidentally*, that is, as the result of the ordinary interactions of natural or physical forces'.[78] Having made this point, Taylor argues that if you believe that *your own cognitive faculties* are the result of nothing but natural forces, it would be just as unreasonable to base this belief on those very faculties:

> It would be irrational for one to say *both* that his sensory and cognitive faculties had a . . . nonpurposeful origin and *also* that they reveal some truth with respect to something other than themselves . . . If, on the other hand, we do assume that they are guides to some truths having nothing to do with themselves, then it is difficult to see how we can, consistently with that supposition, believe them to have arisen . . . by the ordinary workings of purposeless forces, even over ages of time.[79]

If our trust in the stone sign for information beyond itself is to be reasonable, we must not attribute it to chance and/or necessity, but to design. Likewise, if our (inescapable) trust in our own cognitive faculties for information beyond them is to be rational, then we must not attribute those faculties to chance and/or necessity. Rather, we must attribute those faculties to design. Hence Taylor's argument closely combines the anti-naturalism argument from reason and the argument from reason for design.

Epistemology and evolution

> *. . . the idea of a natural sympathy between the deepest truths of nature and the deepest truths of the human mind . . . makes us more at home in the universe than is secularly comfortable.*
> THOMAS NAGEL[80]

In Dawkins' view: 'We are jumped-up apes and our brains were only designed to understand the mundane details of how to survive in the Stone Age African savannah.'[81] Although he says that our brains were 'designed', Dawkins means nothing of the sort. He means that a combination of unintended natural laws and unguided contingent happenstance (chance, or luck) just happened to throw up an ape with a brain that tended to keep its gene-machine of a body alive long enough to reproduce and look after its progeny in the conditions of Stone Age Africa, and that jumped-up ape is us. How bold, how iconoclastic, how amazing are the truths revealed to us when we bravely abandon the 'medieval' view of man as a rational animal whose being was intended and brought about by the God in whose image we are made, and turn 'into the keen wind of understanding'[82] provided to us by that great prophet of modern science Charles Darwin! Indeed, exactly in so far as Dawkins' description of humanity as jumped-up apes is *amazing*, so too is it *unlikely* and therefore *self-defeating*. For isn't it unlikely that brains only 'designed' (i.e. evolved *without design*) to understand the mundane details of how to survive in the Stone Age African savannah should be capable of understanding the far from mundane details of evolutionary theory as it applies to themselves thousands of years ago? Hasn't Dawkins laid claim to a position analogous to the man who trusts the 'Welcome to Wales' sign whilst believing that it is the result of nothing but natural forces? The more seriously we take Dawkins' assessment of human origins, the less seriously it seems we can take it.

Faced with the anti-naturalism argument from reason, Anthony Flew actually appeals to evolution, objecting that: 'it looks as if evolutionary biology and human history could provide some reasons for saying that it need not be a mere co-incidence if a significant proportion of men's beliefs about their environment are in fact true'.[83] However, it is, at the very least, an open question whether or not evolutionary biology and human history provides *sufficient* reason for believing that men's beliefs about their environment are likely to be reliable, even in the minimal sense of being true *more often than not*. As Stephen Stitch contends: 'there are major problems to be overcome by those who think that evolutionary considerations impose interesting limits on irrationality'.[84]

Plantinga's evolutionary anti-naturalism argument

Alvin Plantinga argues that we should be doubtful of the sort of epistemological claim Flew makes for evolution, and has developed an 'evolutionary anti-naturalism argument' on the grounds that: 'The fact that my behaviour (or that of my ancestors) has been adaptive . . . is at best a third-rate reason for thinking my beliefs mostly true and my cognitive faculties reliable . . .'[85] As Richard Rorty argues: 'The idea that one species of organism is, unlike all the others, oriented not just towards its own increased propensity but toward Truth, is as un-Darwinian as the idea that every human being has a built-in moral compass . . .'[86] However, Plantinga points out an obvious problem with this sort of claim: in undermining reason it undermines itself. On the one hand, if we accept that an orientation towards truth is un-Darwinian, and we accept Darwinism, we thereby provide ourselves with a reason to doubt our orientation towards truth, and hence the Darwinian theory that those capacities have produced. On the other hand, if we accept that an orientation towards truth is un-Darwinian, and we accept (as we must on pain of self-contradiction) that we are in fact orientated towards truth, we thereby provide ourselves with a reason to doubt Darwinism. Either way, Darwinism is in trouble.

Plantinga dubs the sort of self-defeating proposition affirmed by Rorty 'Darwin's Doubt', because Darwin wrote that: 'the horrid doubt always arises whether the convictions of man's mind, which has been developed from the mind of the lower animals, are of any value or at all trustworthy'.[87] Plantinga argues that Darwin's Doubt does indeed follow from a belief in naturalistic evolution, and that it is self-defeating, in that it gives one reason to doubt the naturalism from which it follows. Plantinga goes on to argue that the self-contradictory nature of Darwin's Doubt provides us with reason for accepting a theistic worldview.

Naturalistic evolution certainly can't *guarantee* that our beliefs are true, because the 'Blind Watchmaker' of evolution is concerned with adaptive bodily behaviour and not with truth. As Moreland observes: 'it is not clear that the ability to know truth from falsity is necessary to survive. As long as an organism interacts consistently with its environment it need not interact accurately . . . our capacities to sense and think accurately about the world go far beyond what is needed to survive.'[88] Stephen Clark reminds us: 'that it has often been advantageous to live by "false" beliefs'.[89]

Even if Flew is right when he says that evolution can provide an explanation for 'men's beliefs about their environment', we might well question whether evolution can adequately account for men having reliable beliefs about anything beyond their immediate physical environment – about things like evolutionary history for example! As Clark suggests: 'The problem for us is that we insist (and must insist) that we can get things right (do get things right) about the universe in ways that had no possible advantage to our ancestors.'[90]

Physicalism and the failure of Darwinian epistemology

William Hasker takes matters one step further when he argues that: 'if we accept the physicalist premise of causal closure and the supervenience of the mental, Darwinist epistemology flunks out completely: it has no ability whatever to explain how any of our conscious mental states have even the most tenuous hold on objective reality'.[91] C. S. Lewis prefigured Hasker when he considered the relationship between reason and evolution:

> . . . natural selection could operate only by
> eliminating responses that were biologically
> hurtful and multiplying those which tended to
> survival. But it is not conceivable that any
> improvement of responses could ever turn them
> into acts of insight . . . The Naturalist [gives] a
> history of the evolution of reason which is
> inconsistent with the claims that he and I both
> have to make for inference as we actually practise
> it. For his history is . . . an account, in Cause and
> Effect terms, of how people came to think the way
> they do. And this of course leaves in the air the
> quite different question of how they could possibly
> be justified in so thinking. This imposes on him
> the very embarrassing task of trying to show how
> the evolutionary product which he has described

could also be a power of 'seeing' truths. But the very attempt is absurd.[92]

Hasker argues that the attempt is absurd because, on the assumption of the causal closure of the physical domain, 'the conscious state of the organism, as such, can have *no influence whatever* on the organism's behaviour and thus on its propensity to survive'.[93] The heart of the problem is that, given physicalist assumptions:

> . . . *the occurrence and content of conscious mental states such as belief and desire are irrelevant to behaviour and are not subject to selection pressures.* On this assumption, *natural selection gives us no reason to assume that the experiential content of my mental states corresponds in any way whatever to objective reality.* And since on the physicalist scenario Darwinist epistemology is the *only* available explanation for the reliability of our epistemic faculties, the conclusion to be drawn is that physicalism not only *has not given* any explanation for such reliability, but it *is in principle unable to give* any such explanation. And that, it seems to me, is about as devastating an objection to physicalism as anyone could hope to find . . . Darwinian evolution, constrained by the closure of the physical, cannot possibly be correct; it fails entirely to account for any correspondence between physical reality and the content of our subjective experience.[94]

Consequences of the anti-naturalism argument from reason

Ironically, the more vociferous a naturalist like Richard

Dawkins is in affirming naturalism, the reduction of mind to matter, and the truth of Darwinian (naturalistic) evolution, the more they sink themselves into the mire of self-contradiction that points not only to the necessity of belief in a naturalism-busting 'dualism of fundamental explanations, the idea that we cannot expunge purpose from the basic level of explanation',[95] but to a naturalism replacing theism: 'There are, in this area, a number of "theoretical advantages" for a theistic account of the world over a naturalistic one.'[96] As Robert C. Koons argues:

> . . . materialism, without a designer who intended man to be equipped with an aptitude for truth, leads inexorably to an epistemological catastrophe, the 'epistemic defeat' of all the materialist's aspirations for knowledge . . . There is a price to be paid for scientific realism, for the conviction that our scientific theories provide models of the real world, models that we have some reason to believe may be approximately correct. This price is our admission that the physical realm does not exhaust reality, but that it is instead the artifact of a reasonable God who has fitted us to the task of investigating it.[97]

Contra Bertrand Russell's belief that humans are 'subordinated to nature, the outcome of natural laws',[98] the anti-naturalism arguments from reason show that humans are *not* wholly subordinated to nature, but partially transcend its explanatory capacities:

> . . . an act [of reasoning], to be what it claims to be – and if it is not, all our thinking is discredited – cannot be merely the exhibition at a particular place and time of that total . . . system of events

called 'nature' . . . acts of reasoning are not interlocked with the total interlocking system of Nature as all other items are interlocked with one another. They are connected with it in a different way; as the understanding of a machine is certainly connected with the machine but not in the way the parts of the machine are connected with each other. The knowledge of a thing is not one of the thing's parts. In this sense something beyond Nature operates whenever we reason.[99]

Since acts of reason must transcend the explanatory capacity of physical cause and effect, since chance is an unreliable basis for correctly relating logical ground and consequent, and since the addition of chance to cause and effect cannot therefore account for rationality either (we may define rationality as intentional mental states related by a freely chosen submission to rational *oughts*), it helps the naturalist not one jot to explain human rationality as the effect of nothing but chance variation and natural selection.

Lewis criticises naturalists for a dogmatic insistence on reducing everything to materialistic realities when such reductionism is not only self-defeating, but is based upon something known from thinking (i.e. matter) rather than upon the basic fact of thinking itself, which is immediately and certainly known, for: 'Reason is given before Nature and upon reason our concept of Nature depends.'[100] Naturalism insists on putting the material cart before the thinking horse, and the result is self-defeating: 'Naturalists have been engaged in thinking about Nature. They have not attended to the fact that they were *thinking*. The moment one attends to this it is obvious that one's own thinking cannot be a merely natural event, and that therefore something other than Nature exists.'[101] As Anthony O'Hear argues: 'there are aspects of our experience and existence more fundamental than science, and on which science depends for its possibility. So science cannot be used, as it often is, to undermine those features of our natures.'[102] To rephrase the warning of Moser and Yandell, what naturalistic monism gains by unification of multiplicity in data is lost by neglect of genuine recalcitrant data:

> The validity of rational thought, accepted in an utterly non-naturalistic, transcendental (if you will), supernatural sense, is the necessary presupposition of all other theorizing. There is simply no sense in beginning with a view of the universe and trying to fit the claims of thought in at a later stage. By thinking at all we have claimed that our thoughts are more than mere natural events. All other propositions must be fitted in as best they can round that primary claim.[103]

When we ask which worldview makes the best sense out of the irreducible nature of rationality, the matter first view of naturalism is revealed as a complete non-starter, whereas the Mind first view of theism provides a coherent explanatory context for our rational capacities.

Broadening our options

We need to reduce the scientistic recourse to reductionism and to liberate science to follow the evidence wherever it leads. As C. S. Pierce wrote: 'The only end of science, as such, is to learn the lesson that the universe has to teach it . . . it simply surrenders itself to the force of facts.'[104] To approach the study of biology without Dawkins' self-defeating naturalistic assumption doesn't entail ruling out evolution as an adequate (or even the best available) explanation of biology, but it does mean letting the evidence speak for itself and realizing that, either way, the results of our inquiry will be compatible with belief in design and, indeed, with seeing evidence for design in nature.

An agnostic or theistic scientist can be much more open to following the evidence where it leads than an atheistic scientist, because while they will be rightly *biased* in favour of natural explanations *when they are adequate*, they will not *rule out* supernatural explanations where natural explanations fail to suffice – as they do in the case of human reasoning, upon which science depends.

The slippery slope away from a divine foot in the door of nature

The slippery slope from science to scientism, from explanation to reductionism, observed by Lewis and embraced by Dawkins, is followed all too easily. The world of the natural sciences 'is neither good, nor beautiful, nor holy, nor just. There is nothing in nature which justifies or answers to our ethical, aesthetic and religious aspirations . . .'[105] In so far as we only understand the world through science, then, we will see a world without goodness or beauty. But as J. P. Moreland points out, for many people in Western culture: 'knowledge is obtained solely by means of the senses and science . . . knowledge is identical to *scientific* knowledge . . . Science is the measure of all things, and when a scientist speaks about something, he or she speaks *ex cathedra*.'[106] It is, therefore, hardly surprising that the false identification of knowledge with *scientific* knowledge results in the widespread assumption that matters of goodness, beauty and religion are not matters of truth or knowledge, but of mere subjective opinion. Keith Ward observes:

> Good scientists like . . . Richard Dawkins . . . have published books that openly deride religious beliefs, and claim the authority of their own scientific work for their attacks. Their claims are seriously misplaced. Their proper scientific work has no particular relevance to the truth or falsity of most religious claims. When they do stray into the fields of philosophy, they ignore both the history and the diversity of philosophical viewpoints, pretending that materialist views are almost universally held, when, in fact, they are held by only a fairly small minority among philosophers . . . The form of materialism they espouse is open to very strong, and standard, criticisms, particularly in respect to its virtual total inability to account for the facts of consciousness and for the importance of ideas of truth and virtue . . . Ironically, their attitudes are often anti-scientific in temper as well as anti-religious, since they do not consider carefully and rigorously the claims of major theologians, but are content to lampoon the crudest versions of the most naïve religious doctrines they can find. Their treatment of religion shows no dispassionate analysis, but a virulent contempt which can only be termed prejudice.[107]

The materialistic conclusions of these scientific atheists only follow in so far as we agree to only understand the world through science (a science restricted to natural explanations), and to ignore the fact that even this restricted form of inquiry relies upon rational capacities that don't fit within naturalistic categories. Why, aside from 'a virulent contempt' for non-scientific facts, would anyone want to do such an odd thing as that? To focus on what science has to say about the world in this way is like viewing the world through a window and concluding that wetness doesn't exist, because it can't be sensed through the window. The whole point of a window is that it lets in some elements (e.g. light) while excluding others (e.g. rain). To conclude from a window that the things it ignores in order to work don't exist would be to make a rather basic logical mistake. Likewise, to conclude from science that the things science ignores when it describes reality (goodness, beauty, meaning, God, etc) don't exist would be to make an equally basic mistake.

Looking through a window is a really useful way of looking at the world (it keeps you warm and dry while you look), but there is more to the world than can be discovered by looking through windows. Science is a really useful way of looking at the world (it can tell you how rainbows are formed by the refraction of light through water droplets), but there is more to the world than can be discovered by looking at it through science (for example, the fact that rainbows are beautiful): 'Unable within its borders to find room for moral and aesthetic experiences . . . science has had to leave them outside the pattern. Yet in actual concrete experience [indeed, in the very practice of science] they refuse to remain outside; they insist on being taken into account.'[108] Indeed, the desire to reduce reality to nothing but its scientifically describable constituents is fundamentally at odds with the historical origin and logical pre-conditions of science itself. As Phillip Johnson writes:

> The very idea of natural laws stems from the concept that the world is ruled by a rational lawgiver, just as it is a historical fact that modern science grew out of a worldview guided by biblical theism . . . the rationality and reliability of the scientific mind rests on the fact that the mind was designed in the image of the mind of the Creator, who made both the laws and our capacity to understand them.[109]

The Emperor's old clothes

Scientiftic explanations have variously been taken to be the best, or even the only legitimate explanations. Such a practice draws upon an imperialistic view of scientific knowledge left over from the heyday of positivism in science and logical positivism, its philosophical partner.
MICHAEL POOLE[110]

The belief that 'knowledge is identical to scientific knowledge' is not something that can be known scientifically. Rather, it is a *philosophical* dogma called 'positivism', a dogma that 'relegates religious, theological, ethical and aesthetic knowledge to the realm of mere fantasy'.[111] Alister McGrath detects an 'unstated (and outdated) philosophical positivism that seems to underlie [Dawkins'] statements on the working methods of the natural sciences'.[112] Dawkins: 'draws a line in the intellectual sand, defined by the assumptions of what seems to be an outdated scientific positivism typical of the late nineteenth century, but which is not taken with any great seriousness by the philosophers of science of the twenty-first century, who tend to regard this as an oddity of largely historical interest'.[113]

Physicist and theologian Paul Haffner explains that: 'August Comte (1798–1857), the founder of positivism, formulated the "positive philosophy," which in conjunction with the positive sciences would give the complete answer to all the questions concerning man and the cosmos. For Comte, knowledge is obtained solely from sense experience through the scientific method . . . The philosophical heir to positivism . . . is scientism.'[114] Positivism is nothing but a form of reductionism, in that it reduces knowledge to 'nothing but' *scientific* knowledge. However, such a philosophy is inconsistent with the assertion that it is true, for as J. P. Moreland asks: 'Can you give me one single scientific test that offers a definition of truth itself or that shows me that there is such a thing?'[115] The answer, of course, is 'No': 'scientism is self-refuting [because] scientism is not itself a proposition of *science*, but a proposition of *philosophy about science* to the effect that only scientific propositions are true and/or rational [and yet] scientism is itself offered as a true, rationally justified position to believe'.[116] Besides which:

> . . . some propositions believed outside science (e.g., 'red is a colour,' 'torturing babies for fun is wrong,' 'I am now thinking about science') are better justified than some believed within science (e.g., 'evolution takes place through a series of very small steps'). It is not hard to believe that many of our currently held scientific beliefs will and should be revised or abandoned in one

> hundred years, but it would be hard to see how
> the same could be said of the extra-scientific
> propositions just cited.[117]

However: 'scientism does not allow for this fact, and it is therefore to be rejected as an inadequate account of our intellectual enterprise'.[118]

R. Douglas Geivett notes that: 'More than any other predecessor, Hume was an inspiration to the empiricism-intoxicated proponents of logical positivism.'[119] According to Hume:

> When we run over our libraries, persuaded of
> these principles, what havoc must we make? If we
> take in our hand any volume, of divinity or school
> metaphysics, for instance; let us ask, Does it
> contain any abstract reasoning concerning
> quantity or number? No. Does it contain any
> experimental reasoning concerning matter of fact
> and existence? No. Commit it then to the flames:
> for it can contain nothing but sophistry and
> illusion.[120]

But if we take the volume in which Hume makes this claim in hand, what havoc must we make? Hume's statement does not contain any abstract reasoning concerning quantity or number. Nor does it contain any experimental reasoning concerning matter of fact and existence. If we wish to act consistently with Hume's positivism, we ought to commit his statement to the flames on the basis that it can contain nothing but sophistry and illusion! Positivism is both philosophically and practically self-defeating.

Comte's Hume-inspired positivistic dogma lay behind the now infamous 'verification principle' of the 'logical positivist' school of philosophy, popularized in Britain by A. J. Ayer's 1936 publication: *Language, Truth and Logic*.[121] Ayer said that the meaning of any declarative statement that was not true by definition (such as $2 + 2 = 4$) lay in its ability to be *verified* (at least in principle). To 'verify' something simply means to check it out with the senses: 'some possible sense-experience should be relevant to the determination of its truth or falsehood'.[122] For example, the statement 'This is a book' is meaningful because you can verify it by touching and reading the book, but the statement 'God exists' is (supposedly) not meaningful because you can't verify it by touching or looking at God. According to Ayer: 'If a putative proposition fails to satisfy this principle, and is not a tautology, then I hold that it is metaphysical, and that, being metaphysical, it is neither true nor false but literally senseless.'[123] For the verificationist, it isn't that the proposition 'God exists' is *false*, but that it is *meaningless*. When you stop to consider that millions of people, both believers and non-believers, have gone about using the term 'God' as if it meant something for thousands of years, the claim that it does not might appear somewhat counter-intuitive, but there you go.[124] As Ayer admitted, logical positivism actually entails that the atheist's denial of God's existence is just as meaningless as the theist's affirmation of His existence: 'If the assertion that there is a god is nonsensical, then the atheist's assertion that there is no god is equally nonsensical.'[125]

Ironically, given that the proponents of logical positivism were materialistic atheists, 'materialism would have to be rejected as nonsense by a strict interpretation of logical positivism'.[126] That matter is objectively real is neither true by definition nor something that can be verified by sense data, since it is the nature of what the senses perceive that is in question. The reality of the natural world is something intuited and assumed by scientists, not something proven by science.

Not only does Ayer's verification principle exclude all objective talk of God (theistic *or* atheistic) and matter from the realm of meaningful utterances, but all talk of objective goodness and beauty as well:

> Such aesthetic words as 'beautiful' and 'hideous' are employed, not to make statements of fact, but simply to express certain feelings and evoke a certain response. It follows, as in ethics, that there is no sense in attributing objective validity to aesthetic judgements, and no possibility of arguing about questions of value in aesthetics . . . there is nothing in aesthetics, any more than there is in ethics, to justify the view that it embodies a unique type of knowledge. It should now be clear that the only information which we can legitimately derive from the study of our aesthetic and moral experiences is information about our own mental and physical make-up.[127]

Things soon unravelled for the verification principle. Its supporters had trouble formulating it in such a way as to allow science but exclude religion, a fact demonstrating that the verification principle was a piece of self-justification built upon the desire to be rid of God, rather than the conclusion of a disinterested search for truth.[128] Moreover, it was pointed out that the principle itself was neither true by definition, nor open to verification – even in principle. The verification principle ruled itself to be meaningless!

Ayer tried to get around this problem by admitting

that the verification principle wasn't a meaningful *proposition* but saying that it was a *rule* for using language. But why pay attention to such an arbitrary rule?[129] Keith Ward reports the following conversation between Ayer and a student:

> A student once asked [Ayer] if you could make any true general statement about meaningful statements. 'Yes,' he replied. 'You can say that all meaningful statements must be verifiable in principle.' 'I see what you mean,' said the student. 'But how can I verify that?' 'I am glad you asked that,' said the philosopher. 'You cannot verify it. But it is not really a meaningful statement; it is just a rule for using language.' 'Whose rule?' 'Well, it's my rule, really. But it is a very useful one. If you use it, you will find you agree with me completely. I think that would be very useful.'[130]

If we adopt the rule, then of course we will agree with Ayer, and of course Ayer will find that useful! But he can't provide us with a *reason* for adopting his rule (certainly not one that doesn't implicitly contradict the rule he wants us to adopt). Instead, he recommends it on the basis of its usefulness. Usefulness for what? Usefulness for supporting scientism (as the verificationist's attempts to produce a version of the principle capable of drawing a line of demarcation between science on the one hand and matters of religion, morality and aesthetics on the other hand, shows). In other words, the motivation for adopting the verification rule is the self-contradictory assumption that reductionistic science is the only path to objective truth about reality. Indeed, at heart I suspect that the motivation behind verificationism is the desire to exclude God by excluding talk about God. Verificationism is a form of atheistic censorship. However, the younger generation of philosophers, like Ward, who opposed this baseless peer-pressure were well within their rights to point out that the Emperor of logical positivism had no clothes, but brazenly walked the halls of academia with nothing but a smile of fashionable popularity to disguise his self-contradicting ways.

William Lane Craig writes: 'Fifty years ago philosophers widely regarded talk about God as literally meaningless . . . but today no informed philosopher could take such a viewpoint.'[131] Ronald H. Nash agrees: 'Today, it is quite difficult to find any philosopher who is willing to claim publicly the label of logical positivism. The movement is dead and quite properly so.'[132] Ayer himself later mused that: 'I just stated [the verification rule] dogmatically and an extraordinary number of people seemed to be convinced by my assertion.'[133] By 1973 Ayer was admitting in print that: 'the verification principle . . . has never yet been adequately formulated . . . the verification principle is defective . . .'[134] Talking about logical positivism in an interview for *The Listener* in 1978, Ayer admitted, 'Nearly all of it was false.'[135] In the book *Great Thinkers on Great Questions*, Ayer says: 'Logical Positivism died a long time ago. I don't think much of *Language, Truth and Logic* is true. I think it is full of mistakes.'[136]

Dawkins doesn't go as far as Ayer did. For Dawkins, it would appear that 'God exists' is a straightforwardly false statement, rather than a meaningless one. Nevertheless, Dawkins does appear to be committed to a form of positivism, and all forms of positivism make the same basic reductionistic mistake of issuing the

self-contradictory philosophical assertion that only scientific claims deserve (significant) respect. Thus scientism self-destructs even as it attempts to de-construct
any belief that falls outside its scientistic tunnel vision.
As C. E. M. Joad concluded: 'in order that science may
be possible, there must exist more in the world than science admits to occur'.[137]

This isn't to say that science has nothing to contribute to our thinking about the really big questions –
questions like: 'Does God exist?', 'What is a human
being?', and 'What is our place in the grand scheme of
things?' But it does mean that science can't be our sole
guide to reality. And it does mean, as Bryan Appleyard
argues, that there are some legitimate questions that
science can neither answer *nor dismiss*: 'science itself
has no morality . . . and can tell us nothing about the
meaning [or] significance of our own lives'.[138] The fact
that science has nothing to say about such matters
doesn't mean that there is nothing to say about them,
only that science is the wrong tool for the job: 'The
world of science is a world from which value has been
completely eliminated. Yet . . . the intimations of the
ethical [and] consciousness have as much right to be
treated as objectively valid as the perceptions of the
external world upon which science is based . . .'[139]

Given that scientism commits such a basic logical
mistake as self-contradiction, what is its continuing
appeal to undoubtedly intelligent scientists like
Dawkins? Harvard University geneticist Richard
Lewontin, a materialist who says that science is 'the
only begetter of truth', has let the cat out of the bag:

> We take the side of science [i.e. scientism] in spite
> of the patent absurdity of some of its constructs . . .

in spite of the tolerance of the scientific community for unsubstantiated just-so stories, because we have a prior commitment to materialism. It is not that the methods and institutions of science somehow compel us to accept a material explanation of the phenomenal world, but, on the contrary, that we are forced by our a priori adherence to material causes to create an apparatus of investigation and a set of concepts that produce material explanations, no matter how counterintuitive, no matter how mystifying to the uninitiated.[140]

'Moreover', says Lewontin: 'that materialism is absolute, *for we cannot allow a Divine foot in the door* . . .'[141] Now, as Victor Reppert comments: 'a certain amount of tenacity in the face of apparently contrary evidence is necessary for anyone who holds to a worldview. However, when one insists on padlocking one's belief system against the possibility of evidence that the belief system might be in error, I am inclined to suspect that all is not well from the point of view of rationality.'[142] Moreover, in keeping God outside our scientific ring-fence, we inevitably end up keeping out everything that cannot make it past that same dogmatic barrier. And that includes reason, goodness, beauty, and meaning.

Conclusion

Thus far we have analyzed the ways in which the realities of goodness and rationality subvert the worldview of Dawkins' naturalistic nihilism. It's time we turned to beauty, for as C. S. Lewis wrote:

. . . if our minds are totally alien to reality then all

our thoughts, including this thought, are worthless. We must, then, grant logic to reality; we must, if we are to have moral standards, grant it moral standards too. And there is really no reason why we should not do the same about standards of beauty. There is no reason why our reaction to a beautiful landscape should not be the response . . . to a something that is really there. The idea of a wholly mindless and valueless universe has to be abandoned at one point – i.e. as regards logic: after that, there is no telling at how many other points it will be defeated nor how great the reversal of our nineteenth-century philosophy must finally be.[143]

[1] Baggini, Julian and Stangroom, Jeremy, *What Philosophers Think* (London: Continuum, 2003), p.6.

[2] Dawkins, Richard, *The Blind Watchmaker* (London: Penguin, 1988), p.13.

[3] Hasker, William, 'How Not To Be A Reductivist', *PCID*, 2.3.5, October 2003 at www.iscid.org/papers/Hasker_NonReductivism_103103.pdf

[4] *ibid.*

[5] Dawkins, Richard and Pinker, Steven, 'Is Science Killing the Soul?' at www.edge.org/3rd_culture/dawkins_pinker/debate_p11.html

[6] Moreland, J. P. and Craig, William Lane, *Philosophical Foundations For A Christian Worldview* (Downers Grove: IVP, 2003), p.199.

[7] Dawkins, *op. cit.*, p.151, my emphasis.

[8] Dawkins, Richard, 'Genes and Determinism', in Julian Baggini and Jeremy Stangroom (eds), *What Philosophers Think* (London: Continuum, 2003), p.51.

[9] Moser, Paul K. and Yandell, David, 'Farewell to philosophical naturalism', in William Lane Craig and J. P. Moreland (eds), *Naturalism: A critical analysis* (London: Routledge, 2001), p.3.

[10] *ibid.*, p.3.

[11] 'Nick Pollard talks to Dr. Richard Dawkins' at www.damaris.org/content/content.php?type=5&id=102

[12] Hasker, *op. cit.*

[13] Dawkins and Pinker, 'Is Science Killing the Soul?', *op. cit.*

[14] C. S. Lewis, 'The Empty Universe', in *Present Concerns* (London: Fount, 1991), p.81.

[15] *ibid.*, p.81.

[16] *ibid.*, p.83.

[17] *ibid.*, p.85.

[18] Purtill, Richard, *Thinking About Religion* (Longman, 1978), p.6.

[19] *ibid.*, p.10.

[20] Hasker, *op. cit.*

[21] Dembski, William A., 'Kurzweil's Impoverished Spirituality', in *Are We Spiritual Machines?* (Discovery Institute, 2002), p.107.

[22] Reppert, Victor, 'Several Formulations of the Argument from Reason', *Philosophia Christi*, Volume 5, Number 1, 2003, p.10-11.

[23] Dembski, *op. cit.*, p.108.

[24] *ibid.*, p.108.

[25] Hasker, William, *The Emergent Self* (Cornell University Press, 1999), p.59.

[26] Lovell, Steven, 'C.S. Lewis' Case Against Naturalism' at http://myweb. tiscali.co.uk/cslphilos/CSLnat.htm

[27] Reppert, Victor, *C.S. Lewis's Dangerous Idea* (Downers Grove: IVP, 2003), p.51.

[28] Russell, Bertrand, 'What I Believe', in *Why I Am Not A Christian* (London: Routledge, 1996), p.42, 47.

[29] Hasker, 'How Not To Be A Reductivist', *op. cit.*

[30] Churchland, Paul M., *Matter and Consciousness* (MIT Press, 1988), p.21.

[31] Eccles, John and Popper, Karl, *The Self and Its Brain* (New York: Springer-Verlag, 1977), p.546, quoted by Roger Forster and Paul Marston, *Reason & Faith* (Eastborne: Monarch, 1989), p.183.

[32] 'Lewis himself encountered the Argument from Reason in conversations with Owen Barfield, became persuaded that the argument was a good one, and in consequence rejected the naturalistic realism he had hitherto accepted . . .' – Victor Reppert, 'Some Supernatural Reasons Why My Critics Are Wrong', *Philosophia Christi*, Volume 3, Number 1, 2003, p.77.

[33] Lewis, C. S., *Miracles* (London: Fount, 1998), p.11.

[34] *ibid.*, p.14.

[35] Morris, Thomas V., *Francis Schaeffer's Apologetics: A Critique* (Chicago: Moody Press, 1976), p.42.

[36] Lewis, *op. cit.*, p.14.

[37] *ibid.*

[38] *ibid.*, p.15.

[39] *ibid.*

[4] *ibid.*

[41] *ibid.*, p.15-20.

[42] Lewis, *op. cit.*, p.26.

[43] Hasker, *op. cit.*, p.71.

[44] Lewis, C. S., 'Religion Without Dogma?', in *Timeless at Heart* (London: Fount, 1991), p.92.

[45] Hasker, *op. cit.*, p.67-68.

[46] 'Dr. Reppert on the "Argument from Reason"' at http://go.qci.tripod.com/ Reppert-interview.htm

[47] Thanks to Angus Mengue for correspondence on this issue.

[48] Reppert, 'Several Formulations of the Argument from Reason', *op. cit.*, p.24.

[49] *ibid.*, p.23.

[50] Madell, Geoffrey, *Mind and Materialism* (Edinburgh University Press, 1988), p.11.

[51] Lewis, *op. cit.*, p.16.

[52] *ibid.*

[53] Moreland, J. P., *Scaling the Secular City* (Grand Rapids: Baker, 1987), p.87.

[54] Lewis, C. S., 'De Futilitate', *Christian Reflections* (London: Fount, 1991), p.87-88.

[55] Lewis, C. S., *The Discarded Image* (Cambridge University Press, 1964), p.165-166.

[56] Willard, Dallas, 'Knowledge and Naturalism', in William Lane Craig and J. P. Moreland (eds), *Naturalism: A critical analysis* (London: Routledge, 2001), p.39.

[57] Searle, John, *The Rediscovery of the Mind* (Cambridge: MIT Press, 1992), p.51.

[58] Moreland, *op. cit.*, p.96.

[59] Willard, *op. cit.*, p.44.

[60] Moreland, *op. cit.*, p.93.

[61] *ibid.*

[62] Clark, Stephen R. L., *God, Religion and Reality* (SPCK, 1998), p.98.

[63] Clark, Stephen R. L., *From Athens to Jerusalem* (Oxford University Press, 1984), p.96-97.

[64] Geach, Peter, *The Virtues* (Cambridge University Press, 1977), p.52.

[65] Lewis, *op. cit.*, p.18.

[66] Dawkins, *The Blind Watchmaker* (Penguin, 1990), p.10.

[67] Hasker, 'How Not To Be A Reductivist', *op. cit.*

[68] Reppert, *C.S. Lewis's Dangerous Idea*, *op. cit.*, p.87, 101.

[69] *ibid.*, p.53.

[70] Lewis, *Miracles*, *op. cit.*, p.28.

[71] *ibid.*

[72] *ibid.*, p.29.

[73] Moreland, *op. cit.*, p.103.

[74] Reppert, *op. cit.*, p.104.

[75] O'Hear, Antony, *Philosophy* (London:: New Century, 2001), p.125.

[76] Lewis, 'Religion Without Dogma?', *op. cit.*, p.93.

[77] Taylor, Richard, *Metaphysics* (Englewood Cliffs, New Jersey: Prentice Hall, 1974).

[78] *ibid.*

[79] *ibid.*

[80] Nagel, Thomas, *The Last Word* (New York: Oxford University Press, 1997), p.130.

[81] Dawkins, Richard, *Sunday Telegraph*, 18 October 1998.

[82] Dawkins, Richard, *A Devil's Chaplain*, (London: Weidenfeld & Nicolson, 2003), p.13.

[83] Flew, Anthony, 'Determinism and Validity Again', *The Rationalist Annual*, 1958, p.47.

[84] Stitch, Stephen, 'Evolution and Rationality', in *The Fragmentation of Reason* (Cambridge: MIT Press, 1990), p.56.

[85] Plantinga, Alvin, *Warranted Christian Belief* (New York: Oxford University Press, 2000), p.235.

[86] Rorty, Richard, 'Untruth and Consequences' in *The New Republic*, 31 July 1995, p.36.

[87] Charles Darwin, letter to William Graham, 3 July 1881, in *The Life and Letters of Charles Darwin*, Francis Darwin (ed.), (University Press of the Pacific, 2001).

[88] Moreland, *op. cit.*, p.50.

[89] Clark, *Reason, Religion and God, op. cit.*, p.99.

[90] *ibid.*, p.100.

[91] Hasker, *op. cit.*, p.76.

[92] Lewis, *Miracles, op. cit.*, p.18, 20-21.

[93] Hasker, *op. cit.*, p.78.

[94] *ibid.* p.79, 197.

[95] Reppert, 'Several Formulations of the Argument from Reason', *op. cit.*, p.32.

[96] *ibid.*

[97] Koons, Robert C., 'Science and Theism', in Paul Copan and Paul K. Moser (eds), *The Rationality of Theism* (London: Routledge, 2003), p.83.

[98] Russell, Bertrand, 'What I Believe', in *Why I Am Not A Christian* (London: Routledge, 1996), p.42, 47.

[99] Lewis, *Miracles, op. cit.*, p.23, 25.

[100] *ibid.*, p.23.

[101] *ibid.*, p.43.

[102] O'Hear, Anthony, *Philosophy* (London: Continuum, 2001), p.13.

[103] Lewis, 'Religion Without Dogma?', *op. cit.*, p.95.

[104] Pierce, C. S., quoted by Hasker, 'How Not To Be A Reductivist', *op. cit.*

[105] Joad, C. E. M., *Guide to Philosophy* (London: Victor Gollancz, 1946), p.565.

[106] Moreland, J. P., *Love Your God With All Your Mind* (Colorado Springs: NavPress, 1997), p.33.

[107] Ward, Keith, *op. cit.*, p.11-12.

[108] Joad, *op. cit.*, p.571.

[109] Johnson, Phillip E., 'The Intelligent Design Movement' in William A. Dembski and James M. Kushner (eds), *Signs of Intelligence: Understanding Intelligent Design* (Grand Rapids, Brazos, 2001), p.36-37.

[110] Poole, Michael, 'Explaining or Explaining Away?', *A Guide to Science and Belief* (Lion Manual) (Lion Publishing, 1997).

[111] Pope John Paul II, Encyclical Letter *Fides et Ratio* 88.

[112] McGrath, *op. cit.*, p.162-163.

[113] *ibid.*, p.163.

[114] Haffner, Paul, *The Mystery of Reason* (Leominster: Gracewing, 2001), p.14.

[115] Moreland, *op. cit.*, p.149.

[116] *ibid.*, p.146.

[117] Moreland, J. P., 'Science and Theology', in *Evangelical Dictionary of Theology*, second edition, (Baker, 2001), p.1072.

[118] Moreland, *Love God With All Your Mind, op. cit.*, p.147.

[119] Geivett, R. Douglas, 'The Evidential Value of Religious Experience', in *The Rationality of Theism, op. cit.*, p.200.

[120] Hume, David, quoted by H. D. Lewis, *Philosophy of Religion* (London: The English Universities Press, 1965) p. 62-63.

[121] Ayer, A. J., *Language, Truth and Logic* (London: Victor Gollancz, 1936).

[122] *ibid.*, p.9.

[123] *ibid.*

[124] 'The very fact that [the verification principle] denied meaning to statements which many people regarded as meaningful could be taken as evidence that it was false.' – A. J. Ayer, *The Central Questions of Philosophy* (London: Penguin, 1973), p.34.

[125] *ibid.*, p.175.

[126] Reppert, *C.S. Lewis's Dangerous Idea, op. cit.*, p.20.

[127] Ayer, *op. cit.*, p.118-119.

[128] Many religious claims are verifiable either in fact (e.g. Jesus' resurrection is a historically investigable occurrence) or in principle (e.g. John Hick noted that the existence of heaven was *in principle* verifiable: after death). One might also think that there is a sound version (or elaboration) of the ontological argument for God that proves his existence as a matter of definition (e.g. 'God' means 'the greatest possible being'. The concept of 'the greatest possible being' includes having necessary existence, that is, existing if its existence is possible. It is possible that God exists. Therefore, God exists.) cf. C. Stephen Evans, *Philosophy of Religion* (Leicester: IVP, 1985).

[129] 'why should anyone follow the prescription if its implications were not to his taste?' – A. J. Ayer, *The Central Questions of Philosophy*, (London: Penguin, 1973), p.34.

[130] Ward, Keith, *God: A Guide for the Perplexed* (Oxford: OneWorld, 2002), p.184.

[131] Craig, William Lane, 'Advice to Christian Apologists' at www.baptist pastors.org.au/Mosaic/Spring_Summer_2002/lane_advice_to_apologists.htm

[132] Nash, Ronald H., *Faith and Reason* (Zondervan, 1988), p.53.

[133] Ayer, quoted by Keith Ward, *The Turn of the Tide* (London: BBC Publications, 1986), p.59.

[134] Ayer, A. J., *The Central Questions of Philosophy* (London: Penguin, 1973), p.22-34.

[135] Ayer, A. J., *The Listener*, 2 March 1978.

[136] Ayer, A. J., in Roy Abraham Vargese (ed.), *Great Thinkers on Great Questions* (Oxford: OneWorld, 1998), p.49.

[137] Joad, *op. cit.*, p.566.

[138] Appleyard, Bryan, *Understanding The Present* (London: Picador, 1993), p.xii.

[139] Joad, *op. cit.*, p.567-568.

[140] Lewontin, Richard, 'Billions and Billions of Demons', *New York Review of Books*, January 9, 1997.

[141] *ibid.*, my italics.

[142] Reppert, *op. cit.*, p.126.

[143] Lewis, C. S., 'De Futilitate', *Christian Reflections* (London: Fount, 1991), p.96-97.

CHAPTER 6

Unweaving Beauty

Writing in the preface of his 2003 album *Out There*, prog-rock keyboard maestro Rick Wakeman explains: 'I have long held the belief that whilst we readily accept the five senses . . . the true missing sense is that of music. I firmly believe that the origins of all music do not begin in this world as we understand it, but are subconsciously taken from . . . somewhere "Out There" . . .' Wakeman's comments place him in a long tradition of artists who experience the creative process as originating from contact with objective aesthetic realities that inform and constrain their own expression, and as being empowered by this inspiration in a way that cannot be explained away as nothing but the outcome of naturalistic processes. Wakeman testifies that: 'Being a confirmed Christian I also believe that music is very much a gift from God . . . to be enjoyed, developed and shared amongst all races, religions and creeds.'

. . . maybe we have too quickly abandoned the sense of our forefathers that beauty, truth and the good are indissolubly related, so that beauty well deserves its former status as the aesthetic value par excellence.
DAVID E. COOPER[1]

One way or another, directly and indirectly, Richard Dawkins talks a lot about beauty. In an article for the *Telegraph* Dawkins affirmed that: 'The real world, properly understood in the scientific way, is deeply beautiful and unfailingly interesting.'[2] In *Unweaving the Rainbow* he says:

. . . the urge to know more about the universe seems to me irresistible, and I cannot imagine that

anybody of truly poetic sensibility could disagree.
I am ironically amused by how much of what we
have discovered so far is a direct extrapolation of
unweaving the rainbow. And the poetic beauty of
what that unweaving has now revealed, from the
nature of the stars to the expansion of the
universe, could not fail to catch the imagination of
Keats; would be bound to send Coleridge into a
frenzied reverie . . . [3]

However, Dawkins pays little if any attention to unweaving beauty itself (that is, to understanding the nature of beauty and considering its metaphysical implications).[4] I'd like to spend this chapter doing just that; for unweaving the beauty of the rainbow (as opposed to unweaving the physics of the rainbow) subverts Dawkins' whole attempt to offer a poetic defence of scientism. It will also help us to appreciate far more important truths about the rainbow than physics can reveal.

According to Thomas Dubay: 'science and theology agree on the objectivity of beauty. While there is a subjective readiness in us, greater or lesser, for perceiving the splendid, both disciplines assume and insist that beauty is not merely in the eye of the beholder; it is primarily something "out there".'[5] Not everyone would agree. The Greek philosopher Protagoras wrote that: 'Man is the measure of all things; of those things that are, that they are; of those things that are not, that they are not.'[6] However, it is only recently, with the 'death of God', that Protagoras' relativism has become culturally influential. C. E. M. Joad explains:

The current view of values is that they are
subjective. To say 'this is good' or 'this is
beautiful' means, on this view, that I, or most

people who have ever lived, or most of those who have the knowledge and experience which entitles them to pass judgement, or most of the governing classes of the community to which I belong, approve of it or appreciate it or derive enjoyment from it. Thus good, bad, beautiful, ugly (and, presumably, true, false) are relational qualities, that is to say, they are related to human beings. They are also psychological in that they are defined with reference to mental states. It follows that if there were no human minds and no feelings, therefore, of appreciation, approval and the reverse, nothing would be good, bad, beautiful, ugly, true or false.[7]

And as Douglas Groothuis warns: 'If there is no beauty beyond the eye of the beholder, art becomes merely a tool for social influence, political power and personal expression; the category of obscenity is as obsolete as the ideal of beauty.'[8]

C. S. Lewis, in *The Abolition of Man*, relates how the authors of an English textbook, whom he names 'Gaius' and 'Titus', comment upon a story about the poet Coleridge and a waterfall. Imagine the scene, as the water majestically cascades over the precipice, plunging into the still waters below, sparkling in the sunlight. Perhaps the waterfall sustains a fine, airy mist that catches the sun and produces a rainbow. Two tourists were present besides Coleridge: one called the waterfall 'sublime',[9] the other said it was 'pretty'. Coleridge 'mentally endorsed the first judgement and rejected the second with disgust'.[10] Gaius and Titus comment:

When the man said *This is sublime*, he appeared to be making a remark about the waterfall . . .

> Actually . . . he was not making a remark about
> the waterfall, but a remark about his own feelings.
> What he was saying was really *I have feelings
> associated in my mind with the word
> 'Sublime'*, or shortly, *I have sublime feelings*.[11]

According to Gaius and Titus, this confusion is common: 'We appear to be saying something very important about something: and actually we are only saying something about our own feelings.'[12] Hence beauty is reduced to nothing but subjective feelings.

I suspect that Dawkins would agree with Gaius and Titus. He certainly thinks this way when it comes to moral values, as revealed in an interview with the *Skeptic* magazine:

> **Skeptic:** Can we turn to evolution to answer not
> what is, but what ought to be?
> **Dawkins:** I'd rather not do that . . . In my opinion,
> a society run along 'evolutionary' lines would not
> be a very nice society in which to live . . .
> **Skeptic:** But then isn't what we ought to do (as
> David Hume argued a long time ago) just a matter
> of preference and choice, custom and habit?
> **Dawkins:** I think that's very likely true . . .
> **Skeptic:** So once again the discussion goes back
> to how do you determine whether something is
> good or not, other than by just your personal
> choice?
> **Dawkins:** I don't even try.[13]

J. L. Mackie was clear that the claim that values are subjective includes not only moral goodness, but 'nonmoral values, notably aesthetic ones, beauty and various kinds of aesthetic merit [for] clearly much the same considerations apply to aesthetic and to moral values, and there would be at least some initial implausibility in a view that gave the one a different status from the other'.[14] Indeed, in an interview with Keith Ward, Dawkins admitted that: 'My view, if you think about its aesthetic . . . connotations, is a bleak and cold one.'[15] As theologian Colin E. Gunton muses: 'if only science tells us the truth, what remains to art? A doctrine of the meaninglessness of material particulars combines with scientism to deprive the artistic object of its inherent meaning and substantiality.'[16] In *River out of Eden* Dawkins announces that 'Beauty is not an absolute virtue in itself.'[17] Ward comments: 'I do not think he really means it, since he places so much emphasis on simplicity and beauty in scientific theories that he must regard it as a virtue. However . . . One of the most destructive ploys of atheism is to suggest that facts are there, in the outside world, while values are just subjective reactions, which vary from one person to another, matters of personal taste.'[18] It seems that Dawkins, like Gaius and Titus and like Mackie, has adopted a philosophy of value represented by the sceptical Scottish philosopher David Hume (mentioned in the *Skeptic*'s interview), who argued that:

All sentiment is right; because sentiment has a reference to nothing beyond itself, and is always right, whenever a man is conscious of it. But all determinations of the understanding are not right; because they have a reference to something beyond themselves, to wit, a real matter of fact; and are not always conformable to that standard . . . Beauty is no quality in things themselves: it exists merely in the mind which contemplates them; and each mind perceives a different beauty.[19]

For Hume: 'beauty is nothing but a form which produces pleasure'.[20] So, if masochistic acts produce in me a feeling of aesthetic pleasure, then masochism is 'beautiful', *for me*. Beauty depends upon *my* pleasure, and is thus relative to me as a subject. No aesthetic judgements can be false, because no one can be mistaken about their own subjective aesthetic reactions. Beauty 'does not reside in any of the things of nature, but only in our own mind'.[21] This is the common, subjective view of beauty that I think is very ugly. The end result of this view, as Lewis saw, is that: 'the emotion, thus considered by itself, cannot be either in agreement or disagreement with reason . . . the world of facts, without one trace of value, and the world of feelings, without one trace of truth or falsehood, justice or injustice, confront each other, and no rapprochement is possible'.[22]

Beauty strikes back

Does the emerald lose its beauty for lack of admiration?
MARCUS AURELIUS

To me, as to Lewis, the theory of value adopted by Hume, Gaius, Titus and Dawkins looks very much like putting the cart before the horse. After all, aesthetic value, like moral value, is experienced as a reality beyond ourselves that impinges upon us: 'Beauty belongs, *prima facie*, to things. It is not emotions which are beautiful but that which arouses them.'[23] This objective view of beauty represents the common sense presumption of human tradition: 'in *pre-modern* aesthetics . . . aesthetic objects and values are generally taken to be prior, with aesthetic responses and attitudes being held to be posterior to and explicable in terms of these . . .'[24]

In aesthetic experience we perceive something that draws us towards itself as an end rather than as a means. This pleasurable sense of 'being drawn' is derived from the perception of the object as one that can be appreciated *for its own sake*. What sort of pleasure are we considering here? Plotinus put the matter well when he observed that: 'These experiences must occur whenever there is contact with any sort of beautiful thing, wonder and a shock of delight and longing and passion and a happy excitement.'[25] The subjectivist confuses their pleasurable experience of beauty with the beauty that they experience as pleasurable. As Augustine wrote: 'If I were to ask whether things are beautiful because they give pleasure, or give pleasure because they are beautiful, I have no doubt that I will be given the answer that they give pleasure because they are beautiful.'[26] How times have changed. Norman L. Geisler reckons that nowadays belief in 'the relativity of beauty may be more widespread than the relativity of truth or the relativity of morality'.[27] Jerry Solomon concurs, noting that 'one of the most prevalent ways of approaching art is to simply say that "beauty is in the eye (or ear) of the beholder"'.[28] However, while the pleasurable *experience* of beauty is obviously in the eye (or ear) of the beholder, it hardly follows that the beauty thus experienced is similarly subjective. Indeed, like our experience of moral value, our aesthetic experience appears, *prima facie*, to have an objective referent: 'Just as my experience of roundness when I see an orange is not itself round, my experience of aesthetic excellence has an objective reference beyond the experience itself,' observes Douglas Groothuis, 'To think otherwise is to fundamentally confuse the perceiving subject with the perceived object.'[29] Mortimer J. Adler made a crucial distinction when he wrote that: 'admirable beauty is objectively present, but enjoyable beauty is in the eye of the beholder, who gets pleasure from beholding it'.[30] As Groothuis puts it: 'Beauty is not *only* in the eye of the beholder.'[31]

The objectivity of admirable beauty

> . . . *whatever is true, whatever is honourable,*
> *whatever is right, whatever is pure, whatever is*
> *lovely, whatever is of good repute, if there is any*
> *excellence and if anything worthy of praise, let*
> *your mind dwell on these things.*
> PAUL (PHILIPPIANS 4:8)

Philosopher E. R. Emmet, who was a subjectivist, accepted that:

There is not much doubt that the view [of beauty] that has been most strongly held by philosophers in the past, from Plato onwards, has been the objective one – that is that beauty in a sense is something that is there, that whether an object is beautiful or not is a matter of fact and not a matter of opinion or taste, and that value judgements about beauty are true or false, right or wrong.[32]

To believe in objective beauty is to be philosophically orthodox, and despite the current fashion for abandoning this orthodoxy, there are many recent and contemporary philosophers who hold to the objectivity of beauty.

Lewis began his counterattack on the subjective position propagated by Gaius and Titus by pointing out that: 'the man who says *This is sublime* cannot mean *I have sublime feelings* . . . The feelings which make a man call an object sublime are not sublime feelings, but feelings of veneration.'[33] The correct 'translation' of the tourist's assertion, if a translation must take place, would be 'I have humble feelings.'[34] Otherwise we would end up translating assertions such as 'You are contemptible', as 'I have contemptible feelings', which is ludicrous.

If a humble feeling of veneration prompts Coleridge to agree that the waterfall is sublime, we may ask *whether that feeling was an appropriate response to its object*. In other words, aesthetic delight may be appropriate or inappropriate relative *not to the person doing the appreciating*, but *to the nature of the object being appreciated*. As Lewis explained:

> Until quite modern times all . . . men believed the universe to be such that certain emotional reactions on our part could be congruous or incongruous to it – believed, in fact, that objects did not merely receive, but could merit, our approval or disapproval . . . The reason why Coleridge agreed with the tourist who called the cataract sublime and disagreed with the one who called it pretty was of course that he believed inanimate nature to be such that certain responses could be more 'just' or 'appropriate' to it than others . . . the man who called the cataract sublime was not intending simply to describe his own emotions about it: he was also claiming that the object was one which merited those emotions.[35]

Lewis draws upon Augustine's definition of virtue as *ordo amoris* or 'appropriate love': 'the ordinate condition of the affections in which every object is accorded that kind and degree of love which is appropriate to it'.[36] Hence he says that: 'because our approvals and disapprovals are thus recognitions of objective value or responses to an objective order, therefore emotional states can be in harmony with reason . . . or out of harmony with reason . . .'[37]

Whether the appreciated fact is objective (e.g. a rainbow) or subjective (e.g. a theory about rainbows in Newton's mind), its intrinsic admirability, or lack of admirability (and the moral merit attached to appreciating it) are matters of objective fact. Therefore, beauty is objective: 'To say that the cataract is sublime means saying that our emotion of humility is appropriate or ordinate to the reality, and thus to speak of something else besides the emotion . . .'[38]

Subjectivism about beauty is counter-intuitive

If you are used to the assumption that beauty is subjective, it might appear counter-intuitive to be told that the subjective theory of beauty is counter-intuitive. However, I hope that a few thought experiments might help us to uncover some deeply held intuitions about beauty that are at odds with the assumption of subjectivity. Consider the following amusing snatch of dialogue by Peter Kreeft:

> *Sal:* . . . Look at that beautiful sunset!
> *Chris:* Oh! Thanks, Sal.
> *Sal:* Thanks for the sunset? Who do you think I am, God? I didn't make the sunset.
> *Chris:* No, I mean to thank you for calling my

attention to it. And thanks to God for making it.

Sal: . . . I don't need your God; I have science to explain everything . . .

Chris: Since when is 'beautiful' a scientific term?

Sal: It isn't.

Chris: But you just called the sunset beautiful. You're not being scientific.

Sal: . . . I didn't really mean it.

Chris: You mean the sunset isn't really beautiful?

Sal: Right. It's just a dance of molecules. The beauty isn't really in it. It's in us, in our feelings.

Chris: The beauty is in you, not the sunset?

Sal: Yes.

Chris: But that's silly. You're not that beautiful. The sunset is!

Sal: I mean the beauty is in my feelings, not in my face.

Chris: You *felt* beautiful when you looked at the sunset?

Sal: No. I'm *not* that beautiful. But I feel the sunset is.

Chris: Then according to your feelings, the sunset really is beautiful, there really is beauty out there?

Sal: According to my feelings, yes. But my feelings are wrong. There's no real beauty out there. How can feelings tell you what the real world out there is like?

Chris: Why not? Why can't feelings be just as true as reasoning?

Sal: . . . That's just plain silly.

Chris: Why can't feelings be true?

Sal: I guess I don't know, I feel it.

Chris: And that feeling – is it true?[39]

This dialogue plays on the awkward way in which the subjective theory of beauty says that beauty is just a matter of our feelings, even as our feelings tell us that beauty is a matter of the nature of those things outside of ourselves that we appreciate as beautiful: 'an objectivist account of our aesthetic judgements explains our experience of beauty, ugliness, and other aesthetic properties in a way the subjectivist [account] cannot'.[40] Which should we trust, our feelings about beauty or the subjective theory of beauty? We can't do both: 'when we call a sunset beautiful,' admits Anthony O'Hear, 'we unreflectively take ourselves to be speaking of the sunset and its properties. We do not, as Hume [and his followers] maintain, take ourselves to be speaking about nothing in the object, or to be merely gilding and staining it with projected sentiment . . .'[41] As Richard Swinburne argues:

> When people admire a beautiful work of art, they are not admiring the effect of the work on their consciousness; they do not say 'This is a wonderful painting because it produces these feelings in me and other people who look at it.' Rather, it is because they believe that it has some beautiful feature, which they have been fortunate to notice, that it does produce the *appropriate* feeling. The . . . painting is beautiful in itself . . . it has beauty which it would still have even if no one has the right sensory equipment to notice it. Of course, it is also good that people admire what is beautiful; but the beauty of the beautiful does not depend upon being recognized. How could it? For recognition of beauty, as of anything else, depends upon the existence of the feature before and

independently of being recognized.[42]

Aesthetician Oswald Hanfling makes a similar point:

> In a book about the development of our planet in past ages, we may read that long ago, before the appearance of any 'intelligent minds' on earth, such and such a region, now arid desert, was full of beautiful plants. This would strike us as an interesting and by no means unintelligible statement . . . on [Hume's view] such statements . . . must be nonsensical. They would be like talking about a world in which there is pleasure, but no beings capable of feeling pleasure. Such talk would indeed be 'absurd and contradictory'. But this is not so in the case of beauty.[43]

C. E. M. Joad employed an analogous thought experiment to highlight the presupposition 'that beauty is better than ugliness, even if there is nobody to enjoy it'[44]:

> Let us suppose that all people in the world are abolished but one. Let the sole survivor of humanity . . . be confronted with the Sistine Madonna of Raphael. This picture, it will be said by subjectivists, is still beautiful because it is being appreciated. Suppose . . . that in the midst of the last man's contemplation of the picture he too is abolished. Has any alteration occurred in the picture? Has it experienced any change? Has in fact anything *been done to* it? The only change that has occurred is that it has ceased to be appreciated. Does it, therefore, automatically cease to be beautiful? Those who hold the subjectivist position must maintain that it does . . .[45]

But this subjectivist answer, says Joad, 'requires a certain amount of intellectual hardihood . . . We do, that is to say, believe in our hearts that beauty is better than ugliness, even if there is nobody to enjoy it,'[46] and hence: 'the view that [our appreciation of beauty] is the reflection of some factor in the nature of things to which the human mind responds is by no means lightly to be dismissed'.[47]

The analogy between ethics and aesthetics

> . . . *clearly much the same considerations apply to aesthetic and to moral values, and there would be at least some initial implausibility in a view that gave the one a different status from the other.*
> J. L. MACKIE[48]

Ethics and aesthetics go hand in hand because goodness is a beautiful thing and beauty is a good thing. Albertus Magnus wrote that, 'Beauty calls things to it because it is an end and a good.'[49] Aquinas thought of the beautiful: 'as a way in which the good makes itself manifest',[50] and wrote that 'anyone who desires the good, by that very fact desires the beautiful'.[51] Therefore, if moral values are objective, it would be reasonable to think that aesthetic values are likewise objective. Hence we can argue for the objectivity of beauty by analogy with the objectivity of morality.

The commander of the Belsen concentration camp, observing the Holocaust, may have found himself aesthetically pleased by what he perceived – somewhat, we may suppose, after the manner of a pyromaniac who derives pleasure from burning things. However, I think most people would agree that the Holocaust was not a beautiful event, because (to put it mildly) it was not a good thing. Indeed, most people would agree that the sight of helpless and innocent victims being systematically slaughtered must be an ugly affair, because it is an evil affair. Just as Hitler may reasonably be supposed to have approved of the Holocaust as a good thing, while yet leaving us with the intuition that the Holocaust was a bad thing, so the fact that someone (or some community) finds something 'pleasing when perceived' leaves us with the intuition that this fact alone cannot settle the matter of whether the thing in question really is beautiful or not. I therefore agree with Mortimer J. Adler when he encourages us to recognize that, 'in addition to the enjoyable, there is the admirable',[52] that the enjoyable is not necessarily admirable, the pleasant not always beautiful. So we see that the concept of aesthetic value is inextricably linked to the concept of moral value, and the objectivity of the one guarantees the objectivity of the other. To return to the Belsen commander's supposed approval of the Holocaust, I suggest that, whether moral or aesthetic, this approval says little about the truth of his assertions that the Holocaust is good or beautiful. While aesthetic utterances certainly have a subjective aspect, assertions of the type 'rainbows are beautiful' are matters of objective truth or falsehood. This seems to me to be the most natural and common sense analysis of such utterances, an analysis that I do not believe we should attempt to 'explain away'. Instead, I think we should agree with Norman L. Geisler that: 'Beauty is that which is admirable for its own sake . . . it has intrinsic admirability . . .'[53]

Aesthetic disagreements count for objectivity

Anthony O'Hear observes:

> . . . it is often said that taste is not to be argued

about, and that matters of taste simply reflect personal preference . . . But that is surely false. The arguments we all engage in about the virtues of competing tastes are among the fiercest and most bitterly contested. We know, deep down, that these things do matter. They are important in themselves.[54]

The prime reason given for doubting the objectivity of beauty is that people differ in what they find to be aesthetically pleasing in their subjective experience. How, it is asked, can beauty be an objective quality when people obviously disagree about what is and is not beautiful? This objection parallels the common objection advanced against objective moral values that such values must be subjective because different people hold different moral beliefs. However, the moral objectivist may accept that different people and cultures have different moral *beliefs*, without needing to capitulate over the existence of objective moral *values*. If the objection from differing opinions can be met with regards to moral value, then parallel responses will prevail in the case of aesthetic value.

Some people may simply be wrong about what the standard of morality actually is, so the fact that not everyone agrees about what is right and wrong does not prove that there is no ultimate standard. Besides, we are not here concerned with the recognition of particular ethical rules (e.g. 'Fairness is a good thing'), but with the general and objective distinction between right and wrong. Furthermore, the idea that cultures differ about values does not carry all that much factual weight, for 'No culture ever existed which taught a totally different set of values.'[55]

Indeed, that people disagree about ethics indicates, not that moral values are subjective, but that they are objective. People disagree about matters of objective truth, such as whether moral values are objective or not. When it comes to subjective truths, people don't disagree. (Recall our discussion of my subjective preference for Pepsi Cola over Coca Cola.) The fact that people disagree somewhat about moral values, which is advanced as evidence for the subjectivity of morality, is therefore actually evidence that moral values are objective. To the parallel argument as advanced against the objectivity of aesthetic values we can make parallel responses. Differing subjective opinions about aesthetic matters does not prove that aesthetic assertions have no objective content. As W. R. Sorley noted: 'We must distinguish two things: value and the consciousness of value. They do not necessarily go together.'[56]

No one disagrees with the assertion that rainbows are beautiful, and says instead that they are ugly. In other words, although aesthetic disagreements are real and count in favour of regarding beauty as objective, such disagreement is not as widespread or divergent as the critic assumes. As philosopher Colin Lyas argues:

> . . . it is not clear that there is massive disagreement in aesthetic judgements. When haste, ignorance, prejudice, inexperience and the like are discounted what is striking is the amount of agreement there is about what is good and great in art. Where there is disagreement it is sometimes patchy. Two people may agree on the greatness of Mozart, Beethoven and Shakespeare but disagree over Mahler. Even here the way this is put is significant: one is likely to say 'I cannot

see what you see in Mahler.' This language . . .
suggests that there may be something to be seen,
but that one is *blind* towards it. And this blindness
may be overcome by further experience and
discussion . . . It is . . . possible to overestimate
the amount of disagreement when seeking to show
that aesthetic judgement is less objective than our
ordinary perceptual judgements. Even if it were
not . . . the mere fact of disagreement shows
nothing . . . no more than the fact that a colour-
blind man makes a different claim about the traffic
lights from a fully-sighted man shows anything
about the subjectivity of colour perception.[57]

Discovering 'beauties unthought of now'

Twelve-tone piano music has never been 'my cup of
tea', and perhaps it never will be. This fact is quite consistent with my belief that there is probably something
of intrinsic aesthetic value, and so appreciability, within at least some twelve-tone piano music. There is no
contradiction in my saying that twelve-tone piano music
has intrinsic admirability, and is therefore objectively
beautiful, but that I personally don't 'get it'. Other people clearly find aesthetic pleasure in this music when
they perceive it, and I have no reason to doubt that their
appreciation is ordinate (morally proper), or based
upon a mistaken belief that this music possesses qualities which it is morally good to appreciate. I therefore
have reason to believe that at least some twelve-tone
piano music is beautiful, and this in no way contradicts
the fact that this music gives me no aesthetic pleasure;
or, to put it another way, that I do not find such music
to be beautiful *within my own subjective experience*.

A fascinating illustration of the distinction between acknowledged objective beauty and subjective 'enjoyed beauty' comes from Sir Francis Younghusband, who, moved by the scenery of Kashmir, wrote that:

> There came to me this thought . . . why the scene should so influence me and yet make no impression on the men about me . . . Clearly it is not the eye but the soul that sees. But then comes the still further reflection: what may there not be staring me straight in the face which I am blind to as the Kashmire stags are to the beauties amidst they spend their entire lives? The whole panorama may be vibrating with beauties man has not yet the soul to see. Some already living, no doubt, see beauties we ordinary men cannot appreciate. It is only a century ago that mountains were looked upon as hideous. And in the long centuries to come may we not develop a soul for beauties unthought of now?[58]

The critic may ask: 'What grounds are there for thinking that the correct view [of mountains] wasn't the one of 100 years ago?'[59] If we asked Younghusband this question, he might well reply that his grounds for thinking that his view of the aesthetic value of mountains is the correct one is simply that he finds them beautiful (this is a 'properly basic' belief for him). Since the objective account of beauty can easily accommodate other people simply 'not getting it', Younghusband could simply find himself with the conviction that mountains are beautiful, and presume that the people of 100 years ago simply hadn't noticed. As Jacques Maritain writes: 'however beautiful a created thing may be, it can appear beautiful to some and not to others, because it is beautiful only under certain aspects, which some discern and others do not'.[60] Indeed, Younghusband is quite prepared to accept that there may be unappreciated beauties that neither he, nor anyone of his generation, has 'the soul to see' as yet.

A critic might also pose the following question: 'We find desolate landscapes beautiful; the eighteenth century found them repulsive. What facts would show one or other of us to be wrong?'[61] For example, Dr Johnson was singularly unimpressed with the Scottish scenery:

> [The hills] exhibit very little variety; being almost wholly covered with dark heath, and even that seems to be checked in its growth. What is not heath is nakedness . . . An eye accustomed to flowery pastures and waving harvests is astonished and repelled by this wide extent of hopeless sterility. The appearance is that of matter incapable of form or usefulness, dismissed by nature from her care and disinherited of her favours, left in its original elemental state, or quickened only with one sullen power of useless vegetation. It will readily occur, that this uniformity of barrenness can afford little amusement to the traveller; that it is easy to sit at home and conceive rocks and heath, and waterfalls; and that these journeys are useless labours, which neither impregnate the imagination, nor enlarge the understanding.[62]

What facts would show one or other of us to be wrong? The fact that we are not stepping outside our moral rights in finding aesthetic enjoyment in contemplating desolate landscapes! It may be difficult to *prove* that there is nothing immoral about appreciating desolate landscapes as we now often do, but then we are happy enough to live with the fact that moral judgements are sometimes hard to make, let alone prove. Absence of proof is no direct disproof of a belief. Dr Johnson seems to have been preoccupied with the demand that a beautiful landscape should match up with the familiar beauties of the English countryside. In short, Dr Johnson found the Scottish landscape too different and boring for his tastes. He just didn't 'get it'.

'But what is it about desolate landscapes which we now "see" which people in the eighteenth century couldn't see?' asks our critic, 'Isn't it more reasonable to suppose that our attitudes have simply changed, but that neither of us is objectively correct in our respective aesthetic estimations?' What is it that we now 'see' that people in the past did not 'see'? What else but the *beauty*, that is, the intrinsic aesthetic admirability, of certain qualities that can be found in such landscapes?

Just as the aesthetic sensibility of individuals matures throughout their lives as they gain a wider aesthetic experience, so the aesthetic sensibilities of a civilization can mature as time goes on, because the shared culture which civilization builds up incorporates a greater and greater range of aesthetic experiences. We should expect then, on the objective theory of beauty, that as time goes on people will notice more and more about the world that is beautiful. It is a prediction of the objective theory of beauty that as time goes on, more and more beautiful facts can be discovered. It is therefore a confirmation of this theory that this should be so in, for example, the contrast between eighteenth- and twenty-first-century attitudes to desolate landscapes.

If many people find something beautiful which I find ugly, I am likely to form the opinion that I simply lack good taste in this case, and that the object of dispute probably is beautiful, especially if the people disagreeing with me have a wider aesthetic experience that I do. In this way an objective concept of beauty can easily accommodate the fact that 'Different persons get [aesthetic pleasure] from different objects', that, 'They differ in their tastes', and that 'What one person finds enjoyable, another might behold with no pleasure at all.'[63] Still, as Aldous Huxley wrote:

> An Indian, for example, finds European orchestral music intolerably noisy, complicated, over-intellectual, inhuman. It seems incredible to him that anyone should be able to perceive beauty and meaning, to recognize an expression of the deepest and subtlest emotions, in this elaborate cacophony. And yet, if he has patience and listens to enough of it, he will come at last to realize, not only theoretically, but also by direct, immediate intuition, that this music possesses all the qualities which Europeans claim for it.[64]

And the reverse is surely true of someone brought up in the Western musical tradition listening to Indian music.

In sum, I think we should agree with Cambridge philosopher G. E. Moore, who wrote that: 'the beautiful should be *defined* as that of which the admiring contemplation is good in itself . . . the question whether it is truly beautiful or not, depends upon the *objective* question whether the whole in question is or is not truly good'.[65] As Alvin Plantinga says: 'To grasp the beauty of a Mozart D Minor piano concerto is to grasp something that is objectively there; it is to appreciate what is objectively worthy of appreciation.'[66]

The overwhelming beauty of creation

. . . all things are beautiful and in some way delightful.
BONAVENTURE[67]

I think it clear that on the above definition of beauty, the vast majority of facts are objectively beautiful overall, and that the cosmos is overwhelmingly beautiful overall. Aristotle recognized this when he wrote that scientists contemplate a truth that is 'worth knowing'[68] because it is beautiful, and assured us that scientists may find this beauty 'in the most trivial-seeming circumstances'.[69] 'We must avoid a childish distaste for examining the less valued animals', said the philosopher, 'for in all natural things there is something wonderful . . . we should approach in inquiry about each animal without aversion, knowing that in all of them there is something . . . beautiful.'[70] More recently, mathematical physicist Henri Poincaré wrote: 'The scientist does not study nature because it is useful; he studies it because he delights in it, and he delights in it because it is beautiful. If nature were not beautiful, it would not be worth knowing, and if nature were not worth knowing, life would not be worth living.'[71] French philosopher Jacques Martin explains that:

> Like . . . the true and the good, the beautiful is
> being itself considered from a certain aspect; it is
> a property of being . . . Thus everything is
> beautiful, just as everything is good, at least in a
> certain relation. And as being is everywhere pres-
> ent and everywhere varied the beautiful likewise is
> diffused everywhere and is everywhere varied . . .
> each kind of being is good in its own way, is
> beautiful in its own way.[72]

This is *not* to say that absolutely everything is beautiful 'through and through', or in every aspect of its being. Rather, it is to say that everything is beautiful *in at least one aspect of its being*. This follows from the premise that being *per se* is a good thing in itself; that is, that the judgement that it is better for something rather than nothing to exist, is true. As Swinburne says: 'the existence of any concrete thing is a good . . .'[73] Since goodness is beautiful, every thing is beautiful, at least *in that it exists*, because existence *per se* is good. 'If one thinks of ugliness as a negative quality, as opposed to being the mere absence of beauty,' writes Swinburne, 'one would be hard put to think of any part of the pre-human world which is ugly; ugliness in this sense seems to arrive with the arrival of humans, who, knowingly or unknowingly, make something which could be beautiful ugly instead.'[74] This being so, it follows that only certain facts, such as morally bad actions, are ugly overall. Art critic David Thistlethwaite even testifies that: 'In the Great War . . . unimaginable destruction faced the "official war artists", as they struggled to give meaning to what they saw. This was not a place, of torn trees, pounded mud and rat-occupied corpses, where any shallow belief in order could survive. But the stubborn witness of the great paintings that came out of the unthinkable horror, is to beauty.'[75] Beauty, as well as goodness, can be found in some measure, however small, in any fact.

The relationship between beauty and ugliness (like that between goodness and evil) is asymmetrical. Facts can be beautiful without being ugly in any way, whereas nothing can be ugly without being beautiful in at least one way; although some things are indeed ugly

overall. As Colin McGinn observes: 'The devil is sometimes depicted as having *some* positive aesthetic attributes. He is not always ugly and repulsive, but can be
seductive and charming; he may occasionally have
refined artistic tastes. But he is never, I think, depicted
as genuinely beautiful of soul; his *core* is always repug-
nant.'[76] This observation chimes with the biblical
description of the Devil as a fallen angel who 'masquer-
ades as an angel of light' (2 Corinthians 11:14).[77]

Categories of beauty and aesthetic judgement

Beauty is a general quality of nature . . . the
perceiving mind must also be beautiful and
healthy. The vile or vulgar mind not only cannot
discern beauty, it is a great destroyer of beauty
everywhere.
W.R. INGE, *OUTSPOKEN ESSAYS*

Art critic Sir Herbert Read was surely correct when he
said: 'I do not believe that a person of real sensibilities
ever stands before a picture and, after a long process of
analysis, pronounces himself pleased. We either like it
at first sight, or not at all.'[78] However, this does not
mean that people do not make aesthetic judgements, or
that there are no criteria for aesthetic evaluation, only
that such evaluations are often quickly and subconsciously made. Still, I suppose some people do not have
what Sir Herbert would consider 'real sensibilities', and
that they, or those who wish to check and understand
their sensibilities, might want to take greater care.
Some people have a *knack* of producing the answers to
sums without going through all the working-out; but

even they may on occasion work through a sum step by step to double-check or to help someone else.

The aesthetic equivalent of working through a sum step by step is paying close attention to the different aspects of an object. Objective beauty is dependent upon objective goodness, and there are three general categories of goodness:

1. Ontological goodness (instrumental goodness deriving part of its value from the intrinsic goodness of the end to which it is a means, and including such properties as *efficiency, simplicity* and *elegance*; causal goodness, and the good of 'being' *per se*).

2. Moral or ethical goodness.

3. Epistemological goodness: truth and knowledge (what Victor Cousin called: 'The intellectually beautiful, that splendour of the True'[79]).

It follows from the fact that goodness is beautiful that there are just as many categories of beauty as there are of goodness. It must be remembered during the following discussion that every reference to goodness carries with it a reference to beauty, and vice versa. Unfortunately, unlike the Greek *Kalos*, English has no word for the 'beautiful-good'.[80] There are, then, three general categories of beauty:

● The first is *ontological beauty*. For example, there is the beauty of instrumental goodness, deriving some of its value from the intrinsic beauty of the end to which it is a means and including such aesthetic factors as efficiency, simplicity and elegance.[81] A beautiful machine is a machine that fulfils its purpose well, which means in as efficient, simple, elegant and reliable a manner is possible. Such a machine, be it an engine or a kettle, possesses instrumental beauty: 'There is a beauty of form and function in a piece of delicate and complex machinery like a Rolls-Royce aero engine, as well as in a Bach Fugue; there can be ugliness or beauty in the design of a car, no less than in that of a cathedral.'[82] There is the causal beauty of things that produce beautiful things (things like artists!). Under the maxim that one cannot give what one has not got, producers of beauty (including designers) must themselves be beautiful. There is the beauty of sheer existence, whether that existence is subjective or objective. As Stephen Clark writes: 'to be at all is to be beautiful'.[83]

- The second is *moral or ethical beauty* (the moral beauty of a thing's *telos* contributes to its instrumental beauty). A truly beautiful building or machine (e.g. a cathedral or its organ) is a beautiful means towards a beautiful end, which will often mean a *morally* good end. As William Dembski says: 'God's intentions are intelligible. Moreover that intelligibility is as much moral and aesthetic as it is scientific.'[84]

- The third is *epistemological beauty* (the beauty of truth embodied in or communicated by an object). As Winfried Corduan reminds us: 'A work of art is a piece of communication.'[85] Stephen F. Brown explains how Franciscan theologian Bonaventure (1217–1274) 'never viewed the world in a hard-nosed, factual way. A rose, for him, was always more than a rose. Or, perhaps, we might better say that for Saint Bonaventure a rose, while remaining a rose, tells an attentive viewer a richer story of its reality.'[86] William Dembski picks up on the communicative nature of beauty:

I look at a blade of grass and it speaks to me. In the light of the sun, it tells me that it is green. If I touch it, it tells me that it has a certain texture. It communicates something else to a chinch bug intent on devouring it. It communicates something else still to a particle physicist intent on reducing it to its particulate constituents. Which is not to say that the blade of grass does not communicate things about the particles that constitute it. But the blade of grass is more than any arrangement of particles and is capable of communicating more than is inherent in any such arrangement.[87]

In other words, because everything exists in relationships (whether conscious, unconscious, or non-conscious), everything communicates truths about the relationships in which it stands. This communication of truth is *kalos* (both good and beautiful). According to Thomas Dubay: 'The awareness that the universe is stunningly beautiful wherever we turn our eye is now so much a conviction of our most productive scientists that objective grandeur is considered a warrant of truth . . . Beauty has an immediately evidential power pointing to the discovery and pursuit of truth.'[88]

These criteria are founded in the belief that truth and goodness are beautiful, and in the recognition that the fundamental good and beauty is the goodness and beauty of being *per se* (this gives the lie to Dawkins' attempt to detach the question of cosmic truth from the question of meaning). To put it more simply, *to make an aesthetic judgement about an object it is necessary to delineate the different types and degrees of objective value that it possesses.*

A work of art that possesses beauty in all of these aspects will be objectively more beautiful (more deserving of aesthetic appreciation and praise), all things being equal, than a work of art lacking beauty in one of these aspects. However, these aspects need to be placed in order: ontological goodness (rooted in being) is the most fundamental value, followed by the beauty of moral goodness and the beauty of truth (which is both good and beautiful). Thus moral beauty, as a subcategory of the beauty of goodness, is more important to the overall beauty of a work of art than epistemological beauty, although the two are related.

Truth in art need not mean the photographic, realistic representation of objects in painting or sculpture. Rather, it primarily refers to the worldview that seeps into a piece of art via the artist. Art that is grounded in truth will possess greater beauty, all other things being equal, than art that is rooted in falsehood: 'Art is truly religious not when it employs traditional religious subjects, still less when it seeks a photographic depiction of reality, but when it probes beneath the surface of the finite and brings to light the ultimate meaning which lies beyond and beneath things.'[89] Art that allows one to grasp truth is, at least in this respect, beautiful: 'Art [can be] a form of knowledge, in which the artist allows you to share his knowing.'[90]

The beauty of instrumental goodness depends in part upon the end to which it is the means. Thus the goodness of the end takes priority in judgements of instrumental beauty, followed by the efficacy of the means as such. This rightly suggests that an instrumentally beautiful motorbike probably has greater instrumental beauty than an instrumentally beautiful bomb, even if the bomb is more efficient than the bike at fulfilling its purpose.

A painting produced with the intention that people come to a disinterested appreciation of the beauty of God or of His creation will be more beautiful, all other things being equal, than a painting produced with the intention that people come to a disinterested appreciation of the glory of an earthly ruler. Of course, whether or not one *recognizes* this will depend upon whether or not one recognizes the value of this assumed theistic *end*, and that will depend upon whether or not one accepts the existence of God. For the Christian, non-Christian art (in so far as it remains true to its creator's worldview) will lack a certain instrumental, moral and epistemological beauty, being orientated on the basis of false worldview assumptions.[91] This point highlights the importance of the relation between art and truth (which, as a good thing, is also a beautiful thing).

An object of appreciation might be beautiful in some of these aspects and ugly in others. Whether or not a thing is beautiful or ugly *overall* will depend upon the relative degrees of beauty possessed by these aspects, and the relative value of those aspects for the thing in question. To ensure that we pay attention to these different aspects is to ensure that an overall immediate impression of beauty or ugliness does not overwhelm the importance of less immediately obvious, but nonetheless important, aesthetic details (we can explain Dr Johnson's failure to appreciate the Scottish countryside as a failure to pay sufficient attention to these details).

A beautiful machine is first and foremost a machine that fulfils its function well, which means in as efficient, simple, elegant and reliable a manner as possible. Such a machine, be it a mousetrap or a bio-molecular motor, possesses instrumental beauty. A truly beautiful machine also possesses causal goodness, in that it produces beautiful results. A beautiful kettle boils water quickly and safely (instrumental beauty) to produce water that is good for making hot drinks (causal beauty). A truly beautiful machine is a beautiful means towards a beautiful end, which will often mean a *morally* good end (drinking tea is, all things being equal, a good thing to do – especially if it is fair trade tea!). Finally, a beautiful machine also possesses the beauty of *being* which is possessed by all facts. A biological machine like the flagellum (more about this later) clearly possesses instrumental beauty (including some value derived from the intrinsic goodness of the end to which it is a means, simplicity, elegance and reliability), and causal beauty.

While an atomic bomb may be (at least in some of its aspects) a beautiful machine (it certainly possesses efficiency), it is (deterrent value aside) the means to the end of killing people. Thus, compared with a machine that is the equally efficient means to an undoubtedly better end (e.g. a baby-incubator), the atomic bomb will be objectively less beautiful. Indeed, if we rate moral goodness as more important than instrumental beauty, even a barely workable machine that is nonetheless the means to a good end will be more beautiful than the efficient means to a less valuable end.

Beauty beyond science

> *Naturalism is inadequate to account for beauty.*
> JOSH MCDOWELL AND THOMAS WILLIAMS[92]

To summarize our results so far, we can say that:
   1. Beauty is an objective feature of reality that cannot be accommodated by a naturalistic metaphysic (hence naturalism is false).
   2. Beauty communicates truths in a way that transcends scientific description (hence scientism, which seeks to reduce all reality to the scientifically describable, is false).
   3. Aesthetic judgements are rationally motivated judgements that can be appropriate or inappropriate, true or false, in accordance with the objective qualities (ontological, moral and epistemological) of the thing being judged.
Having looked at the objective nature of beauty and how we make aesthetic judgements, I'd like to take some time out to examine the distinction between art and craft, because this will illuminate a much more fundamental fact about rainbows than Newton's optics.

Understanding art

It might be said that everyone knows, if only intuitively, what art is. Art is painting, sculpture, literature, music, film, dance, and so on. These are all *examples of arts*, but what common feature justifies us in grouping these examples together under the single concept of 'art'? What is it that means a painting by Renoir is art, but a plain magnolia bedroom wall isn't? After all, an artist might place that magnolia wall in a gallery and call it 'art'. What distinguishes a shopping-list from a poem, especially a poem that reads like a shopping list? Such examples push the envelope of the term 'art' as commonly used, but common usage is based on traditional application, and not necessarily upon any considered theory about the nature of the things to which the term is applied. Someone might hesitate to call an Australian black swan a swan simply because they have never seen a black swan before, but their doubt doesn't show that the swan in question isn't a swan. Rather, their doubt shows that they have an inadequate understanding of what constitutes a 'swan' (having plumage of this or that colour is an accidental, though common, property of swans). Likewise, the question (asked perhaps of a magnolia coloured pile of bricks in a gallery) 'But is it art?' doesn't show that the questioned object is not art. Rather, it shows that the questioner holds an inadequate concept of what constitutes 'art'. (If the questioner had an adequate concept of 'art' they would say that the wall was, or was not, art.)

Mortimer J. Adler points out that the term 'art' comes from the Latin *ars*, and is 'a translation of the Greek word *techne*, which is best rendered in English by the word "skill"'.[93] The fundamental meaning of 'art' is therefore: 'the skills that human beings have in producing something or performing in a certain way'.[94] We still retain this meaning in the phrase 'There must be an art to it', said when trying to accomplish some trying task (e.g. erecting a deck-chair or putting together flat-pack furniture).

Posing the question where the phrase 'fine art' comes from, Adler reckons: 'that it comes from the derivation of the word "fine" from the word "final". Works of fine art are final in the sense that they are not intended as means to ends beyond themselves, but rather to be enjoyed as ends in themselves.'[95] Hence aesthetic pleasure is said to be 'disinterested' pleasure, a pleasure that takes interest in its object as an end in itself: 'To be disinterested concerning something is not the same as being uninterested in it. "Disinterestedness" can describe the absence of the kind of interest that relates to one's own advantage or disadvantage.'[96] Objects of aesthetic value, that is, are never *merely* means to an end, but are always themselves ends: 'when you see beautiful things [you] just want them to exist outside, in themselves, so that you can love them and understand them'.[97] The idea of aesthetic contemplation is the idea 'of *contemplating something for its own sake*'.[98] As Jerome Stolnitz writes:

> We usually see things . . . in terms of their usefulness for promoting or hindering our purposes . . . I see the pen as something I can write with, I see the oncoming automobile as something to avoid . . . Thus, when our attitude is 'practical,' we perceive things only as means to some goal which lies beyond the experience of perceiving them . . . But nowhere is perception exhaustively 'practical.' On occasion we pay attention to a thing simply for the sake of enjoying the way it looks or sounds or feels [i.e. the intrinsic merits of the thing itself]. This is the 'aesthetic' attitude of perception . . . [99]

Something is art if it is the intended object of perception directed towards appreciating the objective, intrinsic value of things; thus 'Disinterested contemplation is said to be object-centred contemplation.'[100] C. S. Lewis explained this well when he wrote that: 'art can be either "received" or "used." When we "receive" it we exert our senses and imagination and various other powers according to a pattern invented by the artist. When we "use" it we treat it as assistance for our own activities.'[101] Works of art are the intended objects of *disinterested*, aesthetic contemplation, such that the artist intends to present people with objective values to appreciate. It is not so much the work of art as a physical entity that is the intended object of contemplation. Rather, it is *the intrinsic values* that the art-entity embodies and communicates that are the intended objects of contemplation.

The disinterested appreciation of intrinsic value

Intrinsic value (as noted above) can be value *relative to an end*, but intrinsic value is never *subjective* value. For example, some of the intrinsic value of a spade is *relative* to the value of digging holes. To aid in the digging of holes, after all, is the defining purpose of a spade. 'Being good for digging holes' is what Aristotle would call the 'final cause' or *telos* of the spade. However, a spade has the intrinsic, objective value of 'being good for digging holes' w*hether or not I subjectively value this end*; I personally might not value such a 'final cause' due to a 'hole phobia'!

If I contemplate a spade in purely practical terms (i.e. 'Will it help me to dig this hole?'), my contemplation of the spade is not 'disinterested', and is therefore not

'aesthetic contemplation'. On the other hand, a disinterested (and therefore aesthetic) attitude of perception
would ask something like: 'Does this spade exhibit
objective values?' An aesthetic appreciation of the
spade (initiated, perhaps, because an artist has placed
it in an art gallery in order to bring it to our aesthetic
appreciation) would undoubtedly *include* perceiving
that the spade has the intrinsic value of being good for
digging holes, but there would be more going on than
that (e.g. an appreciation of its smooth and shinny
blade, the texture of its wooden shaft, etc).

Art is made or presented for aesthetic appreciation

Having given an illustration of how an artist can cause
us to shift from a purely practical to an aesthetic mode
of appreciation by presenting an object in a gallery, we
can see why philosopher Nicholas Wolterstorff defines
art as: '*an entity made or presented in order to serve
as an object of aesthetic contemplation*'.[102] On this
definition a spade in the corner of a building site is not
art, but a spade presented in an art gallery *is* art,
because it is an entity 'presented in order to serve as an
object of aesthetic contemplation'. Art need not be
produced for the purpose of aesthetic contemplation,
although everything produced for that purpose is art.
Art needs to be produced *or presented* (or both) for the
purpose of aesthetic contemplation: 'in the case of
Duchamp's *Fountain*, for example, it makes all the
difference whether the object is left in its normal position as a urinal, or exhibited for appreciation in a
gallery'.[103] The difference is not in the objective value of
the object (things don't become more beautiful just
because you put them in a glass case or hang them on

the wall), but in our openness to appreciating that value.

The distinction between art and craft

Objects of craft, however beautiful, are neither produced nor presented for the purpose of aesthetic appreciation (at least, not primarily). This is what distinguished art from craft: the *intention* behind its creation and/or presentation is quite different. Anything created and/or presented with the intention that it serves as the focus of aesthetic contemplation is art; thus craft can become art, but art cannot become craft. Works of craft may serve an aesthetic function, but the intention that forms them is not primarily artistic.

A good kettle (as a work of craft, or skill) is a kettle that serves well the purpose of a kettle, which is to boil small amounts of water quickly and safely. Fulfilling this purpose gives the kettle a measure of beauty. If a kettle is a beautiful object overall, so much the better. Nevertheless, one would hardly choose a kettle that was beautiful to look at but which took two hours to boil water over a kettle that was less beautiful to look at but which boiled water in two minutes! Conversely, one would not pick a painting *as a painting* purely because it was the right size to hide a crack on your wall, rather than a more beautiful painting of less utilitarian shape.

Craft and aesthetic value

Nevertheless, it is important to recognize that the realm of aesthetic value is not restricted to art, but plays a crucial role in craft. As Wolterstorff says: 'If an artefact occupies a significant place in our perceptual field, then, it is a better artefact if it is an *aesthetically* better artefact.'[104] For example:

> Perhaps the ugly concrete-block flats in lower-class housing developments serve rather effectively the housing needs of those who live in them. Yet they are not *good* houses – not as good as they could be. Something is missing, something of the joy that rightfully belongs in human life, something of the satisfaction that aesthetically good housing would produce in those who dwell there.[105]

In the Christian worldview, humans deserve to be treated with the dignity befitting creatures made in God's image, and that respect includes provision for the aesthetic beatitude of their daily environment. Tastes do indeed differ, but few would choose to live in a drab concrete-block if a more beautiful option were available. As art critic David Thistlethwaite says: 'good design is also good theology'.[106]

Love-spoons and dessertspoons

A carved wooden Welsh love-spoon can be used to fulfil the same function as a dessertspoon, but a dessertspoon will hardly fulfil the same function as the love-spoon (at least, not half so well)! The primary function of a love-spoon is as an artistic expression of love, while the primary function of a dessertspoon is to aid in the eating of food. Now, a dessertspoon has some beauty. For example, it has the beauty of instrumental goodness that comes from contributing to a good and therefore beautiful end (i.e. human nutrition). However, the primary purpose of the dessertspoon is not to facilitate disinterested attention to beauty, but to help people eat.

Similarly, a love-spoon could help someone to eat, but that is not its primary function. Rather, its primary function is to facilitate disinterested attention to beauty; for it is by drawing attention to beauty that the love-spoon acts as a symbol of the value the lover places on his beloved.

From the theistic perspective, the universe is probably more analogous to a dessertspoon than to a love-spoon; but it happens to be a very beautiful dessertspoon that has been presented as a work of art for our aesthetic contemplation and admiration. Particular aspects of creation may be works of craft that are additionally presented for aesthetic contemplation as art, or works of art pure and simple, but to see the world as a work of art is to see the world as theists see it. This is how the Psalmist saw the world when he wrote that: 'The heavens declare the glory [or beauty] of God; the skies proclaim the work of this hands. Day after day they pour forth speech; night after night they display knowledge. There is no speech or language where their voice is not heard' (Psalms 19:1-3). While naturalists like Richard Dawkins look upon creation as neither art nor craft, people who believe in God see both. We see the same universe, but we interpret it very differently. Nor are these interpretations merely different sentiments. It is impossible for both interpretations to be correct, and it is impossible for neither interpretation to be correct. One interpretation is right and the other is wrong.

Reading the rainbow

My heart leaps up when I behold
A rainbow in the sky.
WORDSWORTH[107]

Some theists think that God has taken special care to present particular aspects of the world as works of art. He has, as it were, framed these aspects of reality in one way or another to draw our attention to them. According to the biblical story of the flood,[108] one of those aspects of the world is the rainbow: 'I have set my rainbow in the clouds, and it will be the sign of the covenant between me and the earth' (Genesis 9:13). In other words, while God didn't create the rainbow as a work of art, he has presented it as a work of art and put a title on it saying, 'I Love You.'

Darwin described in his *Autobiography* how he gradually drifted away from belief in the Old Testament, seeing it as a 'manifestly false history of the world',[109] particularly mentioning 'with . . . the rainbow as a sign'[110] and reckoning that it 'was no more to be trusted than . . . the beliefs of any barbarian'.[111] It seems to me that Darwin's belief in the Old Testament foundered, at least in part, upon a false dilemma. As a scientist Darwin would have known that there has never been a time when the laws of physics haven't meant that rainbows will appear under the right physical conditions; but the temptation to de-bunk the biblical understanding of rainbows by reference to this fact is a temptation to miss the point of 'the rainbow as a sign'.[112] As Alister McGrath comments, 'Even before the mind grasps the scientific principles that govern the shape and colours of that rainbow, the human heart has responded at a far deeper intuitive level . . .'[113] There is indeed 'an enhanced sense of appreciation that results from understanding . . . Newton's optical explanation of the colours of the rainbow',[114] but the optical explanation of the rainbow, far from explaining away the rainbow's beauty or message, simply expands the horizon of appreciated objective beauty that requires metaphysical explanation. As McGrath counsels: 'nature points upwards, aesthetically and ontologically, and we fail to appreciate its richness until we become caught up in this upward trajectory'.[115]

You may understand the physics of rainbows as well as Newton, but if you can't look at a rainbow and see it as a work of art signalling that God loves you, then you are missing out on the most important fact about rainbows. This isn't a fact that would be mentioned in a scientific account of rainbows, but that only goes to show the limitations of science. Failing to appreciate the joyful, child-like message of the rainbow is like looking at Tracy Emin's notorious *Unmade Bed* and missing the fact that it had been presented as a work of art that therefore had something to communicate. The message of God's 'rainbow' is very different to Emin's *Unmade Bed* (and the former is surely more beautiful than the latter), but you get the point.

Kermit the Frog once asked, in a song about rainbows, 'Why are there so many songs about rainbows?' I think humans love songs about rainbows because rainbows are a love-letter from God saying, in effect: 'The Lord your God is with you, he is mighty to save. He will take great delight in you, he will quiet you with his love, he will rejoice over you with singing' (Zephaniah 3:17). When children draw pictures of rainbows as gifts for people they love, they are reflecting God's use of the rainbow for the very same end. It is a source of sadness to me that the dogma of naturalism should blind people like Dawkins to this truth.

Let's play Monopoly – the aesthetic argument for God

Beauty exists as an objective reality, and nothing within nature will account for it.
JOSH MCDOWELL AND THOMAS WILLIAMS[116]

Beauty is the gift of God.
ARISTOTLE[117]

In his interview with Nick Pollard, Dawkins said: 'I'd say I have a very positive, I'd almost say poetic, vision of the universe from a scientific point of view . . . Awe and wonder are things which religious people undoubtedly feel, but I get a bit irritated when they imply they have a monopoly of them, I think I can feel wonder as well as the next man.'[118] I wouldn't dream of irritating Professor Dawkins by claiming a religious monopoly on subjective experiences of awe and wonder, but I'm quite prepared to risk irritating him by claiming a philosophical monopoly on a worldview sufficient to justify the objective appropriateness of awe and wonder, whether directed at a rainbow or at the laws of physics which underlie the rainbow. The crux of the matter is that, for Dawkins, all that matters when it comes to giving an objective description of reality, is matter. Dawkins can feel awe and wonder as well as the next man, but *he cannot attribute any objective value to these feelings that tie them to the objects that evoke them.* Nor can he see the rainbow as a work of art that communicates a message of love. Dawkins' scientistic worldview can never accommodate the full communicative reality of beauty, because the rainbow 'is more than any arrangement of particles and is capable of communicating more than is inherent in any such arrangement'.[119]

The fundamental problem with the objective theory of beauty for atheists like Dawkins is that it depends, as G. E. Moore's definition of beauty makes clear, upon an objective theory of goodness, and an objective theory of goodness depends in turn upon the recognition of an objective standard of goodness that, as we have seen, can ultimately only find its home in the character of God. You can't have art without an artist, you can't have goodness without Goodness Himself, and you can't have beauty without Beauty Himself. As Augustine commented:

> . . . beauty . . . can be appreciated only by the mind. This would be impossible, if this 'idea' of beauty were not found in the mind in a more perfect form . . . But even here, if this 'idea' of beauty were not subject to change, one person would not be a better judge of sensible beauty than another . . . This consideration has readily persuaded men of ability and learning . . . that the original 'idea' is not to be found in this sphere, where it is shown to be subject to change . . . And so they saw that there must be some being in which the original form resides, unchangeable, and therefore incomparable. And they rightly believed that it is there that the origin of things is to be found, in the uncreated, which is the source of all creation.[120]

Augustine is saying that our judgements about beauty must be measured against some objective standard that the human mind apprehends and employs. This standard of beauty cannot depend upon any individual finite mental state (or collection thereof), or else it would of necessity be a subjective standard; and objective aesthetic judgements cannot depend upon a subjective aesthetic standard. Therefore, there must exist an objective standard of beauty that is independent of finite minds. However, an aesthetic standard is not the sort of thing that could possibly exist in the physical world. Therefore, the standard of beauty must exist neither in finite minds, nor in the physical world, but in an infinite non-physical reality that perfectly embodies beauty.

Thomas Aquinas' argument from degrees of perfection (from his famous 'five ways') is implicitly aesthetic: 'Among beings there are some more and some less good . . . and the like [e.g. beautiful]. But more and less are predicated of different things according as they resemble in their different ways something which is the maximum . . . so that there is something which is truest, something best, something noblest [and something maximally beautiful] . . . and this we call God.'[121] Tom's argument works with all 'great making properties' (properties that any being is the greater for having), including the property of beauty. Aquinas argues that there can be no non-supreme objective goodness (or beauty) if there is no maximal example of goodness (or beauty); and this maximal example of beauty is God.

More recently, Francis A. Schaeffer suggested that only by beginning with a *personal* ultimate reality can we reasonably aspire to the use of the universal categories of value necessary to a meaningful existence: 'if you begin with the impersonal . . . there is no place for morals as morals [or beauty as beauty]. There is no standard in the universe which gives final meaning to such words as *right* and *wrong* [or beautiful and ugly]. If you begin with the impersonal, the universe is totally silent concerning any such words.'[122] This must be right, for if non-human reality is 'indifferent' as Dawkins claims, then the only home for value is the finite, sub-jective individual: 'The Greeks understood that if we were really to know what was right and what was wrong [beautiful or ugly], we must have a universal to cover all the particulars.'[123] However, while the Greek gods 'were personal gods – in contrast to the Eastern gods, who include everything and are impersonal – they were not big enough. Consequently, because their gods were not big enough, the problem [of universal categories] remained unsolved for the Greeks.'[124] This is where God provides what the Greeks lacked, an objective and per-sonal instantiation of maximal, perfect goodness and beauty by which worldly particulars can be judged.

The postmodern rejection of objective value is a log-ical consequence of the modernistic rejection of God. For while modernism initially attempted to retain belief in the 'permanent things' while rejecting God, such a position is unsupportable, because God is the ground of all value. As Jean Baudrillard, Professor of Philosophy of Culture and Media Criticism at the European Graduate School, writes: 'In the aesthetic realm of today there is no longer any God to recognize his own . . . there is no gold standard of aesthetic judgement or pleasure. This situation resembles that of a currency which may not be exchanged: it can only float, it's only reference itself, impossible to convert into real value or wealth.'[125] Indeed, once God is out of the picture there is no room in reality for objective beauty or goodness, for the objective value of truth or knowledge, or for the expectation that the human mind is capable of reliably grasping anything beyond what is pragmatically useful to our survival:

While on the surface postmodernism seems to reject the artificially truncated rationalism embodied by scientific materialism, it actually adopts the materialist account of man as its starting point. Richard Rorty, dean of American postmodernists, even argues for the importance of 'keeping faith with Darwin.' It is precisely because the materialist account of man is so bleak that it creates fertile ground for postmodernism to grow . . . If human beings (and their beliefs) really are the mindless products of their material existence, then everything that gives meaning to human life – religion, morality, beauty – is revealed to be without objective basis. [In a doomed attempt to] avoid sliding into nihilism as a result of this revelation, postmodernists take a page from Nietzsche and reject reason altogether, urging people to fashion their own reality through an act of the will. In this way, the narrow 'rationalism' of scientific materialism begets utter irrationalism.[126]

There is no way for a modernist like Dawkins to avoid the postmodern nihilistic terminus. As R. C. Sproul explains: 'the existence of God is the supreme *proto*-supposition for all theoretical thought. God's existence is the chief element in constructing any worldview. To deny this chief premise is to set one's sails for the island of nihilism . . .'[127]

The ontological link the aesthetic argument forges between objective beauty and divinity is the same as the link proposed by the moral argument between objective goodness and divinity: namely, that without divinity – which necessarily exemplifies total objective goodness (and hence total objective beauty, because goodness is beautiful) – there would be no objective good. And without objective good, there would be no objective beauty, because nothing can be objectively beautiful that is not objectively good to appreciate: 'If God is dead, so is beauty.'[128] If no being of absolute beauty exists, then the ideal of beauty by which we judge a rainbow to be beautiful cannot transcend our finite consciousness, and our judgements of beauty must therefore be relative and subjective. As Peter Kreeft observes: 'God is objective spirit, and when "God is dead", the objective world is reduced to matter and the spiritual world is reduced to subjectivity . . .'[129] If a rainbow is objectively beautiful, then 'somewhere over the rainbow' there must exist a being of absolute and unsurpassable beauty:

> . . . ideal Beauty . . . resides neither in the individual nor in a collection of individuals. Nature or experience provides the occasion of our conceiving it, yet beauty is essentially a distinct thing. The man who has once conceived it finds all natural figures, beautiful as they may be, only images of a beauty which is not realised in them . . . the true and absolute Ideal is no other than God Himself . . . The physically beautiful serves as an envelope for the intellectually and morally Beautiful . . . God is the principle of all the three orders of the Beautiful . . . God is perfect Beauty . . . He presents to our reason the most elevated idea beyond which there is nothing, to our Imagination the most attractive Contemplation, to our Sentiment an object supremely lovely. He is therefore perfectly the Beautiful . . .[130]

God – the maximally beautiful being

Philosopher Patrick Sherry notes that: 'Beauty is probably today the most neglected of the divine attributes.'[131] This is despite the fact that 'many of the early Christian Fathers and the medievals regarded it as central in their discussions of the divine nature . . .'[132] Although God's beauty is infrequently mentioned in modern discussions of divinity, theists continue to attribute beauty to God. Clark Pinnock and Robert Brow write of 'God's sublime beauty'.[133] Keith Ward speaks of 'the supreme beauty, the supreme value, of the Divine self'.[134] Dallas Willard considers 'the beautiful mind of God'[135]; while Peter Kreeft says that: 'God is infinite Beauty and the inventor of all beauty in creatures.'[136] Jacques Martin wrote: 'God is beautiful. He is the most beautiful of beings . . . He is beautiful through Himself and in Himself, beautiful absolutely.'[137]

The Bible often attributes beauty to God. The book of Isaiah promises that: 'In that day the Lord Almighty will be a glorious crown, a beautiful wreath for the remnant of his people' (Isaiah 28:5). The book of Psalms frequently ascribes beauty to God:

> One thing I ask of the Lord,
> This is what I seek:
> That I may dwell in the house of the Lord
> all the days of my life,
> *To gaze upon the beauty of the Lord*
> (Psalm 27:4, my italics)

The Psalms extol us to pray: 'May the beauty of the Lord our God rest upon us . . .' (Psalm 90:17), and to: 'Ascribe to the Lord the glory due his name [i.e. his nature]' (Psalm 29:2; 96:8). Keith Ward informs us that 'the idea of the glory and majesty of God is the idea of beauty, power and wisdom which is complete . . .'[138] Richard Harries adds: 'When goodness, truth and beauty are combined we have glory. When boundless goodness, total truth and sublime beauty are combined in supreme degree, we have divine glory . . . God is in himself all glory in a sublime conjunction of beauty, truth and love.'[139] God's moral holiness is one component of his beauty: 'Then Moses said, "Now show me your *glory*." And the Lord said, "I will cause all my *goodness* to pass in front of you . . ."' (Exodus 33:18-19, my italics).

A mathematician contemplating Newton's equations may quite legitimately describe the object of their contemplation as beautiful. Similarly, someone accurately conceiving of God may quite legitimately describe the object of their contemplation as beautiful, and sublimely so, for as the medieval theologian Peter Lombard wrote:

> The most exalted philosophers . . . understood the beauty of a body to be sensible and the beauty of the soul to be intelligible, and they preferred intellectual to sensible beauty. We call 'sensible' such things as can be seen or touched and 'intelligible' such as can be perceived by mental vision. Once they perceived various degrees of beauty in mind and body, they realized there was something which produced these beautiful things, something in which beauty was ultimate and immutable, and therefore beyond compare. And they believed, with every right, that this was the source of all things, that source which itself was never made but is that by which all else was made.[140]

Indeed, *to say that God is objectively, maximally beautiful is to imply everything that can be said about the nature of God.* To say that God is maximally beautiful is to say that He is maximally good (since only good qualities are beautiful), that is, that God consists of the greatest set of goods that can exist together in one and the same being. This set of unified goods includes maximal goodness of every possible type. God exhibits maximal ontological goodness (and thus necessary and independent existence). God possesses a maximal capacity for knowledge (since truth is good and truth is a quality of beliefs). Most appropriately, as the best of all possible personal beings (which God must be since the personal is a higher good than the impersonal, knowledge a facet of mind and moral goodness a quality of persons): 'God is love' (1 John 4:8).

Conclusion

Long ago the Greek philosopher Plato ascended in thought from the beauty of the world to the absolute beauty of the divine:

> This is the right way of being initiated into the mysteries of love, to begin with examples of beauty in this world and use them as steps to ascend continually to absolute beauty as one's final aim . . . This above all others is the region where a truly human life should be spent, in the contemplation of absolute beauty . . . One who contemplates absolute beauty and is in constant union with it . . . will be able to bring forth not mere reflected images of goodness but true goodness, because one will be in contact not with a reflection but with the truth . . . What may we suppose to be the felicity of the man who sees

absolute beauty in its essence, pure and unalloyed,
who . . . is able to apprehend the divine beauty . . . ?[141]
The connection between God and objective value means
that the concept of objective beauty loses all coherence
if God is excluded from our worldview. The devaluation
of objective beauty, and the consequent loss of wonder
and meaning felt in society at large, is a logical consequence of the 'death of God'. To reject the absolute
beauty of divinity (whether one begins by rejecting
beauty and ends by rejecting God, or begins by rejecting God and ends with the rejection of beauty) is not to
cast aside a piece of extraneous worldview ornamenta-
tion, but to eschew the one sure foundation of a meaningful existence:

> In Plato, a connection is made between the
> contemplation of beauty, human goodness and
> love. One who contemplates beauty can rightly be
> said to love that which is most worth loving. And,
> since Plato holds that one becomes like what one
> contemplates, the contemplator of beauty is one
> whose life becomes beautiful . . . In this sense,
> God is supreme goodness. To love God is the
> highest goal of human life. To attain God is to
> have one's life enfolded in perfect beauty, and to
> become an image of goodness to others . . . Thus
> we can move from awe and admiration of God to
> love of God.[142]

Dawkins' repudiation of objective beauty makes his
protestation that science doesn't negate our sense of
wonder before the universe ring hollow; for Dawkins'
science is so saturated in atheism that his 'poetic vision
of the universe'[143] can't be presented as being in agreement with reality. For Dawkins, the world of scientific

facts, without a trace of objective beauty, and the world of subjective aesthetic experience, without a trace of objective truth, confront each other, and no rapprochement is possible. Such a view is indeed aesthetically empty and nihilistic. But such a view is wrong: 'beauty is objective and knowable and real', as J. P. Moreland writes: 'it's not in the eye of the beholder, it's objective, it can be known'.[144] The subjective view of beauty is wrong because God, the maximally beautiful being of whom all lesser beauties speak, exists: 'finite beauty as wonderful and intrinsically valuable as it is, functions not only as a good but also as a pointer to a good that lies beyond it that is our ultimate *telos* [goal]. And that is the ultimate beauty – God Himself.'[145] As Thomas Dubay notes: 'The only logical alternative to nihilism is theism and its philosophy and theology saturated with the true, the good, and the beautiful.'[146]

[1] Cooper, David E., *Aesthetics: The Classic Readings* (Blackwell, 1997), p.6.

[2] Dawkins, Richard, *A Devil's Chaplain* (London: Weidenfeld & Nicolson, 2003), p.42.

[3] Dawkins, Richard, *Unweaving the Rainbow* (London: Penguin, 1999), p.63.

[4] Unweaving beauty is the task of aesthetics, a philosophical subject area that takes its name from the Greek for 'perception': *aesthesis*.

[5] Dubay, Thomas, *The Evidential Power of Beauty* (San Francisco: Ignatius, 1999), p.16-17.

[6] Protagoras, quoted by Holmes, *Fact, Value and God* (Eerdmans, 1997), p.8.

[7] Joad, C. E. M., *The Recovery of Belief* (London: Faber & Faber, 1952), p.212.

[8] Groothuis, Douglas, *Truth Decay* (Leicester: IVP, 2000), p.26.

[9] In the Romantic era, 'sublime' replaced 'beauty' as the pre-eminent aesthetic term of praise.

[10] Lewis, C. S., *The Abolition of Man* (London: Fount, 1999), p.7.

[11] Quoted, *ibid.*

[12] Quoted, *ibid.*, p.8.

[13] Miele, Frank, 'Darwin's Dangerous Disciple – An Interview with Richard Dawkins', *The Skeptic*, vol. 3, no. 4, 1995.

14 Mackie, J. L., *Ethics: Inventing Right and Wrong* (London: Penguin, 1990), p.15.

15 Dawkins, Richard, quoted in Keith Ward, *The Turn of the Tide* (London: BBC, 1986), p.32.

16 Gunton, Colin E., *The One, The Three And The Many* (Cambridge University Press, 1996), p.67.

17 Dawkins, Richard, *River out of Eden* (London: Weidenfeld & Nicolson, 1995), p.120.

18 Ward, *op. cit.*, p.142.

19 Hume, David, *On the Standard of Taste, Selected Essays* Oxford Paperbacks, 1993.

20 Hume, David, *A Treatise of Human Nature* Oxford University Press, 1978.

21 *ibid.*

22 Lewis, *op. cit.*, p.16.

23 Joad, *op. cit.*, p.145.

24 Haldane, John, 'Admiring the High Mountains', in T. D. J. Chappell (ed.), *The Philosophy of the Environment* (Edinburgh University Press, 1997), p.81.

25 Plotinus, 'Enneads', in *Aesthetics: The Classic Readings, op. cit.*, p.60.

26 Augustine, quoted by Umberto Eco, *The Aesthetics of Thomas Aquinas*, p.49.

27 Geisler, Norman L., *The Issue of Beauty*, Side One.

28 Solomon, Jerry, 'Art and the Christian' at www.leaderu.com/orgs/probe/docs/artandxn.html

29 Groothuis, *op. cit.*, p.257.

30 Adler, Mortimer J., *Adler's Philosophical Dictionary* (Pocket Books, 1996), p.39.

31 Groothuis, *op. cit.*, p.258.

32 Emmet, E. R., *Learning to Philosophise* (Longmans, 1964), p.119.

33 Lewis, *The Abolition of Man, op. cit.*, p.8.

34 *ibid.*

35 *ibid.*, p.14.

36 *ibid.*

37 *ibid.*, p.16.

38 *ibid.*

39 Kreeft, Peter, *Yes or No?* (San Francisco: Ignatius, 1991), p.41-42.

40 O'Hear, Anthony, *Beyond Evolution* (Oxford: Clarendon Press, 1997), p.187.

41 *ibid.*, p.191.

42 Swinburne, Richard, *Providence and the Problem of Evil* (Oxford: Clarendon Press, 1998).

43 Hanfling, Oswald, 'Aesthetic Qualities', *Philosophical Aesthetics*, p.47-48.

44 Joad, *Guide to Philosophy, op. cit.*, p.347.

[45] *ibid.*, p.346.

[46] *ibid.*, p.347.

[47] *ibid.*

[48] Mackie, *op. cit.*, p.15.

[49] Quoted by Eco, *op. cit.*, p.113.

[50] *ibid.*, p.32.

[51] *ibid.*, p.33.

[52] *Adler's Philosophical Dictionary*, *op. cit.*, p.37.

[53] Geisler, *op. cit.*

[54] O'Hear, Anthony, *Philosophy* (London, New Century, 2001), p.102.

[55] Kreeft, Peter and Tacelli, Ronald, *Handbook of Christian Apologetics* (Crowborough: Monarch, 1999).

[56] Sorley, W. R., *Moral Values and the Idea of God* (Cambridge University Press, 1921), p.124.

[57] Lyas, Colin, 'The Evaluation of Art', in Oswald Hanflung (ed.), *Philosophical Aesthetics – an introduction* (Oxford: Blackwell, 1992), p.371-372.

[58] Quoted by H. E. Huntley, *The Divine Proportion* (New York: Dover, 1970), p.89.

[59] Dr Nicholas Everitt, personal communication.

[60] Maritain, Jacques, *Art and Scholasticism* (University of Notre Dame Press, 1974), p.3.

[61] Dr Nicholas Everitt, personal conversation.

[62] Johnson, S., *A Journey to the Western Islands*, ed. R. W. Chapman, (Oxford University Press, 1994), p.34-35.

[63] Adler, *op. cit.*, p.37.

[64] Huxley, Aldous, *Ends and Means* (Greenwood Press, 1969), p.287.

[65] Moore, *op. cit.*, p.201.

[66] Plantinga, Alvin, 'Two Dozen (or so) Theistic Arguments' at www. homestead.com/philofreligion/files/Theisticarguments.html

[67] Bonaventure, *The Journey of the Mind to God* (Hackett, 1993), p.16.

[68] Aristotle, quoted by Stephen R. L. Clark, 'Platonism and the gods of Place', *The Philosophy of the Environment*, *op. cit.*, p.33.

[69] Aristotle, quoted *ibid.*

[70] Aristotle, *De Partibus Animalium*, 1.645a.

[71] Quoted by Clark, *op. cit.*

[72] Martin, *op. cit.*, p.3.

[73] Swinburne, *Providence and the Problem of Evil*, *op. cit.*, p.52.

[74] *ibid.*, p.53.

[75] Thistlethwaite, *op. cit.*, p.7.

[76] McGinn, Colin, *Ethics, Evil and Fiction* (Oxford: Clarendon Press, 1999), p.98.

[77] On the existence of the Devil, cf. Peter S. Williams, *The Case for Angels* (Carlisle: Paternoster, 2002).

[78] Read, Herbert, *The Meaning of Art* (Faber & Faber, 1951), p.29.

[79] Cousin, Victor, 'God Seen in the Beautiful', in Alfred Caldecott and H. R. Mackintosh (eds), *Selections from The Literature of Theism* (Edinburgh: T&T Clark, 1931), p.310.

[80] The various forms of The Greek term *kalos* can mean, amongst other things: fairest (*kalliste*), comeliest (*kallistos*), fair, noble, wise, sweet, and the beauty of morally good or honourable acts (*kalos*). Jesus says 'Salt is good [*kalos*]' (Mark 9:50). During the transfiguration Peter says: 'Rabbi, it is good [*kalos*] (for) us to be here' (Mark 9:5). Jesus calls himself 'The Good [*Kalos*] Shepherd' (John 10:11). The Greek *agathos* meant instrumentally or morally good, *kalos* adds to *agathos* the idea of objective beauty.

[81] 'For contemporary science the first trait of beauty is an elegant simplicity.' – Thomas Dubay, *The Evidential Power of Beauty* (San Francisco: Ignatius, 1999), p.39.

[82] Whittle, Donald, *Christianity and the Arts* (Mowbrays, 1966), p.145.

[83] Clark, Stephen R. L., *God, Religion and Reality* (London: SPCK, 1998), p.95.

[84] Dembski, William A., *Intelligent Design* (Downers Grove: IVP, 1999), p.229.

[85] Corduan, Winfried, *No Doubt About It* (Broadman & Homan Publishers, 1997), p.265.

[86] Brown, Stephen F., Bonaventure, *The Journey of the Mind to God*, Introduction (Indianapolis: Hackett, 1993), p.ix.

[87] Dembski, William A., 'The Act of Creation: Bridging Transcendence and Immanence' at www.arn.org/docs/dembski/wd_actofcreation.htm

[88] Dubay, Thomas, *The Evidential Power of Truth* (San Francisco: Ignatius, 1999), p.39, 339.

[89] Begbie, Jeremy S., *Voicing Creation's Praise* (Edinburgh: T&T Clark, 1998), p.20.

[90] Thistlethwaite, David, *The Art of God and the Religions of Art* (Carlisle: Paternoster, 1998), p.82.

[91] As much as I appreciate the music of progressive rock-group *Yes*, my appreciation is sometimes detrimentally affected by the New Age worldview they occasionally express. If Christianity is true, the music made by these fine musicians would be even more beautiful if it grew out of, and so expressed, the Christian worldview. Non-Christians would probably find the same aesthetic disquiet listening to the Christian Celtic progressive rock group *Iona*.

[92] McDowell, Josh and Williams, Thomas, *In Search Of Certainty* (Wheaton, Illinois: Tyndale, 2003), p.92.

[93] *Adler's Philosophical Dictionary*, *op. cit.*, p.33.

[94] *ibid.*, p.32.

[95] *ibid.*, p.33.

[96] Collinson, Diane, 'Aesthetic Experience', *Philosophical Aesthetics*, *op. cit.*, p.134.

[97] Murdoch, Iris, *Acastos, 'A dialogue about religion'* (Penguin, 1987), p.103.

[98] *ibid.*, p.35.

[99] Stolnitz, Jerome, *Aesthetics and Philosophy of Art Criticism*, p.137, quoted by Wolterstorff, *op. cit.*, p.35.

[100] Wolterstorff, *op. cit.*, p.47.

[101] Lewis, C. S., *An Experiment in Criticism* (Cambridge, 1961), p.88

[102] Wolterstorff, Nicholas, *Art in Action* (Carlisle: Solway, 1980).

[103] Hanfling, Oswald, 'The Problem of Definition', in *Philosophical Aesthetics* (Oxford: Blackwell, 1992), p.25.

[104] Wolterstorff, *op. cit.*, p.170.

[105] *ibid.*

[106] Thistlethwaite, *op. cit.*, p.20.

[107] Wordsworth, quoted by Alister McGrath, in *The Re-Enchantment of Nature* (Hodder & Stoughton, 2003), p.140.

[108] cf. Norman L. Geisler, 'Noah's Flood' at www.johnankerberg.org/Articles/PDFArchives/theological-dictionary/TD4W0701.pdf

[109] Darwin, Charles, *The Autobiography of Charles Darwin*, (ed.) N. Barlow (London: Collins, 1958), p.85-87.

[110] *ibid.*

[111] *ibid.*

[112] *ibid.*

[113] McGrath, Alister, *The Re-Enchantment of Nature* (London: Hodder & Stoughton, 2003), p.140.

[114] *ibid.*

[115] *ibid.*, p.142.

[116] McDowell and Williams, *op. cit.*, p.79.

[117] Backhouse, Robert, (ed.), *5,000 Quotations for Teachers and Preachers* (Eastbourne: Kingsway, 1994), p.12.

[118] Dawkins, Richard, 'Nick Pollard talks to Dr. Richard Dawkins', *Thirdway*, April 1995, vol 18, no 3.

[119] Dembski, 'The Act of Creation: Bridging Transcendence and Immanence', *op. cit.*

[120] Augustine, *City of God.*

[121] Aquinas, Thomas, *Summa Theologica.*

[122] Schaeffer, Francis A., *He Is There and He Is Not Silent, The Complete Works of Francis A. Schaeffer, Volume One* (Crossway Books, 1994).

[123] *ibid.*

[124] *ibid.*

[125] Baudrillard, Jean, *The Transparency of Evil: Essays on Extreme Phenomena*, trans. James Benedict (New York: Verso, 1990), p.14-15.

[126] West, John G. Jr, 'The Regeneration of Science and Culture', in William A. Dembski and James M. Kushiner (eds), *Signs of Intelligence – understanding intelligent design* (Brazos Press, 2001), p.65.

[127] Sproul, R. C., *The Consequences of Ideas* (Crossway Books, 2000), p.171.

[128] Farley, Edward, *Faith and Beauty: A Theological Aesthetic* (Aldershot: Ashgate, 2001), p.64.

[129] Kreeft, Peter, *Heaven – The Heart's Deepest Longing* (San Francisco: Ignatius, 1989), p.23, 25, 112, 247.

[130] Cousin, *op. cit.*, p.309-311.

[131] Sherry, 'Beauty', in *A Companion to Philosophy of Religion, op. cit.*

[132] *ibid.*

[133] Pinnock, Clark H. and Brow, Robert C., *Unbounded Love* (Wipf & Stock Publishers, 2001), p.178.

[134] Ward, Keith, *Religion & Creation* (Oxford: Clarendon Press, 1996), p.198.

[135] Willard, Dallas, *The Divine Conspiracy* (London: Fount, 1998), p.158.

[136] Kreeft, Peter, *Angels (and Demons)* (San Francisco: Ignatius, 1995), p.72.

[137] Martin, *op. cit.*, Chapter 5.

[138] Ward, *op. cit.*, p.267-268.

[139] Harries, Richard, *Art and the Beauty of God* (London: Mowbray, 1993), p.54.

[140] Lombard, Peter, *The Sentences* i. 3. I. *The Sentences* were a standard medieval university textbook, upon which it was common to make commentaries.

[141] Plato, *Symposium*.

[142] Ward, Keith, *God, Faith & The New Millennium* (OneWorld, 1999), p.97.

[143] Dawkins, Richard, 'Nick Pollard talks to Dr. Richard Dawkins', *Thirdway*, April 1995, vol 18, no 3.

[144] Moreland, J. P., in *Comunique*, Robert K. Garcia, 'Communiqué Interview: J. P. Moreland' at http://communiquejournal.org/q4_moreland.html

[145] *ibid.*

[146] Dubay, *op. cit.*, p.96.

CHAPTER 7

Beauty and the Last Man

Sam Mendes' multi-award winning directorial debut *American Beauty* (Dreamworks, 1999) was a film that contrasted crumbling family life with the sense that beauty communicates something about a transcendent realm of peace. The film is narrated from beyond the grave by Lester Burnham (Kevin Spacey): 'I'll be dead in a year,' he tells us, 'In a way, I'm dead already.' Lester tells the story of his mid-life crisis, a crisis that is finally resolved only moments before his demise. Two scenes in particular stand out in their treatment of beauty. In the first, video-camera-toting next-door neighbour Ricky (Wes Bentley) shows Lester's daughter Jane (Thora Birch) 'The most beautiful thing I've ever filmed', a plastic bag caught in a wind-eddy (something that took the film makers four 'takes' to capture):

This bag was just, dancing, with me. Like a little kid begging me to play with it . . . That's the day I realized that there's this entire life behind things, and this incredibly benevolent force that wanted me to know that there was no reason to be afraid, never . . .

Sometimes there's so much beauty in the world, I feel like I can't take it, and my heart is just going to cave in.

In the second scene, which picks up imagery from the first, Lester's life flashes before his eyes as he dies:

. . . lying on my back at boy-scout camp, watching falling stars . . . the first time I saw my cousin Tony's brand new fire-bird; and Jane, and Jane . . . I guess I could be pretty pissed off about what happened to me, but it's hard to stay mad when there's so much beauty in the world; sometimes I feel like I'm seeing it all at once . . . My heart fills up like a balloon that's going to

> burst . . . And then it flows through me like rain, and I
> can't feel anything but gratitude for every single
> moment of my stupid little life.
>
> There is a sense here that the problem of pain and suffer-
> ing is overwhelmed by the gift of beauty from a transcen-
> dent realm to which beauty testifies.

*Reality as actually experienced contains intuitions
of value and significance, contains love, beauty,
mystical ecstasy, intimations of godhead.*
ALDOUS HUXLEY[1]

It is ironic that, while Richard Dawkins confuses naturalism with science and seeks to defend both from the
charge of nihilism by talking about the beauty of nature,
there is actually a fourfold chain of argumentation that
leads from beauty to God.

Aesthetic reality can be divided between our subjective awareness of beauty and the objective beauty of
which we are aware. Aesthetic arguments may therefore
focus either upon our knowledge of beauty, or upon the
beauty we know. Aesthetic arguments that focus upon
our knowledge of beauty are 'epistemological' arguments; those that focus upon the beauty we know are
'ontological' arguments.

Some of the epistemological arguments (arguments
from the fact of aesthetic experience) begin with the
mere fact that we have aesthetic awareness, and seek to
show that theism provides the best explanation of this
capacity. As William C. Davis writes: 'Humans have
numerous features that are more easily explained by
theism than by metaphysical naturalism, if only because
metaphysical naturalism currently explains all human

capacities in terms of their ability to enhance survival. Among these features are . . . the appreciation of beauty . . .'[2] Other epistemological arguments (arguments *from the content of aesthetic experience*) begin with the particular nature of our aesthetic experience, seeking to interpret this experience as revealing God's existence.

Some ontological aesthetic arguments (arguments *from beautiful things*) ask how good an explanation it is that unintended natural processes should be said to have produced the objective beauty that we discover around us. Other ontological aesthetic arguments (arguments *from the fact of beauty itself*) propose that only the existence of God can ground objective aesthetic value, just as the moral argument proposes God's existence as the ground of objective moral value. We have already examined ontological arguments *from the fact of beauty itself* (in the previous chapter). Therefore, the current chapter will deal with epistemological aesthetic arguments, while the following two chapters will deal with the ontological argument *from beautiful things*.

Arguments from the fact of aesthetic experience

The unreasonable beauty of mathematics

> . . . beauty is widely recognised by physicists as being an important characteristic of the laws of nature, one which has served as a highly successful guide to discovering the fundamental laws of nature . . .
>
> ROBIN COLLINS[3]

In *Unweaving the Rainbow* Dawkins quotes Indian astrophysicist Subrahmanyan Chandrasekhar: 'This "Shuddering before the beautiful", this incredible fact that a discovery motivated by a search after the beautiful in mathematics should find its exact replica in Nature, persuades me to say that beauty is that to which the human mind responds at its deepest and most profound.'[4] J. P. Moreland similarly observes: 'Philosophers of science have often pointed out that one of the criteria for a true (or rational) scientific theory is its elegance or beauty.'[5] For example: 'Albert Einstein and Erwin Schrodinger were guided by the conviction, borne out by previous scientific discoveries, that a good scientific theory would safeguard the beauty of nature and would itself be formally or mathematically beautiful.'[6] Schrodinger and Dirac, two founders of quantum theory, remarked: 'It was a sort of act of faith with us that any equations which describe fundamental laws of Nature must have great mathematical beauty in them. It was a very profitable religion to hold and can be considered as the basis of much of our success.'[7] Physicist Steven Weinberg comments: 'there is simplicity, a beauty, that we are finding in the rules that govern matter that mirrors something that is built into the logical structure of the universe at a very deep level'.[8] Weinberg describes a beautiful theory as one that displays simplicity and a sense of inevitability analogous to the sense of inevitability one can find in a painting or musical score to which we would not want to add or remove anything. Physicist Paul Davies reports: 'It is widely believed among scientists that beauty is a reliable guide to truth, and many advances in theoretical physics have been made by the theorist demanding mathematical elegance of a new theory.'[9] Indeed, 'when laboratory tests are difficult, these aesthetic criteria are considered even more important than experiment'.[10] Robert Augros and George Stanciu conclude that: 'All the most eminent physicists . . . agree that beauty is the primary standard of scientific truth.'[11]

Consider just how amazing it is that a scientist thinking through equations in the office can repeatedly pick one out simply because it is more beautiful than others, and then discover that it is the beautiful equation that accurately describes the way objective reality behaves. Why should it be the case that, as John Polkinghorne writes, 'it has been our experience that the laws of nature are always expressed in equations of unmistakable mathematical beauty'?[12] Many thinkers have observed that, 'The unreasonable effectiveness of mathematics', as Eugene Wigner called this conundrum, lends itself to theistic interpretation. Professor of Mathematics Dr Graham R. Everest of the University of East Anglia writes: 'everywhere you look in mathematics you see beauty, and, although it is a highly technical subject, you will find universal agreement among mathematicians that at the heart of the best theorems lie the simplest ideas. I would reckon this to be a universal principle in science generally and it points gloriously to God's ordinance.'[13]

Douglas Groothuis tells the story of a Russian PhD student in the days of Communism who was so impressed with the beauty of some mathematical equations about the universe that he was moved from atheism to theism – despite the political constraints on such belief. In the late 1980s the Russian student told his story to a visiting Christian professor of physics:

> I was in Siberia and I met God there while
> I was working on my equations. I suddenly
> realized that the beauty of these equations had to
> have a purpose and design behind them, and I
> felt deep in my spirit that God was speaking to
> me through these equations. But I don't
> know much about Him. Could you tell me
> about Him?[14]

The professor obliged and the student became a Christian.

J. P. Moreland argues that: 'Beautiful theories or systems of thought which are mere inventions get their beauty from the superior human intellect which formed them. Similarly, beautiful theories, which are discovered and which accurately reflect the way the world is, get their beauty from the Mind which formed them.'[15] The analogy between examples of beauty created in human thought and the beauty discovered by humans in the cosmos may lead us to infer that aesthetic choice lies behind the structure of the cosmos.

John Polkinghorne has written extensively about the significant role of beauty in the mathematics employed by physicists: 'There is no a priori reason why beautiful equations should prove to be the clue to understanding nature . . . but it does not seem sufficient simply to regard it as a happy accident.'[16] According to Polkinghorne: 'science discerns a world which in its rational beauty and rational transparency is shot through with signs of mind, and the theist can understand this because it is indeed the Mind of God that is partially disclosed in this way'.[17]

Aesthetic awareness and survival value

*From the point of view of usefulness, or of
survival in the natural world, the arts might seem
an inexplicable and irrational activity.*
OSWALD HANFLING[18]

Professor H. E. Huntley, in *The Divine Proportion – A
Study In Mathematical Beauty*, poses the evolutionary puzzle of our aesthetic sense thus:

> . . . we might begin by asking whether the
> universal human thirst for beauty serves a useful
> purpose. Physical hunger and thirst ensure our
> bodily survival. The sex drive takes care of the
> survival of the race. Fear has survival value. But –
> to put the question crudely – what is beauty for?
> What personal or evolutionary end is met by the
> appreciation of a rainbow, a flower or a
> symphony? At first sight, none . . . it appears to
> serve no utilitarian end.[19]

Dawkins thinks that the human capacity for art is the
unintended spin-off of a hypothetical evolutionary
process involving pictorial communication between
hunters, a story that does precious little to explain the
existence of aesthetic awareness (or why our capacity
for appreciating beauty serves to aid the discovery of
nature's underlying structures).

The problems of giving an evolutionary explanation
of aesthetic awareness have been recognized since
Darwin's own day: 'Alfred Russel Wallace, the co-discoverer of the theory of evolution, argued that our . . .
love of beauty could not possibly be explained in terms
of survival promotion. He concluded that this must
mean that there was more to human nature than evolution

could account for and . . . looked for the answer in divine intervention.'[20]

In his Gifford lectures on *Theism and Humanism*, Arthur J. Balfour discussed 'the incongruity between our feelings of beauty and a materialistic account of their origin'.[21] Balfour asserted that: 'our aesthetic sensibilities must be regarded (from the naturalistic standpoint) as the work of chance. They form no part of the quasi-design which we attribute to selection; they are unexplained accidents of the evolutionary process.'[22] However, 'This conclusion harmonizes ill with the importance which civilized man assigns to them in his scheme of values.'[23]

Denis Alexander writes that: 'even the most ardent sociologist might baulk at attributing greater reproductive success to the effects of listening to Brahms rather than to Beethoven. If the universe has no ultimate purpose, as atheism suggests, then the universal experience of being moved by works of great music or by other great acts of human creativity is difficult to explain.'[24] Indian philosopher W. S. Rhodes agrees: 'The sense of beauty in human beings . . . has no obvious survival value. Human sensitivity to beauty cannot be accounted for on materialist lines and the beauty of the world only partly so. Unless there is an intelligence sensitive to beauty in some way directing the course of things the facts must remain without full explanation.'[25]

In his classic treatment of the design argument, F. R. Tennant developed the argument from the inability of evolution to adequately account for our aesthetic sensibilities, pointing out that 'in the organic world aesthetic pleasingness of color, etc., seems to possess survival-value on but a limited scale, and then is not to be identified with the complex and intellectualized aesthetic sentiments of humanity, which apparently have no survival value'[26]:

> From the point of view of science, beauty [is] a biologically superfluous accompaniment of the cosmic process. Once more then lucky accidents and coincidences bewilderingly accumulate until the idea of purposiveness . . . is applied to effect the substitution of reasonable, if alogical, probability for groundless contingency. If we do apply this category of design to the whole time-process, the beauty of Nature may not only be assigned a cause but also a meaning, or a revelational function. It may then be regarded as no mere by-product . . . [27]

Arguments from the content of aesthetic experience

The challenge of atheism, and the nihilism that so often accompanies it, is best countered by a clearer vision of God's fair beauty, not by intellectual arguments. –
CLARK PINNOCK[28]

Thomas V. Morris relates a conversation that took place one night in a restaurant in Nebraska at a table full of professional philosophers:

> One of the philosophers pointed to a fellow thinker across the table, known for his outspoken religious belief, and said, 'If someone asked you to prove that there is a God, what would you do?' The man being questioned took another bite of mashed potatoes, looked up, and replied, 'I'd say,

"Come into my garden and look around."' He took a long drink of iced tea and started cutting his steak. Everyone waited. He kept eating. 'That's *all*?' his interlocutor responded, incredulous. 'Yep,' he said. People at the table looked at each other. The questioner tried again. 'But suppose I'm the one asking the question, and you say that, and I go into your garden and look around like you told me to, and I get no proof at all. What then?' The theistic gardener seemed puzzled at the other philosopher's confession of such possible obtuseness. He sighed aloud and then, with a world-weary professional tone, slowly responded, 'Well, I'd just say, "Look closer."'[29]

'What could be more clear or obvious when we look up to the sky and contemplate the heavens, than that there is some divinity of superior intelligence?'[30] So asked Cicero, and the majority of humanity echoes this insight at one time or another. Even David Hume noted that: 'A purpose, an intention, or design strikes everywhere the most careless, the most stupid thinker; and no man can be so hardened in absurd systems, as at all times to reject it.'[31] G. K. Chesterton calls atheism an 'abnormality' because 'It is the reversal of a subconscious assumption in the soul; the sense that there is a meaning and a direction in the world it sees.'[32] In a study of why people believe in God, Michael Shermer found that the most common reason theists give for their own belief in God (28.6 per cent) is the 'good design' of the universe.[33] Call this the 'intuitive design argument'. A major factor in the intuitive design argument is an appreciation of the aesthetic dimension of reality; hence the philosopher's advice to 'look closer' at his garden. As Moreland says: 'the beauty of the world and many of its aspects points to the existence of a grand Artist'.[34]

Clark Pinnock begins his thoughts on the matter from the fact that, in our appreciation of works of human art, we are familiar with the existence of beauty that we know has not been produced by pure chance. In these cases we experience a 'form of communication'[35] through which we perceive 'intelligence, thought, and feeling'.[36] We often have the same (or at least a similar) experience when we encounter the physical universe; we often find ourselves experiencing the universe 'as a work of art'.[37] On the basis of the principle that like causes produce like effects, Pinnock argues that our experience of the physical universe as artistic beauty, being similar to our experience of human art, gives us reason to infer the existence of an Artist with 'intelligence, thought, and feeling'[38] behind the universe. The rationality of holding to this conclusion is bolstered by the principle of credulity, for as Richard Swinburne explains: 'we ought to believe that things are as they seem to be, until we have evidence that we are mistaken . . . If you say the contrary – never trust appearances until it is proved that they were reliable – you will never have any beliefs at all. For what would show that appearances were reliable, except more appearances?'[39]

Kitty Ferguson points out that:

> If we were somehow able to take the natural world, straighten out the lines, correct the asymmetries and irregularities, make all the tree-trunks into true cylinders, the picture that would emerge would be unnatural, unbeautiful, impossible . . . As important as the concept of

> pattern in nature is, there is also a powerful
> requirement for a pulling out of shape . . . There is
> a tension everywhere between ideal pattern and
> deviation from it.[40]

Such a subtle balance and tension between an 'ideal' pattern and an interesting deviation from it, 'is familiar to artists and musicians',[41] notes Ferguson; 'it is part of their craft to use it, to make it work for them'.[42] Likewise, 'The rationality of the universe goes beyond its manifestation in obvious symmetry, pattern, and cause and effect. It would appear to include the ability to make judgements as to when the symmetry must be broken, when the geometry must be pulled out of shape . . .'[43] Ferguson asks, 'Is that the rationality of the Mind of God?'[44]

The desire for beauty

> . . . absence does not mean non-existence; and a
> man drinking a toast of absent friends does not
> mean that from his life all friendship is absent. It
> is a void but it is not a negation; it is something
> as positive as an empty chair.
> G. K. CHESTERTON[45]

Aesthetic experience plays a significant role in the intuitive design argument as well as in religious experience generally speaking. Augustine lamented: 'I looked for pleasure, *beauty*, and truth not in him but in myself and his other creatures, and the search led me instead to pain, confusion, and error.'[46] Augustine's search eventually led to the belief that God was the true object of his need, the true fountain of beauty, and to the exclamation: 'Oh Beauty so old and so new! Too late have I loved thee!'[47]

This same search for that transcendent something sensed within or through aesthetic experience was a golden thread running through the life of C. S. Lewis. Lewis picked up on the Romantic term *Sehnucht* to describe a family of emotional responses to the world which are linked by a combined sense of longing for and displacement or alienation from the object of desire. *Sehnucht* is 'nostalgic longing', and it arises when experience of something within the world, particularly beauty, awakens in us a desire for something beyond what the natural world can offer as a corresponding object of desire. As C. E. M. Joad put it: 'aesthetic emotion is at once the most satisfying and the most unsatisfying of all the emotions known to us; satisfying because of what it gives, unsatisfying because it gives so briefly, and, in the act of giving hints at greater gifts withheld'.[48] Thus *Sehnucht* directs our attention towards the transcendent, that which 'goes beyond' our present experience. The power of fairy tales lies in their ability to transport us into a world transparently imbued with *Sehnucht*. Consider the experience of beauty that sustains Sam the Hobbit in the midst of Mordor's deathly landscape, from *The Return of the King* by Lewis' friend J. R. R. Tolkein:

> There, peeping among the cloud-wrack above a dark tor high up in the mountains, Sam saw a white star twinkle for a while. The beauty of it smote his heart, as he looked up out of the forsaken land, and hope returned to him. For like a shaft, clear and cold, the thought pierced him that in the end the Shadow was only a small and passing thing: there was light and high beauty forever beyond its reach.[49]

However, warns Lewis: 'The books or the music in which we thought the beauty was located will betray us if we trust them; it was not in them, it only came through them, and what came *through* them was longing . . . Do what we will, then, we remain conscious of a desire which no natural happiness will satisfy.'[50] There is beauty *in* books and music as there is in nature; but these things also stir within us a desire for a beauty greater than themselves that we seem to apprehend *through* their beauty. It is as if their finite beauty is a derived quality that draws our aesthetic attention into the platonic heaven of un-derived and absolute beauty. In Christian theism this 'as if' finds fulfilment:

> . . . we want so much more – something the books on aesthetics take little notice of. But the poets and the mythologies know all about it. We do not want merely to see beauty, though, God knows, even that is bounty enough. We want something else which can hardly be put into words – to be united with the beauty we see . . . to receive it into ourselves . . . to become part of it . . . At present we are on the outside of the world, the wrong side of the door. We discern the freshness and purity of morning, but they do not make us feel fresh and pure. We cannot mingle with the splendors we see. But all the leaves of the New Testament are rustling with the rumor that it will not always be so. Some day, God willing, we shall get *in*. When human souls have become as perfect in voluntary obedience as the inanimate creation is in its lifeless obedience, then they will put on its glory, or rather that greater glory of which Nature is only the first sketch.[51]

Lewis constructed his 'argument from desire' on the basis of *Sehnucht*: 'Creatures are not born with desires unless satisfaction for those desires exists. A baby feels hunger: well, there is such a thing as food . . . If I find in myself a desire which no experience in this world can satisfy, the most probable explanation is that I was made for another world.'[52] A man's hunger does not prove that he will get any food; he might die of starvation. But surely hunger proves that a man comes from a race which needs to eat and inhabits a world where edible substances exist: 'In the same way,' says Lewis, 'though I do not believe (I wish I did) that my desire for Paradise proves that I shall enjoy it, I think it a pretty good indication that such a thing exists and that some men will.'[53]

Rudolph Otto's book *The Idea of the Holy* describes 'the Numinous' as that which causes in those who perceive it a sense of awe. The Numinous is not the subjective experience, but the transcendent object about which one feels this sense of awe. The principle of credulity encourages us to accept the straightforward interpretation that the Numinous is an objective reality truly perceived. Awe of the Numinous is one of the emotional states grouped together under the category of *Sehnucht*. Moreover, a sense of the Numinous often accompanies aesthetic experiences of the 'sublime' variety (i.e. the beauty of the great and majestic), such as a mountain or thunderstorm (this explains why mountains and climatic events feature so widely in the religious experience of the Jewish nation). Neither the aesthetic experience itself, nor the immediate objects of that experience, can be termed 'the Numinous'. The mind of a university-educated prince turned shepherd is quite capable, for example, of distinguishing between a burning bush and the numinous presence of God mediated through that burning bush.[54] Perception of the numinous constitutes a whole new level or depth of experience:

> When we are awed by the intolerable majesty of the Himalaya . . . we are merely receiving through symbols adapted to our size, intimations of the Absolute Beauty . . . . we are – if we receive a genuine aesthetic or religious impression – passing through and beyond this object, to the experience of an Absolute revealed in things.[55]

As Simone Weil suggests, just as every artist is present in their work, so: 'In everything which gives us the pure authentic feeling of beauty there really is the presence of God.'[56]

Beauty as a natural sign

> *As John Keats saw the ornamentation of a Greek urn as mirroring the great human longing for meaning, value and beauty, we must learn to see the present beauty of nature as a sign and promise of the coming glory of God, its creator.*
> ALISTER MCGRATH[57]

Peter Kreeft distinguishes between a 'conventional sign', like letters in an alphabet that could have been different, and a 'natural sign' that 'is a living example of what it signifies'.[58] For example, 'There is happiness in a smile, as there is not a curve ball in the catcher's two fingers signalling it.'[59] Just as the smile is a 'natural sign' of the happiness it signifies, so nature can be seen as a 'natural sign' of the transcendent object of desire that makes itself immanent therein. Is this seeing a true insight into ultimate reality, or a delusion? In the absence of sufficient reason to doubt God, the principle of credulity would suggest that what seems to be the case is the case. One can easily explain how some people fail to 'read the sign', for we know that 'we can look *at* a sign instead of looking along it'[60] to that which it signifies. British philosopher Roger Scruton observes:

> There is an attitude that we direct [or are naturally led to direct] towards the human person, and which leads us to see in the human form a perspective on the world that reaches from a point outside it. That is what we see in a smile. And the experience of the holy, the sacred and the miraculous arises in a similar way, when we direct [or are led to direct] this attitude not to other human beings, but to places, times, and objects . . . Such things have no subjectivity of their own . . . The experience of the sacred is therefore a revelation, a direct encounter with the divine, which eludes all explanation in natural terms . . .[61]

Maybe it is due to a misplaced generalization of the scientific method, looking at the natural world rather than along it, that some people do not experience the world as a natural sign.[62]

Sensitivity to the numinous functions as a variety of *Sehnucht* because beauty acts as a link to the divine source and standard of beauty. On this hypothesis, it is unsurprising to read Roger Scruton affirming that: 'in the sentiment of the sublime we seem to see beyond the world, to something overwhelming and inexpressible in which it is somehow grounded . . . it is in our feeling for beauty that the content, and even the truth, of religious doctrine is strangely and untranslatably intimated to us'.[63] Despite these observations, Scruton apparently remains an atheist (albeit a church-going atheist), recommending a hollow 'let's pretend' philosophy to paper over the cracks of meaninglessness left in his secular worldview by the absence of God. High culture, says Scruton, 'teaches us to live *as if* our lives mattered eternally'.[64]

The art-object of creation is a natural sign of God's creative joy, and as such it requires us to pass beyond the mediating object to appreciate the transcendent beauty that it communicates to us. It is this transcendent beauty that is the ultimate 'object' of aesthetic appreciation, because transcendent beauty is the necessary source and standard of the imminent beauty that is the proximate subject of aesthetic contemplation. Just as the joy transcends the twinkle in an eye, so beauty transcends the artwork, and so God's love transcends the rainbow. This means that *God is the ultimate objective locus of aesthetic appreciation*, whether people recognize this fact or not.

Art and the line of despair

Francis Schaeffer analyzed modern culture in terms of the dichotomy it has set up between the rational realm of (objective, empirical) facts and the non-rational realm of (subjective, opinion relative) values. Schaeffer called the historical crossing-point after which this dichotomy arose 'the line of despair'.[65] Dawkins, like Hume, lives on the wrong side of Schaeffer's 'line of despair'. The theist accepts art 'as the mediation that embodies love for the beauty of this world and desire for those far-off gleams of a higher world'.[66] The atheist doesn't believe in any 'higher world', and so cannot accept such a high view of art. Instead, they must relegate those 'gleams of transcendence'[67] offered by art to the realm of pure subjectivity.

Schaeffer observed that a secular worldview that cuts a transcendent God out of its account of reality leads to the depersonalization of humanity in the realm of fact and the restriction of values (including moral goodness, beauty, and ultimately even truth) to the realm of subjective, relative opinion. As a secular worldview grows, value is increasingly placed in what Schaeffer dubbed 'the upper story', where a leap of blind faith is required to avoid the obvious naturalistic conclusion that the 'death of God' leads to the 'death of value':

> Modern man, says Schaeffer, resides in a two-story universe. In the lower story is the finite world without God; here life is absurd . . . In the upper story are meaning, value, and purpose. Now modern man lives in the lower story because he believes there is no God. But he cannot live happily in such an absurd world; therefore, he continually makes leaps of faith into the upper story to affirm meaning, value, and purpose, even though he has no right to, since he does not believe in God.[68]

Dawkins' personal rejection of social Darwinism is just such a leap of faith, which is ironic given his condemnation of religious faith as 'belief in spite of, even perhaps because of the lack of evidence . . .'[69]

While Schaeffer wrote in the 1970s, postmodernism was in its infancy, and culture as a whole still clung, through a non-rational leap of faith, to the existence of value. Today, the implications of the 'death of God', foreseen by Nietzsche, have finally caught up with us:

> 'Where is God?' [cried the madman] 'I shall tell
> you. We have killed him . . . All of us are his
> murderers. But how have we done this? . . . Who
> gave us the sponge to wipe away the horizon?
> What did we do to unchain this earth from its sun?
> . . . Where are we moving now? Away from all
> suns? Are we not plunging continually backward,
> sideward, forward, in all directions? Is there any
> up or down left? Are we not straying through an
> infinite nothing?'[70]

Postmodernists can tread water for a while, but eventually they will drown in a sea of relativism; for as Nietzsche recognized, one has no right to Christian morality without accepting the Christian worldview:

> When one gives up the Christian faith, one pulls
> the right to Christian morality out from under
> one's feet. This morality is by no means self-
> evident. Christianity is a system, a whole view of
> things thought out together. By breaking one main
> concept out of it, the faith in God, one breaks the
> whole. It stands or falls with faith in God.[71]

The same hard truth holds for aesthetic value.

Peter Kreeft diagnoses Western culture as suffering from an 'eclipse of "the permanent things"'[72]; an eclipse that has followed that of the supreme permanent thing, God. Apart from God, says Kreeft, culture has lost 'permanent truths . . . the objective and unchangeable laws of logic, metaphysics, and mathematics', together with 'permanent, objective moral laws'.[73] (It is now true to say, for example, that: 'There are academic circles in which talk of truth, let alone religious perspectives being true, is about as popular as a teetotal sermon at a local pub.'[74] John F. Walkup goes so far as to suggest that: 'A majority of faculty and students reject the existence of absolute truth.'[75]) We can add to Kreeft's list of cultural casualties the eclipse of objective beauty. It is as if society has become exhausted with the attempt to constantly leap in to the upper storey of objective values in the face of a worldview that provides no basis for their existence. It is this lack of a sufficient metaphysical basis for the affirmation of goodness and beauty that leads to the nihilistic effect of Dawkins' writings upon readers astute enough to notice the inconsistency between his naturalistic worldview and its blithe dismissal as irrelevant to questions of personal meaning.

The supposed 'de-mystification' of nature by science is what we might dub a 'straw herring', an easily defeated but irrelevant opponent brought in and knocked down in the hope that no one notices the real issue is still standing. What is the value of personal meaning in a meaningless universe if personal meaning has no objective value? Objectively speaking, none: 'You cannot have a valid human meaning in a universe which is meaningless . . .'[76] Those who 'see through' the universe inevitably 'see through' their own pretensions to 'personal meaning': 'You cannot go on "seeing through" things for ever. The whole point of seeing through something is to see something through it . . . If you see through everything, then everything is transparent. But a wholly transparent world is an invisible world. To "see through" all things is the same as not to see.'[77]

Postmodernism is the result of the realization that without the transcendent reference point provided by God, the 'upper story' of value has become nothing but an incoherent miscellany of subjective, relative opinions, governed more by fashion than common sense. Consider the similarities between the prophetic words of Nietzsche (above) and Roger Scruton's view of postmodern culture, which recommends that we live 'as if' life mattered:

> To understand the depth of the . . . 'as if' is to understand the condition of the modern soul. We know that we are animals, parts of the natural order, bound by laws which tie us to the material forces which govern everything . . . and that death is exactly what it seems. Our world has been disenchanted and our illusions destroyed. At the same time we cannot live as though that were the whole truth of our condition. Even modern people are compelled to praise and blame, love and hate, reward and punish. Even modern people . . . are aware of self, as the centre of their being; and even modern people try to connect to other selves around them. We therefore see others *as if* they were free beings, animated by a self or soul, and with more than a worldly destiny. If we abandon that perception, then human relations dwindle into a machine-like parody . . . the world is voided of love, [moral] duty and [aesthetic] desire, and only the body remains.[78]

Scruton is openly admitting that *postmodernism necessitates an inconsistent life*. In the realm of fact we 'know' that people are the unintended material products of material necessity, plus time, plus chance. We 'know' that there is therefore no objective value in truth, goodness, or beauty. However, we cannot live as if all this were true. Therefore, we must be inconsistent and live the lie of 'as if'. Schaeffer noted how some naturalists (such as Julian Huxley) admit that man 'functions better if he acts as though God is there', and he pointed out that 'This is not an optimistic, happy, reasonable or brilliant answer. It is darkness and death.'[79] Roger Scruton seems to be repeating history because God-less philosophy has nowhere left to run but the land of illusions.

Richard Dawkins is driven to the same conclusion about love as Scruton by the incisive questioning of Nick Pollard:

> *Pollard:* Jesus said that love is the purpose of life. Does that sound nonsense to you?
>
> *Dawkins:* It sounds like something grafted on, a superfluous excrescence on life, which I feel I understand better. But it doesn't surprise me that, brains being what they are, they have a capacity to invent spurious purposes of the universe which –
>
> *Pollard:* You would say that love is a spurious purpose?
>
> *Dawkins:* Well, love is not a purpose, love is an emotion (which I certainly feel) which is another of those properties of brains.
>
> *Pollard:* A by-product?
>
> *Dawkins:* Well, it's probably more than just a by-product. It's probably a very important product for gene survival. Certainly sexual love would be, and so would parental love and various other sorts of love. But to say that love is the purpose of life doesn't in any way chime in with the understanding of life which I feel we have achieved.[80]

Dawkins' reductionistic comments about love call to mind the prophecy of Nietzsche: 'Behold, I show you the last man. What is love? What is creation? What is longing? What is a star? Thus asks the last man and blinks. The earth has become small, and on it hops the last man who makes everything small.'[81] For the atheist, love cannot function as the fundamental meaning or goal of existence, because love cannot be an objectively good thing in a Godless universe. Dawkins' atheism forces him to reduce love to nothing but a physical act or a subjective 'emotion' which is itself reducible to some property or other of the brain, which in turn only exists because it happens to have been conducive at some point in the past to the survival of selfish genes that it exists.

Indeed, whether Dawkins is thinking about the grand scheme of things or about the individual, 'purpose' is for him nothing but shorthand for purposelessness:

> The [idea that the] purpose of a bird's wing is to keep the bird aloft [is] not cognitively thought out. What it really means is that the bird's ancestors that had wings did, in fact, stay aloft. It was a good [i.e. successful] thing to do, so they had more children and so their descendants inherited the same wings. More fundamentally, to say that the purpose of life is to pass on their DNA means that all living things are descended from a long line of successful ancestors, where success means they have passed on their DNA . . . *There is no purpose other than that.*[82]

None of this means that Dawkins doesn't love his wife (Lalla Ward[83]); but it does raise a serious question mark over the capacity of his naturalism to account for the reality of that love:

> The point that atheist evolutionists refuse to face

is that without a creator, human life makes no sense. When atheists take science beyond its scope, and claim the explanation for all of reality, their science becomes a failure on its own terms. For to be successful, a scientific theory must adequately explain the reality it is addressing. Evolution, when placed within a purely materialistic or atheistic framework, strikingly fails at this point. It does not explain humanity.[84]

Art to the Rescue?

With the rise of naturalism and secularism in the (so-called) Enlightenment, (which Peter Kreeft wryly calls 'the Darkening'[85]), art unsurprisingly came to the fore as a substitute religious experience. As Roger Scruton explains: 'art became a redeeming enterprise, and the artist stepped into the place vacated by the prophet and the priest'.[86] Modernist culture rejected the medieval recognition of the 'face of God' in nature and art, but continued to seek the experience of awe and wonder that it craved in an art devoid of a transcendent reference point:

> The high culture of the Enlightenment . . . involved a noble and energetic attempt to rescue the ethical view of human life . . . which flourished spontaneously in the old religious culture . . . The rescue was a work of the imagination, in which the aesthetic attitude took over from religious worship as the source of intrinsic values.[87]

From the theistic point of view, one could say that the spiritual feelings of modernism were better than its philosophy. One could say the same of Dawkins' *Unweaving the Rainbow*. Faced with the charge of nihilism, Dawkins points to his poetic attitude towards science, as if a subjective emotional response could take over from religion as a source of intrinsic value. However, this Enlightenment rescue attempt is doomed from the start, and the theist has an explanation for this failure: God is the source of aesthetic value as well as ethical value. Cut off from its source, objective aesthetic value (no less than ethical value) is bound to whither and die. Indeed, after the Enlightenment 'death of God' it would not be long before people realized this was so. 'Artistic expression over the past 400 years, the age of science, persistently returns to the man alone, lost and searching for something, though he is seldom sure precisely what'[88] notes Bryan Appleyard; but instead of preserving the meaning of spiritual experience by reacknowledging its transcendent source, postmodernism held on to naturalism and resigned itself to the objective meaninglessness of all value. As Scruton says: 'When religion dies . . . the vision of man's higher nature is conserved by art. But art cannot be a substitute for religion, nor does it fill the void that is left by faith.'[89]

Pictures at an exhibition

Walking through a Cambridge museum I was struck by the changing themes apparent in the historically ordered art collection. Many of the earlier paintings had a religious theme; paintings of nature became more prominent as time went on, but the general impression produced by these artworks was one of artistic beauty and meaning. I could sense that the artists were saying: 'Look, this person/event is important (often theologically so)', or simply, 'Look, this is beautiful.' As I reached the art of the Enlightenment, detailed still-life studies and portraits of wealthy people who had paid to be immortalized on canvas dominated the collection. Art had begun to serve man. Finally, I reached galleries of twentieth-century art. The change of mood was even more pronounced and all the more disturbing, for this art clearly expressed a disturbed mindset. Images of pain and depression filled me with a sense of tragic compassion, in stark contrast with the beauty and hope I had just seen filling the art of so many preceding centuries. Artist Thomas Williams contemplates the affect of naturalism upon art:

> The direction that much art has taken in the past few generations tells us something about the despair of naturalism. There was a time when the goal of the artist was to display beauty. But as naturalistic philosophy became dominant, much of the art produced became increasingly pointless, despairing, and consciously devoid of beauty. The oppressive weight of the philosophy of meaninglessness has squeezed the bright colors from the brushes of many unbelieving artists. In their despair they have dismissed beauty as an illusion that cannot hide the dark void they believe will ultimately engulf all things. And their art reflects that despair.[90]

As theologian Hans Kung put it: 'Art has now become the expression of man's estrangement, his isolation in the world, of the ultimate futility of human life and the history of humanity.'[91]

If God exists, then to worship the beauty of art in the Enlightenment manner is to make art into an idol, to mistake the sign for the subject, the face for the person. As Peter Kreeft warns: 'Since an idol is not God, no matter how sincere or passionately it is treated as God, it is bound to break the heart of its worshipper, sooner or later. Good motives for idolatry cannot remove the objective fact that the idol is an unreality . . . You can't get blood out of a stone or divine joy from nondivine things.'[92]

If, as Roger Scruton claims, healthy art is inseparable from healthy religion, then either God exists and explains this connection, or God does not exist, and the world is absurd. Why absurd? Because a world in which aesthetic value depends upon the retention of belief in a non-existent God is a world that asks us to hypocritically predicate true value on a falsehood. If the world is not thus absurd, God both exists and grounds aesthetic value.

The hypothesis that God is the only sufficient condition of the objectivity and meaningfulness of aesthetic value explains (what otherwise seems inexplicable) why the flower of artistic high culture that flourished under the worldview of Christendom turned to rancour in a secular society: 'if you consider the high culture of modern times', writes Scruton, 'you will be struck by the theme of alienation which runs through so many of its products . . . the high culture of our society, having ceased to be a meditation on the common religion, has become instead a meditation on the lack of it'.[93] What is it that people miss so much that they devote a large proportion of our culture's artistic output to mourning its loss? The answer is simple: God.

The mannishness of man
Schaeffer pointed out how a naturalistic worldview leads to the denial of those aspects of personhood that

are essential to the existence of meaningful aesthetic experience. The denial of any objective reality besides matter includes the denial of what Schaeffer called 'the mannishness of man' (and which, in these more politically correct times, we might call 'the humanness of humans'): 'Those aspects of man, such as significance, love, relationship, rationality and the fear of nonbeing, which mark him off from animals and machines . . .'[94] Dawkins' philosophy very clearly eliminates the mannishness of man. While the confusion between the science of naturalists and the naturalism of scientists goes unchallenged, 'Science, quietly and inexplicitly, is talking us into abandoning ourselves, our true selves.'[95] For example, atheist Francis Crick writes that: 'your joys and your sorrows, your memories and your ambitions, your sense of personal identity and free-will, are in fact no more than the behaviour of a vast assembly of nerve cells and their associated molecules. As Lewis Carroll's Alice might have phrased it: "You're nothing but a pack of neurons."'[96] Dawkins agrees that a human is 'some manifestation of brain stuff and its workings . . . I'd place a very heavy bet (which I realise I could never actually win) that when my brain rots my self will not in any sense exist.'[97] But as Schaeffer said: 'if man has been kicked up by chance out of what is only impersonal, then those things that make him man – hope of purpose and significance, love, notions of morality and rationality, beauty and verbal communication – are ultimately unfulfillable and are thus meaningless'.[98] Naturalism therefore leads to nihilism, of which postmodernism is an expression: 'The existential vacuum which is the mass neurosis of the present time can be described as a private and personal form of nihilism' wrote psychiatrist Victor E. Frankl, 'for nihilism can be defined as the contention that being has no meaning.'[99]

No one, said Schaeffer, has ever worked out how to obtain the personal from the impersonal. Three decades of thought since Schaeffer have not improved matters for naturalists. According to Jerry Fodor ('by common consent the leading philosopher of mind in the world today'[100]): 'Nobody has the slightest idea how anything material could be conscious. Nobody even knows what it would be like to have the slightest idea about how anything material could be conscious.'[101] David Chalmers dubbed this the 'hard problem' of consciousness: 'The hard problem . . . is the question of how physical processes in the brain give rise to subjective experience . . . nobody knows why these physical processes are accompanied by conscious experience at all.'[102] Ned Block concurs: 'We have no conception of our physical or functional nature that allows us to understand how it could explain our subjective experience . . . we have nothing – zilch – worthy of being called a research programme, nor are there any substantive proposals about how to go about starting one . . . Researchers are *stumped*.'[103] Dawkins admits that consciousness is 'philosophically mysterious'[104] and writes: 'we don't yet really have any idea how it evolved and where it fits into a Darwinian view of biology'.[105] It should be clear from these admissions of ignorance that the identification of the human mind with the human brain, far from being a discovery of modern science, is a conclusion deduced from the prior assumption of naturalism. Dawkins allows that: 'If scientists suspect that all aspects of the mind have a scientific [i.e. naturalistic] explanation but they can't actually say what that explanation is yet, then of course it's open to you to doubt whether the explanation ever will be forthcoming. That's a perfectly reasonable doubt.'[106] Nevertheless, Dawkins' commitment to naturalism prevents him from accepting the legitimacy of any non-naturalistic account of consciousness: 'spirit . . . is not an explanation, it's an evasion . . . The scientist may agree to use the word soul for that which we don't understand, but the scientist adds, "But we're working on it, and one day we hope we shall explain it [naturalistically]."'[107] However, having examined some of the powerful philosophical arguments against physicalism (cf. the anti-naturalism arguments from reason), it should be clear that a wholly naturalistic understanding of humanity is inadequate not only *in fact*, but also *in principle*. Humanity is more than merely natural, and it is not the metaphysical concept of spirit that constitutes 'an evasion' of the need for explanation, but the promissory naturalism of Dawkins' scientism.

Philosopher J. Budziszewski recalls the dilemma of self-understanding he experienced as an atheist:

My mind, I supposed, was nothing more than the activity of my brain, my brain nothing more than a computational device. Of course, we do not experience ourselves as machines, but I told myself that we are machines under a double curse – the illusion of being more than machines and the desire for the illusion to be true. How a machine could suffer such things as desires and illusions deeply troubled me. In fact, all the phenomena of consciousness troubled me. I was troubled by the redness of red, the deliberateness of choice, the preciousness of my loves, the sense I sometimes had of exerting my will against an inclination – I was even troubled by the experience of being troubled. I knew that I could not fit these things inside the theory that I was a machine, and I knew that the intuition that I was more than a machine made a better fit with reality. To get around this fact, I told myself that a machine is something that I know, whereas a soul is something that I do not know – conveniently forgetting that I experience myself, unlike machines, directly . . . In a sense, I thought, I did not exist.[108]

Eventually, Budziszewski came to a realization: 'I had reached my conclusions not because of the data but in spite of it.'[109]

As Schaeffer observed: 'Our generation longs for the reality of personality, but it cannot find it. But Christianity says personality is valid because personality has not just appeared in the universe, but rather is rooted in the personal God who has always been.'[110] Dawkins thinks that this explanation is a bad explanation because it doesn't explain the spiritually complex (the mannishness of man) by the physically simple (matter plus time plus chance). However, if the simple explanation doesn't explain 'the mannishness of man', but rather ends up explaining it away, shouldn't we accept the theistic explanation as the more adequate account of the facts? As Richard Swinburne argues: 'why did not evolution just throw up unfeeling robots? . . . Darwinism can only explain why some animals are eliminated in the struggle for survival, not why there are animals and men at all with mental lives of sensation and belief, and in so far as it can explain anything, the question inevitably arises why the laws of evolution are as they are. All this theism can explain.'[111] On the theistic hypothesis, God brings it about that brain events of a certain kind reliably give rise to, or are correlated with, mental experiences of a certain kind. The providence of God can here explain what science is in principle incapable of explaining.[112]

O'Hear gets cold feet but then warms to his topic

It is fascinating to observe how a contemporary non-Christian philosopher, attempting to deal with the question of beauty, can tie himself up in a knot. Anthony O'Hear is an agnostic who rejects scientism and the naturalistic project to reduce human nature and experience to 'nothing but' the result of natural selection. For example, in his 1997 book *Beyond Evolution*, O'Hear argues that 'to find the Rokeby Venus beautiful is to make an objective judgement',[113] and sets out to show that 'our sense of beauty . . . cannot usefully be analysed in biological or evolutionary terms'.[114] O'Hear acknowledges that 'from a Darwinian perspective, truth, goodness, and beauty and our care for them are very hard to explain'.[115] He even acknowledges that, 'For some, speculation about the origin of our non-Darwinian concerns would take a religious direction.'[116] O'Hear observes that 'in experiencing beauty we feel ourselves to be in contact with a deeper reality than the everyday',[117] and passes the following observations upon this experience:

> Art can seem revelatory, just as it does seem to answer to objective standards. It can seem to take us to the essence of reality, as if certain sensitivities in us . . . beat in tune with reality. It is

> as if our . . . appreciation of things external to us
> . . . are reflecting a deep and pre-conscious
> harmony between us and the world from which we
> spring. If this feeling is not simply an illusion . . .
> it may say something about the nature of reality
> itself, as responsive to human desires . . . But how
> could we think of an aesthetic justification of
> experience . . . unless our aesthetic experience
> was sustained by a divine will revealed in the
> universe, and particularly in our experience of it
> as beautiful? It is precisely at this point that many
> or even most will draw back. Aesthetic experience
> *seems* to produce the harmony between us and
> the world that would have to point to a religious
> resolution were it not to be an illusion.[118]

O'Hear has argued that beauty is objective, and that if beauty is understood objectively it points to the truth of 'a religious resolution'. The conclusion that follows is clearly the truth of 'a religious resolution'. However, O'Hear draws back, saying: 'But such a resolution is intellectually unsustainable, so aesthetic experience, however powerful, remains subjective and, in its full articulation, illusory. This is a dilemma I cannot solve or tackle head on.'[119] To summarily dismiss the 'religious resolution' as 'intellectually unsustainable' in this way, involving as it does throwing over everything he has already argued for, seems like an uncharitably off-hand-ed failure to follow the evidence where it leads.

O'Hear's consideration of beauty in *Beyond Evolution* ends with the thought that, 'despite the problems of alienation thrown up by science . . .'[120] we nevertheless have a sense that we are, to some extent, at home in the world; and that nowhere do we meet this intuition quite so strongly as in our experience of beauty: 'From my point of view it is above all in aesthetic experience that we gain the fullest and most vividly lived sense that though we are creatures of Darwinian origin, our nature transcends our origin in tantalizing ways.'[121] Aesthetic experience, says O'Hear, promises to reconcile our particular experiences of beauty 'to what might be thought of as our striving for some transcendent guarantee and consolation'.[122] For O'Hear, this tantalization is literal. The aesthetic experience that calls us home is an illusion, a 'whistling in the dark'[123] as he puts it, and this realization must leave us alone with our alienation. Thus O'Hear finds himself in exactly the same position as the author of Ecclesiastes who saw that everything was 'meaningless . . . under the sun' [i.e. without reference to a transcendent God].

In *After Progress* (1999) O'Hear tentatively follows the evidence further towards the 'religious resolution' he formally derided, writing that: 'Through art . . . we do have intimations of beauty, of order, of divinity, even, way beyond the biological.'[124] Our 'yearning for beauty [points] to a more than material underpinning of matter itself'.[125] Indeed:

> . . . in appreciating the beauty of the world and of things in the world, we are seeing the world as endowed with value and meaning . . . We are seeing the world and our own existence as created, guided and measured by what the religions have referred to variously as God or Brahman or the One . . . We are seeing the world as animated by some higher quasi-personal purpose, operating through and behind the material processes revealed and studied by natural science.[126]

O'Hear even argues that 'salvation [from the loss of value instigated by scientism], if it is to come, will have to come through that higher power'.[127]

In *Philosophy in the New Century* (2001), O'Hear once again defends the objectivity of beauty: 'In saying that one painting is beautiful and another ugly, one is saying something about the paintings, something which can be explained, argued about and discussed. It is also something on which people can be right or wrong.'[128] He goes on to acknowledge that:

> . . . there are intimations of value within our experience which reveal us each to be part of something more significant than our individual life and fate . . . In the past these intimations of value have typically been expressed and understood religiously . . . with the advance of materialism, formal religion has declined. But the intimations of value survive, and they are resistant to being explained away in materialistic fashion . . .[129]

So what does he do with these materialistically inexplicable 'intimations of value'? Nothing: 'Whether these reflections should lead us to consider or reconsider any actual religion is not for philosophy to say.'[130] Why ever not? O'Hear cautions that philosophy 'can at most clear a space for more full-bloodied world-views and commitments'.[131] But this is certainly not how most of the great philosophers have understood their subject. Of course philosophy has limits – just as science has limits – but philosophers have traditionally assumed the task of using philosophy to positively inform, and to organize information from beyond philosophy (especially science) into, a coherent worldview. For many of those philosophers, that worldview has been theistic. O'Hear simply leaves us dangling in mid-air. Doing nothing with our intimations of value is an improvement on dismissing them because they are seen to lead to God, but isn't it better still to follow beauty wherever it leads, even if that 'wherever' is a *Whom*ever? Indeed, the O'Hear of *After Progress* goes further towards that whomever than the O'Hear of *Philosophy* (perhaps because he regards the former as being less a work of philosophy in his unusually narrow sense of the term, than a work of cultural analysis).

Although O'Hear may have called the religious understanding of beauty 'intellectually unsustainable',[132] he did so in the face of his own logically valid argument for just such a religious conclusion, an argument and conclusion that he seems to have warmed to in later writings. O'Hear would certainly encourage us not to be put off accepting such a 'religious resolution' by anything that science has to say: 'To view the world religiously is to see meaning and intelligence and purpose behind its mute physical processes. It cannot be said that doing this is wrong, or that science could show that it is wrong. At bottom there can be no conflict between science and religion.'[133]

[1] Huxley, Aldous, *Ends and Means* (London: Chatto & Windus, 1940), p.267.

[2] Davis, William C., 'Theistic Arguments', in Michael J. Murray (ed.), *Reason for the Hope Within* (Grand Rapids: Eerdmans, 1999), p.37, my italics.

[3] Collins, Robin, 'Design and the Many-Worlds Hypothesis', in William Lane Craig (ed.), *Philosophy of Religion: A Reader and Guide* (Edinburgh University Press, 2002), p.137.

[4] Dawkins, Richard, *Unweaving the Rainbow* (Allen Lane, 1998), p.63.

[5] Moreland, J. P., *Scaling the Secular City* (Grand Rapids: Baker, 1987), p.49.

[6] *ibid.*

[7] Quoted by Denis Alexander, *Rebuilding the Matrix* (Oxford: Lion, 2001), p.249.

[8] Weinberg, Steven, quoted by Alexander, *ibid.*

[9] Davies, Paul, *The Mind of God* (London: Penguin, 1993), p.175.

[10] *ibid.*

[11] Augros, Robert and Stanciu, George, *The New Story of Science* (Lake Bluff, Illinois: Regnery Gateway, 1984), p.39.

[12] Polkinghorne, John, 'Does God exist?', in Harriet Swain (ed.), *Big Questions in Science* (London, Jonathan Cape, 2002), p.6.

[13] Everest, Graham R. in John F. Ashton (ed.), *On the Seventh Day* (Master Books), p.266.

[14] Groothuis, Douglas, *Truth Decay* (Downers Grove: IVP, 2000), p.251.

[15] Moreland, *op. cit.*

[16] Polkinghorne, John, *Belief In God In An Age of Science* (Yale, 2003), p.2.

[17] Polkinghorne, John, *Science & Theology* (SPCK, 1998), p.73.

[18] Hanfling, Oswald, *Philosophical Aesthetics: an introduction*, (Oxford: Blackwells, 1992), Introduction, p.vii.

[19] Huntley, H. E., in *The Divine Proportion – A Study In Mathematical Beauty* (New York: Dover Publications, 1970), p.12-20.

[20] O'Hear, Anthony, *After Progress* (London: Bloomsbury, 1999), p.67.

[21] Balfour, Arthur J., *Theism and Humanism* (Inkling Books, 2000), p.48.

[22] *ibid.*, p.43.

[23] *ibid.*

[24] Alexander, Denis, *Rebuilding the Matrix* (Oxford: Lion, 2001), p.253.

[25] Rhodes, W. S., *The Christian God* (ISPCK, 1998).

[26] Tennant, F. R., *op. cit.*

[27] *ibid.*

[28] Pinnock, Clark H., *Most Moved Mover: A Theology of God's Openness* (Paternoster, 2001), p.2.

[29] Morris, Thomas V., *Philosophy for Dummies* (IDG Books, 1999), p.242.

[30] Cicero, *De Natura Deorum.*

[31] Hume, David, *Dialogues Concerning Natural Religion* (Indianapolis: Bobbs-Merrill, 1946), p.214.

[32] Chesterton, G. K., *The Everlasting Man* (London: Hodder & Stoughton, 1927), p.191.

[33] Only 6 per cent of people believe that other people believe in God because of their perception of design. cf. Michael Shermer, 'Why People Believe in God: An Empirical Study on a Deep Question', *The Humanist*, 59:6:20-26 (Nov/Dec, 1999).

[34] Moreland, *op. cit.*

[35] Pinnock, Clark, *Reason Enough* (Paternoster, 1980), p.64-65.

[36] *ibid.*

[37] *ibid.*

[38] *ibid.*

[39] Swinburne, Richard, *Evidence for God* (Mowbray, 1986).

[40] Ferguson, Kitty, *Fire in the Equations* (Bantam Press, 1995), p.19.

[41] *ibid.*

[42] *ibid.*

[43] *ibid.*

[44] *ibid.*

[45] Chesterton, *The Everlasting Man, op. cit.*, p.106.

[46] Augustine, *Confessions* (Oxford Paperbacks, 1998).

[47] *ibid.*

[48] Joad, C. E. M., *Guide to Philosophy* (London: Victor Gallancz, 1946), p.354.

[49] Tolkein, J. R. R., *Return of the King* (New York: Ballantine Books, 1965), p.244.

[50] Lewis, C. S., *The Weight of Glory* (San Francisco: HarperCollins, 2001).

[51] *ibid.*

[52] Lewis, C. S., *Mere Christianity* (San Francisco: HarperCollins, 2001).

[53] *ibid.*

[54] cf. Humphreys, Colin J., *The Miracles of Exodus: A Scientist's Discovery of the Extraordinary Natural Causes of the Biblical Stories* (London: Continuum, 2003), p.69-81.

[55] Underhill, Evelyn, *Man and the Supernatural* (Methuen, 1934), p.170.

[56] Weil, Simone, *Gravity and Grace* (London: Routledge, 1952), p.137.

[57] McGrath, Alister, *The Re-Enchantment of Nature* (London: Hodder & Stoughton, 2003), p.187.

[58] Kreeft, Peter, *Heaven – the heart's deepest longing* (San Francisco: Ignatius, 1993), p.115.

[59] *ibid.*

[60] *ibid.*, p.112.

[61] Scruton, Roger, *An Intelligent Person's Guide To Philosophy* (London: Duckworth, 1997), p.95-96.

[62] The distinction between 'looking along' and 'looking at' comes from C. S. Lewis' essay 'Meditations in a Toolshed,' in Walter Hooper (ed.), *God in the Dock* (London: Fount).

[63] Scruton, *op. cit.*, p.29.

[64] *ibid.*, p.14.

[65] cf. *The Complete Works of Francis A. Schaeffer, volume 1*, 'A Christian View of Philosophy And Culture', (Crossway Books, 1994).

[66] Blumberg, Janet Leslie, *'The Literary Background of The Lord of the Rings'*, *Celebrating Middle Earth* (Seattle: Inkling Books, 2002), p.79-80.

[67] *ibid.*, p.80.

[68] Craig, William Lane, *Reasonable Faith* (Crossway, 1994), p.65.

[69] Dawkins, Richard, 'A scientist's case against God', speech delivered at the Edinburgh International Science Festival, 15th April 1992, published in the *Independent*, 20 April 1992.

[70] Nietzsche, Frederick, *The Gay Science*. (Random House, 1974).

[71] Neitzsche, quoted by Ravi Zacharias in *A Shattered Visage* (Grand Rapids: Baker, 1990), p.49.

[72] Kreeft, Peter, *op. cit.*

[73] *ibid.*, p.42-43.

[74] Yandell, Keith, *Philosophy of Religion – a contemporary introduction*, (Routledge, 1998), Preface.

[75] Walkup, John, 'From Religion to Relationship', in Paul M. Anderson (ed.), *Professors Who Believe – The Spiritual Journeys of Christian Faculty* (IVP, 1999), p.85.

[76] Peck, W. G., *The Salvation of Man* (London: Centenary Press, 1938), p.83.

[77] Lewis, C. S, *The Abolition of Man* (London: Fount, 1999), p.50.

[78] Scruton, Roger, *An Intelligent Person's Guide To Modern Culture* (London: Duckworth, 1998), p.68.

[79] Schaeffer, *op. cit.*

[80] 'Nick Pollard talks to Dr. Richard Dawkins', *Thirdway*, April 1995, vol 18, no 3.

[81] Nietzsche, *The Portable Nietzsche*, trans. Walter Kaufmann (New York: Viking press, 1954), p.129-130.

[82] 'Nick Pollard talks to Dr. Richard Dawkins', *op. cit.*

[83] cf. The Unofficial Lalla Ward Homepage at www.geocities.com/Area51/Rampart/3947/

[84] Birkett, Kirsten, *The Essence of Darwinism* (Matthias Media, 2001), p.120.

[85] Kreeft, *Back to Virtue, op. cit.*, p.100.

[86] Schaeffer, *op. cit.*, p.36.

[87] *ibid.*

[88] Appleyard, Bryan, *Understanding the Present* (London: Picador, 1993), p.15.

[89] Scruton, *op. cit.*, p.49.

[90] McDowell, Josh and Williams, Thomas, *In Search of Certainty* (Wheaton, Illinois: Tyndale, 2003), p.83.

[91] Kung, Hans, *Art and the Question of Meaning* (SCM Press, 1981).

[92] Kreeft, *op. cit.*

[93] Scruton, *op. cit.*, p.17.

[94] Schaeffer, *op. cit.*

[95] Appleyard, *op. cit.*, p.xviii.

[96] Crick, Francis, *The Astonishing Hypothesis* (Simon & Schuster, 1994), p.3.

[97] Dawkins, Richard, 'Nick Pollard talks to Dr. Richard Dawkins' at www.damaris.org/content/content.php?type=5&id=102

[98] Schaeffer, Francis A., *Whatever Happened to the Human Race?, op. cit.*, p.372.

[99] Frankl, Victor E., *Man's Search For Meaning* (Washington Square Press, 1984), p.152.

[100] McGinn, Colin, *The Making of a Philosopher* (London: Scribner, 2003), p.190.

[101] Fodor, Jerry, 'The Big Idea: Can There be a Science of Mind?', *Times Literary Supplement*, July 3 1992.

[102] Chalmers, David, 'The Puzzle of Conscious Experience', *Scientific American*, special edition, 'The Hidden Mind', 12 (1) (August 2002), 92-93.

[103] Block, Ned, 'Consciousness' in S. Guttenplan (ed.), *A Companion to the Philosophy of Mind* (Oxford, 1994), p.211.

[104] Dawkins, Richard, 'Darwin's Dangerous Disciple' at www.skeptic.com/03.4.miele-dawkins-iv.html

[105] *ibid.*

[106] Dawkins, Richard 'Is Science Killing the Soul?' at www.edge.org/documents/archive/edge53.html

[107] *ibid.*

[108] Budziszewski, J., in Norman L. Geisler and Paul K. Hoffman (eds), *Why I Am A Christian* (Grand Rapids: Baker, 2001), p.55.

[109] *ibid.*, p.55.

[110] Schaeffer, *op. cit.*

[111] Swinburne, Richard, 'The Justification of Theism' at www.leaderu.com/truth/3truth09.html

[112] cf. Adams, Robert 'Flavors, Colors and God', in R. Douglas Geivett and Brendan Sweetman (eds), *Contemporary Perspectives on Religious Epistemology* (New York: Oxford University Press, 1992).

[113] O'Hear, Anthony, *Beyond Evolution* (Oxford: Clarendon Press, 1997), Preface.

[114] *ibid.*, Preface.

[115] *ibid.*, p.214.

[116] *ibid.*

[117] *ibid.*, p.195.

[118] *ibid.*, p.199-201.

[119] *ibid.*

[120] *ibid.*

[121] *ibid.*, p.202.

[122] *ibid.*, p.214.

[123] *ibid.*, p.195.

[124] O'Hear, Anthony, *After Progress* (London: Bloomsbury, 1999), p.239.

[125] *ibid.*, p.245-246.

[126] *ibid.*, p.249-250.

[127] *ibid.*, p.250.

[128] O'Hear, Anthony, *Philosophy* (London: New Century, 2001), p.153.

[129] *ibid.*

[130] *ibid.*

[131] *ibid.*

[132] O'Hear, *Beyond Evolution, op. cit.*, p.201.

[133] O'Hear, *Philosophy, op. cit.*, p.135.

CHAPTER 8

Over the Rainbow

In the 2003 film *Alien Hunter* (Dir. Ron Krauss) James Spader plays linguist Julian Rome, a Berkeley academic who once worked for NASA searching for extra-terrestrial intelligence. Rome is called to the South Pole when a research base chips a truck-sized object out of the ice, an object that emits a radio signal. One of Rome's colleagues suggests this signal could be a natural phenomenon: 'a meteorite would explain the EMP' (electro-magnetic pulse). 'Not a non-random signal', Rome retorts. The unidentified object is emitting a signal that is neither simple and non-random (like that produced by a pulsar) nor complex but random (like 'white noise'). If the signal conformed to either of these two options it could readily be explained away as a natural phenomenon. We know from experience that nature can produce simple, non-random phenomena and complex, random phenomena. However, the radio signal is both complex and non-random (like a computer program or a musical score). In fact, it consists of a long string of 'prime numbers repeated over and over'. In our experience, whenever we know the source of something that is both complex and non-random (like a computer program, a musical score, or a long list of prime numbers in ascending order), it originates from intelligence. Hence the best explanation of the signal coming from the polar object is not that it is a natural phenomenon, as Rome's colleague suggests, but that it is caused by intelligence. That this string of numbers is being produced randomly (without intelligence) is 'a possibility', Rome admits, but the odds against it are just too large to turn this bare possibility into a realistic explanation. Hence Rome concludes: 'I know it's artificial.' What the scientists can't tell from the signal is whether that intelligence is terrestrial or extra-terrestrial. Is their polar object an elaborate hoax, or an alien artefact as Rome believes? Nor can

> they tell whether the object's purpose is aggressive or benign. The only way to find out is to open it up . . .

The order, arrangement, beauty, change and movement of the visible world declare that it could only have been the work of God, who is indescribably and invisibly great and indescribably and invisibly beautiful.
AUGUSTINE

Having examined aesthetic arguments from both the fact and contents of aesthetic experience in Chapter Seven, and having already dealt with arguments from the fact of beauty itself in Chapter Six, this chapter will kick off an examination of aesthetic arguments from beautiful things. I will round off my discussion of aesthetics in these final chapters by examining, in dialogue with Richard Dawkins, the scientific theory of 'Intelligent Design' (ID). This will be done with one eye on how ID relates to the account of beauty developed in Chapter Six, and the other on what ID contributes to our search for the meaning and purpose of life.

Aesthetic arguments from beautiful things

. . . whence arises all that Order and Beauty which we see in the world?
ISAAC NEWTON[1]

Added beauty

Beauty shows that the world is infused with more meaning than mere mechanisms can account for . . .
JOSH MCDOWELL AND THOMAS WILLIAMS[2]

Stuart Burgess, Reader in Engineering Design at Bristol University, writes that, 'Following modern discoveries of the staggering complexity and beauty of nature, the Design argument is stronger than ever before . . . I believe that the beauty of nature . . . presents one of the biggest challenges to the atheist . . .'[3] According to Burgess, 'One of the most positive evidences for a Creator is the existence of profound beauty throughout the natural world.'[4] Burgess distinguishes between 'inherent' and 'added' beauty: 'Inherent beauty is a beauty that exists as a by-product of mechanical design. In contrast, added beauty is a type of beauty which has the sole purpose of providing a beautiful display.'[5] For example, there is no mechanical reason for a classical column to be anything more than a plain cylinder, yet Greek architects decorated their columns with grooves and 'capitals'. When added beauty is seen in objects, says Burgess, 'this represents very strong evidence for design because there is no mechanical reason for the beautiful appearance'.[6] Burgess suggests that nature is replete with examples of added beauty which bespeak artistic design. Palaeontologist Kurt P. Wise likewise argues that nature is too beautiful for naturalistic explanations: 'One striking characteristic of life unexplained by evolution is its aesthetic nature . . . This magnificent beauty . . . cannot be explained by macroevolutionary theory. It is, however, consistent with an intelligent cause for life . . .'[7]

F. R. Tennant begins his classic meditation on the significance of nature's beauty with the obvious assertion that: 'Nature is sublime or beautiful, and the exceptions do but prove the rule.'[8] Tennant's next premise is that: 'In general, man's productions (other than professed works of art), and almost only they, are aesthetically vile . . . We might almost say the one [human agency] never achieves, while the other [nature] never misses, the beautiful.'[9] This generalization applies, says Tennant, to the products *and productive processes* of both humanity and nature (thus Tennant's argument can happily accommodate a process of evolution): 'Compare, e.g., "the rattling looms and the hammering noise of human workshops" with Nature's silent or musical constructiveness; or the devastating stinks of chemical works with Nature's fragrant distillations.'[10] Richard Swinburne would agree, for he writes that: 'one would be hard put to think of any part of the pre-human world which is ugly; ugliness in this sense seems to arrive with the arrival of humans, who, knowingly or unknowingly, make something which could be beautiful ugly instead'.[11] Then comes Tennant's argument: 'If "God made the country" whereas man made the town . . . we have a possible explanation of these things; but if the theism contained in this saying be rejected, explanation does not seem to be forthcoming.'[12]

The beauty of nature, argues Tennant, cannot be co-extensive with either nature's 'mechanicalness', or its (supposed) lack of aesthetic design, 'as man's utilitarian productions shew'.[13] Concrete car parks are utilitarian, but they are ugly. As Balfour pointed out: 'An ill-proportioned building might have been equally fitted for its purpose; a plain sword might have been equally lethal.'[14] Tennant is certainly on to something here, for as W. S. Rhodes writes: 'Beauty may be associated with fitness for function . . . Yet things exactly suited to their function are not necessarily beautiful . . . And it is only in certain cases that the beauty of living things can be attributed to fitness for function.'[15] In other words, nature is full of 'added beauty' that cannot be explained by reference to such mechanical notions as survival value. As Tennant says: 'we may still ask why *Nature*'s mechanism affects us in such wise that we deem her sublime and beautiful, since mere mechanism, as such, is under no universal necessity to do so, and what we may call human mechanisms [produced on purely utilitarian lines] usually fail to do so'.[16] Yet, 'this potency, describable as the Objective factor in beauty, belongs to Nature's very texture'.[17]

The motive of beauty

Richard Swinburne takes up a suggestion from Tennant that beauty provides a motive, meaning, and purpose for creation. Swinburne says that if God exists, then he has: 'apparently overriding reason, for making, not merely an orderly world . . . but a beautiful world – at any rate to the extent to which it lies outside the control of creatures'.[18] Swinburne argues: 'God has a very good reason for making a beautiful Universe, namely that he himself will admire it (not admire it because he made it, of course; but because what he made is admirable).'[19] Moreover, the goodness of subjective, enjoyed beauty constitutes one reason for God to create creatures with an aesthetic sense. As Augustine wrote: 'Then there is the beauty and utility of the natural creation, which the divine generosity has bestowed on man, for him to behold . . .'[20] Swinburne says that while 'the beauty of the beautiful does not depend on being recognized',[21] it is of course 'good that people admire what is beautiful'.[22]

There are two reasons why God might be expected to make a basically beautiful world: that He may appreciate its beauty, and that creatures like ourselves may appreciate the beauty both of God and of God's Creation. God's fundamental motivation for making a basically beautiful world is that 'beauty is a good thing'.[23] The conclusion Swinburne draws is that 'if there is a God there is more reason to expect a basically beautiful world than a basically ugly one . . .'[24]

The next step in Swinburne's argument is to assert that: 'A priori . . . there is no particular reason for expecting a basically beautiful rather than a basically ugly world.'[25] The conclusion to be drawn from this observation is that, if the world is basically beautiful, that would be evidence for the existence of God. It only remains for Swinburne to point out that the world is indeed basically beautiful to complete his argument:

> The existence of all concrete things . . . is good in itself. The more, the better. And better that they be arranged in a beautiful way. Could anyone who has come to admire sculpture possibly deny that? But better still is a moving sculpture – a process whereby trillions of concrete things emerge from simple beginnings. Could anyone who has come to admire dance possibly deny that? And good that they should come in kinds with marvellous patterns of colour, new kinds emerging from old – a living painting. The goodness of the existence and beauty of the non-conscious world . . . is so obvious, and yet it needs a poet to bring it alive . . . But is it not obvious that a good God would seek to bring about such beauty?[26]

In other words, from an aesthetic point of view, the world looks much as we might expect it to look if it were created by God, because 'God has reason to make a basically beautiful world',[27] and because 'he would seem to have overriding reason not to make a basically ugly world beyond the powers of creatures to improve'.[28] This remains true, says Swinburne, 'whether or not anyone ever observes [the beauty of the world], but certainly if only one person ever observes it'.[29] The judgement that the world is basically beautiful is supported by the arguments of Chapter Six, and rounds off a sound aesthetic argument for the existence of God. And while this argument can only carry the strength appropriate to an argument to the best explanation, 'The argument surely works.'[30]

Unevolved beauties

Around AD 210 Father Minucius Felix wrote his *Octavius*, a dialogue between the Christian lawyer Octavius and a pagan who argues that the world is a chaos of nonpurposeful spontaneous generation. Octavius replies:

> I feel the more convinced that people who hold this universe of consummate artistic beauty to be not the work of divine planning, but a conglomeration of some kind of fragments linking together by chance, are themselves devoid of reason and perception . . . For what is so manifest, so acknowledged and so evident, when you lift your eyes to heaven and examine all the things which are below and around you, than that there exists some divine Being of unequalled mental power by whom all nature is inspired . . ?[31]

Which is more likely, that the contingent atomic fragments emerging from the 'Big Bang' should by chance just happen to be such as to conglomerate together, *without any form of planning*, into a 'universe of consummate artistic beauty', or that such an outcome is, as most people believe, the result of a deliberate artistic inspiration?

Employing the same basic argument as Father Felix with more finesse, J. P. Moreland affirms that features of the world such as 'a sun-set, fall in Vermont, the human body, the Rocky Mountains [and] the singing of birds . . . all exhibit real, objective beauty'.[32] Moreland argues that: 'the beauty in the examples cannot be accounted for in terms of survival value, natural selection, and the like'.[33] For this conclusion he gives the following reasons:

> . . . some of the examples (the Rocky Mountains) are not biological organisms. Further, even when one considers biological organisms (the human body) it is not clear that the beauty of those organisms is related to their survival. Since science does not deal with value qualities (aesthetic or moral) in its descriptions of the world, then beauty as an aesthetic property is not a part of evolutionary theory.[34]

Augustine's remarks on this subject have lost none of their relevance:

> . . . *even if we take out of account the necessary functions of the parts*, there is a harmonious congruence between them, a beauty in their equality and correspondence, so much so that *one would be at a loss to say whether utility or beauty is the major consideration in their creation* . . . There is no visible part of the body which is merely adapted to its function without being also of aesthetic value . . . Hence it can, I think, readily be inferred that in the design of the

human body dignity was a more important consideration than utility.[35]

Since naturalistic explanations of the world give no *a priori* reason to expect much if any beauty to arise in either the biological or non-biological realm, a theistic explanation, which can invoke teleology, gains a measure of credibility. W. S. Rhodes muses: 'It is difficult to believe that so many beautiful things came into being without any kind of direction by a power sensitive to beauty.'[36] As Aristotle observed: 'it is unlikely that fire, earth, or any such element [i.e. that any material or efficient causes] should be why things manifest goodness and beauty'.[37]

Attributing biological beauty to a *naturalistic* evolutionary process hardly accounts for the overwhelming *amount* and *degree* of objective beauty produced. As Norman L. Geisler notes:

. . . things in nature . . . move towards an end, be it staying alive or reproducing, and *they move toward secondary purposes that have nothing to do with themselves*. In the big picture *their existence and actions make the world . . . beautiful*, and this implies a designer, because, as Aquinas argued, 'These agents act in predictable . . . ways that seem to work towards the best results [and] whatever lacks knowledge must be directed toward an end.'[38]

'God' provides a more adequate explanation of nature's propensity to produce beauty than does the simpler but less adequate explanation of 'naturalistic evolution', and is therefore to be preferred. Such an explanation does not exclude God working through and within an evolutionary process to obtain this effect. Moreover, as

Moreland says, evolution can hardly account for the beauty of objects that did not evolve. Nor is this a matter of arguing for a 'God-of-the-gaps', because the explanatory gap being referred to is one *inherent* to the structure of scientific explanation. As John Polkinghorne testifies: 'Beauty slips through the scientist's net.'[39] The metaphysical explanation for beauty available to the theist does not rule out scientific explanation, but subsumes it within a wider explanatory teleology capable of providing a more adequate account of the place of beauty in the cosmos. William C. Davies follows the trail to its conclusion:

> . . . consider the data of useless (nonutilitarian) beauty. Is God a better explanation of that feature of the world than metaphysical naturalism? To decide, you must ask whether useless beauty is more likely to exist if God exists or if metaphysical naturalism is true. This is by no means a simple or obvious estimate; but I'm convinced that an honest evaluation leads to the conclusion that God's existence explains this and other features of the world far more successfully . . . Value, both moral and aesthetic, appears to be an objective feature of the world . . . a fact much more likely to have been the case if God exists than if the universe is a grand accident.[40]

Beauty, intuition, analogy and design

Think of the beauty of nature – a sunset – the intricacies of a leaf. It is highly unconvincing to say it has no designer . . .
CARRIE BOREN[41]

The common intuition that nature is the result of a divine design is clearly linked to our aesthetic awareness of reality: 'The teleological argument has great appeal because it fulfills the aesthetic longings *within* us as we view the beauty of the world *around* us.'[42] The design arguments of scientists like Johannes Kepler, Robert Boyle, Robert Hooke and Isaac Newton all included an appreciation of beauty. Abraham Lincoln said: 'I can see how it might be possible for a man to look upon the earth and be an atheist, but I cannot conceive how he can look up into the heavens and say there is no God.'[43] Design arguments build upon this intuition of design, seeking to tease it out into an explicit set of premises supporting the conclusion of design.

Can evolution expel design?

It is popularly thought that the theory of evolution decimated Paley's design argument. Pre-Darwinian apologists may be forgiven for mistaking eyes and such-like for the products of intelligent design, but now science has stepped into the explanatory gap, and swept away the 'God-of-the-gaps'. However, theists needn't deny that natural processes made objects such as the eye, because they can easily deny that natural processes act without teleological direction. Science is incapable of ruling out 'personal explanations'. It is only *naturalistic* evolution that contradicts the intuition of and inference to design, but since evolution can only be naturalistic if God does not exist to intend the process of evolution, and since this is not something science is able to rule out, the suggestion that evolution undermines design begs the question. Moreover, the theist may simply argue that the *naturalistic* evolutionary explanation, although simple, is not adequate enough to overturn the *overwhelming intuitive impression* that the universe is a work of art.

Besides, evolution cannot explain all examples of watch-like order, because it: 'presupposes the *existence* of certain entities with specific potential behaviours and an *environment* of some specific kind that operates upon those entities in some specifically ordered fashion'.[44] The evolutionary challenge therefore fails to contradict the design paradigm. As Balfour wrote: 'there is nothing in the mere idea of organic evolution which is incongruous with design'.[45]

Indeed, *if* the universe produces 'watches' through a natural process, *then* it seems reasonable to construe that process itself as the product of design, just as it is reasonable to attribute an automated factory – even one operating on Darwinian principles – to design. Evolution does not destroy the analogical design argument; at most it pushes it back a step, from the objects that make up the world, to the substances and processes that make the objects that make up the world.

Hume's many designers critique

Another major charge levelled against the design argument is that it does not provide warrant for the existence of a single designer. As David Hume put the objection: 'A great number of men join in building a house or a ship, in rearing a city, in framing a commonwealth, why may not several deities combine in framing a world?'[46] But against this, Occam's razor compels us to postulate the least number of entities necessary to explain the available data, and in this instance that number is one. As Stephen T. Davis asks:

'If there is more than one designer, exactly how many are there? And why do they cooperate? Those questions do not need to be asked if there is but one designer.'[47] Given that we already have reason to believe in the existence of a transcendent personal being (as might be concluded from the moral argument and the argument from reason), Occam's razor would encourage us to conflate the source of design with this same being.

Then again, this is a *cosmos*, a coherent structure of 'ordered beauty'. We inhabit a *uni*verse, a unified whole. As J. P. Moreland writes, 'One God is a simpler explanation than the polytheistic one and it makes more intelligible the fact that we live in a *uni*verse and not a plurality of universes.'[48] Most cathedrals (let alone cities) are a conglomeration of architectural styles, renovations, innovations, and re-building. The cosmos, on the other hand, possesses a unity in both its physical 'engineering', and *in its artistic facets*. Here we already begin to see the aesthetic design argument taking part in a mutually supportive 'wider teleology'. Swinburne argues: 'If there were more than one deity responsible for the order [and beauty] of the universe, we should expect to see characteristic marks of the handiwork of different deities in different parts of the universe, just as we see different workmanship in the different houses of a city.'[49]

The aesthetic analogical design argument may have an advantage over the common analogical design argument here, in that while machines and buildings generally do have several builders (although they also generally have only one designer or architect), the artistic creation of worlds is usually the work of one artist, both in inception *and* execution. A Middle-Earth, a Narnia, a

Discworld, is the product of a Tolkein, a Lewis, a Pratchett. Our cosmos is perhaps as much like a Middle-Earth, a Narnia or a Discworld as it is a watch or an automated watch-making factory. The aesthetic, artistic analogy is perhaps as strong as the industrial, engineering analogy; and points more clearly to a single Designer. As Laura L. Garcia writes: 'some have proposed that a better analogy might be between the universe and a work of art, rather than between the universe and a machine, since this would allow a greater appeal to the beauty of the universe and would avoid some of Hume's criticisms . . .'[50]

Intelligent design theory

In the world we find everywhere clear signs of an order which can only spring from design.
IMMANUEL KANT

Intelligent Design (ID) is a scientific research programme embraced by a relatively small but growing group of scientists and other academics (design theorists) who argue that intelligent agency is a better explanation for the complexity of the universe as a whole, and for certain physical systems within the universe, than appeals to the inherent (albeit created) capacities of nature. ID claims intelligent causation is the best explanation for information-rich structures, that intelligent causation is empirically detectable, and that intelligent causation is admissible in scientific theory making. Thanks to developments in information theory, there now exist 'well-defined methods that, on the basis of observational features of the world, are capable of reliably distinguishing intelligent causes

from undirected natural causes'.[51] William Dembski
defines intelligent design as: 'the science that studies
how to detect intelligence'.[52] Many sciences depend
upon detecting intelligence: 'notably forensic science,
artificial intelligence . . . cryptography, archaeology and
the Search for Extraterrestrial Intelligence [SETI]'.[53] ID
suggests 'that we extend these insights, which have
proved so fruitful in other fields, to the world of the natural sciences'.[54]

Whenever the sciences detect intelligence, 'the
underlying entity they uncover is information'.[55] Thus,
ID is properly formulated as a theory of information:
'intelligent design is therefore not the study of intelligent causes *per se* but of informational pathways
induced by intelligent causes. As a result intelligent
design presupposes neither a creator nor miracles . . .
it detects intelligence without speculating about the
nature of the intelligence . . .'[56] It is this minimal metaphysical baggage that keeps ID within the realm of science: 'in science, the question is not between finding
natural causes or supernatural causes, but between natural and intelligent ones'.[57]

Within biology, 'intelligent design is a theory of biological origins and development'.[58] Design theorists
claim that the current dominance of neo-Darwinian theory is a function of the pool of live explanatory options
being artificially restricted by an unjustified methodological constraint, namely, the philosophical presupposition that natural sciences should only explain
things in terms of the inherent capacities of nature
(whether or not those capacities are conceived, as theists conceive of them, as being themselves designed).
Design theorists argue for a more 'open philosophy of

science',[59] and insist that the important question is not whether neo-Darwinism is the best explanation *given a ban on mentioning intelligent agency*, but whether it is *the best explanation*, full stop. Design theorists argue 'that once hypotheses positing Intelligent Design are allowed into the pool of live options, then the explanatory superiority of the neo-Darwinian theory is no longer apparent. On the contrary, its deficiencies, particularly in the explanatory power of its mechanisms of random mutation and natural selection, stand in stark relief.'[60] In sum, ID is a scientific research pro-gramme postulating that:

> The world contains events, objects and structures that exhaust the explanatory resources of undirected natural causes and that can be adequately explained only by recourse to intelligent causes . . . Precisely because of what we know about undirected natural causes and their limitations, science is now in a position to demonstrate design rigorously . . .[61]

Francis J. Beckwith reports that: 'ID proponents have developed highly sophisticated arguments, have had their work published by prestigious presses and in aca-demic journals, have aired their views among critics in the corridors of major universities and institutions, and have been recognized by leading periodicals, both academic and non-academic.'[62] As well as examining the theoretical underpinnings of ID, the current chapter will consider the data of cosmic fine-tuning as an instance of ID, leaving Chapter Nine to examine examples of biological intelligent design, and to sum up the status and import of ID with reference to the search for meaning.

Not 'creation science'[63]

> *Intelligent design theory . . . says nothing about*
> *the Bible.*[64]

Dawkins lumps ID theory together with 'creation science', calling ID a 'euphemism for creationists'.[65] Leonard Krishtalka notoriously slighted ID as 'creationism in a cheap tuxedo'.[66] The PBS documentary *Evolution* contains a scene showing a stack of books critical of Darwinism, while the narrator says: 'Ever since *The Origin of Species* was published, strict believers in biblical creationism have attacked Darwin's vision.'[67] The narration fails to point out that one of the books shown, *Darwin on Trial*, is by design theorist Phillip Johnson, who explicitly says he is *not* a believer in creation science (another, *Darwinism: The Refutation of a Myth*, is by *non-Christian* biologist Soren Lovtrup). Whether pictorial or linguistic, deliberate or subconscious, this rhetorical sleight of hand is a consistent feature of Darwinian apologetics: 'anyone critical of Darwinian evolution risks being stereotyped as a strict believer in biblical creation'.[68] Whether or not they are even a Christian is immaterial! Stephen Jay Gould asserted that the only dissenters from macroevolution are 'protestant fundamentalists who believe that every word of the Bible must be literally true'.[69] In reality, 'some of the strongest critics of Darwin's theory are scientists who happen to be non-fundamentalist Protestants, Catholics, or Jews (as well as agnostics)'.[70]

Historian of science Ronald L. Numbers observes that proponents of evolution tend to conflate ID and creationism: 'They see intelligent design as little more than gussied up creationism, despite the significant differences.'[71] He relates how 'one annoyed critic . . . described [ID] as "the same old creationist bullshit dressed up in new clothes"'.[72] Now, as Francis J. Beckwith observes: 'This accusation, even if true, does not amount to a critique of the actual arguments for ID as a scientific research program.'[73] Nevertheless, as Benjamin Wiker notes: 'intelligent design theorists who are Christians are very careful to distinguish themselves from creationists'.[74] This is not because design theorists necessarily accept Darwinists' low opinion of 'creationism'. Indeed, *some* design theorists are also 'creationists', just as *some* evolutionists are also atheists. However, ID is *not* 'creationism' (anymore than evolution, as opposed to naturalistic evolution, or Darwinism, is inherently atheistic). The story told by ID 'veers away from the usual *theistic evolutionary story* ("based on the evidence, theistic scientists are now concluding that God worked through evolution") *and* from the classic creation science tale ("scientists are recognizing that Genesis is literally true after all")'.[75] Hence the need to draw clear lines of demarcation and to avoid making criticisms of the former that, whether sound or unsound, could only apply to the latter.

Dembski is at pains to stress that ID is *not* 'creationism' as popularly understood:

. . . the design theorists' critique of Darwinism in no way hinges on the Genesis account of creation . . . The design theorists' beef is not with evolutionary change *per se*, but with the claim by Darwinists that all such change is driven by purely naturalistic processes . . . the design theorists' critique of Darwinism begins with Darwinism's failure as an empirically adequate scientific theory, and not with its supposed incompatibility with some system of religious belief.[76]

Phillip Johnson stresses: 'I am not a defender of creation-science . . . The essential point of creation has nothing to do with the timing or the mechanism the Creator chose to employ, but with the element of design or purpose.'[77] Johnson's 1989 'Position Paper on Darwinism' explains: 'The truly fundamental question is whether the natural world is the product of a pre-existing intelligence and whether we exist for a purpose that we did not invent ourselves.'[78] Johnson points out that: 'Creationists are not necessarily Genesis literalists or believers in a young earth, nor do they necessarily reject "evolution" in all senses of that highly manipulable term. A creationist is simply a person who believes . . . that the living world is the product of an intelligent and purposeful Creator rather than merely a combination of [unintended] chance events and impersonal natural laws.'[79] In Johnson's sense of the word, theistic evolutionists (who accept evolution as God's method of creation via secondary causes) are creationists, and a creationist needn't even be a theist. They certainly don't need to accept any of the various interpretations of the Genesis creation story.[80] They simply need to accept the *metaphysical* hypothesis of design. Design theorists accept design as a *scientific* inference to the best explanation: 'design theorists do not defend their position by appealing to esoteric knowledge, special revelation, or religious authority. They make philosophical and scientific arguments whose merits should be assessed by their soundness . . .'[81]

Thomas Woodward, author of *Doubts about Darwin: A History of Intelligent Design*, repudiates the claim that ID is motivated by religious premises:

> . . . hearing how key Design advocates came to their current view, it became clear that their entry into the movement stemmed from intellectual or scientific – not religious – reasons . . . Several of the founders frequently relate a vivid tale of how they previously had assumed the validity of Darwinian scenarios and were later shocked to discover major weaknesses in the case for Darwinism. Typically this intellectual epiphany leads to further reading and research, which cements the new radical doubt about the theory's plausibility.[82]

ID hypothesizes that the religiously unencumbered concept of design (and thus purpose) is a better and more fruitful explanation of certain biological and physical evidence than the assumption that natural regularities and chance are responsible.

Not natural theology[83]

> *ID is a research program whose inferences support, and are consistent with, some belief in a higher intelligence or deity; it is not a creed that contains belief in a specific deity as one of its tenets.*
> FRANCIS J. BECKWITH[84]

While a design paradigm has historically dominated cosmology and biology (from Plato and Aristotle to Newton and Paley), design arguments have traditionally been a part of natural theology, the philosophical project of providing evidence for God's existence. However, design arguments can only provide part of the evidence for God.[85] The ID movement recognizes this

fact and, following Newton's advice about keeping ultimate explanations out of science, distinguishes between
arguing for intelligent design and arguing for *divine*
design (although this is a fact that critics of ID often
obfuscate). Michael Behe writes:

> . . . my argument is limited to design itself; I
> strongly emphasize that it is not an argument for
> the existence of a benevolent God, as Paley's was.
> I hasten to add that I myself do believe in a
> benevolent God, and I recognize that philosophy
> and theology may be able to extend the argument.
> But a scientific argument for design in biology
> does not reach that far. Thus while I argue for
> design, the question of the identity of the designer
> is left open . . . as regards the identity of the
> designer, modern ID theory happily echoes Isaac
> Newton's phrase, *hypothesis non fingo*.[86]

ID argues that there are natural entities that cannot reasonably be explained by chance and/or physical neces-
sities, and only then infers, on the basis of experience,
that the best explanation of these features of reality is
intelligent causation. Whether the intelligence in question is God is yet a further question: 'detecting design
. . . does not implicate any particular intelligence'.[87]

Failure to appreciate the distinction between intelligent design and divine design has contributed to the
scientific establishment throwing out the design paradigm as essentially tied to belief in God when it was not.
After all, one could accept intelligent design and attribute it to the activity of angels, demons, Plato's finite god
(the Demiurge), the gods of Greek polytheism, or to
aliens, rather than to God (hence it is logically possible
for an atheist to support ID[88]).

'Intelligent design is not a form of natural theology',[89] and while every design argument for God is an argument for intelligent design, not every argument for intelligent design need be viewed as an argument for God – at least, not without considerations from outside ID as a scientific theory being brought to bear: 'intelligent design theory by itself makes no claims about the nature of the designer, and scientists currently working within an intelligent design framework include Protestants, Catholics, Jews, agnostics, and others'.[90] As Benjamin Wiker suggests: 'from scientific evidence open to all, we can infer that nature has an intelligent designer. Further, we can extend these arguments philosophically, demonstrating that the intelligent designer is God.'[91]

ID obviously has much to *contribute* to natural theology, in that *divine* design is a plausible and independently supported candidate for the source of scientifically detectable intelligent design. (Theologically speaking, it is interesting to note, given ID's emphasis on the need to explain the origin of information that the Bible portrays God as creating through his Word or 'Logos' [Gen. 1:3; John 1:1-3]: 'Of course God did not physically speak and produce sound waves', writes theologian Terence L. Nichols, 'But the point is that the word conveys information. God's act of creating . . . involves the input of specifying information . . .'[92]) Likewise, natural theology has much to contribute to ID. The two projects are mutually re-enforcing, and are united in their rejection of naturalism. On the one hand, ID furnishes natural theology with powerful new versions of the design argument. On the other hand, anyone who is already impressed by natural theology (e.g.

the arguments from morality and rationality) will be kindly predisposed towards ID.

Intelligent design and aesthetics

Aesthetic design arguments take us further towards theism than non-aesthetic design arguments because they infer the existence of an aesthetically aware artist, and not simply a rational designer. If the cosmos exhibits intelligent design, then it might literally be a *cosmos* – an example of intelligently ordered beauty. If so, aesthetics can help us to round out our understanding of the designer/s and the purpose of creation. (Indeed, deductive aesthetic arguments deduce the existence of a maximally beautiful objective standard of beauty – a description that subsumes Anselm's definition of God as 'the greatest possible being' and leads directly to the theistic God.) A more specific profile of the designer/s takes us beyond the bare scientific assertion of intelligent design, but it also strengthens the explanatory power of the design hypothesis.

Aesthetic design arguments employ theoretical accounts of beauty, art, craft and the criteria of aesthetic judgements that can be applied to ID, for proponents of ID make use of objectively beautiful discoveries made in scientific fields such as cosmology and molecular biology (beauties that were unavailable to past champions of design like Cicero, Newton and Paley). Francis Crick, co-discoverer of DNA, writes of 'the intrinsic beauty of the DNA helix. It is a molecule which has style.'[93] James P. Gills MD writes: 'Each cell expresses an extraordinary and incomparable complexity, beauty really, of form and function.'[94]

Phillip Johnson observes that with the rise of ID: 'We

are talking about a fatal flaw in our culture's creation myth [Darwinian evolution], and therefore in the standard of reasoning that culture has applied to all questions of importance.'[95] He suggests: 'Once we learn that nature does not really do its own creating, and we are not really products of mindless natural forces that care nothing about us, we will have to re-examine a great deal else. In particular, we will need to have a new discussion about . . . what we might mean by . . . the beautiful.'[96] I agree; but it would be a mistake to hold fire on the issue of beauty until the hoped for paradigm shift from naturalistic evolution to intelligent design theory has emerged. It would be a mistake because a discussion about 'what we might mean by the beautiful' can actually contribute to ID here and now. William Dembski asserts: 'The existence of design is distinct from the morality, aesthetics, goodness, optimality or perfection of design'[97] (i.e. the fact that something is evil, ugly, sub-optimal or imperfect does not show that it was not designed). I have two observations about this. The first is that all the additional features mentioned by Dembski can be related to questions about beauty (which is unsurprising because beauty is the widest value concept available to us). The second is that aesthetic considerations can complement and strengthen the case for intelligent design as well as the case for divine design. Several proponents of intelligent design (e.g. Dembski, Johnson and Moreland) have highlighted the close relationship between design and aesthetics, but their observations constitute a 'promissory note' that remains largely unpaid. For example, Dembski notes that 'Contrary to popular accusations by critics, intelligent design theory suggests a number of questions that can be pursued as part of a research program.'[98] He lists fourteen such questions, including: 'Is the design beautiful?'[99]

The 'Explanatory Filter'

> *There exists a reliable criterion for detecting design. This criterion detects design from strictly observational features of the world. Moreover it belongs to probability and complexity theory, not to metaphysics and theology. And although it cannot achieve logical demonstration, it does achieve statistical justification so compelling as to demand assent.*
> WILLIAM A. DEMBSKI[100]

William A. Dembski has been described as 'the leading intellectual theorist of Design and a symbol of the rising generation of young scholars who are joining the movement'.[101] According to Edward Sission: 'If Thomas Huxley was "Darwin's Bulldog", Dembski is the man with the leash and the obedience training technique to bring Darwinism into check.'[102] What is Dembski's leash? It is an 'Explanatory Filter' that identifies intelligent causation by ruling out chance and natural law to decide if an object or event exhibits what chance and natural law alone are *extremely* hard-pressed to produce, namely 'specified complexity' or 'complex specified information' [CSI]: 'Roughly speaking the filter asks three questions in the following order: (1) Does a law explain it? (2) Does chance explain it? (3) Does design explain it?'[103] This follows Plato's observation that: 'all things do become, have become, and will become, some by nature, some by art, and some by chance'.[104] Dembski formally laid out the Explanatory

Filter in *The Design Inference: Eliminating Chance through small probabilities*, published by Cambridge University Press and peer-reviewed as part of the distinguished monograph series, *Cambridge Studies in Probability, Induction, and Decision Theory*.

If something can reasonably be explained by chance and/or necessity, then (by Occam's razor) it should be so explained (although this explanation doesn't rule out a complementary inference by analogy to a 'personal explanation'); but if such an explanation is inadequate, then an inference to the more complex but more adequate hypothesis of design is thereby warranted. Dembski's Filter detects design because intelligent causes easily accomplish what unintelligent causes find all but impossible, the creation of *specified complexity* (that is, the detection of specified complexity does not prove design beyond all possibility of doubt, but it can prove it beyond all reasonable doubt).

A long string of random letters drawn from a Scrabble bag (e.g. 'WDLMNLTDTJBKWIRZREZLMQ-COP') is complex without being specified – that is, without conforming to a *non ad hoc* significant pattern which we can construct from independent background knowledge without simply being read off the object or event in question. A short sequence of letters like 'this' or 'that' is specified (it conforms to a *non ad hoc*, independent pattern) without being sufficiently complex to outstrip the capacity of chance to rationally explain this conformity. (Scrabble players will know that letters drawn at random from the Scrabble bag occasionally form a short word.) A poem like Keats' musings on the rainbow is both specified (conforming to the independent functional requirements of grammatical English language use) and sufficiently complex (doing so at a level of complexity that makes it unreasonable to attribute this match to luck) to trigger a design inference – it would be unreasonable to suggest that Keats produced his poem by drawing tiles from a Scrabble bag. Hence, 'given an event, object, or structure, to convince ourselves that it is designed we need to show that it is improbably (i.e. complex) and suitably patterned (i.e. specified)'.[105] Dembski explains that 'once the improbabilities (i.e. complexities) become too vast and the specifications too tight, chance is eliminated and design is implicated. Just where the probabilities cutoff is can be debated, but that there is a probabilistic cutoff beyond which chance becomes an unacceptable explanation is clear.'[106] As Dawkins admits: 'We can accept a certain amount of luck in our explanations, but not too much.'[107]

William Lane Craig explains the logic of the Filter with a simple illustration:

> Bob is given a new car for his birthday. There are millions of license plate numbers, and it is therefore highly unlikely that Bob would get, say, CHT 4271. Yet that plate on his birthday car would occasion no special interest. But suppose Bob, who was born on 8 August 1949 finds BOB 8849 on the license plate of his birthday car. He would be obtuse if he shrugged this off with the comment, 'Well, it had to have *some* license plate, and any number is equally improbable . . .'[108]

Bob's car having the first license plate was complex (unlikely) but it wasn't noteworthy because it wasn't specified. Bob's car having the second license plate was noteworthy because in addition to being complex it was also specified (it matched the independently given pattern of Bob's name and birth-date).

It is popularly thought that 'if you have enough monkeys banging randomly on typewriters they will eventually type the works of William Shakespeare', but there is a real world limit to the number of 'monkeys' available and the time in which they can type. Indeed, I heard about a zoo that put a typewriter in their monkey cage: the monkeys defecated in the typewriter and hit the same key over and over again! To take the point less literally, the online 'Monkey Shakespeare Simulator' uses logged-on computers to simulate an ever-increasing population of 'monkeys' randomly typing (on simplified keyboards, at a rate of one day's typing per second), and compares the results to Shakespeare's works.[109] As of March 2004, the best result was fourteen 'letters' (if one includes spaces and full stops) from *Coriolanus*, after 4,651,360,000,000,000,000 'monkey-years'![110] Getting better results is clearly going to take a *lot* more monkey-years; but as Dembski would point out, we can't simply keep giving ourselves free 'monkey-years'. A limitation on the explanatory capacity of 'chance' is crucial to the integrity of science: 'If we allow ourselves too many "wildcard" bits of information – either by giving ourselves too many lucky guesses or nature too many lucky occurrences – we can explain anything by reference to chance.'[111] Allowing ourselves too many 'wildcard bits of information' commits the *inflationary fallacy*: 'the problem inherent in the inflationary fallacy is always that it multiplies probabilistic resources in the absence of independent evidence that such resources exist'.[112] Postulating unlimited probabilistic resources makes it impossible to attribute anything with confidence to actual design. Was Shakespeare a great writer, or was it just that whenever he sat down with a quill he happened by chance to move his hand in the right way to produce beautiful scripts? It could happen by chance, if we assume the existence of sufficiently large probabilistic resources: 'Unlimited probabilistic resources make bizarre possibilities unavoidable on a grand scale.'[113]

Judgements about the probability of a given pattern being matched by chance have to be made relative to information about the available probabilistic resources. The relevant resources will be different in different cases, but we can formulate a 'universal probability bound', an upper limit on the probabilistic resources we should take into account. French mathematician Emile Borel proposed 10^{-50} as a universal probability bound below which chance could be precluded as a rational explanation. Dembski calculates a far more stringent probability bound of 10^{-150} based on the number of elementary particles in the universe, the duration of the observable universe and the Plank time. Even with this ultra-conservative criterion, Dembski calculates that nature contains numerous examples of specified complexity.

That nature includes examples of specified complexity is uncontroversial: 'Biological specification always denotes function. An organism is a functional system comprising many functional subsystems. The functionality of organisms can be cashed out in any number of ways. Arno Wouters cashes it out globally in terms of the *viability* of whole organisms. Michael Behe cashes it out in terms of the *minimal function* of biochemical systems.'[114] Leslie Orgel writes: 'Living organisms are distinguished by their specified complexity. Crystals such as granite fail to qualify because they lack complexity; mixtures of random polymers fail to qualify because they lack specificity.'[115] According to Dawkins: 'Complicated things have some quality, specifiable in advance, that is highly unlikely to have been acquired by random chance alone. In the case of living things, the quality that is specified in advance is . . . the ability to propagate genes in reproduction.'[116]

Dembski argues that natural causes are inadequate when it comes to explaining CSI. First, he eliminates necessity: 'Because information presupposes contingency, necessity is by definition incapable of producing information, much less complex specified information . . .'[117] Then he notes: 'Contingency can assume only one of two forms. Either the contingency is a blind, purposeless contingency – which is chance, or it is a guided, purposeful contingency – which is intelligent causation . . .'[118] Dembski argues that 'pure chance . . . is incapable of generating CSI'.[119] He supports this conclusion with a standard inductive argument: Whenever we know the causal history of an object or event that exhibits CSI, we see that it was produced by intelligence. Hence we are justified in concluding that all examples of CSI are probably produced by intelligent design. The conclusion of this inductive argument is intuitively obvious: 'Chance can generate complex unspecified information [e.g. a random string of Scrabble pieces], and chance can generate non-complex specified information [e.g. a short word in Scrabble pieces]. What chance cannot generate is information that is jointly complex and specified . . . [e.g. a poem by Keats]'[120] Dembski's argument requires one more stage:

If chance and necessity left to themselves cannot generate CSI, is it possible that chance and necessity working together might generate CSI? The answer is No. Whenever chance and necessity work together, the respective contributions of chance and necessity can be arranged sequentially. But by arranging the respective contributions of chance and necessity sequentially, it becomes clear that at no point in the sequence is CSI generated.[121]

By a process of elimination then, design is the *best explanation* for CSI: 'Since chance, necessity, and their combination characterize natural causes, it now follows that *natural causes are incapable of generating CSI.*'[122] Dembski calls this conclusion the Law of Conservation of Information (LCI), noting that the phrase 'is due not to me but to the biologist Peter Medawar (see his *The Limits of Science*, 1984)'.[123]

Dawkins, computers, weasels and insects

In *The Blind Watchmaker* Dawkins discusses two 'evolutionary' computer programs, neither of which provides a counter instance to LCI. One begins with a complex but unspecified sequence of letters – 'WDLMNLTDTJBKWIRZREZLMQCOP' – and is programmed to duplicate the sequence with a certain chance of random error, to scrutinize mutant phrases when they occur, and to breed onward from 'the one which, *however slightly*, most resembles the target phrase, METHINKS IT IS LIKE A WEASEL'.[124] The program reached its *pre-specified target* in 64 generations. Not only is the whole program an example of design, its Shakespearean specification has been built into the program by design. As Dallas Willard comments: 'Dawkins recognizes that in this case the selection is guided by a distant ideal form, and is thus unlike natural selection . . .'[125] Dembski points out that Dawkins' program is a 'probability amplifier', because it will always converge on the one target sequence:

> Dawkins' evolutionary algorithm, by vastly increasing the probability of getting the target sequence, vastly decreases the complexity inherent in that sequence . . . Evolutionary algorithms are . . . incapable of generating true complexity. And since they cannot generate true complexity, they cannot generate true specified complexity either . . . the evolutionary algorithm Dawkins uses to produce his target sequence has not so much generated specified complexity as merely shuffled it around . . . invariably when evolutionary algorithms appear to generate specified complexity, what they actually do is smuggle in preexisting specified complexity.[126]

Dawkins' other program randomly mutates a computer generated doodle. Realizing that 'an evolved resemblance to something like an insect was possible',[127] Dawkins says, 'I began to breed, generation after generation, from whichever child looked most like an insect.'[128] Dawkins produced *eight*-legged 'insect' pictures. In this case, the watchmaker was crucially *not* blind ('I began to breed') – but intelligently added preexisting specifications ('whichever child looked most like an insect') into the random complexity generated by his program.

'Richard Dawkins . . . and many other scientists and philosophers are convinced that proper scientific explanations must be reductive', writes Dembski, 'explaining the complex in terms of the simple. The Law of Conservation of Information, however, shows that specified complexity cannot be explained reductively.'[129] Darwinism as an all-embracing biological theory falls foul of LCI:

> Consider the case of trial-and-error (trial corresponds to necessity and error to chance). Once considered a crude method of problem solving, trial-and-error has so risen in the estimation of scientists that it is now regarded as the ultimate source of . . . creativity in nature . . . the Darwinian mechanism of mutation and natural selection is a trial-and-error combination in which mutation supplies the error and selection the trial. An error is committed after which a trial is made. But at no point is CSI generated.[130]

Signs of intelligence

Scientists who ignore LCI and allow an in principle commitment to naturalistic explanations to predetermine their explanatory options when faced with CSI are, to use an example from physicist Robert Kaita, in a similar position to researchers stubbornly committed to a naturalistic explanation for 'crop-circles':

> . . . mysterious patterns were found in wheat fields taking the form of large, distinct geometric patterns . . . speculation ran from intelligent causes, such as ingenious pranksters, or the perennial favorite, extraterrestrial beings, to natural phenomena. Finally a couple of men admitted responsibility and revealed that their equipment consisted of very large versions of the stylus and

string that people have been using to make
geometric figures since antiquity . . . In spite of
this unequivocal evidence for design, some
[people] persisted in suggesting highly improbable
natural causes.[131]

Kaita draws a moral from this episode: 'We need always
to keep in mind two separate questions: how well does
the evidence support design? And, Are we predisposed
to reject design apart from the evidence? The first is a
scientific question. The second is a philosophical question.'[132] For those who wish to exclude the possibility of
intelligent design *a priori*, 'the motive is based not on
"just the facts" but on philosophical prejudice'.[133]

Crop-circles are obviously the product of design (at
least when they are specified and sufficiently complex).
Some people suggest that the source of crop-circle
design is extra-terrestrial. No matter how sceptical we
are about extra-terrestrials, it would be irrational to
argue that because extra-terrestrials don't exist,
crop-circles are not the product of design! Likewise,
however sceptical someone is about the existence of
God, it would be irrational to argue that since God does-
n't exist therefore nothing in nature is the product of
design! The inference to design, whether in the case
of crop-circles or some facet of biology, is prior to the
inference to a particular designer, and stands or falls on
its own merits. Only once design has been established
does the question of what sort of designer best explains
the design (terrestrial, extra-terrestrial or divine?) arise.
In the case of crop-circles, the best explanation is
clearly to attribute the design to human agency. In the
case of design in the texture of nature itself there are
several live explanatory options, including God.

Whether God is the best explanation of such design is a matter for philosophical disputation, but the important point to make at this juncture is that the presumed result of this disputation (whether positive or negative) should not be allowed to prejudice the question of design detection.

Science can rule in design, but it can't rule it out

The 'Explanatory Filter' is only a *positive* test for design.[134] Suppose an ecologically minded artist carefully distributes seaweed on a beach so as to mimic a natural seaweed distribution. The Filter would be unable to detect the activity of intelligence in the distribution of the seaweed. On the other hand, if the seaweed were arranged to form a picture of a human face (as in a recent advert for mobile phone picture-messaging by the Orange phone company), the Filter *would* detect design because such an arrangement of seaweed is both complex *and* specified. Again, consider an inkblot. Dembski's Filter would be unable to decide whether accidentally or deliberately spilled ink had caused an inkblot. On the other hand, present the Filter with a hand-written letter, and it would detect design: 'An inkblot can be explained without appealing to intelligent causation; ink arranged to form meaningful text cannot.'[135] Hence science can rule in design, but it can't rule it out. 'Undirected natural causes' may be 'secondary causes' designed, intended, created, sustained and employed by an intelligent agent for a purpose, just as we can use ink and gravity to create inkblots. As Dawkins admits: 'Science has no way to disprove the existence of a supreme being (this is strictly true).'[136]

Beauty as specification

I suggest that a high degree of objective beauty may be regarded as a specification that, in conjunction with contingent events of sufficiently high improbability, passes through the 'Explanatory Filter' to indicate design. Philosopher Del Ratzsch writes: 'One very characteristic activity of agents . . . is the appreciation of beauty, elegance, and the like. Not only do we experience and appreciate it, but we sometimes attempt to produce it, and often attempt to incorporate some aesthetic dimension into things we are doing . . .'[137] On the basis that something's being designed involves an agent intending to produce some mind-correlative pattern, Ratzsch argues that design arguments should look for 'factors that are *intent relevant*'.[138] After all, 'That some phenomenon is the sort of thing that agents do (or that an agent would or might do) clearly counts . . . in favor of suspicions that perhaps an agent did it.'[139] Given Ratzsch's argument that 'To act for a purpose is to act deliberately with the intent that the action be instrumental in the realization of a specific *value*,'[140] it follows that beauty is a prime candidate for an intent relevant specification. According to Ratzsch: 'complexity, improbability . . . do not by themselves provide strong, obvious evidence for design'.[141] Complexity without specification does not warrant the design inference. However, 'patterns [i.e. specifications] and phenomena that exhibit deep mind correlativity – mind affinity – can constitute varying degrees of evidence for design . . .'[142] Beauty is a good candidate for a design indicative specification. Hence: 'complexity . . . when operating in the service of producing value can constitute evidence for design'.[143] In other words, a highly unlikely pattern of great beauty is indicative of design. Nature is full of such objects and patterns. Moreover, the more beautiful the pattern, the more likely it is that the beauty of the pattern is a reliable guide to the intention of the designer.

The anthropic argument – cracking cosmic fine-tuning

The more I examine the universe and the details of its architecture, the more evidence I find that the universe in some sense must have known we were coming.
FREEMAN DYSON[144]

Dawkins writes: 'Of all the unique and, with hindsight equally improbable, positions of the combination lock, only one opens the lock . . . The uniqueness of the arrangement . . . that opens the safe, [has] nothing to do with hindsight. It is *specified in advance*.'[145] Hence the best explanation of an open safe is not that someone got lucky, but that someone knew the specific unlikely combination required to open it. The so-called 'anthropic fine-tuning' of the universe discovered by cosmologists is identical in nature to the example of cracking a combination lock: 'That the cosmos has been on a path which made possible the later appearance of man is referred to as the 'anthropic principle.'[146] ('Anthropic' comes from the Greek for 'people'.) It has become increasingly apparent that the universe is a most 'specifically constructed entity . . . tuned with extreme precision'.[147] The basic physical laws are 'finely tuned' in the sense that if they were only a little different then the existence of people (or of anything biological) would be impossible. This is a fact that many scientists and philosophers take to indicate design – even if they feel uncomfortable with such an implication. As Stephen Hawking once admitted: 'The odds against a universe like ours emerging out of something like the big bang are enormous . . . I think clearly there are religious implications . . . But I think most scientists prefer to shy away from the religious side of it.'[148] Shying away from a conclusion supported by evidence is hardly a scientific attitude to adopt.

Douglas Adams, author of *The Hitchhiker's Guide to the Galaxy*, thought he had a knockdown response to the anthropic design argument. He likened the fine-tuning argument to a puddle of water arguing that, since the dip in the ground it inhabited seemed to fit it so well, it must have been created with its existence in mind: 'This is . . . an interesting hole I find myself in – fits me rather neatly, doesn't it? In fact it fits me staggeringly well, must have been made to have me in it!'[149] But this analogy is deeply flawed. Water will fit any shape hole – the fit between the hole and the water can be explained wholly by reference to the nature of water. However, life will not fit just any old environment. The fit between our cosmic environment and life cannot be explained wholly by reference to the nature of life: 'In reviewing the physical laws and the numerical values of fundamental constants, one encounters a remarkable precision in these values such that only small changes in the fundamental constants . . . would yield a universe without galaxies, stars, atoms or even nuclei, and consequently, without the capacity for life.'[150] As Moreland and Craig note: 'An observer who has evolved within the universe should regard it as highly probable that he will find the basic conditions of the universe fine-tuned for his existence; but he should not infer that it is therefore highly probable that such a fine-tuned universe exists at all.'[151]

Moreland and Craig illustrate the sense in which the fine-tuning of the universe is a highly improbable fact:

Take a sheet of paper and place upon it a red dot. That dot represents our universe. Now alter slightly one or more of the finely tuned constants and physical quantities which have been the focus of our attention. As a result we have a description of another universe, which we may represent by a new dot in the proximity of the first. If that new set of constants and quantities describes a life-permitting universe, make it a red dot; if it describes a universe that is life prohibiting, make it a blue dot. Now repeat the procedure arbitrarily many times until the sheet is filled with dots. One winds up with a sea of blue with only a few pin-points of red.[152]

The hypothetical question of whether or not universes are possible that have wholly different physical variables but are life permitting is irrelevant to the anthropic argument. Imagine a fly resting on a large, blank area on a wall:

A single shot is fired, and the bullet strikes the fly. Now even if the rest of the wall outside the blank area is covered with flies, such that a randomly fired bullet would probably hit one, nevertheless it remains highly improbable that a single, randomly fired bullet would strike the solitary fly within the large, blank area. In the same way, we need only concern ourselves with the universes represented on our sheet in order to determine the probability of the existence of a life-permitting universe.[153] In the case of Dawkins' cracked combination lock what called out for explanation in terms of an intelligent cause was not merely the fact that an event of small probability had taken place (any long sequence of dialled numbers is equally improbable), but the fact that this small probability was *specified* (as the sequence necessary for opening the lock). In the case of cosmic fine-tuning, what calls out for explanation in terms of design is not the fact that a particular highly unlikely set of physical laws exists, but the fact that this set of laws is *specified* as the set necessary for a life-sustaining universe.

Craig admits: 'fantastically improbable events happen every day. Your own existence . . . is the result of an incredibly improbable union of a certain sperm and a certain egg, yet no one would infer that their union was therefore designed.'[154] (Each outcome here has a comparable objective significance.) However: 'what is at stake in eliminating the hypothesis of chance is what theorists call "specified probability": the demonstration that the event in question is not only improbable but also conforms to an independently discovered pattern'.[155] Any equally long sequence of letters typed at a typewriter is equally improbable, but if we found a string of letters forming a play by Shakespeare we would infer intelligent design (rather than invoking those proverbial typing monkeys): 'In the same way, physics and biology tell us independently of any knowledge of the early conditions of the universe what physical conditions are requisite for life. We then discover how incredibly improbable such conditions are. It is this combination of a specified pattern plus improbability that serves to render the chance hypothesis implausible . . .'[156]

The correct analogy here is not a lottery where any individual's winning is equally improbable and where *someone* has to win, but a lottery in which a single winning green ball is mixed in with several billion non-winning red balls and a single person is asked to reach in once and pull out a single ball. Picking any ball *per se* is equally improbable; nevertheless, it is overwhelmingly more probable that whichever ball you pick, it will be red rather than green: 'Similarly, the existence of any particular universe is equally improbable, but it is incomprehensibly more probable that whichever universe exists, it will be life prohibiting rather than life permitting. It is the enormous, specified improbability of the fine-tuning that presents the hurdle to the chance hypothesis.'[157]

To return to Dawkins' example, the fine-tuning of the universe is like cracking a safe with multiple combination locks, one lock for each cosmic parameter: the matter-anti-matter balance 'had to be accurate to one part in ten billion for the universe to arise'.[158] The expansion rate of the universe from the big bang had to be accurate to one part in 10^{60}, while the force of gravity itself required fine-tuning to one part in 10^{40}.[159] If the strong nuclear force were 2 per cent weaker protons and neutrons wouldn't stick together. If it were 0.3 per cent stronger hydrogen (a crucial component of biological systems) could not exist.[160] Ralph O. Muncaster points out that: 'for physical life to ever be possible at any time in the universe, the overall cosmic mass density must be fine-tuned to a mere 1 part in 10^{60} . . .

Likewise, physicists have calculated that the value of the cosmological constant . . . must be exact to one part in 10^{120} . . .'[161] Oxford physicist Roger Penrose calculated that the original phase-space volume required such exact fine-tuning that the 'Creator's aim must have been [precise] to an accuracy of one part in $10^{10(123)}$'.[162] Penrose was only speaking poetically of the 'Creator's aim', but this sort of data is in fact best explained by the existence of a real Creator. Finely tuned improbabilities compound one another until the overall improbability of cosmic fine-tuning being a fluke becomes unimaginably high. Don N. Page[163] of the Institute for Advanced Study in Princeton, N.J., calculates the odds against the formation of our universe at one in $10,000,000,000^{124}$! As Fred Hoyle complained: 'A common sense interpretation of the facts suggests that a superintellect has monkeyed with physics.'[164]

Some cosmologists attempt to avoid this common sense conclusion by positing the existence of a large number of universes (perhaps an infinite number), each with a different set of laws. However, what guarantees that all these universes have *different* laws is a mystery. Stephen Clark comments:

> It is a mark of desperation that some atheistical materialists have chosen to believe in infinite arrays of universes . . . rather than believe instead that this well-adapted world is founded on intelligence . . . explaining away this world by saying that *all* worlds happen (which does not follow anyway merely from there being, we fantasize, an infinite array of worlds) merely enlarges the problem – and destroys the basis of all explanation (since we could not, on those terms, be right to be

surprised at anything, including Pratchett's Discworld).[165]

The many worlds hypothesis commits the *inflationary fallacy* on a grand scale: 'an arrow is fired at random into a forest and hits Mr Brown. To explain such a chance occurrence it would suffice for the forest to be full of people. The forest being full of people therefore possesses explanatory power. Even so, this explanation remains but a speculative possibility until it is supported by independent evidence of people other than Mr Brown in the forest.'[166] In the absence of such evidence, the best explanation of why the arrow hit Mr Brown remains that someone took careful aim! Likewise, the best explanation of cosmic fine-tuning remains that a designing intelligence took 'careful aim' to produce a life-sustaining universe.

Fine-tuned beauty with a purpose

The fine-tuning of the universe is an example of CSI because it constitutes a sufficiently unlikely (complex) state of affairs that conforms to a specifiable pattern, (the pattern of universal constants necessary for a life-permitting universe). However, these cosmic laws are not only specified considered as finely tuned preconditions of cosmic fruitfulness, but also with respect to their beauty. These fine-tuned laws obviously possess great instrumental and causal beauty, as well as mathematical elegance and simplicity. In other words, given that other sets of physical laws would have been less beautiful than the combination that in fact obtains, this combination constitutes an aesthetic specification. Hitting this aesthetic specification at low probability is an example of CSI. This bears out Moreland's observation that mathematical beauty is an indicator of truth in theoretical physics, and his contention that: 'beautiful theories, which are discovered and which accurately reflect the way the world is, get their beauty from the Mind which formed them'.[167] After all, cosmic 'fine tuning' is just as necessary to the existence of a universe as beautiful as ours, and to the existence of sentient beings capable of appreciating that beauty, as it is to the existence of sentient beings *per se*. This suggests that one of the designer's purposes in creating our finely tuned universe was the production of beauty and beings able to enjoy it.

Paul Davies makes the link between the evidence for design and the existence of a cosmic purpose: 'If physics is the product of design, the universe must have a purpose, and the evidence of modern physics suggests strongly to me that the purpose includes us.'[168] Hence the anthropic argument suggests that human life has an objective purpose. Astronomer Stanley L. Jaki asks: 'Is it reasonable to assume that an Intelligence which produced a universe, a totality of consistently interacting things, is not consistent to the point of acting for a purpose?'[169] Since, as Del Ratzsch argues, 'To act for a purpose is to act deliberately with the intent that the action be instrumental in the realization of a specific *value*,'[170] this evidence for cosmic purpose is also evidence that life is objectively meaningful.

L. Stafford Betty and Bruce Coredell, writing in *International Philosophical Quarterly*, postulate: 'it is a *universal* law that the significantly greater cannot be generated by the significantly less'.[171] (This metaphysical law parallels and prefigures Dembski's LCI.) 'If such a law holds,' argue Betty and Cordell:

. . . it would follow that the [designer] must be superior to us, not only with respect to intelligence (which seems obvious), but in every other important way as well. The mind must be characterized by knowledge, power, beauty, goodness, and love to a degree not known to us mortals . . . it is clear that we are not too far away from a God whom we can at least admire. And if admiration should grow to love – a not unnatural progression – then the God of the great theistic religions is not far away. Religion and science will have joined hands.[172]

Given that there are objective values, this line of reasoning clearly suggests that the designer's intent would indeed have been successfully aimed at the realization of an objectively good value (or set of values), and that life is therefore not only objectively purposeful, but objectively meaningful.

[1] Newton, Isaac, quoted by Richard Westfall, *The Life of Isaac Newton* (Cambridge University Press, 1993), p.259.

[2] McDowell, Josh and Williams, Thomas, *In Search Of Certainty* (Wheaton, Illinois: Tyndale, 2003), p.91.

[3] Burgess, Stuart, *Hallmarks of Design* (Epsom: DayOne, 2002), p.8-9.

[4] *ibid.*, p.73.

[5] *ibid.*

[6] *ibid.*, p.74.

[7] Wise, Kurt P., 'The Origin of Life's Major Groups', in J. P. Moreland (ed.), *The Creation Hypothesis* (Downers Grove: IVP, 1994), p.231.

[8] Tennant, F. R., *Philosophical Theology*, vol. 2.

[9] *ibid.*

[10] *ibid.*

[1] Swinburne, Richard, *Providence and the Problem of Evil* (Oxford University Press, 1998).

[12] Tennant, *op. cit.*

[13] *ibid.*

[14] Balfour, Arthur, *Theism and Humanism* (Seattle: Inkling Books, 2000), p.41.

[15] Rhodes, W. S., *The Christian God* (ISPCK, 1998).

[16] Tennant, *op. cit.*, p.92.

[17] *ibid.*

[18] Swinburne, Richard, *The Existence of God* (Oxford: Clarendon Press, 1991), p.150.

[19] *ibid.*

[20] Augustine, *City of God*, Bk XXII, Chapter 24, p.1075.

[21] Swinburne, *Providence and the Problem of Evil, op. cit.*, p.52.

[22] *ibid.*

[23] Swinburne, Richard, *Is There A God?* (Oxford University Press, 1996), p.54.

[24] Swinburne, *The Existence of God, op. cit.*

[25] *ibid.*

[26] Swinburne, *Providence and the Problem of Evil, op. cit.*, p.51.

[27] Swinburne, *The Existence of God, op. cit.*, p.150.

[28] *ibid.*

[29] Swinburne, *Is There A God?, op. cit.*

[30] Swinburne, *The Existence of God, op. cit.*, p.151.

[31] Felix, Minucius, *Octavius*, quoted by Roger Forster and Paul Marston, *Reason and Faith* (Eastborne: Monarch, 1989), p.420.

[32] Moreland, J. P., *Scaling the Secular City* (Grand Rapids: Baker, 1987), p.48.

[33] *ibid.*, p.49.

[34] *ibid.*

[35] Augustine, *City of God*, Book XXII, Chapter 24, p1073-1074, my italics.

[36] Rhodes, *op. cit.*, p.77.

[37] Aristotle, quoted by John Leslie, *Value & Existence* (Rowman & Littlefield, 1979) p.205.

[38] Geisler, Norman L., *Baker Encyclopedia of Christian Apologetics* (Baker, 1999), p.715, my italics.

[39] Polkinghorne, John, *The Way The World Is* (Triangle, 1992), p.17.

[40] Davis, William C., *op. cit.*, p.36-37.

[41] Boren, Carrie, *Unconditional* (privately circulated publication, 2003), p.12.

[42] Phillips, W. Garry and Brown, Williams E., *Making Sense of Your World* (Salem: Sheffield Publishing Company, 1996), p.74.

[43] Lincoln, Abraham, quoted in Boren, *op. cit.*, p.11.

[44] Willard, Dallas, 'The Three-Stage Argument for the Existence of God', in R. Douglas Geivett and Brenden Sweetman (eds) *Contemporary Perspectives on Religious Epistemology* (Oxford University Press, 1993), p.217. cf. www.dwillard.org/Philosophy/Pubs/language_being.htm

[45] Balfour, Arthur J., *op. cit.*, p.30.

[46] Hume, David, *Dialogues Concerning Natural Religion* (Oxford Paperbacks, 1998), p.39.

[47] Davis, Stephen T., *God, Reason and Theistic Proofs* (Edinburgh University Press, 1997), p.103.

[48] Moreland, *Scaling the Secular City, op. cit.*, p.65.

[49] Swinburne, Richard, 'The Argument for Design', in *Contemporary Perspective on Religious Epistemology, op. cit.*, p.209-210.

[50] Garcia, Laura L., 'Teleological and design arguments', in Philip L. Quinn and Charles Taliafferro (eds), *A Companion To Philosophy Of Religion* (Oxford: Blackwell, 1999), p.339.

[51] Dembski, William A., *Mere Creation* (Downers Grove: IVP, 1996), p.17.

[52] Dembski, 'Three Frequently Asked Questions About Intelligent Design', *op. cit.*

[53] Dembski, *Mere Creation, op. cit.*, p.17. cf. Peter S. Williams, 'Christianity, Space & Aliens' at www.arn.org/docs/williams/pw_christianityspace andaliens.htm

[54] Beckwith, *op. cit.*, p.107.

[55] Dembski, *op. cit.*, p.17. The information content of a structure is simply 'the minimum number of instructions necessary to specify the structure.' – Overman, *A Case Against Accident and Self-Organization* (Rowman & Littlefield, 1997), p.71.

[56] Dembski, *op. cit.*, p.17.

[57] Witham, Larry, *By Design: Science and the Search for God* (San Francisco: Encounter Books, 2003), p.143.

[58] Dembski, *op. cit.*, p.16-17.

[59] cf. Bibliography.

[60] Moreland, J. P. and Craig, William Lane, *Philosophical Foundations For A Christian Worldview* (Downers Grove: IVP, 2003), p.62.

[61] Dembski, *op. cit.*, p.17.

[62] Beckwith, *op. cit.*, p.xvi-xvii.

[63] cf. West, John G. Jr, 'Intelligent Design and Creationism Just Aren't the Same' at www.arn.org/docs2/news/idandcreationismnotsame011503.htm

[64] ARN guide to *Evolution, op. cit.*

[65] Dawkins, Richard, *A Devil's Chaplain, op. cit.*, p.219.

[66] Krishtalka, Leonard, quoted by Glenn Branch in 'Human Nature After Darwin by Janet Radcliffe Richards', *Philosophy Now*, 40, March/April 2003, p.44.

[67] ARN guide to *Evolution, op. cit.*

[68] *ibid.*, p.33.

[69] Gould, Stephen Jay, *Natural History*, March 1997, quoted Woodward, *op. cit.*, p.210.

[70] ARN guide to *Evolution, op. cit.*

[71] 'Intelligent design: The New "Big Tent" for Evolution's critics', *University of Wisconsin – Madison News*, February 19, 2004.

[72] Beckwith, *Law, Darwinism, and Public Education, op. cit.*, p.160.

[73] *ibid.*, p.xxi.

[74] Wiker, B., *Moral Darwinism*, p.77.

[75] Woodward, *op. cit.*, p.196, my italics.

[76] Dembski, 'What Every Theologian Should Know about Creation, Evolution, and Design', *op. cit.*

[77] Johnson, Phillip E., *Darwin on Trial* (Downers Grove, IVP, 19932), p.14, 115.

[78] Woodward, Appendix 2, *op. cit.*, p.223.

[79] Johnson, Phillip E., *Reason in the Balance* (Downers Grove: IVP, 1995), p.74.

[80] cf. Williams, Peter S., 'A Rough Guide to Creation and Evolution' at www.arn.org/docs/williams/pw_roughguidetocreationandevolution.htm; John J. Davis (ed.), *Three Views on Creation and Evolution* (Zondervan, 1999).

[81] Beckwith, *op. cit.*, p.153.

[82] Woodward, Thomas, *Doubts about Darwin: A History of Intelligent Design* (Grand Rapids: Baker, 2003), p.10, 20.

[83] cf. Dembski, William A., 'Is Intelligent Design a Form of Natural Theology?' at www.designinference.com/documents/2001.03.ID_as_nat_theol.htm

[84] Beckwith, *op. cit.*, p.164.

[85] Dembski, William A., 'Does the Design Argument show there is a God?' at www.designinference.com/documents/2003.08.Apol_Stdy_Bib_Entry.htm

[86] Behe, Michael J., 'The Modern Intelligent Design Hypothesis', *Philosophia Christi*, Series 2, Volume 3, Number 1, 2001, p.165.

[87] Dembski, William A., 'Skepticism's Prospects for Unseating Intelligent Design' at www.designinference.com/documents/2002.06.Skepticism_CSICOP.htm

[88] Scientists who accept Fred Hoyle's theory of 'directed-panspermia' (illustrated in the film *Mission to Mars*), the idea that life was engineered and/or brought to earth by extra-terrestrials, might subscribe to ID. Of course, this interpretation of intelligent design theory faces an awkward explanatory regress in explaining the origin of the aliens. cf. Lee Elliot Major, 'Big Enough to Bury Darwin' at http://education.guardian.co.uk/higher/physicalscience/story/0,9836,541468,00.html; Michael J. Behe, 'The God of Science' at www.arn.org/docs/behe/mb_godofscience.htm

[89] Dembski, 'Is Intelligent Design a Form of Natural Theology?', *op. cit.*

[90] ARN guide to *Evolution, op. cit.*

[91] Wiker, *op. cit.*, p.77.

[92] Nichols, Terence L., *The Sacred Cosmos* (Grand Rapids: Brazos Press, 2003), p.61.

[93] Crick, Francis, *Nature* magazine, 1974.

[94] Gills, James P., 'The Magnificently Complex Cell', *Darwinism Under the Microscope* (Lake Mary, Florida: Charisma House, 2002), p.42.

[95] Johnson, Phillip E., *The Wedge of Truth* (IVP, 2000), p.159.

[96] *ibid.*

[97] Dembski, William A., *Intelligent Design* (Downers Grove: IVP, 1999), p.263.

[98] Dembski, William A., 'Design as a Research Program: 14 Questions to Ask About Design' at www.leaderu.com/offices/dembski/docs/db-program.html

[99] *ibid.*

[100] Dembski, *Intelligent Design, op. cit.*, p.151.

[101] Woodward, *op. cit.*, p.24.

[102] Edward Sission at www.designinference.com/documents/2003.09. Endorsements_DesRev.pdf

[103] Dembski, William A., 'The Explanatory Filter' at www.arn.org/docs/dembski/wd_expfilter.htm

[104] Plato, *The Laws* (Book X).

[105] Dembski, William A., 'Another Way to Detect Design?' at www.arn.org/docs/dembski/wd_responsetowiscu.htm

[106] Dembski, Intelligent Design, *op. cit.*, p.166.

[107] Dawkins, *The Blind Watchmaker, op. cit.*, p.139.

[108] Craig, William Lane, *Philosophy of Religion: A Reader and Guide* (Edinburgh University Press, 2002), p.72.

[109] The Monkey Shakespeare Simulator at http://user.tninet.se/~ecf599g/aardasnails/java/Monkey/webpages/

[110] The simulated monkeys typed: '1. Citizen. Be&uox:w6LDn;x&:5"vz (Q'5y6zF!0[A. . .', which matched '1. Citizen. Before we proceed any further, heare me speake . . . '

[111] Dembski, *No Free Lunch, op. cit.*, p.157.

[112] *ibid.*, p.86.

[113] *ibid.*, p.93.

[114] Dembski, *Intelligent Design, op. cit.*, p.149.

[115] Orgel, L. E., *The Origins of Life* (New York: John Wiley, 1973), p.189.

[116] Dawkins, *The Blind Watchmaker, op. cit.*, p.9.

[117] Dembski, 'Intelligent design as a Theory of Information' at www.arn.org/docs/dembski/wd_idtheory.htm

[118] *ibid.*

[119] *ibid.*

[120] *ibid.*

[121] *ibid.*

[122] Dembski, *No Free Lunch, op. cit.*, p.158-159.

[123] Dembski, William A., 'Paul Gross' Dilemma'. It was, perhaps, the formulation of LCI that prompted Robert C. Koons to laud Dembski as 'the Isaac Newton of information theory'.

[124] Dawkins, *op. cit.*, p.47-48.

[125] Willard, Dallas, 'Reflections on Dawkins' *The Blind Watchmaker*' at www.dwillard.org/articles/artview.asp?artID=52

[126] Dembski, *No Free Lunch, op. cit.*, p.183.

[127] Dawkins, *op. cit.*, p.59.

[128] *ibid.*, p.60.

[129] Dembski, William A., *The Design Revolution* (Downers Grove: IVP, 2004), p.163.

[130] Dembski, 'Intelligent Design as a Theory of Information', *op. cit.*

[131] Kaita, Robert, 'Cosmological Principle & Cosmic Imperative?', in William A. Dembski (ed.), *Mere Creation, op. cit.*, p.400.

[132] *ibid.*

[133] Bocarsly, Andrew and Kaita, Robert, in Woodward, *op. cit.*, p.212.

[134] cf. Dembski, *No Free Lunch, op. cit.*, p.23.

[135] *ibid.*

[136] Dawkins, Richard, 'The Great Convergence', *A Devil's Chaplain, op. cit.*, p.149.

[137] Ratzsch, Del, *Nature, Design and Science: The Status of Design in Natural Science* (State University of New York Press, 2001), p.65.

[138] *ibid.*, p.67.

[139] *ibid.*

[140] *ibid.*

[141] *ibid.*, p.70.

[142] *ibid.*

[143] *ibid.*

[144] Dyson, Freeman, *Disturbing the Universe* (New York: Harper & Rowe, 1979), p.250.

[145] Dawkins, *The Blind Watchmaker, op. cit.*

[146] Haffner, Paul, *The Mystery of Reason* (Gracewing, 2001), p.164.

[147] Jaki, S. L., 'Religion and Science: the Cosmic Connection' in J. A. Howard (ed.), *Belief, Faith and Reason* (Belfast: Christian Journals, 1981), p.21.

[148] Hawking, Stephen, quoted by John Boslough, *Masters of Time – Cosmology at the End of Innocence* (New York: Addison-Wesley Publishing Company, 1992), p.55.

[149] Adams, Douglas, *The Salmon of Doubt* (Pan Books, 2003), p.131.

[150] Overman, *A Case Against Accident and Self-Organization* (Rowman & Littlefield, 1997), p.128.

[151] Moreland, J. P. and Craig, William Lane, *Philosophical Foundations For A Christian Worldview* (IVP, 2003), p.487.

[152] *ibid.*, p.486.

[153] *ibid.*

[154] Craig, William Lane, 'Why I Believe in God', *op. cit.*, p.70.

[155] *ibid.*

[156] *ibid.*

[157] *ibid.*, p.71.

[158] Moreland, *Scaling the Secular City, op. cit.*

[159] cf. Meyer, Stephen C., 'Evidence for Design in Physics and Biology' in Michael Behe, William A. Dembski and Stephen C. Meyer, *Science and Evidence for Design in the Universe* (San Francisco, Ignatius, 2000), p.60.

[160] cf. Davies, Jimmy H. and Poe, Harry L., *Designer Universe* (Nashville: Broadman & Holman, 2002), p.85.

[161] Muncaster, *op. cit.*, p.212.

[162] Penrose, Roger, *The Emperor's New Mind* (New York, Oxford, 1989), p.344.

[163] Page's calculation is quoted by L. Stafford Betty and Bruce Cordell, 'The Anthropic Teleological Argument', *International Philosophical Quarterly*, 27, no. 4., (December 1987).

[164] Hoyle, Fred, as quoted in Fred Hereen, *Show Me God* (Search Light Publishing, 1995), p.179.

[165] Clark, Stephen R. L., *God, Religion and Reality* (London: SPCK, 1998), p.106.

[166] Dembski, *No Free Lunch, op. cit.*, p.91.

[167] Moreland, *op. cit.*

[168] Davies, Paul, *Superforce* (New York: Simon & Schuster, 1984), p.234.

[169] Jaki, Stanley, in Roy Abraham Varghese (ed.), *The Intellectuals Speak Out About God* (Chicago: Regnery Gateway, 1984), p.71.

[170] Ratzsch, *op. cit.*, p.67.

[171] Betty, L. Stafford, and Coredell, Bruce, 'The Anthropic Teleological Argument', in Michael Peterson *et al.* (eds), *Philosophy of Religion: Selected Readings* (Oxford, 1996), p.209.

[172] *ibid.*, p.209.

CHAPTER 9
Biological Signs of Purpose

As a child, one of my favourite books was Rudyard Kipling's *Just So Stories* (1902, cf. www.boop.org/jan/just-so/). Modelled on tribal folktales, these tales whimsically explained how various animals gained their defining characteristics. For example, the elephant gained its trunk when an elephant child had its nose pulled by a crocodile! In a famous 1979 article Stephen Jay Gould critiqued biologists' willingness to offer quasi-plausible adaptationistic explanations with little more justification than attached to Kipling's stories. Gould had already used the Kipling analogy in 1977 when he wrote that: 'These tales, in the "Just-So Stories" tradition of evolutionary natural history, do not prove anything . . . concepts salvaged only by facile speculation do not appeal much to me.'[1]

Professor Edward T. Oaks derides evolutionary psychologists for proposing explanations that are 'barely a step up from Kipling's nursery tales'.[2] Oaks attacks Steven Pinker's attempt to 'reverse engineer' the mind, saying he 'veers off into Kipling Land . . . as in his hypothesis that . . . men take women to restaurants on dates because in our hunter-gathering days hunter-men brought home the meat of dead carcasses to gathering-women'.[3] Like Kipling's stories, this tale has some plausibility, but it is clearly a story told:

> . . . to shore up the original hypothesis that was
> supposed to be the question at issue but which
> somewhere along the line got assumed into the fabric
> of the argument the better to justify his reverse-
> engineering project . . . evolutionary biology is . . .
> particularly prone to the lazy assumption that because
> we know the outcome, we know the cause . . . [4]

When evolution stops being the question at issue, but is

assumed into the fabric of argument, it is prone to accept unsubstantiated or even discredited naturalistic 'Just-So Stories' on the basis that because we know naturalism is true (and therefore capable in principle of explaining everything), something naturalistic must have happened.

Consider the theory that a self-replicating molecule arose, 'just-so', from a jumble of primordial chemicals. Is this theory a modern example of the phoenix myth? The phoenix was a fabulous eagle-like bird in the folklore of ancient Egypt. No more than one of these great birds lived at any one time, a fact that presented a problem for its procreative chances. However, at the end of its lifespan (of no less than 500 years), the bird would make a flammable nest and set itself on fire, being consumed by the flames. Then, from out of the ashes, a new phoenix would arise! This is one of the few instances in mythology, writes Lester J. McCann, 'in which something complex is constructed from lifeless matter, completely unaided'.[5] For the naturalist, life   have arisen phoenix-like from the lifeless elements that preceded it, but simply re-telling the phoenix myth in scientific language does nothing to establish that this is anything more than a 'Just-So Story'.

> Complexity, irreducible complexity, magnificent
> complexity . . . The only explanation . . . is in
> design . . . a design shrouded in mysterious
> beauty and predicated on a purpose.
> JAMES P. GILLS[6]

Continuing our examination of aesthetic arguments from beautiful things, when we turn our attention from the cosmic context to the chemical basis of life, we find highly complex contingent arrangements of matter that are specified by their functionality. As Dawkins says: '[For evolution to occur] you need raw materials that can self-replicate . . . The *sine qua non* [that without

which] . . . is self-replication.'[7] The idea that the molecular raw materials required for life could simply 'arise'
from some 'warm little pond' of chemicals, as Darwin
hypothesized, is known as *abiogenesis*, from the Greek
a (without), *bios* (life) and *ginomai* (to form). The concept is popularly known today under the rubric of the
hypothetical 'primal soup', and simply means the supposed naturalistic origin of life from non-life. For example, Isaac Asimov confidently asserts: 'molecules in the
ocean grew gradually more complicated until, eventually, some molecule was somehow formed that could
bring about the organization of simpler molecules into
another molecule just like itself. With that, life began . . .
gradually evolving to the present state of affairs . . .'[8]
The way Asimov presents it, the naturalistic origin of
life sounds like established history. It isn't. As Alan
Hayward comments: 'It all sounds so simple, and so
plausible – as long as you know nothing about microbiology.'[9]

Once upon a time in a warm little pond . . .

The concept of *abiogenesis* was originally held by
ancient Greek thinkers such as Anaximander and
Aristotle, and was revived in the mid-twentieth century
when Stanley Miller and Harold Urey recreated in the
laboratory what they believed to be an accurate representation of the early earth's atmosphere, and managed
(whilst mostly producing oils and tars) to produce some
amino acids by passing an electric spark through their
mixture of gases. If the extrapolation from this experiment to the viability of the naturalistic origin of life
from non-life were sound, one could still ask: 'What
accounts for the existence of a "primal soup" with the

correct 'recipe' for life?' The answer, as Benjamin Wiker points out, would track back to the finely tuned laws of nature, and hence track back to design: 'Since biological evolution depends on stellar evolution . . . the necessity of fine-tuning for biological evolution has already been proven. Even now, Darwinism cannot claim to be designer-free.'[10] A finely tuned 'primal soup' suggests an intelligent 'Primal Cook'! However, 'The "prebiotic soup hypothesis," popularized by Miller's experiment, came under withering criticism from chemists for ignoring the role of competing and destructive cross-reactions . . . that would be expected in any hypothetical ocean or pond.'[11] Moreover, 'Miller and Urey's experiment only works as long as oxygen is absent and certain critical ratios of hydrogen and carbon dioxide are maintained',[12] and scientists now think that oxygen was present in the early earth's atmosphere: 'the early atmosphere looked nothing like the Miller-Urey simulation'.[13] As Dean L. Overman explains: 'The presence of even a small amount of oxygen, assiduously avoided in the laboratories of these experiments, would prevent the formation of amino acids and nucleotides . . .'[14] Of course, if oxygen were not present, the molecules of life would have been unprotected from deadly ultraviolet radiation: 'What we have then is a sort of "Catch 22" situation. If we have oxygen we have no organic compounds, but if we don't have oxygen we have none either.'[15] Hurbert P. Yockey comments: 'The "Warm little pond" scenario was invented *ad hoc* as a materialistic reductionist explanation of the origin of life. It is unsupported by any other evidence and it will remain *ad hoc* until such evidence is found.'[16]

These problems aside, 'The information filled molecules of life are much more complex and structured than previously thought.'[17] As Nobel Prize-winning physiologist George Beadle reports, DNA 'was believed by many to be a rather monotonous polymer built of four kinds of nucleotide units arranged in segments of four that were repeated manifold'.[18] 'At that time,' says fellow Nobel winner Max Delbruck, 'it was believed that DNA was a *stupid* substance.'[19] However, we now know that DNA is very far from being a monotonous polymer, but is in fact an exceedingly complex and 'clever' substance. The amino acids generated by tightly controlled and unrealistic laboratory experiments are far less complex than the simplest protein molecules required for life; 'Miller's optimism has now all but evaporated, as experiments based on his model have failed to produce a number of components essential to life.'[20] Therefore, as chemist Jonathan Sarfati writes: 'the very roots of the alleged evolutionary tree are in very bad shape'.[21]

What is the best explanation for these amazing molecules? How do Dawkins and his fellow materialists think nature managed to flout Dembski's LCI? Dawkins offers the following: 'Nobody knows how it happened but, somehow, without violating the laws of physics and chemistry, a molecule arose that just happened to have the property of self-copying – a replicator.'[22] Here, at least, is a frank admission of ignorance: 'I would have to be more of a chemist that I am to know how likely it is that you are going to get such molecules,' says Dawkins, 'I don't know how difficult it would be to achieve that chemically.'[23] Can we consider for a moment how significant and amazing it is that Professor Dawkins, who regularly accuses Christians of blind faith and who exhorts people to always ask, 'What kind of evidence is there for that?',[24] should believe in what he calls the *sine qua non* of evolution *without a shred of evidence*?[25] As Johnson complains: 'The naturalistic evolution of life from prebiotic chemicals and its subsequent naturalistic evolution into complexity . . . is assumed as a matter of first principle . . .'[26] Benjamin Wiker comments that Dawkins' 'lapse into an irrational faith in the powers of chance to avoid an ID inference . . . is not evidence itself but a telling lapse into a materialist credo *quia absurdum est*'.[27] In fact, there doesn't appear to *be* anything like sufficient evidence for abiogenesis, for as Walter L. Bradley observes: 'the origin of a sophisticated system that is both rich in information and capable of reproducing itself has absolutely stymied origin-of-life scientists'.[28]

Not only does naturalistic science lack an explanation of *how* life is supposed to have arrived on the cosmic scene, it actually lacks any evidence *that* life 'just happened'. As G. A. Kerkut of the Department of Physiology and Biochemistry at the University of Southampton writes, it is 'a matter of faith on the part of the biologist that biogenesis did occur . . .'[29] That abiogenesis 'just happened', as Dawkins' comments make clear, is *a philosophical deduction entailed by the assumption of naturalism*. It is, as chemist Robert Shapiro writes: 'mythology rather than science'.[30] Manfred Schidlowsky argues that: 'the very fact that life sprang up on earth constitutes conclusive proof of a primary reducing environment [i.e. one like the Miller-Urey experiment used] since the latter is a necessary prerequisite for chemical evolution and spontaneous origin of life'.[31] But as Overman comments: 'This is a good example of . . . circular reasoning . . . in which evidence is ignored in order to maintain a myth, and the conclusion is set forth in the premise.'[32]

While theists and agnostics have a healthy bias in favour of naturalistic explanations *when these are adequate* (Dembski's Filter depends upon naturalistic explanations being considered first), they cannot treat such a circular deduction as the unquestionable and absolute certainty that it must be for Dawkins. Rather, they will be open to following the evidence. So just how big a chance is Dawkins' blind faith in the naturalistic origin of life from non-life required to support? Stephen C. Meyer calculates that: 'the probability of constructing a rather short functional protein at random [is] so small as to be effectively zero . . .'[33] In other words, not only does naturalistic science lack an explanation of *how* the chemistry of life arose, or evidence to show *that* life 'just happened', it also flies in the face of evidence that life *didn't* 'just' happen! Biochemist Klaus Dose admits: 'More than thirty years of experimentation on the origin of life in the fields of chemical and molecular evolution have led to a better perception of the immensity of the problem of the origin of life on Earth rather than to its solution.'[34] Of course, this is just what one would expect on the basis of LCI, or the principle that 'the significantly greater cannot be generated by the significantly less'.[35] As Thaxton, Bradley and Olsen note: 'a slowly emerging line or boundary has appeared which shows observationally the limits of what can be expected from matter and energy left to themselves'.[36]

Dawkins admits that the chance origin of life theory 'may seem like a big stroke of luck',[37] but he seeks to mitigate against this admission by saying: 'it had to happen only once . . . it may have happened on only one planet out of a billion billion planets in the universe'.[38] But this is merely optimistic hand waving. The universe 'probably contains no more than one planet for every thousand stars',[39] and 'it is unlikely that there are many, if any, other earth-like planets in the universe'[40] able to sustain life. Benjamin Wiker relates some of the finely tuned conditions that permit life on earth:

> Our sun is not a typical star but is one of the 9 percent most massive stars in our galaxy, and is also very stable. Further, the sun hits the Goldilocks mean for life – neither too hot (like a blue or white star) nor too cold (like a red star) – and its peak emission is right at the visible part of the electromagnetic spectrum – the very, very thin band where not only vision is possible but also photosynthesis. Earth just 'happens' to have the right combination of atmospheric gases to block out almost all the harmful radiation on the electro-magnetic spectrum but, strangely enough, opens like a window for visible light. Jupiter is deftly placed and sized so that it not only helps to balance the Earth's orbit but also acts as a kind of debris magnet keeping Earth from being pummeled. Our moon is just the right size and distance to stabilize earth's axial tilt so that we have seasonal variations but not wildly swinging temperature changes.[41]

Astronomer Hugh Ross lists 200 parameters required for a life-bearing planet. Comparing the chances of a planet falling within these parameters by chance alone with our best estimate of the total number of planets in the universe (10^{22}) he estimates that there is 'less than 1 chance in 10^{215}' of even one habitable planet existing in the universe 'without invoking divine miracles'.[42] Elsewhere, Ross writes that: 'fewer than a trillionth of a trillionth of a percent of all stars will have a planet capable of sustaining advanced life. Considering that the observable universe contains less than a trillion galaxies, each averaging a hundred billion stars, we can see that not even one planet would be expected, by natural processes alone, to possess the necessary conditions to sustain life.'[43] Astrobiologists Peter D. Ward and Donald Brownlee conclude: 'If some god-like being could be given the opportunity to plan a sequence of events with the express goal of duplicating our "Garden of Eden", that power would face a formidable task. With the best intentions, *but limited by natural laws and materials*, it is unlikely that Earth could ever be truly replicated.'[44]

For another thing, to generate a *single* functional protein of 150 amino acids exceeds: '1 chance in 10^{180}, well beyond the most conservative estimates for the small probability bound . . . it is extremely unlikely that a random search through all the possible amino acid sequences could generate even a single relatively short functional protein in the time available since the beginning of the universe . . .'[45] In *The Blind Watchmaker*, Dawkins simply says: 'Given enough time, anything is possible.'[46] But there simply *isn't enough time* available to sustain the plausibility of abiogenesis. Professor of Mathematics at Cardiff University, Chandra Wickramasinghe, concludes: 'Living systems could not have been generated by random processes, within a finite time-scale, in a finite universe.'[47] Hence, as Walter L. Bradley says: 'Today it takes a great deal of faith to be an honest scientist who is an atheist.'[48]

Dawkins' blithe, hand-waving ignorance of the

evidence against the naturalistic origin of life from non-life surely shows, as Michael Behe comments, 'the need to treat Darwinian scenarios . . . with a hermeneutic of suspicion'.[49] As Behe goes on to say: 'Some scientists believe so strongly in Darwinism that their critical judgments are affected, and they will unconsciously overlook pretty obvious problems with Darwinian scenarios, or confidently assert things which are objectively untrue.'[50]

The insuperable complexity problems of originating the cell

DNA is incapable of copying itself unaided: 'What brings DNA to life, so to speak, is the cell in which it is embedded.'[51] Behe notes that: 'joining many amino acids together to form a protein with a useful biological activity is a much more difficult chemical problem than forming amino acids in the first place'.[52] And Overman observes: 'the difficulties in producing a protein from the mythical prebiotic soup are very large, but more difficult still is the probability of random processes producing the simplest living cell which represents an overwhelming increase in complexity'.[53]

We have come a long way in our understanding since Ernst Haeckel described cells as 'homogeneous globules of plasm'[54] in 1905. According to recent research the minimum number of protein-producing genes a single-celled organism needs to survive and reproduce in the laboratory is somewhere between 265 and 350![55] The simplest existing self-reproducing organism known outside the laboratory is the bacterium *Mycoplasma Genitalium*, which has 482 genes. Dr Chris Hutchison and his team experimented on *Mycoplasma*

Genitalium by randomly inserting bits of unrelated DNA into the middle of genes to disrupt their function and seeing if the organism thrived anyway. They found that around a third of the *Mycoplasma*'s genes were unnecessary to its survival in the laboratory. Outside the laboratory, however, *Mycoplasma Genitalium* is 'unable to sustain itself without parasitizing on an even more complex organism . . . Therefore a hypothetical first cell that could sustain itself would have to be even *more* complex.'[56] No wonder Benjamin Wiker concludes: 'there are insuperable problems in trying to explain, via some mode of design-free evolutionary theory, how the first cells could have arisen'.[57]

The chance of an enzyme

The whole subject of the origin of enzymes . . .
bristles with difficulties.
M. DIXON AND E. WEBB[58]

Enzymes are biological catalysts: 'tools the cell uses to maintain, cut up and stick together the molecular raw materials with which it is presented'.[59] In *Climbing Mount Improbable* Dawkins considers Fred Hoyle's conclusion that 'large molecules such as enzymes'[60] are too complex to have come about by chance: 'Enzymes work in cells rather like exceedingly numerous machine tools for molecular mass production', explains Dawkins, 'Their efficacy depends upon their three-dimensional shape, their shape upon their coiling behaviour, and their coiling behaviour depends upon the sequence of amino-acids which link up in a chain to make them.'[61] Dawkins agrees with Hoyle that enzymes could not have come about by chance: 'A typical enzyme is a chain of several hundred links . . . An elementary calculation shows that the probability that any particular sequence of, say 100, amino-acids will spontaneously form is . . . 1 in 20^{100}. This is an inconceivably large number, far greater than the number of fundamental particles in the entire universe.'[62] However, Dawkins is not cowed, because 'Darwinism is *not* a theory of random chance. It is a theory of random mutation plus *non-random* cumulative natural selection. Why, I wonder, is it so hard for even sophisticated scientists to grasp this simple point?'[63] Perhaps it is because Dawkins' simple point is an obvious oversimplification.

Even if we grant that random mutations plus non-random cumulative natural selection can account for what would, on a hypothesis of pure chance, be 'the astronomic impossibility'[64] of the 'eyes and knees . . . and elbow joints . . .'[65] that Dawkins goes on to mention, there are grounds for being more circumspect when it comes to the full package deal Dawkins actually presents of: 'eyes and knees, *enzymes* and elbow joints'.[66] Whether *all* enzymes can be explained by evolution surely depends upon how crucial enzymes *per se* are to the existence of things capable of evolving. Consider Steven Rose's overview of the cell:

> We have pictured raw materials, such as amino acids, entering through the cell wall and being processed on a production line of ribosomes geared to produce proteins on a blueprint laid down by a nuclear planning office. These proteins are then sent to other parts of the cell to themselves perform further operations on fresh raw material. Meanwhile, the cell's fuel, glucose, is pulped down to pyruvic acid and dispatched to the

mitochondrial boiler-house, where it is converted
to useful energy which is distributed throughout
the cell and used to drive the entire machinery
forward. This is a beautiful picture of an elegant
piece of interlocking machinery: each part of the
cell needs all the others in order to survive.[67]

The interlocking and mutually dependent cellular
processes described by Rose all utilize enzymes: 'the
cell requires a different enzyme for practically every
reaction it carries out . . . most cells must have at least
two hundred different enzymes. . .'[68] The first step in
replication (a pre-requisite for evolution by natural
selection) is the unwinding of the DNA double helix,
wherein 'Special enzymes (unwinding proteins) attach
themselves to one of the DNA strands, cause the hydrogen bonds between the bases to break, and bring about
the unzipping of the double helix.'[69] Moreover, while
DNA is ultimately responsible for protein synthesis, it
does not form the immediate template on which proteins are manufactured. This task is reserved for the
single stranded nucleic acid of RNA. The first step in
preparing amino acids for transfer to the RNA template
consists of priming them with sufficient energy to form
peptide bonds. This task is performed 'by a series of
amino acid activating enzymes, one for each amino
acid'.[70] In other words, enzymes are crucial to the functioning of organisms capable of reproduction, as Alan
Hayward explains:

. . . the very first bacterium must have had at least
three components, working together as a team:
nucleic acids, enzymes, and a cell wall. The
problem is, which came first – the chicken, the
egg, or the hencoop? Nucleic acid cannot be

formed without the aid of enzymes. Some enzymes can only be manufactured by other enzymes, and these other enzymes can only be manufactured by nucleic acid. Cell walls are only made by enzymes. And the enzymes cannot do their job unless they are kept in place by the cell wall. So how on earth did it all start?[71]

It can't have *evolved* as Dawkins intimates, because 'natural selection cannot explain the *origin of complex*, self-reproducing life forms . . .'[72] As Jacques Monod admitted, on the Darwinian hypothesis: 'The development of the metabolic system [in the first cells] poses Hereculean problems. So does the emergence of the selectively permeable membrane [the cell wall] without which there can be no viable cell. But the major problem is the origin of the genetic code and of its translation mechanism. Indeed, it is not so much a "problem" as a veritable enigma.'[73] As Hayward explains: 'all the available evidence says that the first nucleic acid molecule would have got nowhere on its own. It could not have reproduced itself until the right enzyme (or enzymes, for it would almost certainly have needed more than one) had been formed in quantity, right next door to it.'[74] In the 1970s, biologist Frank Salisbury mused:

. . . our ideas about the origin of life will have to change radically with the passage of time. Not only is the gene itself a problem: think of the system that would have to come into being to produce a living cell! It's nice to talk about replicating DNA molecules arising in a soupy sea, but in modern cells this replication requires the presence of suitable enzymes. Furthermore, DNA by itself accomplishes nothing. Its only reason for existence is the information that it carries and that is used in the production of a protein enzyme. At the moment, the link between DNA and the enzyme is a highly complex one, involving RNA and an enzyme for its synthesis on a DNA template; ribosomes; enzymes to activate the amino acids; and transfer-RNA molecules. Yet selection only acts upon phenotypes and not upon the genes. At this level, the phenotype is the enzyme itself. How, in the absence of the final enzyme, could selection act upon DNA and all the mechanisms for replicating it? It's as though everything must happen at once: the entire system must come into being as one unit, or it is worthless. There may well be ways out of this dilemma, but I don't see them at the moment.[75]

It does Dawkins no good to counter his calculation that 'the probability that any particular sequence of, say 100, amino-acids will spontaneously form is . . . 1 in 20^{100},'[76] by appealing to the fact that 'Darwinism is . . . a theory of random mutation plus *non-random* cumulative natural selection'[77]; if enzymes are necessary for the existence of a self-replicating organism, and, as Dawkins says, for evolution to occur 'The *sine qua non* . . . is self-replication.'[78]

Moreover, as William Dembski reports, recent research published in the *Journal of Molecular Biology* shows that 'certain enzymes are extremely sensitive to perturbation. Purturbation in this case does not simply diminish existing function or alter function, but removes all possibility of function. This implies that neo-Darwinian theory has no purchase on these systems.'[79] Besides which, Dawkins' calculation applies equally well to other crucial amino-acid chains besides enzymes, such as DNA and RNA.[80] All of which brings us back to chance.

'You stick your left hand in, you stick your left hand out . . .'

A major hurdle faced by the chance hypothesis is the problem of 'chirality', the term given to 'the necessity that all nucleotides in a DNA or RNA chain be of a certain molecular orientation'[81] for the chain to work. Dean L. Overman explains: 'Amino acids are in one of two forms: L-amino acids (left handed molecules) or D-amino acids (right handed molecules), each a mirror image of the other. Only left-handed amino acids (L-amino acids) are contained in biologically functional proteins . . . '[82] For a protein to have a function the amino acids that form it must combine in a sophisticated sequence. This sequence isn't easy to obtain by random processes, because both types of amino acids (L and D amino acids) bond without distinction, and both are equally present in the physical world:

> . . . scientists have not found a single means of *purifying* the mixture – that is, increasing substantially the proportion of left-handed amino acids. (The same problem . . . exists for nucleotides, which must be right-handed.) To create the first cell, *all of the thousands of amino acids in the hundred-plus functional proteins required . . . would suddenly have to show up – the right types at exactly the right place at exactly the right time – all left-handed . . .* Likewise, all 100,000-plus nucleotides

would have to show up at exactly the right time in exactly the right way – all right-handed – to form a functioning DNA molecule.[83]

That would be like flipping a coin and getting 100,000 heads in a row! Getting 10,000 left-handed amino acids together by chance (this is the minimum number of amino acids required for 100 functional proteins) would be like flipping 10,000 tails in a row. Hence: 'randomly getting the correctly orientated compounds for the first, simplest organism would be like correctly predicting 110,000 coin flips in a row'.[84] The probability of each flip being correct, like the probability of each amino acid being left or right handed, is 1 out of 2. The odds of getting all 110,000 flips/amino acids correct works out at 1 chance in $10^{33,133}$!

'You ain't seen nothing yet'

Only 20 of the 80 amino acids on earth are life specific, so each amino acid has only a 1 in 4 chance of being 'the right stuff'. For 10,000 amino acids, that works out at 1 chance in 10^{6021} of randomly obtaining enough life-specific amino acids to form a chain. And since there are 20 life-specific amino acids, any specific chain has a 1 in 20 chance of getting each of its amino acids right, 10,000 times over: which is 1 chance in $10^{13,010}$. By the time we factor in the chances of getting the minimum number of DNA base pairs together for each gene in the simplest organism, and the odds of these genes being workably sequenced, we find that the total odds for the naturalistic origin of the simplest conceivable bacterium (conservatively figured)[85] are 1 chance in $10^{112,827}$! Dr Muncaster points out that this would be: 'like winning 16,119 state lotteries in a row with the purchase of one ticket for each'.[86] If you had a single chance in some cosmic lottery to pick a single pre-designated winning electron out of more than 1300 universes as large as our own, you'd be facing similar odds as those stacked against the chance origin of the simplest conceivable bacterium. As Bernd-Olaf Kuppers says: 'not even the entire space of the universe would be enough to make the random synthesis of a bacterial genome probable'.[87]

Not a snowball's chance
Steven Rose writes that:

> . . . macromolecules . . . are all extremely *unlikely* substances. Those materials which life produces in such abundance still defeat the synthetic techniques of the chemist. In the living cell, such molecules cannot arise purely by random chemical reactions; they must be synthesized according to precisely planned pathways which can achieve a specificity far beyond that of the chemist . . . before it can even begin to act on its external environment, the cell . . . has to provide the mechanisms whereby . . . it can continuously re-synthesize its more complex parts from much simpler molecules.[88]

Faced with such mind-boggling complexity and specificity, Herbert P. Yockey, a pre-eminent authority on information theory and biology, concludes: 'the origin of life by chance in a primeval soup is impossible in probability in the same way that a perpetual motion machine is impossible in probability'.[89] (It is worth noting here with Dean L. Overman that: 'When one couples the probabilities in physics against an accidental universe compossible with life with the molecular biologi-

cal and pre-biological probabilities against the formation of the first form of life from inert matter, the compound calculation wipes the idea of accident entirely
out of court.'[90]) Keith Ward takes stock of the implications of the improbabilities of life 'just happening':

> It seems hugely improbable that, in the primeval
> seas of the planet earth, amino acids should meet
> and combine to form large molecular structures
> capable of self-replication. It is even more
> improbable that long strings of DNA should coil
> into the nuclei of cells, and that cells should
> differentiate to produce organisms, colonies of
> cells which co-operate to form limbs, mouths,
> digestive systems and bodies. The motive for
> positing some sort of intelligent design is almost
> overwhelming.[91]

Likewise, Hoyle and Wickramasinghe conclude:

> . . . the enormous information content of even the
> simplest living systems . . . cannot in our view be
> generated by what are often called 'natural'
> processes . . . There is no way in which we can
> expect to avoid the need for information, no way
> in which we can simply get by with a bigger and
> better organic soup, as we ourselves hoped might
> be possible a year or two ago . . . The correct
> position we think is . . . an intelligence, which
> designed the biochemicals and gave rise to the
> origin of carbonaceous life . . . This is tantamount
> to arguing that carbonaceous life was invented by
> noncarbonaceous intelligence . . .[92]

Hoyle and Wickramasinghe stop short of making the
philosophical identification of their 'noncarbonaceous
intelligence' with God, but they note: 'It is ironic that

the scientific facts throw Darwin out, but leave William Paley, a figure of fun to the scientific world for more than a century, still in the tournament with a chance of being the ultimate winner . . . Indeed, such a theory is so obvious that one wonders why it is not widely accepted as being self-evident. The reasons are psychological rather than scientific.'[93]

Neither by chance nor by law . . .

Darwin had never heard of DNA.
ALAN HAYWARD[94]

Biologist Neil Broom explains that: 'The sequence making up a particular DNA strand is not dependent on any preferred bonding between the individual bases. Each base is the molecular equivalent of the dot or dash in the Morse Code and can be arranged in any linear combination without breaking the rules of chemical bonding.'[95] The sequence of amino acids in DNA cannot be explained by reference to the laws of physics or chemistry any more than the arrangement of ink on a letter can be explained simply with reference to the chemical properties of the ink and paper: 'Because the genetic information is independent from these chemicals, the information did not arise from the chemicals; just as the words in this book did not arise from the ink in my computer printer.'[96] When you consider the information bearing function of DNA this makes perfect sense, for as Nancy Pearcey and Charles Thaxton point out: 'A law produces regular, predictable patterns . . . But a repeating pattern encodes little information . . . if the origin of the DNA sequence were a material force, such as chemical bonding forces . . . The entire DNA molecule would consist of repeating patterns, which would encode very little information.'[97] Hence, as Broom argues: 'The chemical laws that bind each base, A, G, C or T, to its neighbour in DNA are lower-level, slave-like laws that must come under the control of a higher principle in a manner exactly analogous to the *intelligent* sequencing of dots and dashes required in Morse Code to create a *meaningful* message.'[98]

DNA cannot be adequately explained by reference to either chance (as we saw in the previous section), or by law (exactly because DNA is of necessity an *unlikely* arrangement of matter), for 'the genetic code would be impossible if the order in the items in the DNA molecule were chemically necessary'.[99] By its very nature as a code, DNA cannot be explained in terms of physics or chemistry. As Herbert Yokey explains: 'The reason that there are principles of biology that cannot be deduced from the laws of physics and chemistry lies not in some esoteric philosophy but simply in the mathematical fact that the genetic information content of the genome for constructing even the simplest organisms is much larger than the information content of these laws.'[100] The reductionistic attempt to account for the information content of DNA in terms of the laws of nature is a case of trying to derive the greater from the lesser, and hence getting something for nothing: 'Did life arise from non-life?' asks Terry L. Miethe: 'I think this would be tantamount to saying that something came from nothing.'[101] But as the truism runs, 'From nothing, nothing comes.' As Michael Polanyi argued: 'all objects conveying information are irreducible to the terms of physics and chemistry . . . As the arrangement of a printed page is extraneous to the chemistry of the printed page, so is the base sequence in a DNA molecule extraneous to the chemical forces at work in the DNA molecule.'[102] Overman concludes:

> . . . the information in the DNA molecule is independent of the bases of sugars and phosphates which comprise the molecule. If information is independent from these chemicals, the information did not arise from the chemicals; just as a poem written on a blackboard did not arise from the chalk . . . The mathematical probabilities . . . argue against life arising by accident . . . [Therefore] Life appears to be formed only by a guided process with intelligence somehow inserting information or instructions into inert matter.[103]

Nature's regularities just aren't up to the task of creating specified complexity, not because they are the wrong regularities, but simply because they are *regularities*. As Stephen C. Meyer explains:

> Natural laws may well be maintained and have been created by God . . . but the physical and chemical regularities that scientists describe as laws do not (by definition) produce the information-rich configurations of matter that the origin of life requires. God may have created natural law, but he does not use natural laws to create specified biological information.[104]

Too complex for chance, too specific for law

Ruling out chance and law, as Dembski argues, only leaves design. We can rule out chance and law as sufficient explanations for the specified complexity of life not only on their own terms (e.g. DNA is too complex for chance to explain given the probabilistic resources of the universe, and too specific for natural laws to explain), but by noting that any proposed naturalistic explanation of specified complexity falls foul of Dembski's Law of the Conservation of Information. No wonder science writer Fred Heeren reports that: 'Theorists are at a loss to explain how, even in a rich prebiotic soup filled with organic compounds, a sequence that creates the information necessary for life can be produced by any means where intelligence is not already involved.'[105] DNA is a very complex (highly unlikely) arrangement of matter that also conforms to a specific (and beautiful) pattern. That implies intelligent design.

Design or designoid?

Watch out for 'bait and switch' tactics, by which you are led to agree with a harmless definition and then the term is used in a very different sense.

PHILLIP JOHNSON[106]

In *Climbing Mount Improbable* Dawkins draws a distinction between objects that are clearly designed and objects that are not designed but superficially look a bit like they are designed – objects which he calls '*designoid*'.[107] Dawkins illustrates the concept of a designoid with a craggy hillside that suggests the profile of the late President Kennedy: 'Once you have been told, you can just see a slight resemblance to either John or Robert Kennedy. But some don't see it and it is certainly easy to believe that the resemblance is accidental.'[108] Dawkins contrasts this vaguely Kennedy-esque hillside with the four presidents' heads carved into Mt

Rushmore in America: 'They are obviously not accidental: they have design written all over them.'[109] Having given the above examples, Dawkins proceeds to assert that no biological organisms are designed, they are, at most, designoid: 'Designoid objects look designed, so much so that some people – probably, alas, most people – think that they *are* designed. These people are wrong . . . the true explanation – Darwinian natural selection – is very different.'[110]

We need to pay close attention to what's going on here, because the meaning of Dawkins' crucial term just shifted significantly. Dawkins' illustration of a designoid was of something with the superficial appearance of design. People have to have the resemblance between the hillside and Kennedy pointed out to them; some people 'don't see it'[111]; and 'it is certainly easy to believe that the resemblance is accidental'.[112] Now Dawkins wants to convince us that, although some biological objects give such a strong appearance of design that 'most people'[113] intuitively think that they are designed, they are in fact merely designoid. On the face of things, Dawkins' own illustration of the design/designoid distinction supports the majority opinion that some biological objects are designed. It is surely the case that some biological objects are more analogous to Mt Rushmore than they are to the vaguely Kennedy-esque hillside. In which case, what is Dawkins' justification for making the confident, universal negative claim (the hardest sort of claim to prove) that absolutely no biological objects are designed, and that any biological object that gives the appearance, *however strong*, of being designed, is actually designoid? Simply coining a term for 'un-designed objects that look designed', and then applying it to the entire biological realm, hardly settles the matter! If the paradigm 'designoid' object is the Kennedy-esque hillside, then such a broad application of the term is inappropriate. For Dawkins to imply otherwise is 'as though a geologist were to gaze on the four presidential faces carved into Mt Rushmore and then insist . . . that the faces are the product of . . . wind and water erosion'.[114] The meaning of Dawkins' term illegitimately shifts from 'things that look a bit like they might be designed, but on closer inspection obviously are not', to 'things that give every appearance of being designed, but are not'. This shift exhibits a logical fallacy called 'ambiguity' or 'equivocation'.

If Dawkins' elaborately made point is simply, as Alan Keith suggests, that 'some things that appear to be designed are not in fact designed',[115] what justification does he give for thinking that life only *appears* to be designed? It's easy enough to tell design and designoid apart as Dawkins' introduces the distinction, but how are we to tell design from designoid given his implicit re-definition of the distinction? Dawkins clearly applies the first distinction on the basis of observation and the second distinction *on the basis of his commitment to naturalism.* Once again Dawkins assumes that if something has an evolutionary explanation, then it cannot be the result of design. And once again he assumes that everything *must* have a Darwinian explanation because God does not exist.

Dawkins argues that while 'a rock can weather into the shape of a nose seen from a certain vantage point',[116] such a rock would be a *designoid* (in the original sense of the term). Mt Rushmore, on the other hand, is clearly *not* designoid (in the original sense of the term): 'Its four heads are clearly *designed*,'[117] says

Dawkins, because: 'The sheer number of details [i.e. the amount of *complexity*] in which the Mount Rushmore faces resemble the real things [i.e. the complexity fits four *specifications*] is too great to have come about by chance.'[118] In terms of mere possibility, says Dawkins: 'The weather *could* have done the same job . . . But *of all the possible ways of weathering a mountain, only a tiny minority would be speaking likenesses of four particular human beings.*'[119] Hence: 'Even if we didn't know the history of Mount Rushmore, we'd estimate the odds against its four heads being carved by accidental weathering as astronomically high . . .'[120] When Dawkins doesn't rule out design *a priori*, he happily employs a pre-theoretic version of Dembski's design Filter. This Filter leads us to agree with Dawkins about Mt Rushmore being designed, but it also leads us to disagree with him about the supposed absence of scientifically detectable design in nature.[121] Some of the *evidence* argues for design as its best explanation, but Dawkins allows the *dogma* of naturalism to trump the evidence and shoehorn it into the naturalistically acceptable category of 'designoid', even though doing so requires an *ad hoc* redefinition of his own term.

Norman L. Geisler highlights the parallels between Mt Rushmore and DNA, following the evidence where Dawkins will not:

> . . . suppose I come upon a round stratified stone and were asked how it came to be such. I might plausibly answer that it was once laid down by water in layers which later solidified by chemical action. One day it broke from a larger section of rock and was subsequently rounded by the natural erosional processes of tumbling in water. Suppose

then . . . I come upon Mount Rushmore . . . Even
if I knew nothing about the origin of the faces,
would I not come immediately to believe it was an
intelligent production and not the result of natural
processes of erosion? Yet why should a natural
cause serve for the stone but not for the faces?
For this reason, namely, that when we come to
inspect the faces on the mountain we perceive –
what we could not discover in the stone – that . . .
they convey specifically complex information . . .
Suppose also that in studying the genetic structure
of a living organism, we discover that its DNA has
a highly complicated and unique information code,
distinguished by its specified complexity . . .
would we not conclude that it most probably took
intelligence to produce a living organism?[122]

The faces on Mt Rushmore are complex (not something
generally to be expected from erosion!) and specific
(they fit four independent patterns): 'Applying the
explanatory filter, the evidence clearly points to
design.'[123] As with Mt Rushmore, so with DNA.
Undirected natural causes *could* have done the same
job. But *of all the possible ways of arranging amino
acids, only a tiny minority would match the biological specification for functionality*. Hence, even without knowing the history of DNA, we'd estimate the odds
against its occurrence by natural processes as
astronomically high.

Willow seeds and floppy discs

*If . . . computer programs require an intelligent
origin, so too does the message in the DNA molecule.*
NANCY PEARCEY AND CHARLES THAXTON[124]

Dawkins observes that: 'The machine code of the genes is uncannily computer-like.'[125] He says: 'if asked to summarize molecular genetics in a word, I would choose "digital" . . . Genetics today is pure information technology.'[126] In fact, says Dawkins: 'Genes are digital, textual information, and they retain their hard, textual integrity as they change partners down the generations. Chromosomes – long strings of genes – are formally just like long computer tapes.'[127] Dawkins offers the following description of DNA:

> . . . at the bottom of my garden is a large willow tree, and it is pumping downy seeds into the air . . . Not just any DNA, but DNA whose coded characters spell out specific instructions for building willow trees that will shed a new generation of downy seeds. Those fluffy specks are, literally, spreading instructions for making themselves . . . It is raining instructions out there; it's raining programs . . . That is not a metaphor, it is the plain truth. It couldn't be plainer if it were raining floppy discs.[128]

If it *was* raining floppy discs, and those floppy discs, like DNA, carried a digital program (for making other floppy discs perhaps), wouldn't everyone agree that this complex specified information must have originated in some mind or minds? Following Dawkins' own usage, both the floppy disc and the willow seed are physical packets carrying complex, 'specific', 'coded', information. DNA can store information equivalent to that on five high-density computer disks within the space of a thousandth of a millimetre. Bill Gates acknowledges: 'DNA is like a computer program, but far, far more advanced than any software we've ever created.'[129] We know that computer programs come from minds; should we not conclude that the information encoded by DNA originally came from a mind?

Paley's watch and irreducible complexity

The most famous design argument is of course that propounded by William Paley:

> . . . suppose I pitched my foot against a *stone*, and were asked how the stone came to be there, I might possibly answer, that, for anything I knew . . . it had lain there fore ever . . . But suppose I had found a *watch* upon the ground . . . I should hardly think of the same answer which I had given before . . . when we come to inspect the watch . . . the inference, we think, is inevitable, that the watch must have had . . . an artificer or artificers who formed it . . . Arrangement, disposition of parts, subserviency of means to end, relation of instruments to a use, imply the presence of intelligence and mind . . . every manifestation of design which existed in the watch, exists in the works of nature, with this difference, on the side of nature, of being greater and more, and that in a degree which exceeds all computation . . . yet in a multitude of cases, are not less evidently mechanical, not less evidently contrivances, not less evidently accommodated to their end, or suited to their office, than are the most perfect productions of human ingenuity.[130]

In terms of an argument by analogy, the nineteenth-century astronomer John Herschel explained that 'if the analogy of two phenomena be very close and striking, while, at the same time, the cause of one is very obvious, it becomes scarcely possible to refuse to admit the action of an analogous cause in the other, though not so obvious in itself'.[131] Modern knowledge has borne out, and even increased, the strength of Paley's analogy: 'The analogy between humanly crafted mechanical systems and what routinely happens in a single living cell is nothing short of stunning . . .'[132] (Indeed, each cell contains a cellular clock that cycles precisely over periods from two to twenty-six hours.) Michael Denton describes the cell as: 'the complexity of a jumbo jet packed into a speck of dust invisible to the human eye'.[133] Michael Behe notes that: 'Cells swim using machines, copy themselves with machinery, ingest food with machinery . . . highly sophisticated molecular machines control every cellular process.'[134] According to Denton, on a tour of a cell:

> We would see that nearly every feature of our own
> advanced machines had its analogue in the cell:
> artificial languages and their decoding systems,
> memory banks for information storage and
> retrieval, elegant control systems regulating the
> automated assembly of parts and components,
> error fail-safe and proof-reading devices utilized
> for quality control, assembly processes involving
> the principle of prefabrication and modular
> construction.[135]

He argues that:

> Paley was not only right in asserting the existence
> of an analogy between life and machines, but was
> also remarkably prophetic in guessing that the
> technological ingenuity realized in living systems
> is vastly in excess of anything yet accomplished by

man . . . If we are to assume that living things are machines for the purposes of description, research and analysis . . . there can be nothing logically inconsistent . . . in extending the usefulness of the analogy to include an explanation for their origin.[136] Thomas Dubay highlights the strength of this analogy by contrast with a non-controversial instance of analogical scientific reasoning: 'In an archaeological dig, if the investigators find a stone so chipped that it could have served as a knife, they conclude that it was deliberately made, that is, designed for that purpose by a human ancestor. Their inference may well be true, but all the same, it is enormously weaker than . . . design throughout any living cell.'[137]

However, popular summaries of Paley notwithstanding, his argument goes well beyond analogy, however impressive. Although he didn't employ this precise terminology, Paley pointed out that a watch is, at its core, *irreducibly complex*. That is, not only is the watch's purpose carried out by the sum of the watch's parts, but that purpose could not be carried out 'if its different parts had been differently shaped from what they are, or placed after any other manner or in any other order than that in which they are placed . . .'[138] In the contemporary literature of design, a system performing a given basic function (like a watch telling the time), is said to be 'irreducibly complex' if it includes a set of well-matched, mutually interacting, non-arbitrarily individuated parts such that each part in the set is indispensable to maintaining the system's basic function. The set of indispensable parts is the *irreducible core* of the system in question.[139] 'The power of the concept of irreducible complexity', writes John A. Smart, 'is that it invalidates the step-by-step *process* of evolution.'[140] As Behe, Dembski and Meyer explain: 'Natural selection can only act on systems that perform functions that help organisms survive. But "irreducibly complex" systems have no function at all unless all the parts in the system are present. Yet without the aid of natural selection the odds against such systems arising on their own are prohibitive.'[141] The existence of an irreducibly complex system in nature is indicative of design. As atheist Daniel Dennet, who called such systems 'the You-Couldn't-Get-Here-From-There Organ or Organism,'[142] explains: 'If there are designs that cannot be approached by a gradual, stepwise redesign process in which each step is at least no worse for the gene's survival chances than its predecessor, then the existence of such a design in nature would seem to require, at some point in its ancestry, a helping hand from a foresighful designer . . .'[143] And as Arthur J. Balfour said: 'Nice adjustment and fitness exquisitely accomplished are without doubt agreeable objects of [aesthetic] contemplation.'[144] An irreducibly complex mechanism is one that exhibits a functionally necessary degree of 'nice adjustment and fitness exquisitely accomplished', and hence is a thing of beauty.

The irreducible complexities of climbing Mount Impossible

> . . . the belief that an organ so perfect as the eye could have been formed by natural selection, is enough to stagger anyone . . . I have felt the difficulty far too keenly to be surprised at others hesitating to extend the principle of natural selection to so startling a length.
> CHARLES DARWIN[145]

According to Darwinian theory biological systems evolve through the incremental accumulation of beneficial mutations: 'natural selection acts only by taking advantage of slight successive variations; she can never take a great sudden leap, but must advance by short and sure, though slow steps'.[146] Richard Dawkins explains why: 'The larger the leap through genetic space, the lower the probability that the resulting change will be viable, let alone an improvement. [Hence] evolution must in general be a crawl through genetic space, not a series of leaps.'[147] He describes this gradual approach to obtaining biological complexity as 'Climbing Mount Improbable'.[148] Improbable because, as Steven Vogel writes, the theory stipulates that: 'Nature in effect must transmute a motorcycle into an automobile while providing continuous transportation. The need for growth without loss of function can impose severe geometrical limitations.'[149] Phillip Johnson comments:

> Claims that natural selection is a force of stupendous creative power, which is capable of crafting the immense complexity of biological structures that living creatures possess in such abundance, are not supported by experimental evidence or observation . . . Observational evidence (e.g. the famous peppered moth study) shows mainly cyclical changes in the relative frequency of characteristics already present in the population. There is circumstantial evidence pointing to somewhat more impressive changes (e.g. circumpolar gulls, Hawaiian fruit-fly species), but the empirical evidence gives no reason for confidence that natural selection has the creative

power, regardless of the amount of time available, to build up complex organs from scratch or to change one body plan into another . . . The decisive disconfirmation of neo-Darwinism comes from the fossil record. Even if we generously grant the assumption that neo-Darwinist macroevolution is capable of producing basic changes, it does not appear to have done so.[150]

As Stephen Jay Gould admitted: 'Our inability, even in our imagination, to construct functional intermediaries in many cases has been a persistent and nagging problem for gradualistic accounts of evolution.'[151] Gould also pointed out that: 'The fossil record with its abrupt transitions offers no support for gradual change . . . All palaeontologists know that the fossil record contains precious little in the way of intermediate forms; transitions between major groups are characteristically abrupt.'[152] Nevertheless, naturalists, who assume that evolution is true because it fills the explanatory gap left by the exclusion of design, have been content to say that even though we have no idea what path organisms took up Mount Improbable, *they must have done so*. For example, Dawkins says that: 'however daunting the sheer cliffs that the adaptive mountain first presents, graded ramps can be found the other side and the peak eventually scaled'.[153] How does he know that these 'graded ramps can be found' in advance of showing what they are; without even looking for them? Because his justification for this assumption is philosophical rather than scientific: 'Without stirring from our chair, we can see that it must be so',[154] explains Dawkins, 'because nothing except gradual accumulation could, in principle, do the job . . .'[155] What job is that? The job of explaining life *naturalistically*! As Daniel Dennet admits: 'This is a purely theory-driven explanation, argued a-priori from the assumption that natural selection tells the true story – some true story or other – about every curious feature of the biosphere . . . it assumes that Darwinism is basically on the right track.'[156] Once again, Dawkins' conclusion rests upon his presupposition that there is no designer: 'this sort of argument smacks of tautology', complains Michael Denton: 'The only warrant for believing that functional living systems are . . . capable of undergoing functional transformation by random mechanisms, is belief in evolution by the natural selection of purely random changes in the structure of living things. But this is precisely the question at issue.'[157] John Polkinghorne voices the same concern: 'So much of evolutionary argument seems to be that "it's happened and so it must have happened this way".'[158]

Absence of evidence for precise causal histories of how Mount Improbable was supposedly conquered by gradualistic means is not conclusive evidence of an absence of such ascents, and even design theorists are biased in favour of naturalistic explanations (where they are adequate); but the improbability of the gradualistic hypothesis, together with its pervasive lack of evidential support, counts against it as an explanation for anything that looks like the result of design, at least for anyone without an absolute commitment to naturalistic explanations. As Dembski explains:

> Darwinism is committed to a sequence of
> manageable steps that gradually transforms A into
> B. In consequence, there has to be some sequence
> . . . where each transition from one step to the

next can readily be accounted for in terms of natural selection and random variation. Thus, for instance, in a Darwinian explanation of the bacterial flagellum, we know that bacteria lacking a flagellum (and also lacking any genes coding for a flagellum) had to evolve into bacteria with a flagellum (and thus possessing a novel genetic complement for the flagellum). If Darwinism is correct, some step-by-step Darwinian process had to take us from the former type of bacteria to the latter. So how did it happen? How could it have happened? Nature somehow filled in the details, but Darwinists somehow never do.[159]

Dawkins reports '*feeling* . . . that provided the difference between neighbouring intermediates in our series leading to [complex biological structures such as the] eye is sufficiently small, the necessary mutations are almost bound to be forthcoming'.[160] However: 'The DNA replication process for higher organisms includes proofreading to keep error rates at less than one in ten billion [while] errors that do occur are almost invariably neutral or harmful.'[161] Darwinists have failed to provide evidence that any eye could be evolved from scratch though any series of 'sufficiently small' mutations, let alone to provide evidence that any eye historically followed any such evolutionary pathway: 'Ingenious hypothetical scenarios for the evolution of complex adaptations are presented to the public virtually as fact, but sceptics within science derisively call them "just-so" stories, because they can be neither tested experimentally nor supported by fossil histories.'[162] Denton notes that: 'through what intermediate states the reflecting eye evolved is a mystery'.[163] Indeed, cell biologist Franklin

Harold admits: 'There are presently no detailed Darwinian accounts of the evolution of any biochemical or cellular system, only a variety of wishful speculations.'[164] Even these speculations tend to 'artificially isolate a particular component or organ, such as the eye, from the immensely complex system [i.e. the organism] in which it is embedded'.[165] As Johnson complains: 'There is no requirement that any of this speculation be confirmed by either experimental or fossil evidence. For Darwinists, just being able to imagine the process is sufficient to confirm that something like that must have happened.'[166]

Dawkins argues that different forms of eye present in nature can be arranged into a sequence from less to more complex, and that this sequence shows the viability of a Darwinian explanation of the eye: 'modern analogues of every step up the ramp can be found, working serviceably in dozens of eyes dotted independently around the animal kingdom'.[167] However, not only is this sequence of eyes historically hypothetical (showing at best what could rather than what did happen), but its supposedly simple beginning actually assumes the existence of 'a cell sensitive to light and able to react in a specific way to visible radiation . . .'[168] That light sensitive cell, far from being simple, is an example of an 'irreducibly complex' (IC) system that can't have evolved directly by incremental modifications of a precursor system, because all of its parts are necessary to its performing its function. As Jakob Wolf complains: 'far from commanding the resources to explain their emergence, Darwinian explanation consistently presupposes the existence of irreducibly complex systems'.[169] Hence recent discoveries in microbiology mean that the pervasive absence of evidence for the climbing of 'Mount Improbable' has now been transmuted into evidence of absence:

> Climbing Mount Improbable requires taking a slow serpentine route up the backside of the mountain and avoiding precipices. For irreducibly complex systems that have numerous diverse parts and that exhibit the minimal level of complexity needed to retain a minimal level of function, such a gradual ascent up Mount Improbable is no longer possible. The mountain is, as it were, all one big precipice.[170]

For some biological systems (systems exhibiting IC), the task of climbing 'Mount Improbable' is (to all intents and purposes) the task of climbing Mount Impossible. If a biological system exhibits irreducible complexity, then evolution by natural selection is in serious trouble as an adequate explanatory hypothesis (and intelligence, as the only cause known to be capable of originating irreducibly complexity, moves to the fore as the best explanation of IC systems).

Dawkins' bet

Darwin himself admitted that the existence of a single irreducibly complex system would falsify his evolutionary hypothesis: 'If it could be demonstrated that any complex organ existed which could not possibly have been formed by numerous, successive modifications, my theory would absolutely break down.'[171] Dawkins acknowledges that Darwin's remark 'is valid and very wise . . . his theory is indeed falsifiable . . . and he puts his finger on one way in which it might be falsified'.[172] However, he asserts that 'not a single case is known to me of a complex organ that could not have been formed by numerous slight [un-guided] modifications. I do not believe that such a case will ever be found.'[173] Nevertheless, he concedes: 'If it is – it'll have to be a really complex organ, and . . . you have to be sophisticated about what you mean by 'slight' – I shall cease to believe in Darwinism.'[174] Dawkins has a lot riding on his universal negative bet that nothing in nature is irreducibly complex.

The irreducible Behe

Behe's concept of irreducible complexity (IC) has found itself in the peer-reviewed scientific literature . . . and is being taken seriously by scientists.
MIKE GENE[175]

It was Leigh University biochemist Michael J. Behe who reinvigorated the concept of irreducible complexity. Professor Behe received his PhD in biochemistry from the University of Pennsylvania (his dissertation was on sickle cell disease). He worked for four years at the National Institutes of Health on problems of DNA structure, before joining the faculty at Leigh. Behe, a Catholic, reports: 'My religious beliefs haven't influenced my scientific work. I first learned Darwin's theory in parochial school. We were taught that it was God's way of making life through natural laws. That seemed fine with me. It was only when I learned of scientific problems with the theory of evolution that I became skeptical of it.'[176] Behe began to doubt Darwin's theory after reading *Evolution: A Theory in Crisis* by Michael Denton: 'Denton pointed out a number of scientific problems of the theory that I had never considered before,' says Behe, 'Denton talked about what I went on to explore: the great complexity of cellular life, which could not have come about randomly as Darwin believed.'[177] Behe's most notable presentation of irreducible complexity is *Darwin's Black Box: the Biochemical Challenge to Evolution* (1996), where he defined his terms as follows:

> By *irreducibly complex* I mean a single system composed of several well-matched, interacting parts that contribute to basic function, wherein the removal of any one of the parts causes the system to effectively cease functioning. An irreducibly complex system cannot be produced directly . . . by slight, successive modifications of a precursor system, because any precursor to an irreducibly complex system that is missing a part is by definition non-functional.[178]

By definition, any system that is irreducibly complex cannot have evolved directly up a graded ramp round the back of 'Mount Improbable'. Ruling out direct, incremental evolution does not logically exclude what Darwin called 'a sudden leap',[179] but as Dawkins notes: 'The larger the leap through genetic space, the lower the probability that the resulting change will be viable, let alone an improvement.'[180] Behe observes: 'Even if a system is irreducibly complex (and thus cannot have been produced directly) . . . one can not definitely rule out the possibility of an indirect, circuitous route. As the complexity of an interacting system increases, though, the likelihood of such an indirect route drops precipitously. And as the number of unexplained, irreducibly complex biological systems increases, our confidence that Darwin's criterion of failure has been met skyrockets . . .'[181] Sceptics of Behe's hypothesis ideally need to demonstrate the existence of indirect, 'circuitous', evolutionary pathways with the following features: they achieve the gradual assembly of all the components required by a given IC system (in the correct, functionally specific arrangement) through a sufficiently probable series of evolutionary steps wherein each and every step a) has a function, b) either increases the fitness of the preceding functional step or results in a system with a different function, and where c) all of these functional steps are (by definition) different to the function exhibited by the IC end-product being explained. But as William Dembski observes:

> The fact is that for irreducibly complex biochemical systems, no indirect Darwinian pathways are known . . . What's needed is a seamless Darwinian account that's both detailed and testable of how subsystems undergoing co-evolution could gradually transform into an irreducibly complex system. No such accounts are available or forthcoming . . . The absence here is *pervasive* and *systemic* . . .[182]

Critics charge Behe's argument with failing to acknowledge that 'absence of evidence is not evidence of absence', but this truism only holds in the right circumstances. Failing to find one's car keys in the house doesn't indicate they don't exist: after all, they might be in the car and you know you own keys to be discovered. On the other hand, suppose one wasn't sure that keys even existed to be discovered, and had conducted a thorough search anyway, and had come up empty handed. The latter analogy is closer to the scientific reality of explaining IC systems. As Dembski observes: 'If after repeated attempts looking in all the most promising places you don't find what you expect to find and if you never had any evidence that the thing you were looking for existed in the first place, then you have reason to think that the thing you are looking for doesn't exist at all . . . the absence of scientific evidence here is as complete as it is for leprechauns.'[183]

Behe argues that at the biomolecular level of life, which was an unknown 'Black Box' in Darwin's day, there are several irreducibly complex molecular systems 'including aspects of protein transport, blood clotting, closed circular DNA, electron transport, the bacterial flagellum, telomeres, photosynthesis, transcription regulation, and much more'.[184] Given that such systems are resistant to naturalistic explanations, and given our everyday experience that intelligent agents regularly produce irreducibly complex systems, Behe argues that the best explanation of such molecular machines is intelligent design:

> When is it reasonable to conclude, in the absence of firsthand knowledge or eyewitness accounts, that something has been designed? For discrete physical systems – if there is not a gradual route to their production – design is evident when a number of separate, interacting components are ordered in such a way as to accomplish a function beyond the individual components. The greater the specificity of the interacting components required to produce the function, the greater is our confidence in the conclusion of design.[185]

Indeed, we can take this argument further, as Del Ratzsch explains: 'If nature and chance cannot produce some phenomenon, yet there it inarguably is in front of us, it follows that something else did produce it – and agents of various sorts are essentially the only other alternative. And if we have good grounds for thinking that neither humans nor other finite creatures have the relevant capacity, then supernatural agency is the only option left.'[186] Consider just one example of an IC system noted by Behe:

The bacterial flagellum

In 1973 the startling, unexpected discovery was made that some bacteria swim using an outboard motor, spinning their 'flagella' at up to 100,000 rpm like a screw propeller: 'The rotary motor, with a diameter of only 30 to 40 nm [nanometers], drives the rotation of the flagellum at around 300 Hz, at a power level of 10^{-16} W with energy conversion efficiency close to 100%.'[187] The bacterial flagellum has become the mascot for the ID community, because it is irreducibly complex: 'The flagellum includes an acid powered rotary engine, a stator, O-rings, bushings and a drive shaft. The intricate machinery of this molecular motor requires approximately fifty proteins. Yet the absence of any one of these proteins results in the complete loss of motor function.'[188] One can see that a rotary motor without a propeller, or a drive shaft, or a motor, is useless (indeed, it would be less than useless, because it would be a drain on resources): 'Because the bacterial flagellum is necessarily composed of at least three parts – a paddle, a rotor, and a motor – it is irreducibly complex.'[189] In a review article, Robert Macnab comments: 'one can only marvel at the intricacy, in a simple bacterium, of the total motor and sensory system which has been the subject of this review and remark that our concept of evolution by selective advantage must surely be an oversimplification. What advantage could derive, for example, from a 'preflagellum' (meaning a subset of its components), and yet what is the probability of 'simultaneous' development of the organelle at a level where it becomes advantageous?'[190] Experiments have confirmed that eliminating any of the proteins that form the flagellum results in a non-functioning machine.

The bacterial flagellum is irreducibly complex, a fact that rules out explanation by *direct* evolutionary pathways and leaves the Darwinist to fall back on far chancier *indirect* explanations.

How the flagellum evolved? A Just-So story[191]

> *I have learned from my own embarrassing experience how easy it is to concoct remarkably persuasive Darwinian explanations that evaporate on closer inspection.*
> DANIEL DENNET[192]

Christian biologist Ken Miller has argued for an indirect explanation in the case of the flagellum by pointing to the existence of the type III secretory system (TTSS),[193] which is coded for by about ten genes, each of which is homologous (structurally similar) to genes in the bacterial flagellum. Miller sees the TTSS as a functional evolutionary precursor of the flagellum capable of being selected for on its own functional merits and then augmented to produce the flagellum. However, as Dembski points out: 'At best the TTSS represents one possible step in the indirect Darwinian evolution of the bacterial flagellum. What's needed is a complete evolutionary path and not merely a possible oasis along the way. To claim otherwise is like saying we can travel by foot from Los Angeles to Tokyo because we've discovered the Hawaiian Islands.'[194] Two final points nail shut the coffin of Miller's TTSS scenario. The first is that 'The type III system itself is [irreducibly complex], perhaps with ten IC components.'[195] The second is that: 'The best current molecular evidence . . . points to the TTSS evolving from the flagellum and not vice versa.'[196]

H. Allen Orr (a critic of Behe) argues:

> First, it will do no good to suggest that all the required parts of some biochemical pathway popped up simultaneously by mutation. Although this 'solution' yields a functioning system in one fell swoop, it's so hopelessly unlikely that no Darwinian takes it seriously . . . Second, we might think that some of the parts of an irreducibly complex system evolved step by step for other purposes and were then recruited wholesale to a new function. But this is also unlikely.[197]

Nevertheless, the current favourite among indirect explanations being advanced for IC systems is Orr's second option of the wholesale co-option of parts evolved for other functions, an option R. H. Thornhill and D. W. Ussery call 'adoption from a different function'.[198] While the TTSS, for example, contains around ten proteins that are homologous to proteins in the flagellum, the flagellum has another thirty or forty proteins, which are unique to it. As Scott Minnich, Professor of Biology at the University of Idaho, and an expert on the flagellum, says in response to the co-option hypothesis:

> With a bacterial flagellum, you're talking about a machine that's got forty structural parts. Yes, we

find ten of them are involved in another molecular machine, but the other thirty are unique. So where are you going to borrow them from? Eventually you're going to have to account for the function of every single part as if originally having some other purpose. I mean you can only follow the argument so far, until you run into the problem that you're borrowing from nothing . . .'[199]

Stripping away a third of the improbability Dembski calculates for the spontaneous formation of the flagellum (10^{-1170}) doesn't appreciably improve matters for a naturalistic explanation: 'Applied to those remaining two-thirds of flagellar proteins, my calculation yields something like 10^{-780}, which also falls well below my universal probability bound.'[200] As Mike Gene warns: 'The brilliance of Darwin was to minimize the role of chance in apparent design. But once we turn to the co-option explanation, we leave this explanatory appeal behind, as chance reasserts itself into a place of prominence.'[201]

Taking what Joshua A. Smart calls 'a Concessionary approach',[202] Dembski supposes, purely for the sake of argument, that we discover several molecular systems 'like the TTSS that jointly took into account all the flagellar proteins'.[203] Those proteins would be 'similar but, in all likelihood, not identical to the flagellar proteins (strict identity would itself be vastly improbable)'.[204] Such a hypothetical situation, designed to maximize the chances of an indirect explanation by co-option, 'raises the question how those several molecular machines can come together so that proteins from one molecular machine adopt proteins from another molecular machine to form an integrated functional system like the flagellum'.[205] As Minnich says: 'even if you concede that you have all the parts necessary to build one of these machines, that's only part of the problem. Maybe even more complex is the assembly instructions.'[206] Dr John Bracht, managing editor of the journal *Progress in Complexity, Information and Design*,[207] explains:

> . . . biological functionality is turning out to be much more highly specified and precise than we had originally envisioned . . . biology is really a science of engineering, where the constraints for bio-functionality are extreme – to the point that nearly every molecular interaction is remarkably precise and tightly controlled. Molecular biology is much like a jigsaw puzzle where each piece must be specifically shaped to fit with the other pieces around it . . .[208]

Applying these observations to the proposed construction of the flagellum by co-option, Bracht writes:

> The problem is that the proteins which are to become the flagellum are coming from systems that are distinctly non-flagellar in nature . . . and being co-modified from their original molecular interactions into an entirely new set of molecular interactions. Old interfaces and binding sites must be removed and new ones must be created. But given the sheer number of flagellar proteins that must co-evolve . . . the Darwinian explanation is [very unlikely and therefore] really no different from appealing to a miracle.[209]

Dembski concludes: 'We can do the probabilistic analysis at the level of individual proteins . . . Or we can do it at higher levels of organization like functional subsystems [like TTSS] . . . But all such probabilistic analyses still point up vast improbabilities.'[210] Moreover, as

Dembski observes: 'the only evidence we have of successful co-option comes from engineering and confirms that intelligence is indispensable in explaining complex structures like the mousetrap and, by implication, the bacterial flagellum.'[211]

Dawkins' appears to be betting in the face of some long odds: 'Like compulsive gamblers who are constantly hoping that some really big score will cancel their debts, evolutionary biologists live on promissory notes that show no sign of being redeemable . . .'[212] If biologists can discover or construct detailed, testable, indirect Darwinian pathways of sufficiently high probability that account for the emergence of irreducibly and minimally complex biological systems like the bacterial flagellum, 'then more power to them',[213] says Dembski: 'But until that happens, evolutionary biologists who claim that natural selection accounts for the emergence of the bacterial flagellum are worthy of no more credence than compulsive gamblers who are forever promising to settle their accounts.'[214] Dembski summarises the case for design from IC systems:

> . . . irreducible complexity renders biological
> structures provably inaccessible to direct
> Darwinian pathways . . . the failure of evolutionary
> biology to discover indirect Darwinian pathways is
> pervasive and systemic and therefore reason to
> doubt . . . that indirect Darwinian pathways are
> the answer to irreducible complexity . . . it's not
> just that certain biological systems are so complex
> that we can't imagine how they evolved by
> Darwinian pathways. Rather, we can show
> conclusively that direct Darwinian pathways are
> causally inadequate to bring them about and that

indirect Darwinian pathways . . . are utterly
without empirical support in bringing them about.
Conversely, we do know what has the causal
power to produce irreducible complexity –
intelligent design.[215]

Maximally irreducibly complex systems

IC systems like the bacterial flagellum are *in principle*
inaccessible to direct Darwinian pathways, and evolutionary biologists therefore pin their hopes on the possibility that sufficiently probable *indirect* Darwinian
pathways might one day be found to account for them.
(To the best of our knowledge the odds do not favour
such explanations, and hence the best explanation of
such systems is intelligent design.) However, recent
research (which is still at the early stages) points
to the existence of complex biological systems that are
not only inaccessible in principle to direct Darwinian
pathways (making them 'minimally' IC), but inaccessible in principle to indirect pathways as well (making
them 'strongly' or 'maximally' IC). As Dembski
explains:

> . . . there is now mounting evidence of biological
> systems for which any slight modification does not
> merely destroy the system's existing function but
> also destroys the possibility of any function of the
> system whatsoever. (Consult, for instance, the
> research on extreme functional sensitivity of
> various enzymes and on irreducibly complex
> metabolic pathways of enzymes for which each
> enzyme needs to attain a certain catalytic
> threshold before it or its associated pathway can
> serve any biological function at all.) For such

> systems, neither direct nor indirect Darwinian
> pathways could account for them.[216]

Behe's remark that 'if a system is irreducibly complex
(and thus cannot have been produced directly) . . . one
can not definitely rule out the possibility of an indirect,
circuitous route'[217] applies to 'minimally irreducibly
complex' systems, but not to 'maximally irreducibly
complex' systems. When it comes to a maximally IC
system, anyone suggesting that Darwinian mechanisms
alone can offer a sufficient explanation would not only
be betting against the odds, but against an *in principle*
argument to the contrary. As Dembski observes: 'no
Darwinian account could in principle be given for the
emergence of such systems'.[218]

IC and CSI

Dembski points out that irreducible complexity is a special case of specified complexity (Behe and Dembski
have recognized essentially the same problem, Behe's
argument being a concrete example of Dembski's
objection):

> The irreducibly complex systems Behe considers
> require numerous components specifically adapted
> to each other and each necessary for function. On
> any formal complexity-theoretic analysis, they are
> complex in the sense required by the complexity-
> specification criterion. Moreover, in virtue of their
> function, these systems embody patterns inde-
> pendent of the actual living systems. Hence these
> systems are also specified in the sense required by
> the complexity-specification criterion.[219]

Such unlikely (and beautiful) arrangements of matter
bear the hallmark of design.

A group of nutters?

*Anyone who reports anything which displeases
the sceptic will be accused of incompetence,
mental illness or dishonesty, or some
combination of the three, without a single shred
of fact to support the accusations.*
DAVID W. OWENS[220]

Dawkins dismisses ID theorists as: 'a well-organised and well-financed group of nutters'.[221] But this sort of bluster (a debating tactic called 'Poisoning the well') should not intimidate us. Dawkins' bark is worse than his bite (just as his philosophical skills are worse than his rhetorical skills). The fact of the matter is that 'the epistemic status of evolutionary biology is, to say the least, a highly controversial topic'[222] and 'a growing number of highly educated scientists . . . are becoming increasingly sceptical of evolutionary theory'.[223] Thomas Dubay reports: 'The movement in the mainline scientific community to see design in the visible universe, and most particularly in cellular biology, is growing in strength, while its opponents have nothing but feeble and unpersuasive responses.'[224] Professor Frederick Crews grudgingly acknowledges that: 'Intelligent design is thriving in cultural circles where illogic and self-indulgence are usually condemned.'[225]

Dembski counters Dawkins' *ad hominem* attack: 'one can be reasonably well-adjusted, remarkably well-educated (as many design theorists are), and still think Darwinism is a failed scientific paradigm'.[226] Dembski himself has a BA in psychology, an MS in statistics, a PhD in the philosophy of science and a PhD in mathematics (all from the University of Chicago), as well as a

Master of Divinity from Princeton Theological Seminary; and he is currently associate research professor in the conceptual foundations of science at Baylor University. According to Dembski:

> The following problems have proven utterly intractable not only for the mutation-selection mechanism but also for any other undirected natural process proposed to date: the origin of life, the origin of the genetic code, the origin of multicellular life, the origin of sexuality,[227] the scarcity of transitional forms in the fossil record,[228] the biological big bang that occurred in the Cambrian era,[229] the development of complex organ systems and the development of irreducibly complex molecular machines. These are just a few of the more serious difficulties that confront every theory of evolution that posits only undirected natural processes. It is thus sheer arrogance for Darwinists like Richard Dawkins . . . to charge design theorists with being ignorant or stupid or wicked or insane for denying the all-sufficiency of undirected natural processes in biology . . .[230]

Dembski is alluding to a book review by Dawkins in which he affirms: 'It is absolutely safe to say that if you meet somebody who claims not to believe in evolution, that person is ignorant, stupid or insane (or wicked, but I'd rather not consider that).'[231] Dawkins distinguishes between natural selection ('the mutation-selection mechanism') as Darwin's proposed engine of evolution (about which he admits: 'It is still (just) possible for a biologist to doubt its importance, and a few claim to'[232]) on the one hand, and 'the fact of evolution itself, a fact that is proved utterly beyond reasonable doubt',[233] on the other. Hence, by 'the fact of evolution itself' Dawkins appears to mean the multi-faceted belief that life arose millions of years ago due only to (undirected) natural processes and then diversified from a common ancestor over millions of years merely by the operation of (undirected) natural processes. Elsewhere Dawkins circumspectly writes:

> We can now assert with confidence that the theory that the Earth moves round the Sun not only is right for our time but will be right in all future times even if flat-Earthism happens to become revived and universally accepted in some new dark age of human history. We cannot quite say that Darwinism is in the same unassailable class. Respectable opposition to it can still be mounted, and it can be argued that the current high standing of Darwinism in educated minds may not last through all future generations . . . we must acknowledge the possibility that new facts may come to light which will force our successors of the twenty-first century to abandon Darwinism or modify it beyond recognition.[234]

What Dawkins means by 'Darwinism' here probably coincides with the theory of natural selection (which he brackets from 'the fact of evolution itself'), but Dawkins affirms his faith in the survival of what he calls *Core Darwinism*: 'the minimal theory that evolution is guided in adaptively non-random directions by the non-random survival of small random hereditary chances'.[235] And although Dawkins is prepared to concede that evolutionary theory might evolve in the future, he certainly isn't prepared to admit any hint of design or purpose within biology:

> The feature of living matter that most demands explanation is that it is almost unimaginably complicated in directions that convey a powerful illusion ['appearance' would be a less pejorative term] of deliberate design . . . Adaptations, especially complex adaptations, awake such a powerful hunger that they have traditionally provided one of the main motivations for belief in a supernatural Creator. The problem of adaptation, *therefore*, really was a big problem, a problem worthy of the big solution that Darwin provided . . . [236]

Note that the appearance of deliberate design is *assumed* to be 'a powerful illusion', and that this presumed 'illusion of deliberate design' is considered to be a 'big problem' *precisely because* it (indirectly) supports belief in 'a supernatural Creator'. For Dawkins the atheist, the fact of evolution itself must remain staunchly naturalistic, whatever 'new facts may come to light'![237] Once again, Dawkins' conclusion is driven by his philosophy rather than by scientific evidence, a situation that leads him to cast aspersions on the intellectual or moral character of anyone with the timidity to call into question 'the fact of evolution itself' (something that can be done by doubting any of its several facets).[238] Surely we should agree with W. R. Thompson's introduction to the centenary edition of Darwin's *Origin*, which castigated 'scientific men [who] rally to the defence of a doctrine they are unable to . . . demonstrate with scientific rigor, attempting to maintain its credit with the public by the suppression of criticism and the elimination of difficulties, [a situation that] is abnormal and undesirable in science'.[239]

Increasingly common dissent

The truth of the matter is that 'more and more biologists, biochemists, and other researchers have raised serious objections to evolutionary theory in recent years'.[240] For example, Michael Denton, a non-Christian molecular biologist, writes that he is: 'sceptical that major evolutionary changes . . . can be adequately accounted for in terms of the Darwinian model . . .'[241]

Gordon Graham is a Professor of Philosophy at the University of Aberdeen who says he is 'equally unsympathetic to creationism and to any rabidly anti-religious scientism'.[242] According to Graham, 'the intellectual difficulties facing neo-Darwinism are formidable . . .'[243] He quotes David Stove, whom he calls 'a respected philosopher writing in a professional journal'[244] who remarks:

> Most educated people nowadays, I believe, think of themselves as Darwinians. If they do, however, it can only be from ignorance: from not knowing enough about what Darwinism says. For Darwinism says many things, especially about our species, which are too obviously false to be believed . . . at least by any educated person who retains any capacity at all for critical thought on the subject of Darwinism.[245]

Graham observes:

> This is the sort of thing that is frequently said by the 'cultured despisers of religion' (a memorable phrase coined by the theologian Fredrich Schleiermacher), of whom, as a matter of fact, Dawkins is one. Since Darwin is an authority frequently invoked by some of these modern despisers, it is intriguing to find it said of science rather than religion . . . Indeed, in another article

Stove expressly describes Darwinism as a 'new religion'.[246]

'Suffice it to say', concludes Graham, 'that there are dissenting voices, and dissenting voices from within biology itself no less than from anthropology, philosophy, psychology and sociology.'[247]

According to one of those dissenting voices from within philosophy, Norman L. Geisler: 'it is unreasonable to believe that intelligent life was caused by nonintelligent natural forces . . . the odds of life beginning by chance are . . . for all practical purposes, zero . . . it takes more faith to believe in evolution than it does to believe in a supernatural creator'.[248] William Lane Craig concludes that: 'in the absence of a methodological commitment to naturalism, there really does not appear to be compelling evidence for the neo-Darwinian theory. On the contrary, there seems to be pretty persuasive evidence that the neo-Darwinian account cannot be the full story.'[249] Analyzing the theory of evolution without Dawkins' naturalistic assumptions, Alvin Plantinga, one of today's leading philosophers, concludes: 'that it *happened* is doubtful; that it is *certain*, however, is ridiculous'.[250]

Taken in any substantive sense, Dawkins' assertion that 'no qualified scientist doubts that evolution is a fact'[251] is simply incorrect. Jonathan Wells (PhD, Yale; PhD Berkeley) is a qualified scientist, a post-doctoral biologist in the Department of Molecular and Cell Biology at the University of California at Berkley. According to Wells: 'The Darwinian paradigm is in serious trouble, of the kind that matters most in science: it doesn't fit the evidence.'[252] Chemist Cliff Marsh writes:

. . . the factual basis for evolution is, at best, seriously lacking. Knowledge is growing in all fields of science, but, paradoxically, there is less and less solid evidence for evolutionary mechanisms . . . The evidence for evolution being the process by which life originated and developed isn't that convincing. The latest discoveries in biology, chemistry and other areas have raised some serious questions.[253]

According to Robert M. Augros:

. . . key features of Neo-Darwinism, especially gradualism and natural selection, are under serious criticism currently, not from creationists but from within biology itself . . . Neo-Darwinism is far from a conclusive and rigorous demonstration of the sufficiency of random chance in accounting for the origin and structure of living things . . . Darwin's theory may receive its deathblow at the hands of modern palaeontology, ecology, genetics, and molecular biology.[254]

In response to a recent American television series on evolution, 132 qualified scientists signed a joint statement saying: 'We are sceptical of claims for the ability of random mutation and natural selection to account for the complexity of life'[255]:

Signers of the statement questioning Darwinism came from throughout the US and from several other countries, representing biology, physics, chemistry, mathematics, geology, anthropology and other scientific fields. Professors and researchers at such universities as Princeton, MIT, U Penn, and Yale, as well as smaller colleges and the National Laboratories at Livermore, CA and Los Alamos, NM, are included.[256]

As of October 2003 over 300 scientists had signed the sceptical statement.[257]

Physicist Paul Davies moved from promoting atheism in 1983 to realizing in 1984 that 'the laws [of physics] seem themselves to be the product of exceedingly ingenious design',[258] and affirming by 1989 that this fact is 'powerful evidence that there is something going on behind it all. The impression of design is overwhelming.'[259] In his recent book, *The Fifth Miracle: The Search for the Origin of Life*, Davies writes: 'When I set out to write this book I was convinced that science was close to wrapping up the mysteries of life's origin . . . Having spent a year or two researching the field I am now of the opinion that there remains a huge gulf in our understanding . . . This gulf in understanding is not merely ignorance about certain technical details, it is a major conceptual lacuna.'[260] While Davies says he is 'not suggesting that life's origin was a supernatural event',[261] he does think 'that we are missing something very fundamental about the whole business'[262] and confesses: 'My personal belief, for what it is worth, is that a fully satisfactory theory of the origin of life demands some radically new ideas',[263] because 'scientists are currently stumped'.[264]

While many scientists and philosophers (including Christian scientists and philosophers) believe in evolution, many scientists and philosophers (including Christian scientists and philosophers) believe that the neo-Darwinian paradigm is seriously flawed. Huston Smith's arresting verdict may prove to be prophetic: 'We continue to believe in Darwinism, even though it no longer feels right to us. Darwinism is in fact dying, and its death signals the close of our age.'[265]

Time to shift paradigm?

Darwinism is too small to fit the facts it claims to explain, and ID is large enough to include a modified form of Darwinism.
BENJAMIN WIKER[266]

Thomas Kuhn argued that major advances in science have occurred through a succession of 'revolutions' wherein data accumulates that does not fit with the established paradigm of 'normal science'. At first there are, quite naturally, vigorous attempts to absorb this new information into the accepted paradigm: 'but eventually the day comes when the paradigm can no longer stand the burden of its inner contradictions, and a new paradigm is established that makes sense of the new data in a more satisfactory way. This "revolution" in paradigm shifts then makes way for a new period of "normal science".'[267] Design theorists believe that there is a need to subsume Darwin's theory of evolution within the context of a scientific paradigm of intelligent design, because 'Scientific evidence, when evaluated without an overwhelming bias toward materialism, does not support the Darwinian creation story that has effectively become a state-sponsored religion in modernist culture. On the contrary, the evidence actually supports the supposedly discredited view that an intelligent designer . . . had to be involved in biological creation.'[268]

Thomas Woodward argues that Darwinian sceptics like Michael Denton and Phillip Johnson were pre-revolutionary in that they 'attacked Darwinism by piling up scientific anomalies and analyzing the underlying philosophical assumptions', whereas 'Behe and Dembski have made design theory revolutionary in a Kuhnian sense by proposing a new heuristic paradigm that organizes research in a different direction.'[269] Recall how Darwin found himself trapped between seeing *everything* in the biological world as the result of direct and immediate intelligent design, or seeing *everything* as the result of an unintended evolutionary process: 'I am conscious that I am in an utterly hopeless muddle. I cannot think that the world, as we see it, is the result of chance; and yet I cannot look at each separate thing as the result of Design.'[270] One way out of Darwin's muddle is to hypothesize that life is the result of *a combination of* direct, immediate design *and* of an indirect, mediated process of *intended* evolution. This conclusion, I believe, is the best explanation of the available evidence. Darwin considered just such a hypothesis in *The Origin of Species*, but rejected it because, as he said, its proponents 'do not pretend that they can define, or even conjecture, which are the [directly] created forms of life, and which are those produced by secondary laws. They admit variation as a *vera causa* in one case, they arbitrarily reject it in another, without assigning any distinction in the two cases.'[271] ID provides a way out of Darwin's muddle while satisfying the implicit demand of Darwin's objection to limiting the explanatory work done by secondary causes. Dembski's work on CSI allows design theorists to distinguish *nonarbitrarily* between what secondary causes can and can't accomplish. Behe's concept of 'irreducible complexity' performs the same service, albeit in a more limited fashion. As Dembski writes:

> Prior to the rise of modern science all the
> emphasis was on teleological guidance (typically
> in the form of divine design). Now the pendulum

has swung to the opposite extreme, and all the
emphasis is on nature's autonomy . . . Where is
the point of balance that properly respects both,
and in which design becomes empirically evident?
The search for that balance-point underlies all
design-theoretic research. It's not all design or all
nature but a synergy of the two. Unpacking that
synergy is the intelligent design research program
in a nutshell.[272]

ID doesn't hold that the neo-Darwinist theory of evolution is wholly and straightforwardly wrong, but it does
suggest that it is only *a partially successful theory
that needs to be subsumed by a wider explanatory
hypothesis of design*, somewhat as Newton's laws were
subsumed by Einstein's: 'In the heady early days of
Newtonian mechanics,' notes Dembski, 'physicists
thought Newton's laws provided a total account of the
constitution and dynamics of the universe. Maxwell,
Einstein and Heisenberg each showed that the proper
domain of Newtonian mechanics was far more constricted. So, too, the proper domain of the mutation-
selection mechanism is far more constricted than most
Darwinists would like to admit.'[273] As Benjamin Wiker
suggests: 'the application of materialist principles to
nature has been extraordinarily fruitful, insofar as it
represents a half-truth, yet it has ended ultimately in
undermining its own presuppositions'.[274] Putting an
interesting spin on the matter, Joshua A. Smart writes:
'ID is in some sense an evolutionary theory. It is a theory about when evolution is inadequate.'[275]

Dembski acknowledges that 'the Darwinian selection
mechanism constitutes a fruitful idea for biology'.[276] He
also accepts: 'that some speciation occurs in the

manner described by Darwin . . .'[277] However, 'Darwinism is the totalising claim that this mechanism accounts for all the diversity of life. The evidence simply does not support this claim. What evidence there is supports limited variation within fixed boundaries, or what is typically called microevolution.'[278] Moreover, 'Macroevolution – the unlimited plasticity of organisms to diversify across all boundaries – even if true, cannot legitimately be attributed to the mutation-selection mechanism. To do so is to extrapolate the theory beyond its evidential base.'[279] Dembski affirms the existence of a 'considerable overlap'[280] between Neo-Darwinism and Intelligent Design, and points out that: 'intelligent design . . . *does not require that every aspect of biology be designed and is fully capable of assimilating the Darwinian mechanism*'.[281] For example, although some ID theorists doubt common ancestry, Behe states: 'I think common descent remains a reasonable idea.'[282] As Wiker observes: 'ID proponents . . . do not deny many of the marvellous things that Darwinism has uncovered, and so an ID account of biology would include much of what Darwinists have discovered. What they question, however, is the Darwinian assertion that such things are explicable solely as the result of . . . unguided mechanisms.'[283]

A fruitful scientific research programme

> . . . the ID approach is both quite natural and
> scientifically fruitful.
> BENJAMIN WIKER[284]

Dawkins avers that: 'Without evolution, biology is a collection of miscellaneous facts.'[285] Even if he were right about this, wouldn't having a miscellaneous collection of *facts* be better than having the facts distorted by a false theoretical framework? Similarly, Theodosius Dobzhansky propounded the maxim: 'Nothing in biology makes sense except in the light of evolution.'[286] But as Jonathan Wells responds, 'A true scientist would say that nothing in biology makes sense except in the light of evidence.'[287]

Dawkins' fear is doubly unfounded, because ID represents an alternative theoretical framework for biology, a fruitful new 'paradigm' or 'research programme'. Indeed, the ID approach is already paying dividends: 'Design is not a science stopper. Indeed, design can foster inquiry where traditional evolutionary approaches obstruct it.'[288] For example, Benjamin Wiker points out that: 'Since the last half of the 20th century, the discovery of fine-tuning has been the impetus leading to the discovery of more fine-tuning.'[289] Wiker concludes: 'Because the universe is irreducibly complex – not just at one level, but on successive layers of interrelated complexity – accepting the apparent complexity as real does not eliminate science but destroys materialist reductionism so that science may be released from the desire to shrink the universe and instead may inquire ever more deeply into creation . . .'[290] Scott Minnich, Associate Professor of Microbiology at the University of Idaho, is an expert on the flagellum (which he has studied for over 15 years) who says that belief in design has given him many research insights.[291] Dembski concludes: 'Reinstating design within science can only enrich science . . . By eschewing design, science has for too long operated with an inadequate set of conceptual categories. This has led to a constricted vision of reality, skewing how science understands not just the world but also ourselves.'[292] Thomas Woodward likewise welcomes ID as a liberating paradigm:

> To be jarred awake to the powerful role that metaphysical commitments play in cosmology – especially their buttressing and protecting the Darwinian knowledge-claims – can be upsetting and unpleasant, but the cognitive health benefits are enormous. This awakening to the power of hidden metaphysical foundations is the most inevitable and immediately beneficial sort of 'arousing from dogmatic slumber' that Design could achieve. Through such a rude awakening, the power of reason is newly energized. Indeed, such basic notions as rationality, intelligence, and academic freedom are given new impetus, a new breath of life . . .[293]

Darwinists once argued 'that non-protein coding DNA are relics of once-functioning genes or useless "junk" DNA that strongly argued against design of the genome . . .'[294] However, 'new research is beginning to overturn the view that most of the genome has no function',[295] and this is a result that verifies ID in that, unlike Darwinism, ID naturally suggests the hypothesis that so called 'junk DNA' will turn out to have a useful purpose:

> . . . huge stretches of genetic material dismissed in biology classrooms for generations as 'junk DNA' actually contain instructions essential for the growth and survival of people and other organisms . . . scientists said the new discoveries were likely to force them to abandon the term 'junk DNA' and send them back to the drawing board to come up

with sweeping new models for how nature builds and maintains organisms.[296]

Dembski argues: 'ID theorists should be at the forefront in unpacking the information contained within biological systems. If these systems are designed, we can expect the information to be densely packed and multi-layered (save where natural forces have attenuated the information). Dense, multi-layered embedding of information is a prediction of ID.'[297] A similar shift of opinion verifying the design hypothesis has occurred in the case of so-called vestigial structures: 'most of the structures regarded as vestigial in humans a hundred years ago are now known to have a function . . .'[298] Here again: 'we find design encouraging scientists to look for function where evolution discourages it'.[299]

A fledgling breakthrough

As Jonathan Wells says, ID is 'a fledgling program, but there are some promising leads. It could have saved us 25 years if an ID approach to "junk" DNA had been pursued back when it was discovered. There are also applications now being pursued actively in embryology and the study of bacteria.'[300] Further conceptual and experimental work certainly remains to be done (after all, that's the whole point of a scientific research programme),[301] and only time will tell if ID can succeed in prompting a paradigm shift within the natural sciences. Whether or not it does so depends upon overcoming negative philosophical assumptions as much as upon matters of empirical evidence (indeed, it depends upon getting people to approach and evaluate the empirical evidence without a philosophical bias against design). As Dembski writes: 'I'll be the first to admit that intelligent design is an ambitious program and that it may not pan out. But it needs first to be fairly discussed.'[302] Paul Davies comments: 'Dembski's attempt to quantify design, or provide mathematical criteria for design, is extremely useful. I'm concerned that the suspicion of a hidden agenda is going to prevent that sort of work from receiving the recognition it deserves. Strictly speaking, you see, science should be judged purely on the science and not on the scientist.'[303] According to mathematician Wolfgang Smith, a Professor Emeritus at Oregon State University: 'The intelligent design theory is the first rigorous refutation of Darwinism on a scientific and mathematical basis. This impresses me as a major, scientific breakthrough which, hopefully in time, will be recognized by the scientific community at large.'[304] Indeed, despite the deep-rooted naturalistic prejudices of the reigning paradigm of 'normal science', ID research 'is being published and cited in the peer-reviewed scientific literature (including the biological literature)',[305] appearing in such journals as the *Proceedings of the National Academy of Sciences, Journal of Molecular Biology, Journal of Theoretical Biology, Origins of Life and Evolution of the Biosphere* and *Annual Review of Genetics.*

If ID is falsified as a scientific research programme, theism will continue to be the best metaphysical interpretation of the world studied by science (whereas naturalism appears to be a self-defeating metaphysical interpretation). On the other hand, if ID prospers, naturalism will have received a serious blow *from within science itself.* One significant consequence of such an outcome would be that science *as such* would once again affirm belief in the existence of a purpose and intention underlying life.

Conclusion

Dawkins defends scientism from the charge of nihilism by erecting a spurious barrier between cosmic and personal meaning, and by employing an aesthetic defence of science that is either glaring in its nihilistic subjectivity, or which, if understood in terms of the objective theory of beauty, radically subverts its author's atheistic worldview. Far from undermining belief in purpose and design (something they are incapable of doing), modern scientific discoveries and theories actually support an inference to the existence of an aesthetically aware intelligent designer with an objectively good purpose for the cosmos and for human life.

Scientific theories (whether those of Newton's optics, Dawkins' Neo-Darwinian biology, or Intelligent Design) are, strictly speaking, irrelevant to the question of value that lies at the heart of our search for meaning (although ID certainly implies something positive about the question of purpose). What is far from irrelevant is whether or not our appreciation of nature's beauty is taken at face value as an objective intimation of divinity, or interpreted through the 'cold philosophy' of atheism as a 'whistling in the dark'. We can't have it both ways. As F. R. Tennant wrote: 'Values alone can provide guidance as to the world's meaning, structure being unable to suggest more than intellectual power [and thus purpose]. And beauty may well be a meaning . . . If Nature's beauty embody a purpose *of* God, it would seem to be a purpose *for* man, and to bespeak that God "is mindful of him" . . . and thus far the case for theism is strengthened by aesthetic considerations.'[306] And so too is the case for life having an objective meaning.

[1] Gould, Stephen Jay, 'The Return of the Hopeful Monster', *Natural History*, June/July 1977.

[2] Oaks, Edward T., 'The Blind Programmer', *First Things*, March 1998.

[3] *ibid.*

[4] *ibid.*

[5] McCann, Lester J., *Blowing the Whistle on Darwinism* (Independent Pub. Marketing, 1986), p.101.

[6] Gills, James P., *Darwinism Under the Microscope* (Lake Mary, Florida: Charisma House, 2002), p.189.

[7] Dawkins, Richard, 'Darwin's Dangerous Disciple' at www.skeptic.com/03.4.miele-dawkins-iv.html

[8] Asimov, Isaac, *Please Explain*, quoted by Alan Hayward, in *Does God Exist? Science says 'Yes'* (Basingstoke: Lakeland, 1979), p.76.

[9] Hayward, *op. cit.*, p.76.

[10] Wiker, Benjamin, 'Does Science Point to God?' at www.arn.org/docs2/news/doessciencepointtogod040903.htm

[11] Woodward, Thomas, *Doubts About Darwin* (Grand Rapids: Baker, 2003), p.44.

[12] Overman, Dean L., *A Case Against Accident and Self-Organization* (Rowman & Littlefield, 2001), p.41.

[13] Cohen, Jon, 'Novel Center Seeks to Add Spark to Origins of Life', *Science*, 270, (1995), 1925-1926.

[14] Overman, *op. cit.*, p.41.

[15] Denton, Michael, *Evolution: A Theory in Crisis* (Woodbine House, 1996), p.262.

[16] Yockey, Hurbert P., 'A calculation of the Probability of Spontaneous Biogenesis by Information Theory,' *Journal of Theoretical Biology*, 67, (1977), p.377.

[17] Overman, *op. cit.*, p.40.

[18] Beadle, George, 'The Language of the Gene' in *The Language of Science* (New York: Basic Books, 1963), p.62.

[19] Delbruck, Max, interview in Horace Freeland Judson, *The Eighth Day of Creation* (New York: Simon and Schuster, 1979), p.213.

[20] Blanchard, John, *Does God Believe in Atheists?* (Darlington: Evangelical Press, 2000), p.292.

[21] Sarfati, Jonathan, *Refuting Evolution 2* (Master Books, 2003), p.58.

[22] Dawkins, Richard, *Climbing Mount Improbable* (Viking, 1996), p.259.

[23] Dawkins, Richard, 'Darwin's Dangerous Disciple' at www.skeptic.com/03.4.miele-dawkins-iv.html

[24] Dawkins, Richard, *A Devil's Chaplain* (London: Weidenfeld & Nicolson, 2003), p.248.

[25] Dawkins is not alone in his leap of faith. For example, Harvard biologist George Wald dismissed the design explanation for life but candidly admitted: 'I will not believe that philosophically because I do not want to believe in God. Therefore, I choose to believe in that which I know is scientifically impossible: spontaneous generation [that life arose from non-living matter] arising to evolution.' – 'Innovation and Biology', *Scientific American*, 199 (Sept. 1958): 100.

[26] Johnson, Phillip E., 'Positional Paper on Darwinism', in Woodward, *op. cit.*, Appendix 2, p.219.

[27] Wiker, *op. cit.*

[28] Bradley, Walter L., in Strobel, *The Case for Faith* (Zondervan, 2000), p.100.

[29] Kerkut, G. A., *Implications of Evolution* (Pergamon Press), p.150, quoted by John Blanchard, in *Does God Believe in Atheists?* (Darlington: Evangelical Press, 2000), p.297.

[30] Shapiro, Robert, *Origins: A Skeptic's Guide to the Creation of Life on Earth* (New York: Summit Books, 1986), p.112.

[31] Schidlowsky, Manfred, quoted by Overman, *op. cit.*, p.43.

[32] Overman, *ibid.*

[33] Meyer, Steven C., 'The Explanatory Power of Design' in William A. Dembski (ed.), *Mere Creation* (Downers Grove: IVP, 1998).

[34] Dose, Klaus, 'The Origin of Life: More Questions than Answers', *Interdisciplinary Science Review*, 13, (1998), p.348.

[35] Betty, L. Stafford and Coredell, Bruce, 'The Anthropic Teleological Argument', in Michael Peterson *et al.* (eds), *Philosophy of Religion: Selected Readings* (Oxford University Press, 1996), p.209.

[36] Thaxton, Charles, Bradley, Walter and Olsen, Roger, *The Mystery of Life's Origin* (Ashgate, 1987), p.185.

[37] Dawkins, *op. cit.*, p.260.

[38] *ibid.*

[39] Ross, Hugh, 'Astronomical Evidences for a Personal, Transcendent God', in J. P. Moreland (ed.), *The Creation Hypothesis* (Downers Grove: IVP, 1994), p.170.

[40] Astronomer Danny R. Faulkner in John F. Ashton (ed.), *On the Seventh Day* (Green Forrest: Master Books, 2002), p.107.

[41] Wiker, *op. cit.*

[42] cf. Ross, Hugh, 'Fine Tuning of Physical Life Support Body' at www.reasons.org/resources/apologetics/design_evidences/20020502_solar_system_design.shtml?main; and 'Probability for a Life Support Body' at www.reasons.org/resources/apologetics/design_evidences/20020502_life_support_body_prob.shtml?main

[43] Ross, Hugh, 'Astronomical Evidences for a Personal, Transcendent God', *op. cit.*, p.169-170.

[44] Ward, Peter and Brownlee, Don, *Rare Earth* (New York: Springer-Verlag, 2000), p.35, 37.

[45] Meyer, Stephen C., 'Evidence for design in Physics and Biology', in *Science and Evidence for Design in the Universe* (San Francisco: Ignatius, 2000), p.75.

[46] Dawkins, Richard, *The Blind Watchmaker* (London: Penguin, 1990), p.139.

[47] Wickramasinghe, Chandra, cited in Roy Abraham Varghese (ed.), *The Intellectuals Speak about God* (Regnery Gateway), p.33, quoted by John Blanchard, *op. cit.*, p.298.

[48] Bradley, Walter L., in Strobel, *The Case for Faith, op. cit.*, p.111. Bradley is using 'faith' in the same sense that Dawkins uses the term to mean belief without or against evidence.

[49] Behe, Michael J., 'The Modern Intelligent Design Hypothesis', *Philosophia Christi*, Series 2, Volume 3, Number 1, 2001, p.177.

[50] *ibid.*

[51] Rose, Steven, 'Escaping Evolutionary Psychology', in Hilary Rose (ed.), *Alas, Poor Darwin* (Vintage, 2001), p.254.

[52] Behe, Michael J., *Darwin's Black Box* (New York: Free Press, 1996), p.169-170.

[53] Overman, *op. cit.*, p.63.

[54] Haeckel, Ernst, *The Wonders of Life*, trans. J. McCabe, (London: Watts, 1905), p.111.

[55] www.sciencedaily.com/releases/1999/12/991213052506.htm

[56] Sarfati, *op. cit.*, p.155.

[57] Wiker, *op. cit.*

[58] Dixon, M. and Webb, E., *Enzymes*, 2nd edition (London: Longmans, 1964), p.699.

[59] Rose, Steven, *The Chemistry of Life* (Middlesex: Penguin Books, 1975), p.89.

[60] Dawkins, Richard, *Climbing Mount Improbable* (London: Penguin, 1997), p.66.

[61] *ibid.*

[62] *ibid.*

[63] *ibid.*

[64] *ibid.*, p.68.

[65] *ibid.*

[66] *ibid.*, my italics.

[67] Rose, *The Chemistry of Life, op. cit.*, p.187.

[68] *ibid.*, p.89, 91.

[69] Davies, Jimmy H. and Poe, Henry L., *Designer Universe: Intelligent Design and the Existence of God* (Nashville Tennessee: Broadman &

Holman, 2002), p.183.

[70] Rose, *op. cit.*, p.168.

[71] Hayward, *op. cit.*, p.83.

[72] Sarfati, *op. cit.*, p.155.

[73] Monod, Jacques, *Chance and Necessity* (London: Collins, 1972), p.135.

[74] Hayward, *op. cit.*, p.81.

[75] Salisbury, Frank B., from *American Biology Teacher*, Sept. 1971, p.338. cf. 'The DNA-Enzyme System is Irreducibly Complex' at www-acs.ucsd. edu/~idea/DNA-enzyme.htm

[76] Dawkins, *op. cit.*, p.66.

[77] *ibid.*

[78] Dawkins, *Darwin's Dangerous Disciple, op. cit.*

[79] Dembski, William A., 'Three Frequently Asked Questions About Intelligent Design' at www.designinference.com/documents/2003.09.ID_FAQ.pdf: 'the probabilities implicit in such extreme-functional-sensitivity analyses are precisely those needed for a design inference.' (*ibid.*) cf. D. D. Axe, 'Extreme Functional Sensitivity to Conservative Amino Acid Changes on Enzyme Exteriors', *Journal of Molecular Biology*, 301 (2000), p.585-595, at http://nsmserver2.fullerton.edu/departments/chemistry/ evolution_creation/ web/AxeProteinEvolution.pdf

[80] That includes RNA 'ribozymes' postulated as a solution to Hoyle's problem in the 'RNA world' thesis. Ward and Brownlee note: 'The abiotic synthesis of RNA remains the most enigmatic step in the evolution of first life, for no one has yet succeeded in creating RNA.' *Rare Earth* (New York: Copernicus, 2000), p.65.

[81] Muncaster, Ralph O., *Dismantling Evolution: Building the Case for Intelligent Design* (Eugene, Oregon: Harvest House, 2003), p.132.

[82] Overman, *op. cit.*, p.44.

[83] Muncaster, *op. cit.*, p.132.

[84] *ibid.*

[85] cf. *ibid.*, p.142.

[86] *ibid.*

[87] Kuppers, B. O., *Information and the Origin of Life* (Cambridge: MIT Press, 1990), p.60.

[88] Rose, *op. cit.*, p.78-79.

[89] Yockey, Herbert P., *Information Theory and Molecular Biology* (Cambridge University Press, 1992), p.257.

[90] Overman, *op. cit.*, p.196.

[91] Ward, Keith, *God, Faith & The New Millennium* (Oxford: OneWorld, 1999), p.110.

[92] Hoyle, Fred and Wickramasinghe, Chandra, *Evolution from Space* (Dent, 1981), p.24-148.

[93] *ibid.*, p.130.

[94] Hayward, *op. cit.*, p.25.

[95] Broom, Neil, *How Blind is the Watchmaker?* (IVP, 2001), p.54.

[96] Overman, *op. cit.*, p.197.

[97] Pearcey, Nancy and Thaxton, Charles, *The Soul of Science* (Wheaton Illinois: Crossway, 1994), p.231.

[98] Broom, *op. cit.*

[99] Overman, *op. cit.*, p.87.

[100] Yockey, *op. cit.*, p.231.

[101] Miethe, Terry L., *Why Believe? God Exists!* (Joplin Missouri: College Press, 1998), p.79.

[102] Polanyi, Michael, 'Life Transcending Physics and Chemistry', *Chemical and Engineering*, 45, 62, (1967), p.59.

[103] Overman, *op. cit.*, p.89, 101.

[104] Meyer, Stephen C., 'Teleological Evolution: the Difference it Doesn't Make', in *Darwinism Defeated?* (Regent College, 1999), p.95.

[105] Heeren, Fred, *Show Me God* (Wheeling Illinois: Day Star, 2000), p.61.

[106] Johnson, Phillip E., *Testing Darwinism* (Leicester: IVP, 1997), p.44.

[107] Dawkins, Richard, *Climbing Mount Improbable* (TSP: Viking, 1996), p.4.

[108] *ibid.*, p.3.

[109] *ibid.*

[110] *ibid.*, p.4-5.

[111] *ibid.*, p.3.

[112] *ibid.*

[113] *ibid.*, p.4.

[114] Pearcey and Thaxton, *op. cit.*, p.245.

[115] Keith, Alan, *Philosophy Now*, Issue 45, March/April 2004, Letters, p.42.

[116] Dawkins, *op. cit.*, p.3.

[117] *ibid.*

[118] *ibid.*

[119] *ibid.*, my italics.

[120] *ibid.*

[121] Dembski's Filter would not detect design in the Kennedy-esque hillside, and Occam's razor would lead us to agree with Dawkins that it is designoid (in the original sense of the term). However, this would not *prove* that the hillside was *not* designed, since the filter cannot rule out design.

[122] Geisler, Norman L. and Anderson, J. Kerby, *Origin Science* (Grand Rapids: Baker, 1987), p.159-164.

[123] Meyer, *op. cit.*, p.49.

[124] Pearcey and Thaxton, op. cit., p.243.

[125] Dawkins, Richard, *River Out of Eden* (New York, Basic Books, 1995), p.10.

[126] Dawkins, Richard, 'Son of Moore's Law', in *A Devil's Chaplain*, *op. cit.*, p.107.

[127] Dawkins, Richard, 'Genes Aren't Us', *ibid.*, p.105.

[128] *ibid.*, p.111.

[129] Gates, Bill, *The Road Ahead* (Boulder, Colorado: Blue Penguin, 1996), p.228.

[130] Paley, William, *Natural Theology*, Chapter One.

[131] Herschel, J. F. W., *Preliminary Discourse on the Study of Natural Philosophy* (London: Longman, Rees, Orme, Brown and Green, 1831), p.149.

[132] Dubay, Thomas, *The Evidential Power of Beauty* (San Francisco: Ignatius, 1999), p.170.

[133] Denton, Michael, *Nature's Destiny* (New York: Free Press, 1998), p.213.

[134] Behe, *Darwin's Black Box, op. cit.*, p.4-5.

[135] Denton, *Evolution: A Theory in Crisis, op. cit.*, p.329.

[136] *ibid.*, p.341.

[137] Dubay, *op. cit.*, p.185.

[138] Paley, *op. cit.*

[139] cf. Dembski, William A., *No Free Lunch* (Oxford: Rowman & Littlefield, 2002), p.279-289.

[140] Smart, John A., 'On the Application of Irreducible Complexity' at www.iscid.org/papers/Smart_ApplicationOfIC_060503.pdf

[141] Behe, Michael J., Dembski, Michael A. and Meyer, Stephen C., *Science and Evidence for Design in the Universe* (San Francisco: Ignatius, 1999), p.13-14.

[142] Dennet, Daniel C., *Darwin's Dangerous Idea* (London: Penguin, 1995), p.318.

[143] *ibid.*, p.317.

[144] Balfour, Arthur J., *Theism and Humanism* (Inklings Books, 2000), p.41.

[145] Darwin, Charles, *The Origin of Species*, 6th edition (New York: Collier Books, 1962), p.181.

[146] Darwin, *ibid.*, p.184.

[147] Dawkins, Richard, 'Darwin Triumphant', *A Devil's Chaplain, op. cit.*, p.86.

[148] Dawkins, *Climbing Mount Improbable, op. cit.*

[149] Vogel, Steven, *Cat's Paws and Catapults* (Penguin, 1998), p.23.

[150] Johnson, Phillip E., in Woodward, Appendix 2, *op. cit.*, p.219-220.

[151] Gould, Stephen Jay, 'Is a new and general theory of evolution emerging?', *Paleobiology*, Vol. 6 (1), January 1980, p.127.

[152] Gould, Stephen Jay, 'The Return of the Hopeful Monster,' *Natural History*, June/July 1977, p.22, 24.

[153] Dawkins, *A Devil's Chaplain, op. cit.*, p.211-212.

[154] *ibid.*, p.212.

[155] *ibid.*

[156] Dennet, Daniel, 'The Leibnizian Paradigm', in David L. Hull and Michael Ruse (eds), *The Philosophy of Biology* (Oxford, 1998), p.49.

[157] Denton, *op. cit.*, p.228, 315.

[158] Polkinghorne, John, *Science & Christian Belief* (London: SPCK, 1994), p.17.

[159] Dembski, William A., 'Evolution's Logic of Credulity: An unfettered response to Allen Orr' atwww.arn.org/docs/dembski/wd_logic_credulity.htm

[160] Dawkins, *The Blind Watchmaker, op. cit.*, p.146, 179, my italics.

[161] Stone, David H., in John F. Ashton, (ed.), *On the Seventh Day, op. cit.*, p.90.

[162] Johnson, Phillip, 'Daniel Dennett's Dangerous Idea', in *Objection Sustained* (Downers Grove: IVP, 1998), p.62.

[163] Denton, *Nature's Destiny, op. cit.*, p.356.

[164] Harold, F., *The Way of the Cell: Molecules, Organisms and the Order of Life* (New York: Oxford University Press, 2001).

[165] Denton, *op. cit.*, p.331.

[166] Johnson, Phillip, 'What is Darwinism?', in *Objection Sustained* (Downers Grove: IVP, 1998), p.23.

[167] Dawkins, *A Devil's Chaplain, op. cit.*, p.212.

[168] Wolf, Jakob, 'Two Kinds of Causality – Philosophical Reflections on Darwin's Black Box' at www.iscid.org/ubb/ultimatebb.php?ubb=get_topic;f=10;t=000040

[169] *ibid.*

[170] Dembski, *No Free Lunch, op. cit.*, p.290.

[171] Darwin, Charles, *Origin of Species* (1872), 6th edition, (New York University Press, 1988), p.154.

[172] Dawkins, Richard, 'Universal Darwinism', in Hull and Ruse (eds), *The Philosophy of Biology, op. cit.*, p.29.

[173] Dawkins, *The Blind Watchmaker, op. cit.*, p.91.

[174] *ibid.*

[175] Gene, Mike, 'Irreducible Complexity and Darwinian Pathways' at www. arn.org/docs/behe/mb_mg1darwinianpathways.htm

[176] Behe Interview at www.arn.org/docs/behe/mb_pittinterview0201.htm

[177] *ibid.*

[178] Behe, *Darwin's Black Box, op. cit.*, p.39.

[179] Darwin, *Origin of Species, op. cit.*, p.184.

[180] Dawkins, 'Darwin Triumphant', *A Devil's Chaplain, op. cit.*, p.86.

[181] Behe, *op. cit.*, p.40.

[182] Dembski, William A., 'Irreducible Complexity Revisited' at www. designinference.com/documents/2004.01.Irred_Compl_Revisited.pdf

[183] Dembski, William A., 'Irreducible Complexity Revisited' at www. designinference.com/documents/2004.01.Irred_Compl_Revisited.pdf

[184] Behe, Michael J., 'Molecular Machines: Experimental Support for the Design Inference' at www.arn.org/docs/behe/mb_mm92496.htm

[185] Behe, *Darwin's Black Box, op. cit.*, p.194.

[186] Ratzsch, Del, *Science & Its Limits* (Leicester: Apollos, 2000), p.128.

[187] 'Self-Assembly of Bacterial Flagella' at www.aip.org/mgr/png/2002/174.htm

[188] Dembski, William A., 'Reinstating Design Within Science', in Jay Wesley Richards (ed.), *Unapologetic Apologetics* (Downers Grove: IVP, 2001), p.253.

[189] Behe, *op. cit.*, p.72.

[190] Macnab, Robert M., *CRC Critical Reviews in Biochemistry*, Vol. 5, Dec. 1978, p.291-341, quoted at www.parentcompany.com/design_kit/dek1d.htm

[191] 'Here's the recipe for making a just-so story . . . survey the biological world for structures/functions. Find those that seem useful for coming up with a precursor to the system in question and patch them together without much regard for biochemical and/or genetic details. Place the patchwork in an imaginary creature from the distant past that has conveniently gone extinct. Invoke a vague selective pressure thrt selects for the patchwork and then imagine it is plastic and amenable tc further selective modification that just happens to arrive at the systen. in question.' – Julie Thomas, quoted by Mike Gene, 'Evolving the Bacterial Flagellum Through Cooption' at www.idthink.net/biot/flag1/

[192] Dennet, *Darwin's Dangerous Idea, op. cit.*, p.521.

[193] TTSS secrete proteins to establish symbiotic relationships with eukaryotic cells.

[194] Dembski, William A., 'The Bacterial Flagellum: Still Spinning Just Fine' at www.designinference.com/documents/2003.02.Miller_Response.htm

[195] Gene, Mike, 'Evolving the Bacterial Flagellum through Mutation and Co-option' at www.idthink.net/biot/flag1/index.html

[196] Dembski, *op. cit.*, p.3. 'The type III system itself most likely evolved from a flagellum.' – Mike Gene, 'Evolving the Bacterial Flagellum through Mutation and Co-option', *ibid.* Hence, the inclusion of this system as a stage in any supposed indirect evolutionary pathway leading to the flagellum is a non-starter.

[197] Orr, H. Allen, *Boston Review.*

[198] Thornhill, R. H. and Ussery, D. W., 'A classification of possible routes of Darwinian evolution', *Journal of Theoretical Biology* (2000), 203, p.111-116.

[199] Minnich, Scott, in the video *Unlocking the Mystery of Life.*

[200] Dembski, *op. cit.*

[201] Gene, Mike, 'Irreducible Complexity and Darwinian Pathways' at www.arn.org/docs/behe/mb_mg1darwinianpathways.htm

[202] Smart, 'On the Application of Irreducible Complexity', *op. cit.*

[203] Dembski, *op. cit.*

[204] *ibid.*

[205] *ibid.*

[206] Minnich, *op. cit.*

[207] cf. www.iscid.org/pcid.php

[208] Bracht, J. R., 'The Bacterial Flagellum: A Response to Ursula Goodenough' atwww.iscid.org/papers/Bracht_GoodenoughResponse_021203.pdf

[209] *ibid.*

[210] Dembski, 'The Bacterial Flagellum: Still Spinning Just Fine', *op. cit.*

[211] Dembski, William A., 'Gauging Intelligent Design's Success' at www.designinference.com/documents/2003.11.Gauging_IDs_Success.pdf

[212] Dembski, William A., *The Intelligent Design Revolution* (Downers Grove: IVP, 2004), p.112-113.

[213] *ibid.*, p.113.

[214] *ibid.*, p.112-113.

[215] Dembski, 'Irreducible Complexity Revisited', *op. cit.*

[216] Dembski, The Intelligent Design Revolution, *op. cit.*, p.113.

[217] Behe, *op. cit.*, p.40.

[218] Dembski, 'Gauging Intelligent Design's Success', *op. cit.* cf. 'Three Frequently Asked Questions About Intelligent Design', *op. cit.* and Axe, 'Extreme Functional Sensitivity to Conservative Amino Acid Changes on Enzyme Exteriors', *op. cit.*

[219] Dembski, William A., *Intelligent Design* (Downers Grove: IVP, 1999), p.149.

[220] Owens, David W., 'Stupid Sceptic Tricks', *The Skeptic*, Volume 16, Number 3, p.15.

[221] Wakefield, Mary, 'The Mystery of the Missing Links' at www.arn.org/docs2/news/missinglinkmystery102803.htm

(Dawkins made similar but distinct comments about young earth creationists in a *Guardian* article at www.guardian.co.uk/Archive/Article/0,4273,4371166,00.html

[222] Reppert, Victor, *C.S. Lewis's Dangerous Idea* (IVP, 2003), p.116.

[223] ARN guide to *Evolution* at www.arn.org/docs/pbsevolution/vguide.pdf

[224] Dubay, *The Evidential Power of Beauty*, *op. cit.*, p.322.

[225] Crews, Frederick, 'Saving us from Darwin', *New York Review of Books.*

[226] Dembski, William A., 'What Every Theologian Should Know about Creation, Evolution, and Design' at www.arn.org/docs/dembski/wd_theologn.htm

[227] cf. ARN guide to *Evolution*, *op. cit.*

[228] The fossil record does not reveal a gradual development from simple to more complex species with numerous intermittent forms as Darwin predicted: 'the record reveals the sudden appearance at differing times of information-rich organisms within a hierarchical diversity of species with apparently no precursors'. – Francis J. Beckwith, *Law, Darwinism, and Public Education: The Establishment Clause and the Challenge of Intelligent Design* (Rowman & Littlefield, 2003), p.118.

[229] cf. Meyer, Stephen C., Nelson, Paul A. and Chein, Paul, 'The Cambrian Explosion: Biology's Big Bang' at www.discovery.org/articleFiles/PDFs/Cambrian.pdf

[230] Dembski, *op. cit.*, p.231.

[231] Dawkins, Richard, 'BLUEPRINTS Solving the Mystery of Evolution, by Maitland A. Edey and Donald C. Johanson' at www.world-of-dawkins.com/Dawkins/Work/Reviews/1989-04-09review_blueprint.shtml

[232] *ibid.*

[233] *ibid.*

[234] Dawkins, 'Darwin Triumphant', in *A Devil's Chaplain, op. cit.*, p.81.

[235] *ibid.*

[236] *ibid.*, p.79, 81, 84, my italics.

[237] *ibid.*, p.81.

[238] This is what ID theorists tend to mean by 'Darwinism': belief in 'the fact of evolution itself' wedded to a philosophical commitment to the explanatory sufficiency of natural processes (usually expressed as the multifaceted theory that life arose millions of years ago by purely natural processes and then diversified from a common ancestor over millions of years through the undirected but non-random survival of small random hereditary changes).

[239] Thompson, W. R., introduction to *Charles Darwin, The Origin of Species by Means of Natural Selection* (New York: Dutton, 1967), p.xxii.

[240] Strobel, Lee, *The Case for Faith* (Grand Rapids: Zondervan, 2000), p.90.

[241] Denton, Michael, quoted from his professional resume, cf. Woodward, *op. cit.*, p.57.

[242] Graham, Gordon, *Genes: A Philosophical Inquiry* (London: Routledge, 2002), p.ix.

[243] *ibid.*, p.91.

[244] David Stove, quoted by Graham, *ibid.*, p.31.

[245] *ibid.*

[246] Graham, *ibid.*, p.31-32.

[247] cf. www.arn.org/docs2/news/100scientists0929.htm

[248] Geisler, Norman L. and Holden, Joseph, *Living Loud: Defending Your Faith* (Nashville, Tennessee: Broadman and Holman Publishers, 2002), p.55.

[249] Craig, William Lane, 'Tough Questions About Science', in Ravi Zacharias and Norman L. Geisler (eds), *Who Made God?* (Grand Rapids: Zondervan, 2003), p.70.

[250] Plantinga, Alvin, 'When Faith and Reason Clash: Evolution and the Bible' at www.asa3.org/ASA/dialogues/Faith-reason/CRS9-91Plantinga1.html

[251] Dawkins, in *A Devil's Chaplain, op. cit.*, p.220.

[252] Wells, Jonathan, 'The Intelligent Design Movement, Evangelical Scientists, and the Future of Biology,' in *Darwinism Defeated?, op. cit.*, p.137.

[253] Marsh, Cliff, 'Evolution: a theory in terminal decline?', *The Plain Truth*, September-November 2002, p.20.

[254] Robert M. Augros, 'Is Nature Purposeful?', *PSCF*, 48, (December 1996):216, p.2-3.

[255] cf. www.arn.org/docs2/news/100scientists0929.htm

[256] www.reviewevolution.com/press/pressRelease_100Scientists.php

[257] cf. Mark Hartwig, 'Those Annoying Discovery Polls' at www.arn.org/docs/wedge/mh_wedge_031029.htm

[258] Davies, Paul, *Superforce* (Touchstone Books, 1985), p.243.

[259] Davies, Paul, *The Cosmic Blueprint* (London: HarperCollins, 1989), p.203.

[260] Davies, Paul, *The Fifth Miracle: The Search for the Origin of Life* (London: Penguin Press, 1998), p.xvi.

[261] *ibid.*, p.xvi-xvii.

[262] *ibid.*, p.xvii.

[263] *ibid.*

[264] *ibid.*, p.xviii.

[265] Smith, Huston, quoted on the front cover of *On the Seventh Day*, *op. cit.*

[266] Wiker, 'Does Science Point to God?', *op. cit.*

[267] Alexander, Denis, *Rebuilding the Matrix* (Oxford: Lion, 2001), p.21.

[268] Johnson, Phillip E., *The Right Questions* (Downers Grove: IVP, 2002), p.80.

[269] Woodward, *op. cit.*, p.253.

[270] Darwin, Charles, quoted in N. C. Gillespie, *Charles Darwin and the Problem of Creation* (Chicago: University of Chicago, 1979), p.87.

[271] Darwin, Charles, *The Origin of Species* (Ware: Wordsworth Editions Limited, 1998), p.363.

[272] Dembski, 'Three Frequently Asked Questions About Intelligent Design', *op. cit.*

[273] Dembski, *Intelligent Design, op. cit.*, p.113.

[274] Wiker, Benjamin, *Moral Darwinism* (Downers Grove: IVP, 2002), p.295.

[275] Smart, *op. cit.*

[276] Dembski, *No Free Lunch, op. cit.*, p.246.

[277] Dembski, 'On the Very Possibility of Intelligent Design', *The Creation Hypothesis, op. cit.*, p.132.

[278] Dembski, *Intelligent Design, op. cit.*, p.113.

[279] *ibid.*

[280] Dembski, 'Evolution's Logic of Credulity: An Unfettered Response to Allen Orr', *op. cit.*

[281] *ibid.*, my italics.

[282] Behe, Michael J., in *Darwinism Defeated?, op. cit.*, p.107.

[283] Wiker, 'Does Science Point to God?', *op. cit.*

[284] *ibid.*

[285] Dawkins, *A Devil's Chaplain, op. cit.*, p.58.

[286] Dobzhansky, Theodosius, quoted by Wells, *op. cit.*, p.329.

[287] Wells, *ibid.*, p.329.

[288] Dembski, *Intelligent Design, op. cit.*, p.255.

[289] Wiker, *op. cit.*, p.3.

[290] *ibid.*, p.319.

[291] cf. Scott Minnich Homepage at www.ag.uidaho.edu/mmbb/p_minnich_s.htm; Scott Minnich, 'Bacterial Flagella: A Paradigm for Design' at www.arn.org/arnproducts/videos/v021.htm; www.idurc.org/yale-minnich.html; www.iscid.org/scott-minnich.php

[292] Dembski, *op. cit.*, p.256-257.

[293] Woodward, *op. cit.*, p.210.

[294] Bergman, Jerry, 'The Functions of Introns: From Junk DNA to Designed DNA' at www.asa3.org/ASA/PSCF/2001/PSCF9-01Bergman.html

[295] *ibid.* cf. Nesselroade, Paul, 'The Case of the Pseudogenes' at www.arn.org/docs/wedge/pn_wedge_030523.htm

[296] Gillis, Justin, '"Junk DNA" Contains Essential Information' at www.arn.org/docs2/news/junkdnaessential120802.htm

[297] Dembski, William A., 'Becoming a Disciplined Science: Prospects, Pitfalls, and a Reality Check for ID' at www.arn.org/docs/dembski/wd_disciplinedscience.htm

[298] Dembski, William A., 'Ten Question To Ask Your Biology Teacher' at www.designinference.com/documents/2004.01.Ten_Questions_ID.pdf

[299] Dembski, *Intelligent Design, op. cit.*, p.255-256.

[300] Wells, Jonathan, 'Jonathan Wells Lecture Report from Western Michigan University' at www.arn.org/docs/wells/jw_reportfromwmu031401.htm

[301] cf. Dembski, 'Becoming a Disciplined Science', *op. cit.*

[302] Dembski, William A., 'Paul Gross's Dilemma: An Open Letter to the National Association of Scholars in Response to Paul Gross's Article on Intelligent Design in the NAS's September 2003 Issue of *Science Insights*' at www.designinference.com/documents/2003.09.Gross_Response.pdf

[303] Davies, Paul, quoted by Witham, *By Design* (San Francisco: Encounter Books, 2003), p.149.

[304] Martin, Melissa, 'Design Theory: Creationist dogma or evolutionary punk rock?' atwww.ccwv.net/EssayDisplay.asp?recordID=158

[305] Dembski, *The Design Revolution, op. cit.*, p.305.

[306] Tennant, F. R., *Natural Theology*.

Getting a Handle on Hope

At the beginning of the film *The Bourne Identity*, Jason Bourne (Matt Damon) is discovered by fishermen floating in the sea, half-drowned, wounded in the back, and suffering from amnesia. He is literally 'all at sea' with his self-identity. In an early scene he implores his reflection to tell him who he is. He pours over the small number of clues available to him (he is multilingual and good at tying knots), trying to work out who he is supposed to be, but he can't. He is afraid of making shore without even knowing his own name. Names are more than just convenient labels that allow us to refer to people without confusion; ancient cultures considered names to be the key to a person's identity. Even today, we sometimes give children names because of their meaning (for example, Peter means 'like a rock'). Hence the Bible employs many names for God, each of which reveals a different aspect of God's character. And hence the book of Revelation (2:17) promises that God will reveal to those in heaven their name – their true identity. Like Jason Bourne we can spend our time desperately going over and over the small number of clues to the purpose and meaning of our life, or we can ask whether, having created intelligent life for a purpose, our creator might reveal to us the specific answers we need but cannot obtain from simply observing creation.

> . . . *the choice between God and naturalism is not a choice between faith and reason.*
> JOSH MCDOWELL AND THOMAS WILLIAMS[1]

In the Introduction we considered Nola Passmore's eloquent summary of what the human heart longs for:

The heart cry of the human race is for meaning

and purpose, a sense of belonging when human relationships fail to satisfy, a need to know we are unconditionally loved in spite of our circumstances, a need to know that we are not an accident of chance but people of design, a need to know that we have a future and a hope even when everything around us seems to be falling apart.[2]

In the face of this longing, we considered the culturally dominant viewpoint, disseminated by influential public figures like Richard Dawkins, that evolution excludes the truth of any belief in God, 'the pacifier of faith in immortality',[3] the absolute truth of any moral or aesthetic values, or, as a consequence, any cosmic meaning or purpose. According to Dawkins we face a clear choice between caring about the nihilistic truth revealed to us by science, or throwing our brains away in order to embrace the 'warm comfortable lie'[4] that God is not dead and the cosmos is infused with value, meaning and purpose, as intelligent people once believed but Darwin disproved. We must choose to be 'people of intellect, as opposed to people of faith'.[5]

However, Dawkins confuses science with naturalism, and then begs the question by arguing science can 'reveal a world without design'. It is this confusion that results in his dismissing belief in God, purpose and meaning. The theory of evolution is in principle unable to reveal 'a world without design' (or purpose, or meaning), because Dawkins' proposed dilemma of creation or evolution is a false dilemma. Furthermore, naturalism appears to be self-contradictory, in that it is unable to give an adequate account of human rationality. The more Dawkins argues that naturalism and (naturalistically interpreted) evolution are true (or, indeed, that either proves the other), the less we should believe him.

We considered Dawkins' letter of advice to his daughter Juliet on her tenth birthday, where he encouraged her (and us) to think for herself:

> Next time somebody tells you something that sounds important, think to yourself: 'Is this the kind of thing that people probably know because of evidence? . . . next time somebody tells you that something is true, why not say to them: 'What kind of evidence is there for that?' And if they can't give you a good answer, I hope you'll think very carefully before you believe a word they say.[6]

We noted that Dawkins, like the discredited logical-positivist school of thought, circumscribes what counts as evidence so tightly that his definition of evidence ends up suffocating itself, because it cannot be justified with anything that it would count as evidence. Dawkins' assertion that scientists are 'the specialists in discovering what is true about the world and the universe'[7] – an assertion that has profound implications for his worldview and its answer to the question of meaning – is self-defeating, because it leaves no room for metaphysics.

With this point in mind we proceeded to take Dawkins' advice by applying it to his own views. After all, when Dawkins promulgates the message that 'God is dead' because science reveals a world without purpose or design, posing us with a no-brainer choice between scientific truth and spurious religious comfort, he certainly says something that sounds important. So we asked ourselves: Is this the kind of thing that Dawkins knows because of the evidence? Or is it the kind of thing that he only believes because he stands in the atheistic tradition and accepts the authority of fellow atheists that the facts of biology somehow undermine belief in God and thereby belief in cosmic meaning and purpose? We discovered that the latter was closer to the truth, in that evolution is for Dawkins a philosophically certain deduction from his naturalistic worldview (a deduction that elsewhere he presents as if it disproves belief in design!).

When we examined Dawkins' evolutionary views without his naturalistic bias, asking 'What kind of evidence (scientific *and* philosophical) is there for that?', we didn't receive a good answer. Instead we found a series of unsound philosophical assumptions, false dilemmas and invalid arguments intended to bolster a naturalistic worldview that was then used to bypass Dawkins' own requirement for evidence. For example, in considering the origin of life we found that Dawkins exhibits the sort of blind faith in *abiogenesis* (life emerging from non-life by natural means) as he accuses religious believers of having with respect to their beliefs: 'I don't know how difficult it would be to achieve that chemically.'[8] Here, as elsewhere (e.g. the gradualist assumption behind *Climbing Mount Improbable*), we saw how Dawkins' faith in Darwinism actually flies in the face of the evidence for design.

I agree with philosopher Robert C. Koons: 'the new knowledge we have acquired recently, including evidence of the Big Bang, anthropic coincidences, the fantastic complexity and functionality of biological systems, and the deepening intractability of naturalistic explanations for the origin of life and of consciousness, support theism. Indeed, the evidence for theism has never been so clear and strong as it is now.'[9] Against the evidence for design Dawkins was reduced to making evidentially uninformed appeals to 'luck', and to telling hypothetical 'just so' stories. Indeed, in his discussion of Mt Rushmore, Dawkins uses a version of William A. Dembski's 'Design Filter', a filter that demonstrates the existence of design within nature!

Quite aside from the evidence from cosmology and biology for design (and so for purpose), we have in addition to take account of the moral and aesthetic evidence for God's existence (some of which subsumes and reinforces the evidence for design). God and the objective value of goodness and beauty, as we have seen, go hand in glove. One may argue from the existence of God to the objectivity of value, or from the objectivity of value to the existence of God. Alternatively, one may simply intuit both (at least implicitly) in intuiting either.

Our conclusion is that *life is objectively purposeful and meaningful* (in that it realizes the objective existence and subjective appreciation of truth, goodness and beauty), that *God exists*, and indeed, that life is objectively purposeful and meaningful only *because* God exists. Knowing that life is objectively meaningful because God exists is a huge advance on Dawkins' naturalistic nihilism, and cannot but affect how we subjectively experience life. Nevertheless, such a conclusion leaves us with questions about the specific purpose and meaning of life, and how to integrate our lives with that meaning and purpose so as to most fully appreciate and experience the meaningfulness of our existence. As W. Gary Phillips and William E. Brown observe: 'deciding that life *does* have meaning is not the end but the beginning of a quest. Life becomes a continual pilgrimage to find, affirm, and reaffirm a philosophy of life.'[10] We need to know not only *that* life is meaningful (or *that* God exists, or *that* life is meaningful because God exists) but *what* the meaning of life is, and *how* we can connect with that meaning in our lives.

Keith Ward rightly argues that: 'if there is a vast intelligence behind the universe, it is reasonable to think that it has brought the universe into being for some purpose'.[11] And he is right to suggest that 'it will then be natural to try to find some evidence of what that purpose is'.[12] A combination of moral and aesthetic arguments shows that the purpose of life is objectively good and has something to do with the realization of value. The evidence of cosmology and biology combined with the argument from reason implies that the existence of intelligent life is one of the creator's goals. Given that the most significant thing about intelligent life is its capacity to freely form relationships of understanding and love it seems reasonable to suggest that the meaning of life has something to do with such relationships. Beyond these important but nonetheless meagre conclusions, it is hard for the human mind to venture on the evidence of nature alone.

Recall how we empathized with philosopher Peter van Inwagen, reading about the death of the composer Handel, who expressed 'his eagerness to die and to meet his dear Saviour Jesus Christ face to face'.[13] Inwagen's reaction to Handel:

> . . . was negative and extremely vehement, a little explosion of contempt, modified by pity. It might be put in these words: 'You poor booby. You cheat.' Handel had been taken in, I thought, and yet at the same time he was getting away with

something. Although his greatest hope was an illusion, nothing could rob him of the comfort of this hope, for after his death he would not exist and there would be no one there to see how wrong he had been.[14]

Inwagen 'managed simultaneously to believe he was "of all men most miserable" and that he was getting a pretty good deal'.[15] I trust that our investigation thus far indicates that having hope and being a 'poor booby' are not necessarily synonymous, because Dawkins' stark choice between being 'people of intellect, as opposed to people of faith'[16] is a false dilemma. But of course, Handel's hope was founded not only upon the theistic belief that God exists, but upon the Christian belief that God has taken the initiative to relate to humanity in a specific, historically knowable manner that grounds a holistic spirituality (or way of life) suffused with eternal meaning and purpose. It cannot be denied that a perfectly reasonable avenue of inquiry when faced with the quest 'to find, affirm, and reaffirm a philosophy of life'[17] is to wonder whether our creator (who clearly went to incredible lengths to produce a finely tuned, anthropic cosmos) might not have taken the trouble to communicate directly with his creations. As Robert C. Newman says: 'Once you come to believe there is a God, unless you're an idiot, you're going to want to find out more about it. You're going to ask, "Has he intervened in our history? Has he communicated?"'[18] It would not be unreasonable to begin one's search for answers by investigating the historical figure in whom some two billion people believe God has done just that.[19] The website supporting this book (www.IwishICouldBelieve.com) provides an opportunity for readers to critically examine the evidence for themselves.

Next time you see a rainbow, consider the idea that God is presenting it to you as a point of spiritual connection, an artistic message of love. Like all messages of love, like every Valentine's card, this message of love demands an answer (even if that is only to find out more about the offer and the one who made it), and not to respond positively is in the end to respond negatively. As I asked back in that party in Norwich: 'If you wish you could believe in God [and so meaning and purpose], why don't you?'

[1] McDowell, Josh and Williams, Thomas, *In Search Of Certainty* (Wheaton, Illinois: Tyndale, 2003), p.123.

[2] Passmore, Nola, in John F. Ashton (ed.), *On the Seventh Day* (Green Forrest: Master Books, 2002), p.116.

[3] Dawkins, Richard, *A Devil's Chaplain* (London: Weidenfeld & Nicolson, 2003), p.13.

[4] *ibid.*

[5] *ibid.*, p.157.

[6] *ibid.*, p.248.

[7] *ibid.*, p.242.

[8] Dawkins, Richard, 'Darwin's Dangerous Disciple' at www.skeptic.com/03.4.miele-dawkins-iv.html

[9] Koons, Robert C., 'Science and Theism', in Paul Copan and Paul K. Moser (eds), *The Rationality of Theism* (London: Routledge, 2003), p.73.

[10] Phillips, W. Gary and Brown, William E., *Making Sense of Your World* (Salem: Sheffield Publishing Company, 1996), p.21.

[11] Ward, Keith, *God, Faith & The New Millennium* (Oxford: OneWorld, 1999), p.17.

[12] *ibid.*

[13] van Inwagen, Peter, 'Quam Dilecta' at http://honors.org/frcourses/quam/quam_dilecta.html

[14] *ibid.*

[15] *ibid.*

[16] Dawkins, *A Devil's Chaplain, op. cit.*, p.157.

[17] Phillips, W. Gary and Brown, William E., *Making Sense of Your World* (Moody Press, 1991).

[18] Newman, Robert C., in Larry Witham, *By Design* (San Francisco: Encounter Books, 2003), p.218.

[19] 'In 2000, Christians numbered 1,999,600,000 people out of a world population of 6,055,000,000, 33.0%.' – Peter Brierley, *101 Statistics every church leader should know!* (London: Christian Research, 2002), p.5.

Bibliography

- The virtual office of Peter S. Williams at www.peter-s-williams.co.uk
- ARN featured author, Peter S. Williams at www.arn.org/williams/pwhome.htm
- My personal page and links on the Damaris website at www.damaris.org/team.peter.williams

---

The following materials are presented (roughly) in the order in which the relevant topics arise in the reading of this book, and are graded (where appropriate) for accessibility (*not* cogency) with superscripted numbers: [1] for introductory, [2] for intermediate and [3] for advanced reading.

Nihilism

Hibbs, Thomas S., *Shows About Nothing: Nihilism in Popular Culture from the Exorcist to Seinfeld* (Dallas: Spence Publishing, 1999); Hubben, William, *Dostoevsky, Kierkegaard, Nietzsche amd Kafka* (New York: Touchstone, 1997)[1]; Moreland, J. P, *Scaling the Secular City* (Grand Rapids, Michigan: Baker, 1987)[2]; O'Hear, Anthony, *After Progress: Finding The Old Way Forward* (London: Bloomsbury, 1999)[2] and *Philosophy* (London: New Century, 2001)[2]; Scruton, Roger, *An Intelligent Person's Guide to Modern Culture* (London: Duckworth, 1998)[2]; Tolstoy, Leo, *A Confession*, Aylmer

Maude trans. (London: Oxford University Press, 1961)[1]; Zacharias, Ravi, *A Shattered Visage: The Real Face of Atheism* (Grand Rapids: Baker, 1990)[1] and *Can Man Live Without God?* (Milton Keynes: Word, 1994)[1]

Truth and knowledge

Beilby, James, and Clark, David K., 'A Brief Introduction to the Theory of Knowledge' at www.gospelcom.net/rzim/publications/essay_arttext.php?id=12[2]; Koons, Robert C., 'The Relativistic Bog: Two Sources of Knowledge about God' at www.grad resources. org/worldview_articles/bog.shtml[2]; Groothuis, Douglas, *Truth Decay* (Leicester: IVP, 2000)[2]; Holmes, Arthur F., *All Truth Is God's Truth* (Leicester: IVP, 1977)[2]; Kreeft, Peter and Tacelli, Ronald, *Handbook of Christian Apologetics* (Downers Grove: IVP, 1994/Crowborough: Monarch, 1995)[1]

Objective and subjective

Beckwith, Francis J. and Koukl, Gregory, *Relativism: Feet Firmly Planted in Mid-Air* (Grand Rapids: Baker, 2001)[1]; Copan, Paul, *'True for You, But not for Me': Defeating the Slogans that leave Christians Speechless* (Minneapolis: Bethany House, 1998)[1]; Nagel, Thomas, *The Last Word* (Oxford University Press, 1997)[2]

Objectivity of moral value

Beckwith, Francis J., 'Why I Am Not A Relativist' at http://homepage.mac.com/francis.beckwithRELATIVISM.pdf[1]; Kreeft, Peter, 'A Refutation of Moral Relativism' (audio file) at www.peterkreeft.com/ audio/05_relativism/refutation-of-relativism.mp3[1]; Beckwith, Francis

J. and Koukl, Gregory, *Relativism: Feet Firmly Planted in Mid-Air* (Grand Rapids: Baker, 2001)[1]; Chamberlain, Paul, *Can We Be Good Without God?* (Downers Grove, Illinois: IVP, 1996)[1]; Copan, Paul, *'True for You, But not for Me': Defeating the Slogans that leave Christians Speechless* (Minneapolis: Bethany House, 1998)[1]; Kreeft, Peter and Tacelli, Ronald, *Handbook of Christian Apologetics* (Downers Grove: IVP, 1994)[1]; McDowell, Josh and Geisler, Norman L., *Love is Always Right: A Defence of the One Moral Absolute* (Dallas: Word Publishing, 1996)[1]; McGinn, Colin, *Ethics, Evil and Fiction* (Clarendon Press: Oxford, 1999)[3]; Nagel, Thomas, *The Last Word* (Oxford University Press, 1997)[2]; Williams, Peter S., *The Case for God* (Crowbrough, East Sussex: Monarch, 1999)[2]

The moral argument for God

Beckwith, Francis J., 'Moral Law, the Mormon Universe and the Nature of the Right we Choose' at http://homepage. mac.com/francis.beckwith/tnmc.pdf[2]; Beckwith, Francis J., 'Why I Am Not A Relativist' at http://homepage. mac.com/francis.beckwith/RELATIVISM.pdf[1]; Copan, Paul, 'Can Michael Martin be a Moral Realist?: Sic et Non' atwww.gospelcom.net/rzim/publications/essay_arttext.php?id=4[3]; Craig, William Lane, 'The Indispensability of Theological Meta-Ethical Foundations for Morality' at www.leaderu.com/offices/billcraig/docs/meta-eth.html[2]; Holt, Tim, 'The Moral Argument' at www.philosophy ofreligion.info/moral.html[1]; Koons, Robert C. 'Moral Realism and God' at www.leaderu.com/offices/koons/docs/chrphlec13html[2]; Lewis, C. S., 'Right and Wrong as Clues to the Heart of the Universe' at www. mit.edu/~mcguyton/ABSK/ MereChristianity/meretoc.htm[1]; Moreland, J. P., 'The Ethical Inadequacy of Naturalism' at www.afterall. net/citizens/moreland/papers/jp-naturalism2.html[2]; Beckwith, Francis J. and Koukl, Gregory, *Relativism: Feet Planted Firmly in Mid-Air* (Grand Rapids, Michigan: Baker, 2001)[1]; Copan, Paul, *'True for You, But not for Me': Defeating the Slogans that leave Christians Speechless* (Minneapolis, Minnesota: Bethany House, 1998)[1]; Craig, William Lane (ed.), *Philosophy of Religion: A Reader and Guide* (Edinburgh: Edinburgh University Press, 2002)[3]; Davies, Brian, *Philosophy of Religion: A Guide and Anthology* (Oxford: Oxford University Press, 2000)[3]; Hick, John (ed.), *The Existence of God* (New York: Macmillan, 1964)[2]; Lewis, C. S., *Mere Christianity* (London: Fount, 1997)[1]; Williams, Peter S., *The Case for God* (Crowbrough, East Sussex: Monarch, 1999)[2]

Aquinas

'Lux Veritatis' at www.catholicforum.com/luxveritatis/; Thomistic Philosophy at www.aquinasonline.com; Chesterton, G. K, *Thomas Aquinas* (Hodder & Stoughton, 1933)[1]; Copleston, F. C., *Aquinas* (Pelican Books, 1957)[2]; A collection of essays on different aspects of Tom's thought, written by a clutch of modern-day Thomists (and including a delightful essay by Peter Kreeft) is *The Ever Illuminating Wisdom of St. Thomas Aquinas* (Ignatius, 1999)[2]; Several books containing extracts from Aquinas' volumous writings are available: McDermot, Timothy, (ed.), *Aquinas – Selected Philosophical Writings* (Oxford, 1998)[3];

McInery, Ralph, (ed. and trans.), *Thomas Aquinas – Selected Readings* (Penguin Classics, 1998)[3]

Properly basic beliefs

Plantinga, Alvin, 'Theism, Atheism and Rationality' at www.leaderu.com/truth/3truth02.html[3]; Clark, James Kelly, 'How real People Believe – a Defence of Reformed Epistemology' at www.modernreformation. org/mr98/janfeb/mr9801defense.html[2]; Plantinga, Alvin, *Warranted Christian Belief* (Oxford, 2000)[3]

Newton

Bragg, Melvyn, *On Giant's Shoulders* (London: Sceptre, 1998)[1]; Pearcey, Nancy R. and Thaxton, Charles B., *The Soul of Science: Christian Faith and Natural Philosophy* (Wheaton Illinois: Crossway Books, 1994)[2]; Westfall, Richard S., *The Life of Isaac Newton* (Cambridge University Press, 1993)[2]

Naturalism and scientism

Ayer, A. J., *Language, Truth and Logic* (London: Penguin, 1990)[2]; Baggini, Julian, *Atheism: A Very Short Introduction* (Oxford, 2003)[1]; Dennett, Daniel C., *Darwin's Dangerous Idea* (London: Penguin, 1995)[3]; Russell, Bertrand, *Why I Am Not A Christian* (London: Routledge, 1996)[1]

Richard Dawkins

The Selfish Gene (Oxford, 1989)[2]; *The Blind Watchmaker* (London: Penguin, 1988)[2]; *River Out of Eden* (Pheonix, 1996)[2]; *Climbing Mount Improbable* (Viking, 1996)[2]; *Unweaving the Rainbow* (Penguin, 1999)[2]; and *A Devil's Chaplain* (London: Weidenfeld

& Nicolson, 2003)[2]; Barr, Steven M., review of *Unweaving the Rainbow* at http://catholiceducation. org/articles/science/sc0009.html[1]; Bohlin, Raymond G., 'Up a River without a Paddle: A Darwinian View of Life' at www.leaderu.com/orgs/probe/docs/dawkins.html[1]; Johnson, Phillip E., 'The Robot Rebellion of Richard Dawkins' at www.arn.org/docs/johnson/pj_robotrebellion. htm[1]; Johnson, Phillip E., review of *Climbing Mount Improbable* at http://catholiceducation.org/articles/ science/sc0014.html[1]; Miele, Frank, 'Darwin's Dangerous Disciple: An Interview with Richard Dawkins' at www.skeptic.com/03.4.miele-dawkins-iv.html[1]; 'Nick Pollard talks to Dr. Richard Dawkins' at www.damaris.org/content/content.php?type=5&id=10 2#[1]; Orr, H. Allen, 'A Passion for Evolution: A Devil's Chaplain' at www.nybooks.com/articles/16920; Rex Finley, Darel, 'Freely Chosen Dogmatism' at www.alien-ryderflex.com/evolution/Dawkins.html[1]; Sarfati, Jonathan, 'Stumbling over the Impossible: Refutation of *Climbing Mt. Impossible*' at www.answersingenesis.org/docs/ 3750.asp[2]; Willard, Dallas, 'Reflections on Dawkins' *The Blind Watchmaker*' at www.dwillard.org/ articles/artview.asp?artID=52[2]; Williams, Peter S., 'Darwin's Rotweiller & the Public Understanding of Scientism' at www.arn.org/docs/williams/pw_ dawkinsfallacies.htm[2]; McGrath, Alister, *The Re-Enchantment of Nature: Science, Religion and the Human Sense of Wonder* (London: Hodder & Stoughton, 2002)[1]; Steer, Roger, *Letter to an Influential Atheist* (Carlisle: Authentic Lifestyle/ Paternoster Press, 2003)[1]; Ward, Keith, *God, Chance & Necessity* (Oxford: OneWorld, 1996)[3]

General critiques of naturalism

Johnson, Philip E., reviews Daniel Dennett's *Darwin's Dangerous Idea* at www.arn.org/docs/johnson/dennett.htm[1]; Koons, Robert C., 'The Incompatibility of Naturalism and Scientific Realism' at www.leaderu.com/offices/koons/docs/natreal.html[3]; Plantinga, Alvin, reviews Daniel Dennett's *Darwin's Dangerous Idea* at http://id-www.ucsb.edu/fscf/library/plantinga/dennett.html[2]; Vitz, Paul, 'The Psychology of Atheism' at http://catholiceducation.org/articles/religion/re0384.html[1]; Craig, William Lane and Moreland, J. P. (eds), *Naturalism: A Critical Analysis* (London: Routledge, 2001)[3]; Johnson, Phillip E., *The Wedge of Truth: Splitting the Foundations of Naturalism* (Downers Grove, Illinois: IVP, 2000)[1]; Nichols, Terence L., *The Sacred Cosmos: Christian Faith and the Challenge of Naturalism* (Grand Rapids: Brazos Press, 2003)[2]; Ward, Keith, *God, Chance & Necessity* (Oxford: OneWorld, 1996)[3]

The anti-naturalism argument from reason

Craighead, Houston A., 'C. S. Lewis' Teleological Argument' http://faculty.winthrop.edu/craigheadh/articles/csl.htm[2]; Groothuis, Douglas, 'The Great Cloud of Unknowing' www.arn.org/docs/groothuis/dg_greatcloud.htm[1]; Hasker, William, 'How Not to be a Reductivist' at www.iscid.org/papers/Hasker_NonReductivism_103103.pdf[3]; Koons, Robert C., 'The Incompatibility of Naturalism and Scientific Realism' at www.leaderu.com/offices/koons/docs/natreal.html[3]; Plantinga, Alvin, reviews Daniel Dennett's *Darwin's Dangerous Idea* at http://id-www.ucsb.edu/fscf/library/plantinga/dennett.html[2]; Plantinga, Alvin, 'An Evolutionary Argument

Against Naturalism' at http:// hisdefense.org/articles/ap001.html[2]; Plantinga, Alvin, 'Naturalism Defeated' at www.homestead.com/philofreligion/files/alspaper.htm[3]; Listen to Plantinga lecturing on his anti-naturalism argument at www.hisdefense. org/audio/ap_001.ram[2]; Reppert, Victor, 'The Argument from Reason' www. infidels.org/library/modern/victor_reppert/reason.html[3]; 'Interview with Dr. Reppert' at http://go.qci.tripod.com/Reppert-interview.htm[2]; Willard, Dallas, 'Knowledge and Naturalism' at www.dwillard.org/Philosophy/Pubs/knowledge_and_ naturalism.htm[3]; Clark, Stephen R. L., *God, Religion and Reality* (London: SPCK, 1998)[2]; William Hasker, *The Emergent Self*, (Ithica: Cornell University Press, 1999)[3]; Lewis, C. S., *Miracles* (London, Fount, 19982)[2]; Koons, Robert C., 'The Incompatibility of Naturalism and Scientific Realism' and Willard, Dallas, 'Knowledge and Naturalism', in William Lane Craig and J. P. Moreland (eds) *Naturalism: A critical analysis* (London: Routledge, 2001)[3]; Lewis, C. S, *Miracles* (London: Fount, 1998)[1]; Menuge, Angus J., *Agents Under Fire: Materialism and the Rationality of Science* (Rowman & Littlefield, 2004)[2]; Miethe, Terry L., *Shepherd's Notes – Christian Classics: C.S. Lewis's Miracles* (Nashville, Tenessee: Broadman & Holman, 2000)[1]; Moreland, J. P., *Scaling the Secular City* (Grand Rapids, Michigan: Baker, 1987)[2]; Nash, Ronald H., *Worldviews in Conflict: Choosing Christianity in a World of Ideas* (Grand Rapids, Michigan: Zondervan, 1992)[1]; Plantinga, Alvin, *Warrant and Proper Function* (Oxford, 1993)[3]; Plantinga, Alvin, *Warranted Christian Belief* (New York: Oxford University Press, 2000)[3]; Reppert, Victor, *C.S. Lewis's Dangerous Idea* (Downers Grove: IVP,

2003)[2]; Taylor, Richard, *Metaphysics* (Engelwood Cliffs, New Jersey: Prentice Hall, 1974)[2]

Philosophy of mind

Beloff, John, 'Minds or Machines' at www.leaderu.com/truth/2truth04.html; Dembski, William A., 'The Act of Creation: Bridging Transcendence and Immanence' at www.designinference.com/documents/1998.08.act_of_creation.htm; Dembski, William A., 'Converting Matter into Mind' at www.arn.org/docs/dembski/wd_convmtr.htm; Dembski, William A., 'Conflating Matter and Mind' at www.arn.org/docs/dembski/wd_conflating.htm; Dembski, William A., 'Are We Spiritual Machines?' at www.designinference.com/documents/1999.10.spiritual_machines.htm; Dembski, William A., 'The Primacy of the First Person: Reply to Ray Kurzweil' at www.designinference.com/documents/2002.07.kurzweil_reply.htm; Koukl, Gregory, 'All Brain, No Mind' at www.str.org/free/commentaries/philosophy/nomind.htm; Larson, Erik, 'Rethinking Deep Blue: Why A Computer Can't Reproduce a Mind' at www.arn.org/docs/odesign/od182/blue182.htm; Moreland, J. P., 'Human Persons as a Test Case for Integrative Methodologies' at www.leaderu.com/aip/docs/moreland1b.html; Willard, Dallas, 'Non-Reductive and Non-Eliminative Physicalism?' at www.dwillard.org/articles/artview.asp?artID=48; Williams, Peter S., 'Why Naturalists Should Mind About Physicalism, and Vice Versa' at www.arn.org/docs/williams/pw_whynaturalistsshouldmind.htm; Craig, William Lane and Moreland, J. P., *Philosophical Foundations for a Christian Worldview* (Downers Grove: IVP, 2003)[2]; Habermas, Gary R. and Moreland, J. P., *Beyond Death*

(Crossway, 1988)[2]; Hasker, William, *The Emergent Self* (Cornell University Press, 1999)[3]; Craig, William Lane (ed.), *Philosophy of Religion* (Edinburgh University Press, 2001)[2]; Popper, Karl and Eccles, John C., *The Self & Its Brain* (Routledge, 1990)[2]; Moreland, J. P., *Scaling the Secular City* (Grand Rapids, Michigan: Baker, 1987)[2]; Moreland, J. P. and Rae, Scott B., *Body & Soul: Human Nature & the Crisis in Ethics* (Downers Grove: IVP, 2000)[2]; Richards, Jay W. (ed.), *Are We Spiritual Machines?: Ray Kurzweil Vs. the Critics of Strong AI* (Discovery Institute, 2002)[2]; Swinburne, Richard, *The Evolution of the Soul* (Oxford: Clarendon Press, 1997)[3]; Taliaferro, Charles, *Consciousness and the Mind of God* (Cambridge University Press, 1994)[3]

Christian philosophy

Beaty, Michael D., 'God Among the Philosophers' at www. religion-online.org/cgi-bin/relsearchd.dll/show article?item_id=53[2]; Clark, Kelly James, foreword to *Philosophers Who Believe* at www.calvin.edu/academic/philosophy/writings/pwbintro.htm[2]; Craig, William Lane, 'The Resurrection of Theism' at www.leaderu.com/truth/3truth01.html[2]; Hill, Daniel, 'What's New in Philosophy of Religion' www.philosophy now.org/archive/articles/21hill.htm[1]; Smith, Quentin, 'The Metaphilosophy of Naturalism' www.philoonline. org/library/smith_4_2.htm[2]; Craig, William Lane (ed.), *Philosophy of Religion: A Reader and Guide* (Edinburgh University Press, 2002)[2]; Craig, William Lane and Moreland, J. P., *Philosophical Foundations for a Christian Worldview* (Downers Grove: IVP, 2003)[2]

Christianity and science

Access Research Network at www.arn.org; Kreeft, Peter, 'Science & Religion' at http://catholiceducation. org/articles/apologetics/ap0063.html[1]; Moreland, J. P., 'Is Science a Threat or a Help to Faith? A Look at the Concept of Theistic Science' at www.afterall.net/ citizens/moreland/papers/jp-threatscience.html[1]; Moreland, J. P., 'Complimentarity, Agency Theory, and the God-of-the-Gaps' at www.afterall.net/citizens/ moreland/papers/jp-complementarity.html[2]; Moreland J. P., 'Scientific Creationism, Science, and Conceptual Problems' at www.afterall.net/citizens/moreland/ papers/jp-conceptual.html[2]; Moreland, J. P., 'Scientific Naturalism and the Unfalsifiable Myth of Evolution' at www.afterall.net/citizens/moreland/papers/jp-naturalism1.html[2]; Plantinga, Alvin, 'Methodological Naturalism?' at http://id-www.ucsb.edu/fscf/library/ plantinga/mn/home.html[2]; Plantinga, Alvin, 'When Faith and Reason Clash: Evolution and the Bible' at www. asa3.org/ASA/dialogues/Faith-reason/CRS9-91Plantinga1.html[2]; Plantinga, Alvin, 'Evolution, Neutrality, and Anticedent Probability: a Reply to Van Till and McMullen' at www.asa3.org/ASA/dialogues/ Faith-reason/CRS9-91Plantinga2.html[2]; Plantinga, Alvin, 'On Rejecting the Theory of Common Ancestry: A Reply to Hasker' at www.asa3.org/ASA/dialogues/Faith-reason/ PSCF12-92Plantinga.html[2]; Williams, Peter S., 'A Rough Guide to Creation and Evolution' at www.arn. org/ docs/williams/pw_roughguidetocreationandevolution. htm[1]; Craig, William Lane and Moreland, J. P., *Philosophical Foundations for a Christian Worldview* (Downers Grove: IVP, 2003)[2]; Birkett, Kirsten, *Unnatural Enemies: An introduction to science and Christianity* (Kingsford: Matthias Media, 1997); Colson, Charles and Pearcey, Nancy, *Developing a Christian Worldview of Science and Evolution* (Wheaton, Illinois: Tyndale House, 2001)[1]; Menuge, Angus J., *Agents Under Fire: Materialism and the Rationality of Science* (Rowman & Littlefield, 2004)[2]; Moreland, J. P., *Christianity and the Nature of Science* (Grand Rapids, Michigan: Baker, 1989)[2]; Moreland, J. P. and Reynolds, John Mark (eds), *Three Views on Creation and Evolution* (Grand Rapids, Michigan: Zondervan, 1999)[2]; Nichols, Terence L., *The Sacred Cosmos: Christian Faith and the Challenge of Naturalism* (Grand Rapids: Brazos Press, 2003)[2]; Pearcey, Nancy R. and Thaxton, Charles B., *The Soul of Science: Christian Faith and Natural Philosophy* (Wheaton Illinois: Crossway Books, 1994); Ratzsch, Del, *Science & Its Limits: The Natural Sciences in Christian Perspective* (Leicester: Apollos, 2000)[2]

William Paley and the classical design argument
Paley, William, Natural Theology at www.hti.umich.edu/cgi/p/pd-modeng/pd-modeng-idx?type=HTML&rgn=DIV1&byte=53054870[2]; Paley, William, *Natural Theology*, (R A Kessinger Publishing Co, 2003)[2]; Hick, John (ed.), *The Existence of God* (New York: Macmillan, 1964)[2]

Beauty
The place to begin is C. S Lewis' classic work *The Abolition of Man* (Fount)[2]. See also: Dubay, Thomas, *The Evidential Power of Beauty: Science and Theology Meet* (San Francisco: Ignatius, 1999)[2]; Groothuis, Douglas, *Truth Decay* (Leicester: IVP,

2000)[2]; Harries, Richard, *Art and the Beauty of God* (London: Mowbray, 2000)[2]; Joad, C. E. M., *Guide to Philosophy* (London: Victor Gollancz, 1946)[2]; McGinn, Colin, *Ethics, Evil and Fiction* (Clarendon Press: Oxford, 1999)[3]

Aesthetics and Art

Cooper, David E., (ed.), *Aesthetics: the Classic Readings* (Oxford: Blackwell, 1997)[2]; Dubay, Thomas, *The Evidential Power of Beauty: Science and Theology Meet* (San Francisco: Ignatius, 1999)[2]; Harries, Richard, *Art and the Beauty of God* (London: Mowbray, 2000)[2]; Sherry, Patrick, *Spirit and Beauty* (London: SCM, 2002)[2]; Thistlethwaite, David, *The Art of God and the Religions of Art* (Carlisle: Solway, 1998)[2]; Wolterstorff, Nicholas, *Art in Action: Toward a Christian Aesthetic* (Carlisle: Solway, 1997)[3]; Zacharias, Ravi, *Sense and Sensuality: Jesus Talks with Oscar Wilde on the Pursuit of Pleasure* (Orlando: Multhnomah Publishers, 2002)[1]

Aesthetic arguments for God's existence

Plantinga, Alvin, 'Two Dozen (or so) Theistic Arguments' at www.homestead.com/philofreligion/files/Theisticarguments.html[2]; Williams, Peter S., 'Aesthetic Arguments for the Existence of God' at www.quodlibet.net/williams-aesthetic.shtml[2]; Williams, Peter S., 'Intelligent Design, Aesthetics and Design Arguments' at http://iscid.org/papers/Williams_Aesthetics_012302.pdf[2]; Dubay, Thomas, *The Evidential Power of Beauty: Science and Theology Meet* (San Francisco: Ignatius, 1999)[2]; Moreland, J. P, *Scaling the Secular City* (Grand Rapids, Michigan:

Baker, 1987)[2]; O'Hear, Anthony, *Beyond Evolution: Human Nature And The Limits Of Evolutionary Explanation* (Oxford: Clarendon Press, 1997)[3]; O'Hear, Anthony, *After Progress: Finding The Old Way Forward* (London: Bloomsbury, 1999)[2]; O'Hear, Anthony, *Philosophy* (London: New Century, 2001)[2]; Pinnock, Clark H., *Reason Enough: A Case for the Christian Faith* (Exeter: Paternoster, 1980); Rhodes, W. S., *The Christian God* (Delhi: ISPCK, 1998); Swinburne, Richard, *The Existence of God* (Oxford: Clarendon Press, 1991); Swinburne, Richard, *Is There A God?* (Oxford University Press, 1996); Tennant, F. R., *Philosophical Theology*, vol. II (Cambridge, 1930)

The argument from desire

Armstrong, Dave, 'Romanticism, Wagner, C.S. Lewis, Christianity, & Me' at http://ic.net/~erasmus/RAZ63.HTM[1]; Armstrong, Dave, 'C.S. Lewis & the Romantic Poets on Longing, *Sehnsucht*, and Joy' at http://ic.net/~erasmus/RAZ40.HTM[1]; Brown, Dave, 'Real Joy and True Myth' at www.geocities.com/Athens/Forum/3505/LewisJoy.html[1]; Endara, Miguel, 'An Argument from Desire for the Possibility of an Afterlife' at http://irenaeus.truepath.com/journals/v5i1-2.html[1]; Evans, C. Stephen, 'The Mystery of Persons and Belief in God' at www.leaderu.com/truth/3truth07.html[1]; Kreeft, Peter, 'The Argument from Desire' at www.peterkreeft.com/topics/desire.htm[1]; Lovell, Steven, 'All in the Mind?' at www.csl-philosophy.co.uk/[2]; McAllister, Stuart, 'The search for transcendence' at www.gospelcom.net/rzim/publications/slicetran.php?sliceid=216[1]; Carnell, Corbin Scott, *Bright Shadow of Reality: Spiritual Longing in C.S. Lewis* (Eerdmans,

2000); Geisler, Norman L. and Corduan, Winfried, *Philosophy of Religion* (Wipf & Stock, 2003); Kreeft, Peter, *Heaven: the heart's deepest longing* (Ignatius, 1989)

The anthropic argument

Bradley, Walter L., 'The Designed, "Just So" Universe' at www.leaderu.com/offices/bradley/docs/universe.html[2]; Bradley, Walter L., 'Is There Scientific Evidence for the Existence of God? How the Recent Discoveries Support a Designed Universe' at www.origins.org/articles/bradley_existenceofgod.html[2]; Collins, Robin, 'The Fine-Tuning Design Argument: A Scientific Argument for the Existence of God' at www.discovery.org/viewDB/index.php3?program=CRSC&command=view&id=91[3]; Corey, Michael A., 'The Anthropic Principle' at www.michaelacorey.com/article.html[1]; Corey, Michael A., 'Humanity at the "Centre" of the Universe: A Defence of Moderate Anthropocentris' at www.michaelacorey.com/article_violin.html[1]; Craig, William Lane, 'The Teleological Argument and the Anthropic Principle' www.leaderu.com/offices/billcraig/docs/teleo.html[2]; Craig, William Lane, 'Barrow and Tipler on the anthropic principle vs Divine Design' at www.leaderu.com/offices/billcraig/docs/barrow.html[2]; Craig, William Lane, 'Review: The Design Inference – Eliminating chance through small possibilities' at www.leaderu.com/offices/billcraig/docs/design.html[2]; Koons, Robert C., 'Do Anthropic Coincidences require Explanation?' at www.leaderu.com/offices/koons/docs/lec11.html[2]; Leslie, John, 'The Pre-Requisites of Life in Our Universe' at www.leaderu.com/truth/3truth12.html[2]; Pearcey, Nancy, 'Our "Tailor-Made" Universe' at

www.arn.org/docs/pearcey/np_tailormade090200.
htm[1]; Ross, Hugh, 'A "Just Right" Universe' at www.
leaderu.com/science/ross-justright.html[1]; Ross, Hugh,
'Design and the Anthropic Principle' at www.reasons.
org/resources/apologetics/design.shtml?main[1]; Ross,
Hugh, 'Probability for a Life Support Body' at www.
reasons.org/resources/apologetics/design_evidences/
20020502_life_support_body_prob.shtml?main[1]; Behe,
Michael J., Dembski, William A. and Meyer, Stephen C.,
Science and Evidence for Design in the Universe
(San Francisco: Ignatius, 2000)[2]; Dembski, William A.
(ed.), *Mere Creation* (Downers Grove, Illinois: IVP,
1998)[2]; Davies, Paul, *The Mind of God* (London:
Penguin, 1992)[2]; Denton, Michael J., *Nature's Destiny:
How the Laws of Biology Reveal Purpose in the
Universe* (New York: Free Press, 1998)[2]; Gonzalez,
Guillermo and Jay Richards, *The Privileged Planet:
How Our Place in the Cosmos Is Designed for
Discovery* (Regnery, Jan. 2004); Ward, Peter D. and
Brownlee, Donald, *Rare Earth: Why Complex Life is
Uncommon in the Universe* (Springer-Verlag, 2000)[2]

'Pre-revolutionary' critiques of Darwinism

Bergman, Jerry, 'Why Abiogenesis Is Impossible' at
www.trueorigin.org/abio.asp[2]; Mills, Gordan C. and
Dean Kenyon, 'The RNA World: A Critique' at
www.arn.org/docs/odesign/od171/rnaworld171.htm[3];
Newman, Robert C. *et al.*, 'The Status of Evolution as a
Scientific Theory' at www.arn.org/docs/newman/rn_
statusofevolution.htm1; Wells, Jonathan, 'Survival of
the Fakest' at www.discovery.org/articleFiles/PDFs/
survivalOfTheFakest.pdf[1]; Denton, Michael J.,
Evolution: A Theory in Crisis (Besthesda: Adler &

Adler, 1986)[3]; Johnson, Philip E., *Darwin on Trial* (Downers Grove: IVP)[1]; Thaxton, Charles B., Bradley, Walter L. and Olsen, Roger L., *The Mystery of Life's Origin* (Dallas: Lewis and Stanley, 1992)[3]; Swift, David, *Evolution Under the Microscope: A Scientific Critique of the Theory of Evolution* (Leighton Academic Press, 2002)[2]; Wells, Jonathan, *Icons of Evolution* (Washington: Regnery Publishing, 2000); Wiker, Benjamin, *Moral Darwinism: How We Became Hedonists* (IVP, 2002)[2]

On Video or DVD: Johnson, Phillip, *Darwinism on Trial* (ARN); Wells, Jonathan, *A Critique of Darwinist Icons* (ARN)

('Post Revolutionary') Intelligent Design

Access Research Network at www.arn.org; International Society for Complexity, Information, and Design at www.iscid.org/; Beckwith, Francis J., 'Review: *Darwin's Black Box & The Design Inference*' at http://homepage.mac.com/francis.beckwith/JLR.pdf[1]; Dembski, William A., 'Intelligent Design as a Theory of Information' at www.arn.org/docs/dembski/wd_idtheory. htm[2]; Dembski, William A, 'The Logical Underpinnings of Design' atwww.designinference.com/documents/ 2002.10.logicalunderpinningsofID.pdf[3]; Meyer, Stephen C., 'DNA and Other Designs' at www.arn.org/docs/ meyer/sm_dnaotherdesigns.htm[2]; Meyer, Stephen C., 'The Origin of Life and the Death of Materialism' at www.arn.org/docs/meyer/sm_origins.htm[3]; Meyer, Stephen C., Nelson, P. A. and Chein, Paul, 'The Cambrian Explosion: Biology's Big Bang' at www. discovery.org/articleFiles/PDFs/Cambrian.pdf[3]; Behe, Michael J., Dembski, William A. and Meyer, Stephen C.,

Science and Evidence for Design in the Universe (San Francisco: Ignatius, 2000)[2], is the best introduction to ID arguments. An excellent cartoon guide to ID is Newman, Robert C. and Wiester, John L., *What's Darwin Got to Do with It?* (Downers Grove, Illinois: IVP, 2000).[1] Two superb introductions to ID covering the legal/educational perspective are: Beckwith, Francis J., *Law, Darwinism, and Public Education: The Establishment Clause and the Challenge of Intelligent Design* (New York: Rowman & Littlefield, 2003)[2] and Campbell, John Angus and Meyer, Stephen C., *Darwinism, Design, And Public Education* (East Lansing: Michigan State University Press, 2003).[3] For an engaging overview of the main players, history and arguments of the ID movement cf: Woodward, Thomas, *Doubts About Darwin: A History of Intelligent Design* (Grand Rapids: Baker, 2003)[2]

See also: Broom, Neil, *How Blind is the Watchmaker?* (Leicester: IVP, 2001)[2]; Colson, Charles and Pearcey, Nancy, *Developing a Christian Worldview of Science and Evolution* (Wheaton, Illinois: Tyndale House, 2001)[1]; Dubay, Thomas, *The Evidential Power of Beauty: Science and Theology Meet* (San Francisco: Ignatius, 1999)[2]; Geisler, Norman L. and Bucchino, Peter, *Unshakable Foundations* (Minneapolis, Minnesota: Bethany House, 2001); Gills, James P. and Woodward, Tom, *Darwinism under the microscope* (Lake Mary, Florida: Charisma House, 2002)[1]; Moreland, J. P, *Scaling the Secular City* (Grand Rapids, Michigan: Baker, 1987)[2]; ReMine, Walter James, *The Biotic Message: Evolution versus Message Theory* (St. Paul Science, 1993)[2]

On Video or DVD: *Unlocking the Mysteries of Life* (Illustrated Media); Johnson, Phillip, *Blind Watchmaker? A Skeptical Look at Darwinism* (ARN)

William A. Dembski

ARN featured author, William A. Dembski at www.arn.org/dembski/wdhome.htm; Design Inference Website at www.designinference.com/; Beckwith, Francis J., 'Review: *Darwin's Black Box & The Design Inference*' at http://homepage.mac.com/francis. beckwith/JLR.pdf[1]; Craig, William Lane, review of 'The Design Inference' at www.leaderu.com/offices/ billcraig/docs/design.html; *The Design Revolution: Answering the Toughest Questions about Intelligent Design* (IVP, 2004); *No Free Lunch: Why Specified Complexity Cannot be Purchased without Intelligence* (Lanham: Rowman & Littlefield, 2001)[3]; *Intelligent Design: The Bridge between Science & Theology* (Downers Grove: IVP, 1999)[2]; *The Design Inference* (Cambridge: Cambridge University Press, 1999)[3]

Dembski has edited and/or contributed to a number of books: Dembski, William A. (ed.), *Uncommon Dissent: Intellectuals Who Find Darwinism Unconvincing* (Wilmington, Del: ISI Books, 2004); Behe, Michael J., Dembski, William A. and Meyer, Stephen C., *Science and Evidence for Design in the Universe* (San Francisco: Ignatius, 2000)[2]; Dembski, William A. and Kushner, James M. (eds), *Signs of Intelligence* (Grand Rapids, Michigan: Brazos Press, 2001)[1]; Dembski, William A. (ed.), *Mere Creation* (Downers Grove, Illinois: IVP, 1998)[2] and Moreland, J. P (ed.), *The*

Creation Hypothesis (Downers Grove, Illinois: IVP, 1994)[2] – which is an excellent volume in its own right, especially on the philosophical arguments over the legitimacy of the design paradigm within science.

Michael J. Behe and irreducible complexity

Behe, Michael J., *Darwin's Black Box* (Free Press, 1998)[3]; Dembski, William A., *No Free Lunch: Why Specified Complexity Cannot be Purchased without Intelligence* (Lanham: Rowman & Littlefield, 2001)[3]; ARN featured author, Michael J. Behe at www.arn.org/behe/behehome.htm; Behe, Michael J., 'Darwin Under the Microscope' at http://catholiceducation.org/articles/science/sc0017.html*1*; Behe, Michael J., 'A Response to Critics of *Darwin's Black Box*' at www.iscid.org/papers/Behe_ReplyToCritics_121201.pdf; 'Interview with Dr. Michael Behe' at http://id-www.ucsb.edu/detche/video/biology/behe/interview/behe.html; Beckwith, Francis J., *'Review: Darwin's Black Box & The Design Inference'* at http://homepage.mac.com/francis.beckwith/JLR.pdf[1]; Dembski, William A., 'Irreducible Complexity Revisited' at www.designinference.com/documents/2004.01.Irred_Compl_Revisited.pdf[3]; Dembski, William A., 'Biology in the Subjunctive Mood: A Response to Nicholas Matzke' at www.arn.org/docs/dembski/wd_biologusubjunctive.htm; Gene, Mike, 'Irreducible Complexity ReVisited' at www.idthink.net/back/ic/index.html[3]

On Video or DVD: Behe, Michael, *Irreducible Complexity: The Biochemical Challenge to Darwinian Theory* (ARN); Behe, Michael, *Opening Darwin's Black Box: An Interview with Dr. Michael*

Behe (ARN); *Unlocking the Mysteries of Life* (Illustrated Media)

The Bacterial Flagellum

ARN Design Museum: The Bacterial Flagellum at www.arn.org/docs/mm/flagellum_all.htm; 'Bacterial Flagella: An Example of Irreducible Complexity' at www.id.ucsb.edu/fscf/library/origins/graphics-captions/Flagellum.html; See E. Coli swimming using flagella at www.mtmi.vu.lt/pfk/funkc_dariniai/ nanostructures/bacteria.htm; *Physics Today*, 'Motile Behaviour of Bacteria' at www.aip.org/pt/jan00/ berg.htm; 'Self-Assembly of Bacterial Flagella' at www.aip.org/ mgr/png/2002/174.htm; Bracht, John, 'The Bacterial Flagellum: A Response to Ursula Goodenough' at www.iscid.org/papers/Bracht_ GoodenoughResponse_021203.pdf[3]; Dembski, William A., 'Irreducible Complexity Revisited' at www. designinference.com/documents/2004.01.Irred_Compl_ Revisited.pdf[3]; Dembski, William A., 'Still Spinning Just Fine: A Response to Ken Miller' at www.designinference. com/documents/2003.02.Miller_Response.htm[3]; Dembski, William A., 'Evolution's Logic of Credulity' at www.arn.org/docs/dembski/wd_logic_credulity.htm[3]; Dembski, William A., 'Biology in the Subjective Mood: A Response to Nicholas Matzke' at www.arn.org/docs/ dembski/wd_biologusubjunctive.htm[3]; Gene, Mike, 'Irreducible Complexity and Darwinian Pathways' at www.arn.org/docs/behe/mb_mg1darwinianpathways. htm[3]; Gene, Mike, 'Evolving the Bacterial Flagellum Through Mutation and Cooption' atwww.idthink. net/biot/flag1/index.html[3]

On Video or DVD: Minnich, Scott, *Bacterial Flagella:*

Paradigm for Design (ARN); *Unlocking the Mysteries of Life* (Illustrated Media)

Debates on God's existence

Craig, William Lane at www.leaderu.com/offices/billcraig/menus/index.html; Craig, William Lane and Sinnot-Armstrong, Walter, *God?* (Oxford University Press, 2004); Craig, William Lane and Flew, Antony, *Does God Exist? The Craig-Flew Debate* (Ashgate, 2003)[2]; Miethe, Terry L. and Flew, Antony, *Does God Exist? A Believer and an Atheist Debate* (San Francisco: HarperCollins, 1991)[2]; Moreland, J. P. and Nielson, Kai, *Does God Exist?* (Amerherst, New York: Prometheus, 1993)[2]; Russell, Bertrand and Copleston, F. C., 'A Debate on the Existence of God', in Hick, John (ed.), *The Existence of God* (New York: Macmillan, 1964)[1]; Smart, J. J. C. and Haldane, J. J., *Atheism & Theism* (Oxford: Blackwell, 1996)[3].

The problem of evil (cf. The moral argument for God)

Bahnsen, Greg, 'The Problem of Evil' www.salemreformed.org/TheProblemofEvil.html; Clark, Kelly James, 'I Believe in God, the Father, Almighty' at www.calvin.edu/academic/philosophy/writings/ibig.htm[2]; Koukl, Gregory, 'Evil as Evidence for God' www.str.org/free/solid_ground/SG0105.htm[1]; Kreeft, Peter, 'The Problem of Evil' at http://catholiceducation.org/articles/religion/re0019.html[1]; Williams, Peter S., 'Terror from the Skies and the Existence of God' at www.damaris.org/writing/articles/other_articles/worldtradecentre3.htm[2]; Clark, Kelly James, *Return to Reason* (Grand Rapids, Michigan: Eerdmans, 1998)[2]; Howard-Snyder, Daniel (ed.), *The Evidential*

Argument from Evil (Bloomington: Indiana University Press, 1996)[3]; Lewis, C. S., *The Problem of Pain* (London: Fount, 1977)[1]; McGrath, Alister, *Suffering* (London: Hodder & Stoughton, 1992)[1]; Miethe, Terry L. and Habermas, Gary R., *Why Believe? God Exists!* (Joplin, Missouri: College Press, 1998)[2]; Perry, John, *Dialogue on Good, Evil, and the Existence of God* (Indianapolis: Hackett, 1999)[2]; Peterson, Michael *et al.*, (eds), *Philosophy of Religion: Selected Readings* (New York: Oxford University Press, 1996)[2]; Plantinga, Alvin, G*od, Freedom, and Evil* (Grand Rapids, Michigan, Eerdmans, 2001)[2]; Strobel, Lee, *The Case for Faith: A Journalist Investigates the Toughest Objections to Christianity* (Grand Rapids, Michigan: Zondervan, 2000)[1]; Swinburne, Richard, *Providence and the Problem of Evil* (Oxford, 1998)[3]; Williams, Peter S., *The Case for God* (Crowborough, East Sussex: Monarch, 1999)[2]

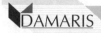